PRAISE FOR THE

CW01647505

"Asra Nomani is a honey badger, not to b

—Gad Saad, … of *The Saad Truth*

"Her Rosa Parks-style civil disobedience has won change."

—New York Times

"You are a hero of mine. You really are. The way you stand up for the things that I have been trying to say but it means so much more coming from you because I am not a Muslim and you are."

—Bill Maher, Host of *Real Time with Bill Maher* on HBO

"A former *Wall Street Journal* reporter who calls herself a liberal feminist, Nomani has become the face of what she describes as 'hopping mad' parents in Virginia, and a central figure in the education culture wars."

—Mother Jones

"Asra Nomani is a hero for education. She demonstrated remarkably effective strategies and tactics in Fairfax County, which can now be deployed across the nation. Parents are revolting against critical race theory and Asra Nomani has demonstrated the courage and intelligence to win the fight."

—Christopher Rufo, Journalist and Manhattan Institute Senior Fellow

"I've come to realize that Muslim reform takes time. Sincere people, like Asra Nomani, are working on it and give me hope."

—Ayaan Hirsi Ali, Author of *Prey*

"What a great country it is, that a Muslim-American woman who arrived here not speaking our language, is far better versed in the guarantees of our constitution and the meaning of our declaration than countless native-born DEI [Diversity Equity and Inclusion] experts."

—Laura Ingraham, Host of *The Ingraham Angle* on FOX News

"Asra Nomani's life story is so inspiring!"

—Janice Dean, Author of *I Am the Storm*

"I am a huge fan of your courage and I truly believe courage is contagious. We just have to see more examples from around us and people will join in."

—Glenn Beck, Radio Host

"Asra Nomani is fearless."

—Larry O'Connor, Host of *O'Connor & Company* on WMAL

WOKE ARMY

THE RED-GREEN ALLIANCE THAT IS DESTROYING AMERICA'S FREEDOM

ASRA Q. NOMANI

BOMBARDIER
BOOKS

Published by Bombardier Books
An Imprint of Post Hill Press
ISBN: 978-1-63758-004-2
ISBN (eBook): 978-1-63758-005-9

Woke Army:
The Red-Green Alliance That Is Destroying America's Freedom
© 2023 by Asra Q. Nomani
All Rights Reserved

Cover Design by Tiffani Shea

Interior Design by Yoni Limor

No part of this book may be reproduced, stored in a retrieval system, or transmitted by any means without the written permission of the author and publisher.

BOMBARDIER
BOOKS

Post Hill
PRESS

Post Hill Press
New York • Nashville
posthillpress.com

Published in the United States of America
1 2 3 4 5 6 7 8 9 10

To my family by birth—my mother, Sajida Nomani, and father, Zafar Nomani; my son, Shibli; brother, Mustafa; and niece, Safiyyah, and nephew, Samir—for your unconditional love.

To my family by destiny—Lily and the accidental activists from school boards to the streets of Tehran who triumph over fear with moral courage for goodness upon this earth.
Woman. Life. Freedom.

TABLE OF CONTENTS

LETTER TO THE READER

Mahsa Amini's death sentence was written decades ago.

When the twenty-two-year-old student emerged from the Shahid Haqqani Metro Station, just off Haghani Highway in Iran's capital of Tehran, the so-called morality policy blocked her path. She was a victim of not only the security forces in Iran but decades of disinformation by a dangerous network of academics, activists, ideologues, and others who have been the propaganda arm of extremists within the Muslim world who push an interpretation of Islam that denies the woman the freedom to feel the wind in her hair.

I call them the Woke Army.

Mahsa Amini's blood is on their hands.

Starting with my first encounter with their character assassins in 2002 and ending with our battle cry in 2022—Woman. Life. Freedom.—our lived expertise fighting the Woke Army is a guide for you into its sick, depraved operations in the West over the past two decades. And a guidepost for how we can defeat it with the moral courage and intellectual clarity we see on the streets of Iran today, among girls also declaring death to tyranny.

May you be inspired to action and truth.

Asra Nomani

October 25, 2022

Morgantown, West Virginia

CAST OF CHARACTERS

The Woke Army is an organized, well-financed global network of Muslim radicals and leftist activists who exploit the freedoms of the West to promote a system of beliefs that runs counter to any values of freedom.

Today, Woke Army adherents exploit the ideas in "critical race theory," a philosophy that is at its heart a form of cultural Marxism—whereby slavish adherence to orthodoxy and ideology, however dangerous or stifling, is equated with "justice." All cultures and societies have been marked by a hierarchy of human value in which people have been devalued and denied fundamental human rights because of identity, from race to religion, gender, and other elements of humanity. What has happened is that ideologues from this new ideology have created a *new* hierarchy of human value that denigrates people based on new biases, prejudices, and bigotry. In this upside-down system, peoples of color are the perpetual victims of "systemic racism" that can be traced directly to the incorrigible "white supremacist" views of the Caucasian majorities throughout history.

Never mind that America fought a war to end slavery, abolished Jim Crow segregation, integrated its military and public schools, enacted landmark civil rights legislation barring racial discrimination, and elected a black president. This is all blithely ignored or written off by the Woke perpetual grievance-mongers as the propaganda of the "patriarchy" undergirded by the bogeyman of "white supremacy." Because the Woke Army asserts that its arguments are unassailably correct, any and all who oppose them are branded—often by well-organized social media mobs or actual ones—as recalcitrant racists.

The cancer of "cancel culture" spreading throughout America, the West, and even my motherland of India—with people singled out for firing, ridicule, or shaming for statements that to the sane majority represent the parameters of necessary debate—can be directly laid at the feet of the silencers. Atop this, the Woke Army has embraced all forms of identity politics so that the list of uncriticizable interest groups—gays, the transgendered, women (well, women of color and liberal women, at least), and Muslims of a certain stripe (and particularly anti-Semitic Muslims)—grows larger every day. While activists in the Woke Army vow they wish to have an "honest conversation about race" in America, they in fact want the exact opposite.

Their edict is clear: you *will* comply with our views of "systemic racism" and our cures for it—granting slavery reparations, enforcing quotas, defunding the police, and indoctrinating your kids, for starters—or we will shut you up and shut you down.

There are some brave free thinkers who resist the Woke Army.

The Woke Army must be stopped to save America—and the world.

THE WOKE ARMY

Muslim Ideologues and Their Allies

1. Hatem Bazian—Director of the Islamophobia Research and Documentation Project, at the University of California, Berkeley; Students for Justice in Palestine cofounder
2. John Esposito—Founding director of the Prince Alwaleed bin Talal Center for Muslim-Christian Understanding and the Bridge Initiative at Georgetown University
3. Khaled Beydoun—Associate professor at Wayne State University Law School
4. Jonathan Brown—Alwaleed bin Talal Chair of Islamic Civilization at Georgetown University

5. Nathan Lean—Former research director at the Bridge Initiative at Georgetown University
6. Omid Safi—Professor in the Department of Asian and Middle Eastern Studies at Duke University

Donors

1. Open Society Foundations
2. Proteus Fund

Woke Organizations

1. Antifa
2. African American Policy Forum
3. Black Lives Matter
4. Center for American Progress
5. Emgage
6. International Institute of Islamic Thought
7. Justice Democrats
8. ReThink Media
9. Southern Poverty Law Center (SPLC)

Muslim Organizations

1. Council on American-Islamic Relations
2. Dream Defenders
3. Electronic Intifada
4. Islamic Networks Group
5. MPower Change

6. MoveOn.org
7. Muslim Advocates
8. MuslimMatters

Council on American-Islamic Relations (CAIR)

1. Nihad Awad—CAIR cofounder, executive director
2. Zahra Billoo—CAIR San Francisco Bay Area executive director
3. Arsalan Bukhari—Former CAIR national strategic communications manager
4. Ibrahim Hooper—CAIR cofounder, national communications director
5. Robert McCaw—CAIR government affairs department director
6. Corey Saylor—Former director of the Department to Monitor and Combat Islamophobia at CAIR; deputy director of strategy at ReThink Media
7. Imraan Siddiqi—CAIR Washington executive director

LoonWatch

This is an online blog where anonymous writers smear people they oppose as "racist," "anti-Muslim," and "Islamophobic." These bloggers refer to their targets as "loons," or lunatics.

1. Muhammad Tauseef Akbar a.k.a. "Garibaldi"—CAIR Chicago research director
2. Javad Hashmi a.k.a. "Danios" at LoonWatch, a.k.a. "J. Hashmi" at MuslimMatters, a.k.a. "DrMaxtor," a.k.a. "1DrM"—Physician and Harvard University PhD student
3. Ahmed Rehab a.k.a. "Emperor"—CAIR Chicago executive director

Writers and Allies

1. Wajahat Ali—Contributing *New York Times* Opinion writer; former co-host, Al Jazeera America
2. Amani Al-Khatahtbeh—*MuslimGirl* founder
3. Shahed Amanullah—Cofounder, numerous blogs; former Obama administration senior technology advisor
4. Reza Aslan—Author
5. Hamdan Azhar—Muslim Writers Collective cofounder
6. Glenn Greenwald—The Intercept cofounder
7. Mehdi Hasan—Former Al Jazeera host; MSNBC host
8. Murtaza Hussain—The Intercept reporter
9. Arsalan Iftikhar—Former national legal director at CAIR; *The Muslim Guy* blog founder
10. Hoda Katebi—Writer
11. Sheila Musaji—*The American Muslim* blog founding editor
12. Aziz Poonawalla—Brass Crescent Awards cofounder
13. Cenk Uygur—The Young Turks founder; Justice Democrats cofounder

Activists

1. Maha Elgenaidi—Islamic Networks Group founder
2. Farhana Khera—Muslim Advocates founding president and executive director
3. Linda Sarsour—Women's March cochair; MPower Change cofounder

Politicians

1. Keith Ellison—Minnesota attorney general
2. Ilhan Omar—Minnesota congressional representative
3. Rashida Tlaib—Michigan congressional representative
4. Atif Qarni—Former Virginia Secretary of Education
5. Abrar Omeish—Fairfax County, VA, School Board member

MuslimMatters

This is a website established by the founders of AlMaghrib Institute, which promotes the hard-line interpretation of Islam called Salafism.

1. Yasir Qadhi a.k.a. "ibn al Hyderabadee"—AlMaghrib Institute and MuslimMatters cofounder
2. Amad Shaikh a.k.a. "Amad"—MuslimMatters cofounder
3. Amir Saheb a.k.a. "Mujahideen Ryder," a.k.a. "ibn Percy"—Blogger

PREFACE

Born in Bombay, India, in the early summer of 1965 to a Muslim family, I am part of the first postcolonial generation of my family, following the end of almost a century of white British rule of the subcontinent's brown and black people of color from 1858 to 1947. During that time, the British showcased the worst of colonialism, pillaging the treasures, people, and spirit of the land, while also offering a glimpse of British organizational acumen, building railroads, educating students, and managing civil services.

From his humble home office in the city of Wardha, India, my paternal grandfather was a court-appointed defense attorney for "freedom fighters," usually young Indian men fighting against British rule, even in one case torching a police station. He lost most of his cases. The British exiled his clients across the "black waters" of the Indian Ocean off the nation's southern coast to a prison in the Andaman and Nicobar Islands.

My father, Mohammad Zafar Alam Nomani, was born in June 1933 in British India. He climbed a banyan tree as a boy to cheer Mahatma Gandhi, an original architect of the nonviolent movement, as he marched for India's freedom from British rule. My father survived the Bengal famine of 1943, standing in line for US food aid that came in the form of sorghum wheat meant for livestock. He still remembers the coarse scratch of the wheat as he swallowed every morsel he got from his mother.

My mother, Sajida Nomani, was born in British India in 1940, in the northern state of Uttar Pradesh, not far from my father's ancestral village. When she was two years old, her father, also an attorney, suddenly died, leaving her mother a widow with nine children and no income. Growing up in the village of Jaigahan, my mother lived separate from the touch of British rule but remembers the curiosity she'd hear from some family members when they caught an occasional glimpse of a white woman, not as a symbol of oppression but rather a curiosity. Sent to live with family in the hill station of Panchgani, India, not far from Bombay, she studied as a day student at a British convent, St. Joseph's High School, despite the protestations of a cousin who thought the family's children should be educated at a Muslim school.

Months before Indians won freedom from British rule on August 14, 1947, my grandfather went to the state capital and turned over his British title, medal, and honors to the British leaders representing the queen of England.

On Independence Day 1947, my mother remembers the sweet taste of Cadbury that the kind white British nuns at her school handed out in celebration. Standing at the Wardha District court square, my father remembers watching a family friend, a government official, pull the Union Jack down from a flagpole as the Indian flag ascended. Joyful locals handed out sweets that those gathered, including my father, enjoyed, smiling widely at their new freedom.

After my parents married in 1962, my older brother, Mustafa, was born, and then I was born in the summer of 1965, less than two decades after India's liberation. My father left for America as a PhD student at Rutgers University, with a scarce few dollars in his pocket. My mother left two years later, raising the money for my brother's and my airfare on TWA, making fifty cents an hour babysitting other people's children. When I arrived, I learned English as a second language and ate free breakfasts for children living in poverty. At home, when we woke up for water at night, we waited after turning on the light switch to give the cockroaches time to scamper under the cupboards. On weekends, we sold cotton *kurtas*, or tunics, at the local Englishtown Flea Market.

My father, eighty-eight, and my mother, eighty, oppose colonization. They oppose imperialism. They certainly oppose oppression, injustice, and "systemic racism."

But they did not teach me to hate white people.

They did not teach me to blame white people for any setbacks I face.

They absolutely did not teach me to expect reparations, quotas, or handouts because of any grievances of "systemic racism" that my people have faced.

Rather, they intuitively understood one of America's greatest gifts: the impulse of the country and its citizens to reward an easy acceptance to those willing to work hard and embrace the pluralistic values that make America a fundamentally decent and prosperous place to live.

That makes me an enemy of a dangerous, well-funded radical cult that is subverting fundamental American values of democracy, meritocracy, and progress with tainted, flawed philosophies about "systemic racism," "white privilege," and "intersectionality" packaged in an ideology of "critical race theory" that blames "white supremacy" and "whiteness" for the world's racial injustices.

* * *

Growing up in Morgantown, West Virginia, reading the Qur'an and the girl detective mystery series, *Nancy Drew*, I embraced liberal American values of freedom, self-determination, and secular governance. The wind blows in my hair. I shake hands with men. I believe a Muslim woman can marry anyone she chooses. I brought into my home and family a puppy named Lily despite a religious edit that angels will not visit a home with a dog inside. When Lily died in January 2021, my family wept. I live by the positive values of honesty, integrity, and compassion that I learned from my parents. I also refuse to be blind to the wrongs committed in the name of Islam by those who interpret the religion to discriminate against girls and women, practice virulent anti-Semitism, and carry out violent jihad against the West while trying to bully and harass Muslims like me who disagree with their ideas of hate. And I am firmly against any religion in political governance.

As an immigrant and a journalist, I feel an allegiance to the pluralistic and secular country that has sheltered my family and given me the freedom to speak and write freely. Of course, America is imperfect. I've read the troubling parts of its history, and I am as dismayed as the next person about the fractious nature of contemporary politics. But I roundly reject the notions—widely promulgated in certain echo chambers these days—that America at its core is racist, anti-immigrant, and anti-Muslim.

My own experience tells me otherwise. Our family's experience has shown that there is no conflict between being a Muslim and an American so long as we understand that respect and tolerance is a two-way street—that as we build and attend our mosques, we also embrace the concepts of freedom of religion, freedom of speech, freedom of the press, and the live-and-let-live social attitude that has served America so well for so long. To ask this of all newcomers to America is hardly "racist" or "oppressive." It's a tried-and-true recipe for success, assimilation, and happiness.

I also believe in the value of owning up. A cadre of dedicated Muslim extremists carried out the 9/11 attacks. Muslim terrorists kidnapped and beheaded my colleague and friend, *Wall Street Journal* reporter Daniel Pearl, in Pakistan in 2002. Then, they lay their prayer rugs upon the quickly washed bloodied floor and laid their heads in prayer in prostration to Mecca, Saudi Arabia. The murderous thugs of ISIS carried out their rape and carnage in the name of a theocracy tied to fundamentalist Islam. Islamic terrorism does not define Islam. But it is real and cannot be denied away by exhortations of "Islamophobia" or "racism."

Yet, while I believe my views fall well within the mainstream of the vast majority of ordinary Americans, they have gotten me pilloried by my coreligionists and their allies. Starting seventeen years ago in 2004, I have been viciously attacked as a "Zionist media whore," "racist," "American apologist," and "Islamophobe" by a network of anonymous character assassins. I undertook a multiyear investigation to uncover the people behind these attacks, their network, their goals, and their funding, and this book is based on more than three hundred interviews with sources, twenty subpoenas, thousands of pages of documents, emails, texts, court filings, and transcripts, and hundreds of hours of video and audio. I contacted the individuals named in the book for comment, and I included their statements in the narrative when they responded and noted that they declined interviews when they did not. If they refused to comment, I attempted to incorporate public statements to fairly reflect their positions. When quoting written material, I have included the original text, including grammatical and spelling errors, because literary forensics—the science of identifying writing and word patterns—has been a critical part of my investigation.

My critics and those who continue to hound me might surprise you. They are politicians, academicians, and the officials of a powerful network that much of the media today characterizes as "mainstream" when, in fact, they are anything but. They grab headlines as representatives of organizations with an alphabet soup of names, such as the Council on American-Islamic Relations, MPower Change, Emgage, Muslim Advocates, the International Institute of Islamic Thought, Muslim Public Affairs Council, and many others. I call this loose coalition the Honor Brigade, for its members feel at every turn the need to defend the "honor" of Islam against any and all who would have the temerity to criticize it.

* * *

The Honor Brigade has embedded itself in America's race conflict, promoting the flawed argument that Muslims are a "race," and they are part of a new Woke Army.

After the tragic murder of George Floyd under the knee of a Minneapolis, Minnesota, police officer, its intersection with groups like Antifa and Black Lives Matter activists moved forward full steam ahead. The Muslim network I had been investigating is part of a radical ideological cult that subscribes to the thesis of "critical race theory" and is hell-bent on throwing America into a class and race war. Muslims have tried to do to me what radical activists are now attempting to do to so many Americans: shaming to silence.

This dangerous cult is "woke" in sheep's clothing because it purports to stand for the admirable and commonly shared principles of racial justice and equality, but under the soft wooly surface lurks a wolf—a wolf that seeks power by humbling the United States by branding as "racist" its institutions, its history, and its people—a wolf that is willing to savagely attack anything and anybody that stands between it and its goals.

I wrote this book to give you a primer on how this dangerous network works and arm you with the intellectual and psychological tools to protect and inoculate yourself, your family, your community, and your country from its diabolical plot.

This is some of what I learned: for the Woke Army, no slight must go unchallenged while the most heinous crimes are explained away as devoid of any connection to the "cause." Those who make the obvious connection between the cult and violence are branded "racist." To be clear, the ideologues in this cult have as much right to speak freely as you and I do and to criticize their critics. But their tactics are often not the tactics of those of us who value free speech. Borrowing from the playbook of identity politics, they use social media mobs, anonymous trolls, and other forms of intimidation to attempt to silence those who oppose them in a classic disinformation campaign of subterfuge, suppression, and manipulation. They get away with this because much of America's mainstream media—loathe to be seen as "politically incorrect"—gives cover to their phony "moderate" and "activist" labels.

Clinical neuropsychologist Orli Peter, who specializes in the assessment and treatment of trauma survivors, explains how the Woke Army exploits empathy through its manipulation of the "narrative" and "storytelling" to essentially hijack the parts of our brain that process emotions, limiting cognitive, rational, logical processing in the prefrontal cortex. "They create a phenomenon of suicidal empathy, shaming people to subsume themselves to their own destruction," says Peter. "If you resist, they set out to destroy you because you stand in the way of their campaign of manipulation."

I know this firsthand. This network has waged a relentless and often vicious character assassination campaign against Muslim reformers and others with similar viewpoints. Their goal: to discredit and silence those who have the gall to question *their* narrative that all the ails of our society can be reduced to "racism," or in the case of Muslims, "Islamophobia." Their tactics are the tactics of bullies and authoritarians, not democrats. Their Twitter mobs and blog posts are staffed by tenured, high-placed academics at prestigious universities, activists at "civil rights" and "social justice" organizations, and writers at "mainstream" media outlets, all the while many of them also hiding behind pseudonyms to hound their targets on social media.

I have used forensic cyber-investigative measures, a civil lawsuit, subpoenas, and old-fashioned gumshoe reporting to unmask them. Using my experience as a former *Wall Street Journal* reporter, my hunt to unmask anonymous trolls harassing Muslim reformers for our calls for women's rights and tolerance within my Muslim community led me to uncover a wider network of ideologues hijacking good intentions and empathy to usurp our nation's democratic ideals.

It has led to one organization: the Council on American-Islamic Relations, known as CAIR. It poses as the Muslim version of the NAACP, claiming to be a civil rights group dedicated solely to protecting the rights of Muslim Americans. But my multiyear investigation into this network is a probe I undertook to get a better understanding of the group that was clearly helping to organize my critics, and the results of my probe suggest far more sinister goals. At its core, this network is anti-Semitic and has contempt for secular American values. It supports a dangerous worldview that Islam ought to be at the center of politics, setting laws, public policy, and regulatory rules. Substitute the word "Islam" with Christian, and a Christian theocracy that espoused these ideas would be just as disturbing (and five hundred years ago it was), and yet its members enjoy legitimacy in the wider network of the Woke Army. This network sponsors campaigns to help political movements, such as the Muslim Brotherhood, founded in Egypt in 1928, to win control of Muslim countries, with draconian laws that criminalize women, girls, and gay and transgender men and women. Its sympathies for purveyors of Islamic terrorism are more than theoretical. Members of the CAIR network have been working to bring ISIS brides back to America, free Guantanamo Bay detainees, free al-Qaeda prisoners in US jails, and destroy Israel even by violent means.

All the while, the real needs of disadvantaged minority groups in America to psychologically progress suffers while being forced into a backseat by the bizarre politics of the Woke Army, and the youth suffer because of the failures of this network of community leaders and their hijinks. This network's reputation as "mainstream" among much of the American media is baffling to anyone who has seriously looked behind its often slick and well-funded public relations façade. When this network and its fellow travelers decided to go after me and just recently also tried to topple my son's magnet high school in Northern Virginia for lack of "diversity," even though its ranks are filled with mostly Asian immigrant families of color—I decided to look into them.

This book is a guide to the Woke Army—an unholy alliance of Muslim radicals with mostly radicalized elites from the professoriate and professional classes, indoctrinated college kids, anarchy-inclined Antifa thugs, and perpetual race-baiters. They mean business, and their business is a radical transformation of America in which noble-sounding ideas like "social justice," "income equality," "equity," and protections against "hate speech" are code for upending the very pillars of American democracy with principles of censorship, racial division, polarization, and Islamism, or Islamic governance. They would do away with the First Amendment, the concept of equal treatment under the law, and the concept of your ability to confront your accuser. How do we know this? You need only to look to the college campuses for a preview: the draconian speech codes, the sexual harassment kangaroo courts, and the mobbing and cancelling of speakers whose views they despise. Look at K-12 indoctrination to see how the Woke Army is racializing every issue and turning classrooms into ideological indoctrination centers, and faculty and staff training into struggle sessions, akin to the Cultural Revolution of Communist China.

And now they're coming for you—your schools, your city councils, your police departments, your employers. Do we really want the people who are sowing chaos and ruining the livability of cities like

Seattle, Minneapolis, and New York City in charge of the bedrock institutions of our country? Do we want superintendents and school boards changing curriculum so that they indoctrinate rather than educate our children? Do we want a new hierarchy of human value that replaces old racism with new racism?

With the 2020 defeat of Donald J. Trump as US president, the arrival of President Joe Biden and Vice President Kamala Harris, the 2024 elections looming before us, and years of battles to come, this book offers you a blueprint to the power brokers, their battle plan and tactics.

What follows is my journey of investigation into the shadowy world that this network and its supporters would rather you not know...

CHAPTER 1

Establishing Legitimacy in the "Resistance"

In early November 2016, as Donald J. Trump claimed victory, an Egyptian American in Southern California took to Twitter to issue a battle cry to overthrow the democratically elected president of the United States of America.

Hussam Ayloush, a leader at the Southern California chapter of the Council on American-Islamic Relations, a Muslim organization known as CAIR, wrote: "Repeat after me: *Al-Shaab yureed isqat al-nizaam* (Arab Spring chant)."

The translation was potent: "The people want to overthrow the regime."

Protesters had shouted the chant at Tahrir Square in Cairo to remove Egyptian leader Hosni Mubarak from power. Ayloush had supported the rise of the extremist Muslim Brotherhood political party to power and its leader, Mohamed Morsi, to the presidency. The Muslim Brotherhood and its expression of Islamism, or political Islam, preaches an ideology of Muslim supremacy, arguing that Islam should be the center of political governance and Islam should be the heart of a nation's legal system.

Over the next weeks, Ayloush worked closely to activate a network of like-minded Islamist sympathizers in his Muslim community, all of them motivated to wield political power with one objective in mind: the destruction of Israel. They traded emails and rushed phone calls. They knew that they had the opportunity of a lifetime. Then, over the next four years, they would join forces with politically liberal activists over a common enemy—Donald Trump—using a little-known ideology called "critical race theory" like a Trojan horse to racialize their Islamist issues and backdoor their religious priorities to the top of the Democratic agenda.

A little over four years later, in mid-January 2021 with the election of Joe Biden as president of the United States, Ayloush convened a victorious video call with some of his great allies in the struggle—Palestinian American activist Linda Sarsour, CAIR cofounder Nihad Awad, CAIR leader Zahra Billoo, Rep. Ilhan Omar, and others—to celebrate their victories and assail the January 6, 2021, assault on the Capitol by Trump supporters.

In a moment of political irony, Ayloush lashed out at the attackers on the Capitol, the image of an empty meeting room behind him, "CAIR California" emblazoned across the wall. "What we witnessed ten days ago was not merely a riot or a violent assault," he declared. "This was an attempted coup on our democracy. The terrorists who led the insurrection in our country's capital were aiming to spark a massacre or probably a deadly conflict that could lead into a civil war, maybe martial law, or a military coup, a military coup similar to the many ones our CIA has orchestrated around the world, but, anyway, they were hoping possibly for a coup that would have prevented the peaceful and democratic transition of power in our country. Thank God, *alhamdulillah*, they failed, at least for now."

From his perch, where he has pressed frequently for ideas of Muslim nationalism and Muslim supremacy, overlooking the bigotry of his own ideology, he said, "The violent actions of the past two weeks are rooted in the long history of white nationalism and white supremacy in our country and not merely something to do with... being unhappy with the results of an election." He continued, "Also, second, the assault on the US Capitol was not an isolated act. It is actually the culmination—the culmination—of an expected result of many years of fueling and normalizing bigotry, promoting conspiracy theories, fostering divisiveness, and undermining our democratic process by President Trump."

Their allies in liberal communities liked and shared the video.

How had these Muslim activists managed to forge this unholy alliance between Islamism, the ideology of the Islam's radical religious right, and Wokeism, the ideology of America's extreme political left?

The answer: they had waged their own years-long disinformation campaign, "fueling and normalizing bigotry promoting conspiracy theories, fostering divisiveness, and undermining our democratic process."

* * *

As CAIR's Hussam Ayloush issued his battle cry, activist Linda Sarsour rallied her followers to march the next day in Manhattan as part of a new campaign organized around a hashtag, #Resistance, admonishing them: "BE THERE!"

She sent the call out to her friends in the American left. The next day, hundreds of disgruntled folks filled the streets of Columbus Circle in Manhattan in one of many anti-Trump rallies to sweep the country over the next days, and Sarsour shouted at them, "If you're not ready to give it all to the movement, get the hell out of our way."

The day after, in San Francisco, Farhana Khera, executive director of nonprofit Muslim Advocates, told other nonprofit leaders in a nationwide conference call that Muslim children were "worried, fearful and some even crying, asking if they have a place in Trump's America." Later, she told a *Politico* reporter that the appointment of retired Lt. Gen. Michael Flynn as national security advisor was an extension of the "bigoted and divisive rhetoric" of the Trump campaign.

Over the next days, a former CAIR official, Zainab Chaudary, senior media associate of the Security and Rights Collaborative at ReThink Media, a Berkeley, California–based media machine with offices outside Washington, DC, that had created a literal "echo chamber" for far-left causes. Chaudary shared anti-Trump article after article on social media, one of the articles calling on President Barack Obama to "shut down" the National Security Agency's surveillance program before it "fell into Trump's hands."

At Duke University in Raleigh-Durham, North Carolina, Omid Safi, professor in the Department of Asian and Middle Eastern Studies, huddled with friends, including Luke Powery, dean of the Duke Chapel, and William "Bill" Hart, whom he had once described as "my critical race theory professor." As a professor of religious studies at University of North Carolina Greensboro, Hart called himself a "critical theorist of religion," teaching "race" was a "euphemism for white supremacy."

"This is not just about Trump," Safi wrote. "This is what racism in America has been like. What is new about it is that it is now merged with the state apparatus at the highest level."

Significantly, much like many conservative groups are funded by donors, this network's national security influence was funded by a common donor: Hungarian American billionaire George Soros. It's counterintuitive that Soros, who survived the Holocaust as a teen born into a Jewish family in Hungary, was financing a great deal of this network, most of them anti-Semitic and anti-Israel. But during the last chapter of the Bush administration, the executive director of Muslim Advocates had convinced the billionaire's Open Society leaders that counterterror policies disproportionately impact Muslims. And it paid well. With Soros's support, revenue at Muslim Advocates jumped from about $78,000 in 2006 to almost $500,000 in 2007, according to the organization's IRS 990 tax forms. By 2019, its revenue had increased to $1.7 million.

While pro–Hillary Clinton and pro–President Obama groups might have been expected to oppose a Trump administration, the "intersection" of illiberal Muslim special-interest groups with liberal activist organizations, like the ACLU and Southern Poverty Law Center, to create an anti-Trump resistance was important for another reason. Illiberal Muslims had enjoyed an incredible influence during eight years of the Obama administration, in a strategic, orchestrated campaign, impacting national security policy from issues of surveillance to the silencing of any discussion on the Islam in Islamic extremism, acting like an Honor Brigade, defending perceived offenses against the dignity of Muslims as "Islamophobia."

Now that they weren't going to enjoy front-door access to the White House, they had to figure out another way to backdoor their influence on America.

* * *

The answer came thousands of miles away in Hawaii.

There, retired attorney Teresa Shook unwittingly set the stage for the rise of not only Sarsour but also CAIR in liberal Democratic politics. Commiserating with friends over Facebook, she tapped five words on her keyboard, "I think we should march." She created a Facebook event page, inviting friends to a Million Woman March on Washington, DC, the day after President Trump's inauguration.

A wave of women from across the country shared the event. One woman in Brooklyn, Mari Lynn Foulger, a clothing manufacturer, created another event page. Foulger was a heterosexual woman, married to her high school boyfriend and pregnant, but, confusingly, she used the name "Bob Bland" professionally.

Shook connected with Foulger on Facebook Messenger, and they agreed to work together. But at one point, when Shook tried to open her page, she was shocked to see it had disappeared. Foulger nonchalantly told her that she had deleted the page and created a new one where she was the administrator.

"Why?" Shook asked.

"I didn't think you'd mind," Foulger responded.

In Brooklyn, a website editor, Vanessa Wruble, messaged Foulger to offer her help. Some black women were calling the "Million Women March" a "white woman's march" that had usurped the name of the "Million Man March," held on October 16, 1995, by the Nation of Islam for black men. Wruble, a white Jewish woman, was the founder of a website, OkayAfrica, publishing news from Africa, and she reached out to contacts to find leaders who were "women of color." She suggested they rename the protest "Women's March on Washington," to avoid the criticism of "cultural appropriation."

Unbeknownst to the others, Foulger bought www.womensmarch.com and www.womensmarch.org. Wruble reached out to a contact, Michael Skolnik, political director for black rap mogul Russell Simmons. Skolnik suggested Carmen Perez, a Mexican American activist, and Tamika Mallory, a black activist and executive director of the National Action Network, a local nonprofit established by shock activist Al Sharpton. Skolnik was chairman of the board of a nonprofit organization, The Gathering for Justice, where Perez was the executive director and Mallory was a board member.

Wruble contacted the two women, and they said yes, but they wouldn't do it without their pal Linda Sarsour, who had marched with them the summer before on the twentieth anniversary of the Million Man March. Wruble agreed, having never heard of Sarsour.

The women met the next day, Saturday, at 2:30 p.m. at the Chelsea Market, in New York City, a busy tourist destination. They found a spot nearby at a luxury hotel, the Gansevoort Meatpacking NYC, and sat in the upstairs bar.

The women shared their stories about what inspired their sense of social justice. Perez, born in Oxnard, California, had grown up around gang culture. She told the group her sister had been killed in a car crash, with her funeral on Perez's seventeenth birthday, and her son's father had been shot years earlier. When Wruble said she was inspired by her Jewish roots, Perez turned to her and said, "The Jews were behind the slave trade. They made money off the backs of brown and black people."

Wruble stared at Perez, stunned.

Wruble let it drop, and the conversation turned to business. Wruble proposed a horizontal organizational structure without a hierarchy.

The women decided to use The Gathering for Justice—the nonprofit where Skolnik, Perez, and Mallory held office—as a fiscal sponsor to take donations. In less than two months, they collected $266,662 for the Women's March and were on track to raise millions.

* * *

Perez, Sarsour, and Mallory started using the language of "intersectionality" as a club to silence women who didn't fit their ideas of intersection: specifically, white women and Jewish women. Just a month earlier, one of the founders of "critical race theory," Kimberlé Crenshaw, had popularized her ideas at a TEDWomen talk titled "The urgency of intersectionality." By April 2022, her talk had five million views.

When Mallory first met Evvie Harmon, a white yoga instructor from South Carolina and local Women's March leader, Mallory told Harmon: "There isn't a white woman from the South that I'd trust."

Often, when someone would challenge Mallory, Perez, or Sarsour, they would respond with a sharp rebuttal: "And how is it going to look that you didn't let women of color lead?"

"It was racial blackmail," said a former organizer, who declined to be identified for fear of reprisal.

The organizing team sometimes met at the offices of The Gathering for Justice on Manhattan's West Side, and within days of first meeting, Mallory, Perez, Sarsour, and Foulger named themselves cochairs, along with another leader, Fontaine Pearson. This wasn't the horizontal leadership model they had agreed to use. Wruble didn't push it.

Later, when Pearson was removed as cochair over a petty spat, Wruble asked Mallory, "Is there room for me now as a cochair?" arguing it would be a powerful image to have a Jewish woman leader beside a Muslim woman.

Mallory responded bluntly, "We can't center Jewish voices too much because Black Lives Matter might have an issue with it."

* * *

The march was getting big—fast.

A new volunteer, Sarah Sophie Flicker, arranged a *Vogue* spread, shot in the South Bronx neighborhood of Hunts Point. A branding company, Amplifier, created march posters. One of the posters included a woman in an American flag headscarf. A symbol of freedom had been appropriated to act as a symbol of political Islam. The cochairs retained Ken Sunshine, celebrity publicist to singer Harry Belafonte, or "Mr. B," as they called the Jamaican American pop star. While most of them worked remotely, one day Mallory called a meeting at The Gathering for Justice office. Team members filed past the murals painted outside the building on W. 43rd Street in Hell's Kitchen and took the elevator to the fourteenth floor suite of offices, only to be greeted by a CNN crew and the cochairs dolled up by professional makeup artists, complete with false eyelashes.

CNN filmed the staged meeting, the women gathered around a living room set like a slumber party, and included the scene in a feature, *The Making of the Women's March on Washington*.

Sarsour was front and center.

The last day of November, the four cochairs did a conference call with a friendly *Huffington Post* reporter, Sarah Ruiz-Grossman, who published an article the next day with the first paragraph, "The Women's March On Washington is happening come hell or high water, march leaders say, and it's largely thanks to three women: Tamika Mallory, Carmen Perez and Linda Sarsour."

Despite her ideological contradictions, Sarsour had successfully embedded herself in the Woke Army's "anti-racist" feminist narrative. And white and Jewish women were sidelined.

* * *

After Trump's election, national Muslim organizations, their liberal allies, and numerous media outlets condemned an alleged attack by Trump voters on a Muslim woman wearing a headscarf as she walked in the NYC subway system. Weeks later, the NYPD revealed the young Muslim woman had fabricated the story to avoid punishment from her conservative Egyptian American parents for breaking curfew.

A police source told the *New York Daily News*, "Nothing happened, and there was no victim." The woman had fabricated the hoax because she been drinking late with friends and didn't want to get in trouble with her parents.

She was sentenced to six months of counseling and three days of community service.

The prosecutor read a letter from the teen, "I was stupid. I plan to continue to find ways to better myself."

Albert Cahn, an attorney at CAIR New York, told the *Daily News* the hoax shouldn't "detract" from the "numerous" reports of "Islamophobia" coming from the Muslim community.

Muslim activists were writing the postelection narrative: Muslims as victims.

* * *

Building a post-Trump narrative of "hate" in America became a lucrative business, constructed by people adept at hate themselves.

In early January, before Trump was inaugurated, Lori Saroya, national director of chapter development, rallied CAIR staff to a conference call to learn about an initiative, "Communities Against Hate," funded by the Open Society Foundations. It allocated local grants to local groups "grappling with the spike in hate incidents." The Leadership Conference Education Fund and the Lawyers' Committee for Civil Rights Under Law led the initiative. The Southern Poverty Law Center was a "strategic adviser," with CAIR Florida and CAIR New York each a "partner." (Saroya later left CAIR and launched a website, Muslims Documenting Sexism, alleging a "pattern of discrimination and abuse inside CAIR.")

* * *

Turned out the conversation about hate was a one-way street.

In Canada, Yusra Khogali was the Muslim cofounder of Black Lives Matter Toronto and cofounder of Black Liberation Collective Canada, a black student movement to "build power, using an intersectional lens, to eliminate anti-Blackness on campus." Born in 1991, she was the daughter of parents from Sudan and a graduate student at the University of Toronto pursuing a master's degree in "social justice education."

"Whiteness is not humxness [humanness]. in fact, white skin is sub-humxn," she wrote, "...white ppl are recessive genetic defects. this is factual. white ppl need white supremacy as a mechanism to protect their survival as a people because all they can do is produce themselves. black ppl simply through their dominant genes can literally wipe out the white race if we had the power to." She later deleted the post.

The year before, Khogali took to Twitter late one morning with a disturbing prayer: "Plz Allah give me strength to not cuss/kill these men and white folks out here today. Plz plz plz." She later complained in a column about being "vilified" for her "rage." She didn't apologize.

* * *

When word spread that Linda Sarsour was a leader of the Women's March, many people understandably cringed.

On March 8, 2011, at 5:38 p.m., Sarsour had launched a crude attack on ex-Muslim author Ayaan Hirsi Ali, equating her to critic of Islam, Brigitte Gabriel, and tweeting that Ali—a victim of female genital mutilation—should have her vagina removed as punishment for her views. She wrote: "Brigitte Gabriel= Ayaan Hirsi Ali. She's asking 4 an a$$ whippin'. I wish I could take their vaginas away – they don't deserve to be women." Sarsour had also publicly supported sharia, or Islamic law, which is wildly sexist in its modern-day applications, even ruling that two women equal one man as witness in criminal law. Sarsour was also fiercely anti-Israel, allied with deeply anti-Semitic Muslims, and opposed to Muslim reformers. (In late December 2015, Sarsour had called an Egyptian American Muslim writer and me "fringe" when we published a *Washington Post* column arguing that Muslim women and girls aren't Islamically required to cover their hair.)

"Intersectional feminism" employed race-baiting rhetoric to advance. And, of course, a network of Muslims—the Honor Brigade—who believed the "honor" of Islam had to be defended, used slurs such as "House Muslim," "Islamophobe," and "Uncle Tom" to discredit Muslim reformers, interjecting themselves in "intersectional feminism" to build unsuspecting, naive "partners" to do the dirty work for them. While Islamist sympathizers like Sarsour fooled Western progressives, Muslim reformers who actually embraced interpretations of Islam compatible with modernity were still vilified within Muslim circles.

* * *

The day after Inauguration Day, Friday, January 20, 2017, an estimated one hundred thousand people descended on DC under the banner of the Women's March on Washington, many wearing pink "pussy hats." They said they marched for "inclusion," "compassion," "transparency," "economic justice," and "democracy." An estimated five million people joined from around the world. A field marshal in the movement called the march organizers "Team Supreme." And Team Supreme enjoyed five-star accommodations at the posh Watergate Hotel off the Potomac River.

On the morning of the march, Teresa Shook, the woman in Hawaii who had initially conceived of a march, only got one minute of stage time.

The cochairs nixed the idea of Vanessa Wruble, the Jewish organizer who had first brought them into the effort, giving a speech. Wruble was only allowed to introduce feminist leader Gloria Steinem. If anyone departed from the script, organizer Paola Mendez scolded the group, "You will be taking time from an Indigenous woman."

The four cochairs walked casually on the stage in black Patagonia down jackets the retailer had sent them for free. Nearby, followers from the controversial Nation of Islam, led by fiery black Muslim convert Louis Farrakhan, stood as security. Leaders from Planned Parenthood and NARAL, which both supported a woman's right to have an abortion, got moments on stage due to their large sponsorships.

Madonna, the pop star, stepped forward in a black "pussy hat." "No opposing force stands a chance in the face of true solidarity," she said, flipping a note card. "And to our detractors who insist our march will not add up to anything…Fuck you."

She paused, looked down. Audible gasps could be heard.

She smiled: "FUCK you!"

* * *

Into the morning, the crowd thundered with applause as an icon in protest movements stepped onto the stage, packed shoulder-to-shoulder with people and it seemed as many camera people as march leaders. With her distinct Afro and gap in her top front teeth, she was Angela Davis, professor emeritus in the History of Consciousness program at the University of California at Santa Cruz. A member of the Black Panther Party in the 1960s, she was arrested in October 1970 for aggravated kidnapping and first-degree murder in the August 1970 killing of a judge in a San Raphael, California, courtroom. She was accused of supplying weapons to the assailant and later acquitted. The radio program *Democracy Now!* carried her Women's March speech with "Legendary Activist" below her name.

"At this very challenging moment of history," she said, remember: "We represent the powerful forces of change that are determined to prevent the dying cultures of racism, heteropatriarchy from rising again."

Without any sense of irony, she declared, "History cannot be deleted like web pages." Behind her, march leaders mingled, chatted, stared into space, and did any host of things but pay attention to the speaker. Men, wearing black beanies emblazoned with "Security," darted their eyes through the crowd.

"We cannot be made to forget that black lives do matter!" she said, to cheers.

"This is a country anchored in slavery and settler colonialism," she said, reading from her speech and waving her arms widely, before laying out her grievances about clean water accessibility from Flint, Michigan, "to the West Bank and Gaza."

Activist Linda Sarsour, in a trademark tight headscarf, this one white, now popped up a few feet behind Davis, speaking adamantly to a march organizer, as Davis roused the crowd to use "intersectional feminism" to protest "racism," "Islamophobia," "anti-Semitism," "capitalist exploitation," "state violence" by police and prisons, and "gender violence," "especially against trans women of color."

Sarsour was now deep in conversation with march organizer Tamika Mallory, both in their new Patagonia jackets, as Davis continued: "Women's rights are human rights all over the planet, and that is why we say, 'Freedom and justice for Palestine.'"

The year before, Davis had published a short book, *Freedom Is a Constant Struggle: Ferguson, Palestine, and the Foundations of a Movement*, with Frank Barat, author of a book, *Corporate Complicity in Israel's Occupation*, and president of the Palestine Legal Action Network, a Chicago-based organization founded in 2012 to challenge "efforts to threaten, harass, and legally bully activists into silence and inaction." It was a project at the Tides Foundation, a 501(c)(3) nonprofit in San Francisco that housed liberal groups. Academic Cornel West, author of *Race Matters*, had penned the foreword. Davis had joined an "indigenous and feminist-of-color, scholar activist delegation to Palestine," as she told the story.

At the march, the crowd cheered.

Davis called for the release from prison of cop killers, including "Mumia Abu-Jamal," born Wesley Cook, a young black teen in the 1960s drawn to the Blank Panther Party. By 1975, as Islamists were building an empire at Temple University, he was working in radio newscasting at Temple's WRTI radio station. He was convicted in the murder of a white police officer in Philadelphia, quoted saying, "I shot the motherfucker, and I hope the motherfucker dies."

Then, she said, "Over the next months and years, we will be called upon to intensify our demands for social justice, to become more *militant* in our defense of vulnerable populations. Those who still defend the supremacy of white male heteropatriarchy had better watch out!"

The Trump presidency would be "1,459 days of resistance," she said.

Across the world, the anti-Israel platform of the Women's March reverberated. At a Women's March rally in Oakland, California, Lara Kiswani, a Palestinian American activist in the anti-Israel Boycott, Divestment, Sanctions (BDS) movement and executive director of the Arab Resource and Organizing Center, an anti-Israel group in San Francisco, stood on stage and declared, "Let us remember that just like racism has no place in the women's movement, displacement, occupation, war, imperialism, and Zionism have absolutely no place in the women's movement."

Linda Sarsour had done it. With the Women's March, she had embedded herself in the American feminist movement, bringing with her fellow Muslim radicals. The new era of "intersectionalism" was born. It was an unholy alliance between illiberal Islamists and liberal Democrats.

CHAPTER 2

Building a Base at 500 Grove Street

Born in the seventh century, Islam was a progressive faith for its time and circumstances but regressive in the terms of orthodoxy that also plagued the history of Judaism and Christianity, including codified religious laws that sanctioned slavery and sexism.

By the tenth century, in the Middle Ages, Islam was a religion of art, science, tolerance, high culture, and critical thinking, a concept in Islam called *ijtihad*, led by rationalists called Mutazalites. While Christians were burning witches at the stake during their Dark Ages, Muslims were charting new ground in electricity, poetry, art, astronomy, and mathematics. Under Muslim control, Spain experienced centuries of progress, prosperity, and peace, with Muslims, Jews, and Christians living side by side without much conflict. In fact, Christian forces ended Islam's Golden Age with reactionary, religiously motivated violence. Muslims responded by closing the gates of *ijtihad*, and dogmatism usurped critical thinking.

For many radical Muslims, like future al-Qaeda leader Osama bin Laden, the defeat of the Ottoman Empire on October 29, 1914, marked the dawn of an era of "humiliation" for Muslims. By the early twentieth century, with the dismantling of the Ottoman Empire, a handful of radical thinkers took advantage of turmoil in the Middle East and undid any surviving remnants of progress and enlightenment in the Muslim world by promoting a belief system of rigidity, orthodoxy, and extremism that is antithetical to the positive values in Islam. In this historical moment, Islam moved from being a potential beacon for culture and tolerance to a reactionary ideology.

In the 1920s, they challenged the dictators who came to power in the nations carved out of the Ottoman Empire. While the West confronted Nazism and Communism, a generation of Muslims quietly crafted a response to seize control of their countries—and expand into the West: "Islamism," or political Islam. In Egypt in 1928, Hassan al-Banna founded the Muslim Brotherhood with the goal of creating an Islamic caliphate. In India in 1941, Muslim scholar Abul A'la Maududi established Jamaat-e-Islami with ambitions to establish a caliphate in South Asia. In 1953, Palestinian scholar Taqi al-Din al-Nabhani founded Hizb ut-Tahrir to create a global caliphate. These groups spread Islamist propaganda with pamphlets, monographs, cassettes, and books, including *Milestones*, published in 1964 by the Muslim Brotherhood's spiritual leader, Sayyid Qutb, inspiring Muslims to violent jihad. Then, in response to the Israeli defeat of Arab armies in 1967, the heads of Muslim countries met in Mecca in 1969 and created the Organization of Islamic Conference, renaming it later to Organization of Islamic Cooperation to "work for revitalizing Islam's pioneering role in the world," "support the struggle of the Palestinian people," and "defend the true image of Islam, to combat defamation of Islam," according to its mission statement.

The Muslim Brothers—and they were mostly men—first started arriving in the United States in the 1950s, finding refuge in the ivory towers of college campuses from the University of Indiana to Temple University in Philadelphia.

In the 1960s, more Muslim immigrants, including my family, arrived in the West.

In October 1965, President Lyndon Johnson signed the Hart-Celler Act, lifting national immigration quotas that benefited Northern Europeans. Muslims from around the world started arriving in the United States. Many, like my parents, were drawn by the values in the West that they wanted to emulate and nurture in their families. Others brought the political ambitions of the Muslim Brotherhood, Jamaat-e-Islami, Hizb ut-Tahrir, and the Organization of Islamic Cooperation to the West.

The most orthodox members of this first generation of twentieth-century Muslim immigrants to America established a foothold for Western radicalization by creating groups that ensconced their dogmatic values to advance Islam in the West. In the 1960s, they started with the Muslim Students Association and the Islamic Circle of North America.

In 1978, a young scholar of literature, Edward Said, gave Islamists the language they needed to advance their cause in a book he published, *Orientalism*. While born into a Christian family, he gave Muslims, like Hamid Dabashi, a young Iranian American Muslim colleague at Columbia University, just the words he needed to attack the West as the "colonizer" and the "oppressor," in a new field called "post-colonialism."

* * *

In early 1979, a revolution in the country of Iran shook the world. It heralded the rise of an extremist interpretation of the minority Shia sect of Islam that brought a repressive theocracy to Iran. In Saudi Arabia, where the government was controlled by an equally repressive interpretation from the Sunni sect of Islam, the monarchs watched the developments in Iran with alarm. In response, they started increasing the exportation of their rigid Wahhabi ideology of Sunni Islam to the world. They had the perfect excuse in late 1979 when the Soviet Union invaded Afghanistan. To inspire fighters in Afghanistan and Pakistan to take up arms against the Soviets, Saudi Arabia exported its extremist Wahhabism to the region, supported by the United States and the government of Pakistan. The fighters took the name *mujahideen*, or warriors for *deen*, the Arabic word for "faith." It was the perfect synergy with the Islamist revivalism of Abul A'la Maududi, a cleric turned theocrat or *maulana*. It was also a recipe for disaster. The Pakistani dictator at the time, General

Zia-ul-Haq, brought Islamic law to the country. In 1979, the King Faisal Foundation, named for the Saudi leader assassinated in 1975 by his nephew, gave Maududi its first King Faisal Award.

With an oil boom, Saudi Arabia pumped millions of dollars into its mission for *dawah*, or "invitation to Islam," through proselytizing, not just to non-Muslims, but Muslims, promoting Saudi's tyrannical strain of rigid Wahhabism.

From 1979 to the present day, the Muslim theocracies of Saudi Arabia and Iran—followed by Qatar and now Turkey—poured billions of dollars into exporting toxic interpretations of Islam to Muslims around the world.

* * *

These early leaders in America happily took money from foreign donors and governments, striving for hegemony in the world, setting the stage for decades of foreign influence in American Muslim practices. They called themselves "brothers." And they were absolutely a Muslim brotherhood.

One of them was a Palestinian immigrant, Ismail al-Faruqi, born in 1921 in Jaffa in British Mandate Palestine. By 1945, he became district governor of Galilee, but with the 1948 establishment of the state of Israel, he moved to Lebanon. As a friend later wrote, "The Zionist occupation and Israel's subsequent independence in 1948 came as both a national catastrophe and an economic blow to him. His job disappeared, and he decided to immigrate to Lebanon."

Al-Faruqi was drawn to the emerging Muslim Brotherhood movement. "His hostility toward Israel could not be quenched by his father's, as well as the mosque's, passive form of Islam." He arrived in the United States in the 1970s to study at Indiana University in Indianapolis, Indiana. There he met Muslim students from around the world who could "sway a renowned professor to revolutionize his longstanding ideological perspective," his friend wrote. He became a scholar of Islam and comparative religions and moved to Temple University to teach and expand his influence. In the 1980s, the friend said, al-Faruqi "invited me to attend a large meeting of Palestinians, some of whom later became leading figures in Hamas," the militant Palestinian organization designated a terrorist organization years later. "It was obvious that the organizers wanted to transform him into an Islamic spokesman for the Palestinian cause in the United States."

In 1980, one group of professional immigrants from the Middle East started the American-Arab Anti-Discrimination Committee. That year, one of the early immigrants, Muhammad Shafiq, later recalled that the Muslim Brothers, including al-Faruqi, made a decision: "It was finally decided to launch the International Institute of Islamic Thought."

Al-Faruqi created a project, the Islamization of Knowledge. He secured $25 million from the Saudi Islamic Development Bank to establish the institute. He was by then the founder of the Islamic Studies program in the Department of Religion at Temple University. He and his wife, Lois al-Faruqi, a scholar of Islamic art, wrote *The Cultural Atlas of Islam*. She went by the name of Lamya as her Muslim name.

That year, he flew to the University of Alberta in Edmonton, Canada, for a conference, Dimensions of Islam in North America.

In his lecture, titled "Islamic Ideals in North America," he said Muslim immigrants to the West had two duties: calling non-Muslims to Islam and transforming the North American reality so that it conforms to Islamic standards.

"Nothing would be greater than these...peoples of the West marching forward under the banner of Allahu Akbar!" he said.

* * *

The next year, al-Faruqi drove the few hours from Philadelphia to Northern Virginia with Muhammad Shafiq, his trusted aide from Tora Bora, Afghanistan. Al-Faruqi wanted to pay some of the brothers in Islam a visit and show Shafiq some real estate they had just bought.

They stopped in front of a building at 500 Grove Street in a small town called Herndon in Fairfax County, Virginia. It was just about a forty-five-minute drive from the White House in America's rural countryside. Nearby towns like Great Falls, Sterling, and Leesburg had dairy farms on acres of rolling hills next to woodlands. It sat inland, just a few miles from the bucolic Potomac River and one of the widest roads cutting through Fairfax Country heading westward, a two-lane road, Route 7, or Leesburg Highway. It went west to the city of Leesburg in neighboring Loudoun County, which bordered West Virginia and its rural roads and byways. Local officials had just built a new international airport minutes away, named after former Secretary of State John Dulles. It was a quiet place, affordable with solid public school education, run by Fairfax County Public Schools. It was an immigrant's dream.

But Shafiq saw only barren land. "Faruqi, there is nothing here! You are buying these buildings? For what?" Shafiq exclaimed.

Al-Faruqi explained that this was where they would realize their vision for decades to come.

The next day, on December 7, 1981, the Muslim Brothers had their first official meeting of their new organization—the International Institute of Islamic Thought—at the nearby home of Jamal al-Barzinji on Safa Court. Al-Barzinji had gotten $8 million from a Saudi family. He wanted to provide the Muslim movement in the United States a wellspring of Islamic scholarship. The Brothers had bought up acres of land and called their street Safa Court, named after one of the hills in Mecca where Hajar was said to have run with her baby Ishmael after Abraham dropped her in the desert. The Brothers who were neighbors in his quiet cul-de-sac walked across the street to the meeting. They elected Ismail al-Faruqi, the Temple University professor, as the treasurer and secretary-general of the institute. Muhammad Shafiq was there. They drafted a constitution and a brochure.

They learned how to set up the organization and registered it in Pennsylvania, where al-Faruqi lived. But everyone knew their organizational base was in the building at 500 Grove Street in the sleepy town of Herndon, Virginia. Al-Faruqi also became a cofounder of the Association of Muslim Social Scientists. Yaqub Mirza, a young immigrant from Pakistan, became an officer.

Nestled among dairy farms and rolling fields, the Muslim Brothers were hiding in plain view. They established a spider's web of organizations, using the International Institute of Islamic Thought to press their agenda of their founders for "the Islamization of thought" in not only the US but the world.

Among the cofounders of IIIT, as it has been called, was a one-time State Department consultant, Abdurahman Alamoudi. He later pled guilty to plotting with Libya to assassinate the ruler of Saudi Arabia, as well as financial crimes related to terrorism, according to the US Department of Justice. Another Muslim Brother was Sami Al-Arian, who would later be deported in a plea-arrangement deal for allegedly assisting a Palestinian terror organization. In an obituary he later wrote for his friend on *CounterPunch*, a self-described "radical" online magazine, Al-Arian credited al-Barzinji for raising "millions of dollars" and establishing "endowed chair positions and centers in some of the most prestigious universities in the US and around the world, including Georgetown University, Harvard University, Hartford Seminary, George Mason University, Cambridge University, California State University, and many others." He wrote: al-Barzinji was involved in the "establishment of every major Islamic organization in the US in the four decades where he either headed the organization, served on its board, or helped in building its programs and outreach, including the Islamic Society of North America (ISNA), the Muslim Students' Association (MSA), the North American Islamic Trust (NAIT), the Association of Muslim Scientists and Engineers (AMSE), the Association of Muslim Social Scientists (AMSS), The World Assembly of Muslim Youth (WAMY), The American Muslim Council (AMC), the American Muslim Alliance (AMA), Council on American Islamic Relations (CAIR), the Graduate School of Islamic and Social Sciences (GSISS), The Fairfax Institute; the Center for the Study of Islam and Democracy Inc. (CSID), a 501(c)3 nonprofit based in Arlington, Virginia; as well as many other organizations and institutions from all over the world, big and small...."

Another IIIT founder, Iqbal Unus, later told *Washington Post* religion reporter Michelle Boorstein that the group's goals were to understand "why Muslims were having trouble fully contributing to contemporary culture." He acknowledged some of their opinions reflected a "very insular worldview, not language that was appropriate in a multicultural, pluralistic environment."

From this outpost for decades to come, the Muslim Brothers launched, funded, and supported organizations such as the Council on American-Islamic Relations, the Holy Land Foundation for Relief and Development, the Safa Group, and politicians from the school board and state house to the US House of Representatives. This was the base for the Honor Brigade that was to come, defending the "honor" of Islam and Muslims.

* * *

The Muslim Brothers saw an exciting opportunity to help fund their vision: buying a chicken farm in Gainesville, Georgia, named Mar-Jac Poultry Inc.

At one point, in a January 4, 2019, letter, Mulham Shbeib, vice president of finance, outlined their "halal" process. Mar-Jac contracted with an Islamic organization to provide Muslim laborers to "start and back up the killing machine while uttering the Tasmiyah & Takbir." *Tasmiyah* is the name for an Arabic phrase, *bismillah*, which means "in the name of Allah." *Takbir* is the name of another Arabic phrase, "Allahu Akbar." The chicken went through a low-voltage stunner that didn't kill the birds but "only calms them down to be ready for the mechanical slaughtering knife which has a sharp rotating blade," he added.

"The slaughtering knife cuts the jugular vein as well as the windpipe without severing the head from the body and causes the chicken to be fully drained of blood," he wrote.

The workers examined the chicken, and Muslim workers manually cut their necks if the machine hadn't done it properly. They killed about twenty-five thousand chickens per hour on three lines. The process is accepted, he said, by the "majority of Muslim Ulema," or scholars, for "wholesale mechanical killing."

Any customers requesting a "Halal certificate" would get one signed on behalf of the International Institute of Islamic Thought on Grove Street.

* * *

The next year, the Muslim Brothers met in Lugano, Switzerland. They circulated a document, dated 1982, called "The Project," outlining a twelve-point plan for building mosques, opening Islamic schools, and adopting "the Palestinian cause as part of a worldwide Islamic plan…by means of *jihad*." The Brothers understood that Yousef al-Qaradawi, a rising star in their global network, had written the document.

The 1982 document called for "the establishment of an Islamic state." The Islamic Society of North America was launched that same year, followed by the Muslim Public Affairs Council. The Muslim Brothers claim the document can't be authenticated, but the FBI included the original document, written in Arabic, and a translation as part of its evidence in a case against the network of organizations at 500 Grove Street. With peace evading Israelis and Palestinians, a new Palestinian organization was born in 1987 called Hamas, whose charter—to this day—seeks the destruction of the state of Israel. Later that year, Palestinians launched their first *intifada*, the Arabic word for "resistance," in Israel and the Palestinian territories.

* * *

One day, shocking news spread from Pennsylvania to Virginia. In the early morning of May 27, 1986, police found the bloody bodies of Ismail al-Faruqi; his American-born wife, Lois, a convert to Islam; and their pregnant daughter, Anmar al-Zein, twenty-seven, in their home in Wyncote, Pennsylvania. Al-Faruqi and his wife had been stabbed to death with a fifteen-inch survival knife. When police arrived, al-Zein was barely conscious; the mother and baby both survived.

The *Straits Times* in Malaysia, citing a British publication, said the murders were the work of "Zionist fundamentalists." In a 2013 article published on al-Faruqi's life in the *American Journal of Islamic Social Sciences*, a psychologist friend, Malik Badri, wrote that he last met al-Faruqi in the early 1980s when he introduced him to "distinguished Palestinians, some of whom later became leading figures in Hamas."

"Unfortunately," he noted, "the Zionists were aware of the potential danger he represented to their continued occupation of Palestine and ongoing atrocities.... This tragedy was not due to his work as an Islamizer, but because of his future anti-Zionist writings and work."

In fact, a black convert to Islam, Joseph Louis Young, forty, confessed to the murder in 1987. He went by the name Yusuf Ali, and he said that another Muslim student had convinced him to murder al-Faruqi for allegedly forcing Malaysian students at Temple to perform "homosexual acts" with al-Faruqi in exchange for scholarships to Temple. The student denied the charges. Two psychiatrists for the defense testified that the victims were not involved in illicit conduct with students but that Young was anti-gay and his belief that the victims were involved in gay relationships triggered this attack. Young died of natural causes at the age of fifty on death row at Greene County Memorial Hospital.

In shock over his mentor's murder, Muhammad Shafiq returned to the US from Pakistan in 1986 on a Fulbright scholarship. He lived in the Northern Virginia suburb of Herndon, near his trusted friends.

There, the Muslim Brothers kept meeting. They were the forefathers of Muslim nationalism in America: Jamal Barzinji and Hisham Altalib from Iraq; Abdul Hamid Ahmad AbuSulayman from Saudi Arabia; Yaqub Mirza and Iqbal Unus from Pakistan; and Sayyid Saeed from India. "I saw that if you really want to build institutions, you need a teamwork," recalled one of the men years later.

In 1989, Barzinji told the group that Muslims had to participate in the political process. He created the American Muslim Council to engage in politics.

* * *

By the early 1990s, the new generation of Muslims in America had established their hub in Northern Virginia.

In 1991, Muslim leaders issued a document that outlined a "stable Islamic Movement led by the Muslim Brotherhood" and a

"Civilization-Jihadist Process" with the US as a "settlement" for "the *jamaat*," or Islamic community. The paper's subtitle: "On the General Strategic Goal for the Group in North America." It was signed "Your brother/Mohamed Akram."

Addressed to "my brothers," he wrote that "what is between your hands is not strange or a new submission without a root, but rather an attempt to interpret and explain some of what came in the long-term plan which we approved and adopted in our council and our conference in the year (1987)." He wrote, "What might have encouraged me to submit the memorandum in this time in particular is my feeling of a 'glimpse of hope' and the beginning of good tidings which bring the good news that we have embarked on a new stage of Islamic activism stages in this continent."

He continued, "The papers which are between your hands are not abundant extravagance, imaginations or hallucinations which passed in the mind of one of your brothers, but they are rather hopes, ambitions and challenges that I hope that you share some or most of which with me. I do not claim their infallibility or absolute correctness, but they are an attempt which requires study, outlook, detailing and rooting from you."

* * *

In 1993, a small group of Muslims met in Philadelphia. The FBI recorded the meeting.

They agreed they would refer to the new anti-Israel group, Hamas, as "Samah."

Inside, Holy Land Foundation CEO Shukri Abu Baker warned the group. "Please don't mention the name Samah in an explicit manner. We agree on saying it as 'Sister Samah.'"

When someone accidentally mentioned Hamas, Baker interrupted the meeting and said, "Didn't we say not to mention that term?"

The man fixed his statement and continued, "Is it against the movement...."

A man joked about using the word "Samah." He said, "What movement?"

Another man, identified by the government as "Gawad," responded, "Hamas..., the Samah Movement," the crowd breaking into laughter. "...I mean Samah."

A young Palestinian, Nehad Awad Hammad—later adopting the name of Nihad Awad—spelled out his vision for spreading the Hamas mission, saying, "If there is a political issue, a Samah's input, for instance, about this or that, we inform people to contact their representatives...."

In early 1994, Awad delivered a speech at Barry University, a private college in Miami, Florida, where he responded to an audience question about humanitarian efforts in the Palestinian territories. He was quoted saying, "I used to support the PLO, and I used to be the President of the General Union of Palestine Students which is part of the PLO here in the United States, but after I researched the situation inside Palestine and outside, I am in support of the Hamas movement more than the PLO."

Three months later, in June 1994, Awad and other leaders of the Islamic Association for Palestine—including the president, Omar Ahmad, and Awad's convert friend, Cary "Ibrahim" Hooper—founded the Council on American-Islamic Relations, or CAIR. They named Awad its executive director. In mid-September 1994, CAIR filed its original articles of incorporation. Its first state chapter was in the San Francisco Bay area.

One of CAIR's first campaigns was to go after a journalist, Steve Emerson. The next year, 1995, Emerson established the Investigative Project on Terrorism, reporting on the Islamists. For the founders of CAIR, destroying Emerson became a priority, no matter how many years it would take. And it would take many years.

For forty years, the Muslim Brothers had enjoyed virtually unfettered expansion in the West. They were the institutions in the "Civilization-Jihadist Process," established to exploit Western civil liberties, the culture of political correctness, and later, the new influence of the radical ideology of "critical race theory" to expand their influence.

* * *

At Georgetown University, John Esposito was hard at work using the Jesuit Catholic campus as the staging ground for another part of the vision of Muslim leaders. He was an Italian American and Catholic. He had studied at Temple University with Ismail al-Faruqi, the Muslim Brother murdered by his student, as his mentor. In 1993, Esposito started the Center for Muslim-Christian Understanding at Georgetown University.

There was no inclusion of "Jewish" in the center's name. Years later, Esposito said in a speech, "I often don't say this publicly... you will all forget what you hear...my center is called Center for Muslim-Christian Understanding, and that's because of the people who originally established it, what they wanted to do...until Palestine is resolved, one cannot talk about this kind of official, I think, trialogue in the kind of effective way in which one would want to."

At one point, his original donor moved on to other projects.

"We were running down on our finances," Esposito later recalled. "It was kind of like an *inshallah* moment," he said, invoking the Arabic term that means "God willing."

One of the original Muslim Brothers who had set up a hub in Herndon, Virginia—Jamal Barzinji—introduced an important member of the Saudi ruling family, Saudi Prince Alwaleed bin Talal, to his friend, Esposito. Bin Talal wanted to expand his footprint in the West. In 2005, he gave Georgetown University $20 million, and Georgetown renamed the center the Prince Alwaleed bin Talal Center for Muslim-Christian Understanding.

* * *

The Muslim Brothers needed a home for their engagement with the US State Department, pressing their vision for political Islam within the cover of democracy.

In 1998, Esposito worked with the International Institute for Islamic Thought for a new project that served just that mission. He helped start the Center for the Study of Islam and Democracy Inc.

The Muslim Brothers now had just the platform to press one of their critical arguments in the West: the US government and other Western democracies should support Islamist movements in foreign countries in the spirit of democracy. Islam was a way of life, they argued, to get around the notion of secularism and the separation of church and state. You weren't going to separate Islam from politics, so wouldn't it be better to have it emerge in a democracy?

The argument was fine in theory, if you didn't pay attention to the details of what fundamentalist Islam in governance looks like: denial of human rights to women, persecution of minority sects and religions, and so many other transgressions on fundamental human rights, such as, for example, the right of a person to reject religion.

Indeed, later, an investigative reporter, Paul Sperry, now a columnist for the *New York Post*, dubbed nearby Route 7 "Wahhabi Corridor," because community leaders, think-tanks, mosques, businesses, and nonprofits, many of them funded by the business entities at 500 Grove Street, had established themselves along Route 7 through the 1980s and 1990s, embracing the extremist Saudi interpretations of Islam called Wahhabism.

Two of the 9/11 hijackers had even lived in an apartment complex, Skyline Towers, off Route 7, praying at Dar Al-Hijrah Islamic Center, a block off Route 7, where the mosque leadership had hired Yemeni American preacher Anwar al-Awlaki to be their imam. After the 9/11 attacks, al-Awlaki abandoned the strip malls that line Route 7 and returned to his native Yemen where he joined al-Qaeda. Knowledge of American life helped him become an effective propagandist. His YouTube videos enticed young Muslims to violent jihad—until he was silenced in 2011 by missiles fired from US military drones on the orders of then-President Barack Obama. Today, with Saudi Arabia having alienated many of these American Muslim leaders by opposing the Muslim Brotherhood, the attachment to the Wahhabi ideology has morphed into an advocacy for Islamism, or political Islam, embraced by groups such as the Muslim Brotherhood in Egypt and the governments of Turkey and Qatar.

In 2002, the *Wall Street Journal* published an article "Funds Under Terror Probe Flowed from Offshore," allegedly supporting nefarious activities in Herndon, Virginia, off Wahhabi Corridor.

"Large sums from two offshore financial havens flowed through the accounts of several US-based companies and charities raided Wednesday by Treasury Department agents investigating terrorism financing, tax and corporate records show," the article read.

The companies had the same address: 500 Grove Street.

CHAPTER 3

Parallel Ideological Movement Emerging

Another movement was afoot in America. Through the 1950s, 1960s, and 1970s, Marxist theory had taken root in America in many communities.

In 1973, a black law professor at Harvard University College of Law, Derrick Bell Jr., published a book *Race, Racism, and American Law*. Little could he know he was laying the groundwork for a revolution that would one day topple the statues of even abolitionist leaders. He would earn a place in history as "Godfather Provocateur," as one fan called him, influencing not only law students and scholars but also hip-hop group Public Enemy and its star rapper, Chuck D, along with other hip-hop artists of the 1970s and 1980s, including Grandmaster Flash and the Furious Five, Tupac Shakur, and N.W.A.

By the late 1970s, Bell had introduced new courses to the curriculum at Harvard Law School, based on his book, examining American law through a racial lens. In 1980, Bell published a sixteen-page article in *Harvard Law Review* called "*Brown v. Board of Education* and the Interest-Convergence Dilemma." Soon after, he left Harvard to become the dean of the University of Oregon School of Law. And black students at Harvard Law School marched to protest for his curriculum to remain at the law school.

Two of Bell's Harvard Law students would carry the mantle decades later for the revolution that Bell envisioned. They were Kimberlé Crenshaw and Mari Matsuda. They organized boycotts and developed a new class called "Alternative Course," with Bell's *Race, Racism, and American Law* as the course textbook and guest speakers including young lawyer activist scholars Richard Delgado and Neil Gotanda.

Born in 1939, Delgado went to public school and earned an AB in philosophy and mathematics at the University of Washington and a JD from the University of California's Berkeley School of Law. He was an editor at the *California Law Review*. He'd later be called a father of "critical race theory." Slightly younger, Gotanda was Asian American, graduating with a BS from Stanford University in 1967, a JD from the University of California Berkeley School of Law in 1980, and an LLM from Harvard University in 1980.

In 1987, Crenshaw invited like-minded thinkers to a retreat, "New Developments in Critical Race Theory." Joining her were Matsuda, Gotanda, law professor Chuck Lawrence, and several others. She later wrote that "critical race theory" was "made up as a name," adding, "Sometimes you gotta fake it until you make it."

In July 1989, the group held its first "Workshop on Critical Race Theory" at the St. Benedict Center, a convent outside Madison, Wisconsin. The luminaries of this new movement were there: Bell, Crenshaw, Delgado, Matsuda, and attorney Patricia William. They even had T-shirts made for the workshop.

In describing her life, Matsuda said in a videotaped interview, "I was raised by actual Marxists," who faced the "demon" of capitalism. In a book, Crenshaw wrote that "one might say that CRT was the offspring of a post-civil rights institutional activism that was generated and informed by an oppositionalist orientation toward racial power."

By their own acknowledgment, the movement tapped the principles of Marxism, along with several other inspirations: "critical theory"; "critical legal studies," which argues that the law is corrupt and part of a larger institution of society designed to keep the establishment of existing power and white elite; "feminist jurisprudence," which teaches that the entire system is stacked against women with patriarchal inequity, promoting only men; "postcolonial theory"; and "postmodernism," a belief that the entire system from philosophy to government is corrupt.

The scientific method has dominated natural science since the seventeenth century and holds that a hypothesis cannot be considered "correct" unless it is challenged by systemic observation and experimentation. The scientific method relies upon rigorous skepticism and criticism to avoid so-called confirmation bias—the tendency to interpret and seek out new evidence as confirmation of the correctness of one's existing hypothesis and beliefs.

"Critical race theory" could not exist were it subject to the scientific method of any of the natural sciences or even softer sciences such as economics. "Critical race theory" starts with a hypothesis that institutional racism is responsible for all ills of disadvantaged minorities, explains all contrary findings as further evidence of racism, and discourages skepticism and criticism by questioning the motives and morals of its critics—branding them racists.

It is not an exaggeration to say that "critical race theory" could not withstand even the most basic criticism were skeptics permitted to speak freely. Accordingly, instead of being a science or taxonomy, "critical race theory" is a religious cult—a self-perpetuating, self-confirming ideology premised on faith, promoted by charismatic leaders who punish and silence any questioning members with risk of excommunication and brand nonbelievers as racist, the same way fundamentalist Islam brands nonbelievers as infidels.

Classic liberalism says that you have to prove your theory, but "critical race theory" is like a self-perpetuating, self-confirming ideology promoted by a cult that says anyone who doesn't believe in it is heretical. They found they were able to overwhelm intellectual people with their allegations of being "racist." It's like a religious orthodoxy.

After graduating with her LLM from Harvard in 1986, Crenshaw joined the faculty of UCLA School of Law. One of the courses on her class schedule: "critical race theory." These new ideologues set about establishing their body of literature. In 1988, Crenshaw published an article, "Race, Reform and Retrenchment: Transformation and Legitimation in Anti-Discrimination Law," in the *Harvard Law Review*.

In 1994, University of San Diego law professor Roy Brooks published an article, "Critical Race Theory: A Proposed Structure and Application to Federal Pleading," in the *Harvard Black Letter Law Journal*. The next year, in 1995, the godfather of "critical race theory," Derrick Bell, published an article, "Who's Afraid of Critical Race Theory?" in the *University of Illinois Law Review*.

That same year, in 1995, law professors Kimberlé Crenshaw, Neil Gotanda, Gary Peller, and Kendall Thomas published a tome, *Critical Race Theory: The Key Writings that Formed the Movement*, with The New Press. With a bright red cover, it became like a Bible for the new movement.

And they started establishing institutions. In 1996, Crenshaw started a 501(c)(3) nonprofit, called the African American Policy Forum, with Luke Charles Harris, a professor of political science at Vassar College. It would become a vehicle for Crenshaw to spread "critical race theory" and its ideology. Meanwhile, the parallel Islamist movement developed by the Muslim Brothers, seething with hate for Israel, was developing.

* * *

A young Palestinian student, Hatem Bazian, arrived in Northern California in the 1980s with one goal: destroy Israel.

"Boycott Israel!" Bazian declared one day to fellow protesters on the campus of the University of California at Berkeley.

Born in the 1960s in Jordan to a father from Nablus on the West Bank and a mother from Jerusalem, Bazian had gone to high school across the border in Amman, Jordan, like Nihad Awad, the cofounder of the Council on American-Islamic Relations. In Jordan, Bazian was a member of the General Union of Palestinian Students, the student arm of the Palestinian Liberation Organization, eventually becoming its president. When he moved to the United States and settled in the San Francisco Bay area, he rose to become president of the San Francisco State University Associated Students and the governing board of the student union. Jewish students complained that Bazian fomented anti-Semitism on campus, including attacks on Hillel, the largest Jewish organization on campus. His nickname became "Hate 'Em Bazian."

One day, in fact, Bazian led a group of students to the campus newspaper, *Golden Gator*, and accused its staff of being Jewish spies. Another day, when artists painted a mural of Malcolm X with dollar signs surrounded by Jewish stars, the *Golden Gator* reported that Bazian spoke in support of the mural at a press conference, but Jewish students were barred from the press conference. Later, he spoke at a fundraiser for KindHearts for Charitable Humanitarian Development, an organization linked to Hamas and investigated by the US Treasury Department for designation as a terrorist organization and successor to the Holy Land Foundation for Relief and Development, established at 500 Grove Street in Herndon, Virginia. KindHearts was effectively shut down by an executive order signed by President Bush in 2001. Bazian graduated with a BA in international relations and speech and communication and an MA in international relations from San Francisco State University. On the board of the United States Student Association, he authored resolutions, later adopted by the organization's national conference, to cut US aid to Israel and impose sanctions on Israel for its sale of military equipment to apartheid South Africa. By the early 1990s, Bazian started as a PhD student in philosophy and Islamic studies at UC Berkeley, where he became very involved with the Muslim Students Association, not just as a student—as a mentor.

In town, Bazian was to meet an unexpected ally who would help him leverage the new ideas of "critical race theory" to his obsession: destroying the state of Israel.

* * *

Born into a reform Jewish family in Cleveland, Ohio, with her father a dentist and her mother from a family that owned movie theaters, Judith Butler had joined the faculty at the University of California at Berkeley after publishing a book, *Gender Trouble*, in 1990 that had made her a key thinker in the emerging field of "critical race theory," extending its sweeping ideas to feminism and "gender theory." In her book, Butler wrote about "performativity," or the notion that gender isn't something that we are but rather something we do, "confounding the very binarism of sex, and exposing its fundamental unnaturalness."

She popularized words like "trope," "problematic," and "heteronormative." Importantly, for Bazian, she was a Jew who was a vocal critic of Israel.

* * *

Bazian was learning quickly how to tap racial politics to further his anti-Israel agenda.

In early April 2000, he organized a conference called "The Forgotten Roots," featuring two black writers, one a New York University faculty member. That fall, Bazian stood before a crowd of anti-Israel protesters, arguing for divestment of academic funds in Israel. He had just learned that a cousin, fourteen, had been killed in a confrontation with Israeli soldiers. The next year, in 2001, Bazian and a UC Berkeley pal, Snehal Shingavi, from India, cofounded a group, Students for Justice in Palestine, which immediately launched a campaign to press UC Berkeley to divest school investments in Israel. Importantly, they recruited young students to their cause. And they would emerge as a dangerous vehicle for anti-Semitism on college campuses.

One afternoon in late April 2001, about thirty-two protesters staged a mock Palestinian refugee camp on the UC Berkeley campus, complete with "Israeli military checkpoints." The protesters occupied Wheeler Hall, blocking access to the building by locking all but three of the building's twelve doors and linking arms to block the three open entrances. By 5:00 p.m., about thirty police officers pulled students and other protesters from the doorways. The police set up a booking station in the lobby and gave the protesters citations, photographing them before releasing them. Shingavi told the college newspaper, "Now it's largely a symbolic action, in solidarity with Palestine."

Will "Iron Sheikh" Youmans, a Palestinian American student at UC Berkeley's law school, was in the crowd. His mother, a schoolteacher, had met and married his father, a white American attorney, in the 1970s in Michigan. She had moved there in her twenties after growing up in Nazareth, in northern Israel. Her ancestral roots traced to nearby Yaffa. During the 1948 war, her father had left home for work. Years later, Youmans said in an interview, "He wanted to get back home, but he could only get back to Nazareth...which means his family ended up losing all their land to Israel." His maternal family became one of Israel's Arab Palestinian population. Born in 1978 in Detroit, Youmans started rapping as a teenager, writing lyrics about prejudice, identity, and his anti-Israel views. He took his "Iron Sheikh" moniker from a 1980s World Wrestling Federation villain character who wore a traditional Palestinian keffiyeh headscarf with black-and-white checkers and a long moustache as he battled stars such as Hulk Hogan. Youmans said, "To be Middle Eastern in this country is to be a villain."

* * *

At the protest pressing for a boycott of Israel, Youmans told a student journalist interviewing him, "The situation in Palestine is getting exponentially worse for Palestinians. The Palestinian death toll is rising at the hands of the Israeli army." He told allies on a Google listserv, "Today, Wheeler hall was transformed to 'Muhammad Al-Durra Hall.' A banner announcing the new name flew from the second floor of the building."

Muhammad al-Durrah was a twelve-year-old boy filmed in September 2000 in Gaza during the second intifada, wailing as his father shielded him from behind a concrete cylinder amid crossfire between Israeli and Palestinian security forces. Days earlier, Israeli leader Ariel Sharon had walked onto the grounds of the al-Aqsa mosque, which sits next to the Dome of the Rock, the mosque with a golden dome in the heart of Jerusalem. Al-Durra's father later said the Israel Defense Forces, or IDF, had killed his son and footage of his burial was broadcast around the world. The IDF said its soldiers did not kill the boy. Later, Pakistani militants who created a murder video of journalist Daniel Pearl included images of the boy to justify Pearl's murder.

On campus, as Youmans marched, another one of Bazian's mentees, Javad Hashmi, a young Muslim from Fremont, California, and a UC Berkeley freshman, wrote a pointed attack against Israel in *Al-Bayan*, a UC Berkeley Muslim student publication where he was a staff writer. Hashmi was born on July 16, 1982, in Santa Clara County, California. His father, Tauseef Hashmi, worked at Cisco, the technology company, and on September 11, 2006, his father had received patent No. 7106731 for a "router with class of service mapping." They were from Pakistan. His older sister, Sarah Qureshi, would emerge into an activist in her own right under her married name, Sarah Deen. His mother, Talat Hashmi, carried the maiden name of Ansari, the name of a tribe in the city of Medina that helped Muhammad in the seventh century when he fled the wrath of enemies in Mecca. Hashmi majored in electrical engineering and computer science at UC Berkeley. A first wave of refugees arrived in Fremont after the 1979 Soviet invasion of Afghanistan led to the flight of Afghans to the West, and a second wave came in the 1990s when the Taliban took control of the country. Many immigrants from India and Pakistan also called Fremont home as they arrived during the dotcom boom of the 1990s in Silicon Valley, buying the more affordable homes in the quiet town. Bazian had once spoken at the local mosque on the topic, "Islamophobia in America and Muslim Responsibility."

The Hashmi family did well in America, eventually moving into one of the more expensive neighborhoods, where one winter blow-up figures of a gingerbread family filled the yard across the street, Mr. Gingerbread, Mrs. Gingerbread, and Boy Gingerbread bobbing and weaving in the cool winter air. Hashmi came from privilege, enjoying entitlements like most people in America never enjoyed. And yet he attacked the West.

The headline on Hashmi's article read: "A Fake Peace for Palestine." He called Palestinian leader Yasser Arafat an "Uncle Tom" for negotiating a peace settlement with Israel. It was a slur in the black community. It would be a smear he would return to using.

He wrote: "Arafat and all of the other Uncle Tom Palestinians are assigned as the spokespeople for the Palestinians."

He quoted Bazian as saying, "...But let these Israelis know that in fifty years we will demand EVERY SINGLE PENNY that they stole from us! We will demand retribution for every one of the more than 800 businesses they liquidated of ours in 1948! We will demand every single tree they uprooted of ours! We will demand every house they burned down of ours! We will demand every inch of land they stole from us!"

Hashmi ended his article as dramatically as Bazian had punctuated it, writing, "Although the military, economic, and political Uprising to capture people's lost labor, capital and and [*sic*] is waged in the Middle East, the moral, intellectual, and spiritual uprising to capture people's lost hearts, minds and souls will be waged the world over!"

Bazian was successfully inculcating this young generation of students with his fiery brand of activism, and they were learning a dark art in the new internet age: being keyboard warriors.

* * *

That summer of 2001, friends of Hatem Bazian at the Arab Anti-Discrimination Committee, founded twenty-one years earlier, launched a new task force called "Right of Return." It advocated for the Palestinian "right to return to their original homes, have their property restored to them and receive compensation for any losses incurred as a result of displacement or dispossession."

Later that summer in Chicago, another friend—Palestinian American writer Ali Hasan Abunimah—registered a new website, ElectronicIntifada.com, with an address on N. State Street in downtown Chicago, on the same block as the headquarters of the fledgling CAIR Chicago chapter.

Born in 1971 in Washington, DC, Abunimah grew up in the United Kingdom and Belgium before returning to the United States to study at Princeton University. There, he became an activist for Palestinians. His mother was from the village of Lifta, now in modern-day Israel. His father, from the village of Battir, now in the

West Bank, was a Jordanian diplomat who served as ambassador to the United Nations. Some of the Abunimah family said their ancestors moved to Palestine from Spain after the expulsion of Muslims from Spain in 1492. Abunimah received a second degree from the University of Chicago, where he worked as a researcher for a community-based organization that surveyed the city's Arab community, becoming vice president and a board member of the Arab American Action Network, before starting Electronic Intifada.

* * *

Meanwhile, while these younger activists were securing their foothold in America, the older generation of Muslims was fighting for their right to stay in America—and out of jail.

Through careful negotiations with Republican operatives including Bush administration senior advisor Karl Rove, the elder American Muslim leaders had possibly secured a way to save their futures in America. They had arrived in the US in the 1960s and 1970s as young students and professionals, before Islamic extremism was on the radar of law enforcement, and they were now entering their fifties and sixties facing growing scrutiny and criminal investigations for their activities allegedly accepting foreign influence and funding foreign entities, including Hamas and Palestinian Islamic Jihad. One of these men was Sami Al-Arian, a professor at the University of South Florida. In discussions with Rove and other Republican leaders, brokered in part by a conservative thinker, Grover Norquist, Al-Arian and his Muslim friends had convinced the Bush administration to ditch something used in national security cases called "secret evidence," so that defendants could know all the evidence against them. (Norquist was married to a Palestinian American Muslim, Samah Alrayyes.) The year earlier, the Muslim Brothers had celebrated when Bush had mentioned his policy shift during a presidential debate in exchange for Muslim support for Bush's candidacy in the 2000 election. Rove later acknowledged the deal in a memoir.

That September 2001, after almost nine months in office, Bush was going to announce his policy shift in a Rose Garden ceremony at the White House.

Al-Arian and his Muslim colleagues readied the morning of the scheduled ceremony to enter the White House, but the ceremony never happened. It was scheduled for the afternoon of September 11, 2001.

As Al-Arian's daughter, Laila Al-Arian, later related in a video, "You know the rest of the story."

* * *

That Tuesday, September 11, 2001, as most of the world was glued to shocking images of the attack on the World Trade Center, the campus of UC Berkeley shook with the news, with students hugging each other and breaking down in tears.

Three days later, about eight hundred people flocked to the Martin Luther King Student Union for a *juma'a*, or Friday, prayer service, marking the holy day of the week for Muslims.

The Palestinian American lecturer, Hatem Bazian, now a popular figure among the Muslim students, stepped forward to lead the prayer and deliver the *khutba*, or sermon.

Bazian warned: "Don't scapegoat others but rise up from the depth of anger to help the community out of despair."

A young student, Wajahat Ali, stood by to deliver closing remarks. Special liaison to the UC Berkeley Muslim Students Association, Ali was born in 1980 in Santa Clara County, California, to parents from Pakistan. He grew up in nearby Fremont, along with Javad Hashmi, calling their hometown "Fremontistan." His parents sold software—it turned out, illegally—and they lived in an expensive house on Canyon Creek Terrace in an upscale neighborhood of Fremont, near the city's picturesque hills.

The activists didn't keep the moral high ground for long.

* * *

Four days later, just one week after the 9/11 attacks, student Wajahat Ali was among about 120 students who stormed the office of the UC Berkeley student newspaper, the *Daily Californian*, demanding an apology for a cartoon by Darrin Bell, a UC Berkeley graduate and the first black cartoonist to be syndicated nationally.

Bell had drawn two bearded men with turbans and long robes, sitting in the hands of the devil, surrounded by flames, a flight manual at their feet, rather than the seventy-two virgins they were expecting in paradise. One man said to the other: "We made it to Paradise! Now we will meet Allah."

Ali told a reporter, "They have to be held accountable. The false representation by the media is directly responsible for the current hostile, angry and fearful attitude of average Americans toward Muslims and Arabs, and this is unacceptable." (Bell later won the Pulitzer Prize in 2019 "for beautiful and daring editorial cartoons that took on issues affecting disenfranchised communities, calling out lies, hypocrisy and fraud in the political turmoil surrounding the Trump administration.")

Two other Muslim leaders, Will "Iron Sheikh" Youmans and Basim Elkarra, president of the UC Berkeley Muslim Students Association, joined the protests. Youmans complained to a student newspaper reporter about the cartoon, "Look on page five of Tuesday's *Daily Californian*. You will see the most vile form of ethnic characterization because it comes during a time when many people are suffering a severe backlash." He groused: "I thought when I came to Berkeley that hate, hateful speech was not to be permitted."

All day long, the student activists spun out soundbites. "We set an example to the whole nation, and if our own paper does this," said Elkarra, "what do we expect from the rest of the nation?"

Another moment he said, "Feeling bad is one thing, but we want action. This is hate speech, not free speech."

Police arrested nineteen students, who were later released.

The *Daily Californian* didn't cave to the protesters' demands, and the newspaper's editors refused to apologize.

Mysteriously, the *Daily Californian* website was hacked with a fake apology for the cartoon on its homepage, and newspaper copies disappeared. The student senate of the Associated Students of the University of California approved a bill demanding an apology and mandatory sensitivity training for the newspaper's staff. Another bill proposed increasing the newspaper's rent.

Sajid Khan, a leader with the Muslim Students Association and a student senator, was a co-author of a bill, alleging a "direct correlation" between the cartoon and attacks on Muslims. No such attacks were reported on the Berkeley campus, however, while the FBI's official hate crimes statistics reported eight times the number of attacks on Jews as on Muslims.

* * *

The experience of Muslim Americans after 9/11 meant that some leaders exploited the new sense of vulnerability.

The data on bias incidents and hate crimes reveals that there was an increase of anti-Muslim bias, but it was infinitely less than discrimination against African Americans or Jews. Muslim leaders consciously fanned the flames of this fear, however, in order to increase their power in the Muslim community and national politics. With the help of George W. Bush, CAIR and other unsavory groups successfully positioned themselves as spokesmen for Muslim Americans. Very little attention was paid to their links with extremist and violent elements in the Middle East. Even less attention was paid to their tacit alliance with the left—something we also saw happening in Europe. The term "Islamophobia" hadn't yet come into vogue, but the concept of victimization was taking root.

The *Oakland Tribune* even wrote: "The coalition of students, mostly but not exclusively Muslims, have used their minority status and a glass-shattering shrillness of tone first to try to muzzle the *Daily Californian* student newspaper, then to punish it through a student government bill and finally to shut it down with theft."

Without skipping a beat, UC Berkeley academic activist Hatem Bazian and the anti-Israel organization he had established, Students for Justice in Palestine, hosted a three-day event, "Intifada 2001: Understanding the Palestinian Quest for Justice," the next week, staged to mark the one-year anniversary of the intifada by Palestinians against Israel.

* * *

In the building at 500 Grove Street in Herndon, Virginia, the Muslim Brothers were in trouble.

A senior special agent of the US Customs Service filed an affidavit in the US District Court for the Eastern District of Virginia alleging that the Safa Group, based out of 500 Grove Street, and "associated individuals" were "ardent supporters" of the Palestinian Islamic Jihad and Hamas. On March 22, 2002, in "Operation Green Quest," federal agents raided nineteen offices and residences in Virginia and Georgia and seized computers and boxes of data and records. Their stops included the building at 500 Grove Street and another building across the street at 555 Grove Street. The network's tax accountant listed the organizations for which he'd filed tax returns on Grove Street.

The list was long: Horizons Education Foundation, The Heritage Education Trust Inc., African Muslim Agency, The Child Development Foundation, American Institute for Societal Sciences, Sanabel Al Kheer Inc., Heritage Holding Inc., International Islamic Charitable Organization, The Graduate School of Islamic and Social Sciences, International Institute of Islamic Thought, York Foundation, Safa Trust Inc., and Sterling Charitable Gift Fund, a donor-advised fund.

That year, according to its IRS Form 990 filing, Sterling Charitable Gift Fund had received one thousand shares of the halal chicken company, Mar-Jac Investments Inc., that Jamal Barzinji and the Muslim Brothers had established in 1986, with the same name as the poultry slaughterhouse. The fund's president was Yaqub Mirza, one of the original Muslim Brothers from Pakistan, living on nearby Safa

Court. Muhammad Ashraf, living around the corner, was the secretary/treasurer. Brother Waseem Zafar kept the books at Grove Street.

They valued the shares at $2.65 million. They also got one thousand shares of Mena Corp., valued at zero dollars. They gave $1 million to the All Dulles Area Muslim Society to build a mosque on Sugarland Road in Sterling, Virginia, around the corner from the cul-de-sac on Safa Court. It would be the mosque that halal chicken built. Over the years, they set up a treasure trove of business with near-identical officers from their roster of Muslim Brothers businesses and similar, innocuous names, including: Center Street Condo LLC, Herndon Associates LLC, Mena Investments LLC, Sterling Advisory Services Inc., Sterling Stock Investments, and Sterling Technology Fund. They doled out millions of dollars to fund the growing network of influence of the Muslim Brothers from Shenandoah University in Virginia to Georgetown University and the Islamophobia Studies Center at the University of California at Berkeley, started by academic activist Hatem Bazian. At Shenandoah University, the Muslim Brothers had funded the Barzinji Project, named for one of the original founders of their network in the United States, with a mission in education.

* * *

The next month, in early April 2002, a year after Hatem Bazian formed Students for Justice in Palestine, he organized a protest to mark the deaths of Palestinian villagers at a village outside Jerusalem, Deir Yassin, in 1948. They launched an "occupation" of UC Berkeley's Wheeler Hall, as they had done the year before. Police arrested some seventy-nine members of Students for Justice in Palestine as they attempted to disturb Holocaust Remembrance Day by American Jewish students. At a rally to protest the arrests, Bazian told protesters to "take a look at the type of names on the building around campus—Haas, Zellerbach—and decide who controls this university."

A 1910 graduate of UC Berkeley, Walter Haas was president of Levi Strauss & Co., and the UC Berkeley Regents voted in 1989 to rename the business school the Haas School of Business after the Haas family gave the university a large gift. Zellerbach Hall was named for Isadore and Jennie Zellerbach after they gave a $1 million gift for the completion of the building. Haas and the Zellerbachs are Jewish.

* * *

That month, Hatem Bazian's protégé, UC Berkeley student Wajahat Ali, got disturbing family news.

The FBI had just arrested his parents.

The US Justice Department announced the arrest of twenty-seven people in a two-year undercover investigation, Operation Cyberstorm, that alleged a "large, loosely affiliated group of dealers in counterfeit software" in the San Francisco Bay area. Among the arrested: Ali's parents, Mirza, then fifty-four, and Sameena Ali, then forty-eight, owners of Samtech Research Inc. The Justice Department accused them of buying about $29 million worth of software through Microsoft's educational program and selling the software to nonacademic sources, including several counterfeit software dealers. The couple was charged with "laundering the proceeds of this scheme." The story even landed in Pakistan's leading English daily, *Dawn*.

According to the indictment, the Alis pirated $1.5 million. They allegedly bought about $430,000 in real estate property in their son's name and wired $319,000 to a bank account in Karachi, Pakistan, from a Fremont bank. Microsoft estimated the scheme forced it to lose $100 million. The criminal complaint charged that the Alis inappropriately sent money to a family "fugitive" and his wife. The Justice Department also accused Ali's parents of defrauding Microsoft by concealing their identities with aliases they used to benefit from an academic discount program from which Microsoft had banned them. Earlier they had faced charges of defrauding the US Air Force; while those charges were dropped, the shadow of fraud hung over the family name in Fremont where gossip traveled fast. A federal jury found the couple guilty of using fake names and bogus applications to win contracts.

That summer, Wajahat Ali's parents got more bad news.

A federal judge ordered the couple to turn over $261,000 allegedly held in a Pakistani bank.

* * *

Around that time, in May 2002, Hatem Bazian was the only speaker at a two-day "cultural assembly" on the Middle East at George Washington High School in San Francisco.

That month, he was about to receive his PhD in philosophy with a major in Near Eastern studies and begin teaching at UC Berkeley. He would be named a senior lecturer and later an adjunct professor of Near Eastern studies and religious studies.

But that day, school administrators sent parents letters of apology for the inflammatory rhetoric Bazian expressed at the assembly, including comparing Zionists to Nazis, as students paraded with Palestinian flags.

That same month, the *New York Times* published an article about a course, "The Politics and Poetry of Palestinian Resistance," that Bazian's cofounder at Students for Justice in Palestine, Snehal Shingavi, twenty-six, was planning to teach in the fall. He was a fifth-year graduate student in English.

That night, he went on the MSNBC show *Hardball*, where liberal host Chris Matthews asked him about the course. Mathews read the course description on air: "The brutal Israeli military occupation of Palestine, an occupation that has been ongoing since 1948, has systematically displaced, killed, and maimed millions of Palestinian people. And yet, from under the brutal weight of the occupation, Palestinians have produced their own culture and poetry of resistance. This class will examine the history of the Palestinian resistance and the way that it is narrated by Palestinians in order to produce an understanding of the Intifada...." Mathews continued: "This class takes as its starting point the right of Palestinians to fight for their own self-determination. Conservative thinkers are encouraged to seek other sections."

He asked Snehal, "Professor, how do you defend a course that advises people with different political views from the ones you take, or offer in the course, to go to somewhere else to learn their American education?"

In a testy back-and-forth with David Horowitz, a supporter of Israel, Sarah Eltantawi, public affairs director at the Muslim Public Affairs Council, defended the course.

* * *

That fall, UC Berkeley law student Will "Iron Sheikh" Youmans, one of the students who had stormed the UC Berkeley student newspaper over a cartoon, published an article on the ultraliberal website CounterPunch with a new grievance.

This time, he announced a strategy to debunk the efforts of the Middle East Forum, a think-tank started fourteen years earlier in 1988 by Jewish American historian Daniel Pipes. Middle East Forum had created a website, Campus Watch, to document academic criticism of Israel.

In the article, Youmans accused Middle East Forum of "cyber-idiocy," and he suggested sending complaints to Campus Watch under "fake names."

He wrote: "Campus-Watch is essentially forming a paramilitary thought police, a private TIPS program for pro-Israel advocates." The US Justice Department had launched Operation TIPS in 2002, asking truckers, train conductors, utility employees, and others to report suspicious activities.

* * *

Days before the first anniversary of the 9/11 attacks, a network of American Muslim scholars, writers, and leaders issued a statement "denouncing violence and terrorism, in the name of Islam, a religion of peace." It coupled the condemnation to a position on Israel and Palestine, noting the "unbearable" condition of life for Palestinians because of the "continued occupation of Palestinian territories."

The statement read like a textbook example of what *not* to say in the face of a public relations disaster. It began okay: "As American

Muslims and scholars of Islam, we wish to restate our conviction that peace and justice constitute the basic principles of the Muslim faith."

It went downhill from there: "We wish again to state unequivocally that neither the al-Qaeda organization nor Usama bin Laden represents Islam or reflects Muslim beliefs and practice," they wrote.

Al-Qaeda and Osama bin Laden might not have represented their Muslim beliefs and practice. But they definitely did represent *some* Muslim beliefs.

Specifically, some extremist Muslim beliefs.

The statement continued: "Rather, groups like al-Qaeda have misused and abused Islam in order to fit their own radical and indeed anti-Islamic agenda. Usama bin Laden and al-Qaeda's actions are criminal, misguided and counter to the true teachings of Islam. We call on people of all faiths not to judge Islam by the actions of a few."

In a Muslim culture defined by honor and shame, the statement was now attempting to save face.

They went on: "We believe in justice and peace for both Israelis and Palestinians."

Within one year, these Muslim leaders had hijacked the 9/11 narrative to pursue their Palestinian agenda.

"We are convinced that security for Israel can only be achieved by justice for Palestinians," the statement continued. "Today, a modicum of justice requires the establishment of an independent Palestinian state through the exercise of Palestinian self-determination. We believe that the continued occupation of Palestinian territories, and Israel's repeated disregard of international law, have made life in the occupied territories unbearable. We say most clearly, however, that the killing of innocent civilians, whether Christian, Muslim, or Jewish, is always wrong and is forbidden in Islamic law and ethics. Illegitimate means can never be justified by a desirable or noble goal."

Most of the statement was now devoted to their grievance with Israel.

The statement ended with an empty platitude: "On this first anniversary of the tragedy of September 11, we call on all people of conscience to denounce violence and to work peacefully for the creation of a better world. We also urge our government leaders to work for peace, justice, liberty, and democracy around the globe."

The signatories included the board members of the nonprofit, the Center for the Study of Islam and Democracy Inc., founded in 1999 by Jamal Barzinji, the Iraqi American living on Safa Court in Herndon, Virginia. The organization supported movements promoting political Islam throughout the Muslim world. Its board of directors had included a list of the VIPs in the American Muslim community: Radwan A. Masmoudi, executive director at the Center for the Study of Islam and Democracy; Louay Safi, a Syrian American leader; Muqtedar Khan, a Pakistani American professor of Islam at Adrian College; John Esposito, the Catholic founder of the Prince Alwaleed bin Talal Center for Muslim-Christian Understanding at Georgetown University; and Svend A. White, a Muslim convert and researcher at the Center for the Study of Islam and Democracy.

The forty-five representatives from Islamic organizations and mosques included VIPs from the Muslim community: Muzammil Siddiqi, a cofounder of the Islamic Society of Orange County, California; Sheila Musaji, editor of *The American Muslim*, established earlier that year; Shahed Amanullah, a Muslim tech guru with a plethora of Muslim websites, listed in the statement as being with United Muslims of America in Fremont, California; Mohamed Nimer, research director at the Council on American-Islamic Relations; and Muhammed Sayeed, secretary general of the Islamic Circle of North America.

The list included several representatives from the Islamic Society of North America and the Muslim Public Affairs Council.

There were forty-four academics who signed the declaration, including Asma Afsaruddin from the University of Notre Dame, and there were thirty-two people from "around the globe," including Tariq Ramadan, an Islamic scholar at University of Fribourg and the grandson of the founder of the Muslim Brotherhood.

The fifty-one "concerned citizens" who signed the declaration included someone named A. L. Poonawalla of North Brunswick, New Jersey, a young man by the full name of Aziz Poonawalla. He would one day become important in legitimizing an anti-American disinformation campaign.

* * *

There was one name who hadn't yet made the roster of VIPs. He was a young up-and-comer in the American Muslim community, and he would later prove to be essential in the fusion of the radical ideology of Islamism with leftist radicalism.

His name was Khaled Beydoun, and he was just two weeks into his first year as a law student on the campus of UCLA when the 9/11 attacks happened. He was looking for direction, and he'd find it in a young law professor with a big mission. Under her tutelage, Beydoun would create a pipeline for other Muslims with grievances to join the Woke Army and its legion of "critical race theory" ideologues.

Beydoun had grown up on the West Side of Detroit in a mostly Arab and black community, raised by an Egyptian single mother. By self-admission, he had "flunked freshman year of high school," becoming "a better boxer than I was a writer."

Still, he earned his degree in political science and Near Eastern studies at the University of Michigan. He later said he chose the UCLA School of Law because it was the only law school at the time with a concentration in "critical race theory." UCLA had the movement's leaders on its faculty as professors, including: Cheryl Harris, the author of *Whiteness as Property*; Devon Carbado, who had done work on "identity performance theory"; and Kimberlé Crenshaw, one of the godmothers of "critical race theory." He later called Crenshaw "my mentor" during a book launch and thanked her as one of two women, the other being his mother, from whom he "learned virtually everything."

Beydoun said: "So I was in law school at this time, examining critical race theory in a range of questions that were grappling with the experience of African Americans, Latinx populations, Native Americans, the struggle of LGBTQ communities, the importance of gender in how it interacts with the law. And I was finding that there was a dearth, if not a complete nonexistence of literature examining what was happening with Muslim Americans in real-time."

He saw a void, and he stepped in. "I was very much, I think, maybe one of the first, if not the first, Muslim American critical race theorists," he said, "that, you know, really tried to merge the canon of critical race theory with what was happening with Muslim Americans and how Islam was also being demonized as a religion in real-time during the war on terror, but also well before the war on terror moment."

"It was transformative for me to see brilliant scholars of color talking about the law in ways that I had never heard before," Beydoun later said. "That really left an impression on me."

Beydoun's law school entry also coincided with the heightened scrutiny that law enforcement directed toward Muslim Americans—or those perceived to be Muslims—in the wake of 9/11.

"I began to see a lot of gaps and opportunities in the legal scholarship," Beydoun said. "A lot of the legal scholarship didn't focus on the racial construction of Arab and Muslim Americans and the special legal crises faced by them after 9/11 but also before 9/11."

"That's when I realized, 'Hey, someone's gotta write about this stuff. Maybe I should be the one.'"

By 2002, over twenty American law schools and at least three overseas law schools taught "critical race theory," showing up in courses related to education, political science, women's studies, ethnic studies, communication, sociology, and American studies.

At UCLA, Beydoun made a critical connection. He met a powerful friend of Crenshaw, Alvin Starks, who would become program manager at Open Society Foundations, the partisan, hard-left-agenda-driven philanthropy started by billionaire George Soros. Starks had his hands on the purse strings of millions of dollars. It was one thing to embrace an ideology. It was critical to have a patron. Starks was that important patron for "critical race theory" ideologues to evangelize and win new converts.

Starks had earned his undergraduate degree at State University of New York and did graduate work at Columbia University. Formerly a staffer at Echoing Green Foundation, a New York City donor launched by a growth equity firm, General Atlantic, awarding human rights fellowships, Starks had just joined Open Society in

2000. There, he directed the New York City Community Fellowship and Initiative program, focused on "policy, organizing, legal reform, and arts and culture." In 2004, he would establish Open Society's "Racial Justice Initiative," focused on "dismantling the structural and systemic barriers that perpetuate race and class exclusion." He would proceed to develop the Racial Justice and Gender Identity program at the Arcus Foundation, financing projects at the "intersections of race, sexuality, and gender identity," and he would later serve as program officer for "racial equity" at the W. K. Kellogg Foundation. By 2020, Starks became the director of the "Equality Team" of Open Society US, overseeing grant making related to "racial justice" and "racial narrative." He'd join the board of Crenshaw's African American Policy Forum.

Beydoun later earned an LLM from the University of Toronto.

And the revolutionaries established themselves further in academia: Derrick Bell, Patricia Williams, Richard Delgado, Kimberlé Crenshaw, Mari Matsuda, Camara Phyllis Jones (an epidemiologist who pushed the idea of racism as a "public health crisis"), and—their newest initiate—Khaled Beydoun.

* * *

When it came to actual defense of issues like women's rights in Muslim communities and progressive interpretations of Islam, Muslim reformers got one response from the Islamists running the labyrinth of organizations built by the Muslim Brothers at 500 Grove Street: silence, shaming, and intimidation.

I learned this in the fall of 2003 as I stood in front of a green front door to a new mosque my father and other men had raised funds to build in my hometown of Morgantown, West Virginia, eager to find a quiet space to heal my grieving spirit. A reporter at the *Wall Street Journal* since I was twenty-three, I was on book leave when the 9/11 attacks happened, and I flew to Pakistan to report on the war in Afghanistan for *Salon* magazine. In Karachi, Pakistan, a friend from the *Journal* visited a home I had rented, and I waved goodbye to him on January 23, 2002, as he left for an interview from which he never returned. He was Daniel Pearl, the journalist kidnapped and then brutally beheaded by Pakistani militants. My boyfriend—a young Pakistani financial analyst—abandoned me, in fear of getting caught in the international dragnet to find Danny. For four weeks, my dining room turned into a command center in the search for Danny, and I worked beside FBI agents and Pakistani counterterrorism police officers trying to find my dear friend. In the fourth week of our search, I learned I was pregnant from my boyfriend—and a criminal, according to the Islamic laws of Pakistan that criminalize unwed motherhood. In the fifth week, we learned the tragic news that militants had murdered Danny, brutally beheading him. I returned to the safe haven of America and my parents' home in Morgantown, where I brought my son into the world on October 16, 2002. We did the pilgrimage to Mecca together with my parents and niece and nephew when my son, Shibli, was three months old, and I decided then that I would not live with shame about the circumstances of Shibli's birth but rather fight to repeal the laws that criminalized unwed motherhood.

That evening, I carried Shibli on my hip, and I wore over my hair the white headscarf I had worn in Mecca. Instead of welcoming us with a warm greeting, the president of the mosque board, an elderly Egyptian American, yelled at me: "Sister, take the back door!"

In shock, I knew I had a quick decision to make.

Would I step forward and affirm my belief that women have a right to enter as first-class citizens, not second-class? Or would I cower to fear and accept my place as a woman deserving of only the back door?

I stepped forward and walked through the front door.

I stepped into my role in a gender jihad, or struggle for women's rights, tolerance, and social justice in Islam.

I phoned an organization that I sincerely thought would help me: the Council on American-Islamic Relations. I hadn't heard the controversy surrounding their birth or the allegations against them as an unindicted coconspirator in the case of an organization, Holy Land Foundation for Relief and Development, that had allegedly funneled money to Palestinian extremists. CAIR said that it protected the civil rights of Muslims. I was a Muslim woman whose civil rights to the front door and into the main hall of my mosque were being denied. I believed them.

Muslim convert Ibrahim Hooper, then forty-five, had been the group's spokesman since its start in 1995. I called him.

He answered his mobile phone at a rally in front of the French Embassy in Washington, DC, to protest a government order that girls wouldn't be allowed to wear headscarves in public schools in France. He couldn't hear me over the shouts of the rally.

I told him about the struggle at my mosque to win the right the prophet Muhammad even allowed in his mosque in Medina: entry of women into the main hall.

"What?" he said, shouts of "*Allahu akbar*" (God is great) behind him. "I can't hear you."

He called me back later. He heard my story. His response disappointed me deeply.

"You should find a new community," he told me, laughing. "Sounds like you need a new mosque."

I said: "What? A new mosque?"

I couldn't believe what I was hearing. He would never tell a woman bullied at a college to transfer. Her complaint would invite a lawsuit—filed by CAIR.

He explained that he felt inclusivity at his mosque, the ADAMS Center, the mosque in Sterling, Virginia, built by funds from the Muslim Brothers at 500 Grove Street.

I responded that if I was a Muslim with a protest against a teacher in my son's school because of disrespect to Islam, he wouldn't tell me to move but would take my complaint to the school board.

"We are the Council on *American-Islamic* Relations," he said, "not the Council on *Islamic-Islamic* Relations."

* * *

I went to group after group established by the Muslim Brothers at 500 Grove Street. The Islamic Society of North America worked with many mosques in the US. Its leaders dispatched Louay Safi, a

Syrian American and executive director of its Leadership Development Center in Plainfield, Indiana. He had signed the declaration on the first anniversary of 9/11, condemning extremists—and the state of Israel. He came to Morgantown and tried to mediate with the men at the mosque who wanted women using a back door and praying in a separate section. I thought he could help. He worked with an organization, the Center for the Study of Islam and Democracy, that I thought would want to uplift the voices of women and girls in the spirit of democracy. Established in 1999 by former staffers of the now-defunct American Muslim Council, it had spent twenty years as a gateway for Islamist leaders in America. A more accurate name would have been the "Center to Promote Political Islam." Seven years earlier, its founder, Radwan Masmoudi, a Tunisian American engineer, had hosted the leader of Tunisia's Islamist political party, Al-Nahda, a man identified by Egyptian media as the leader of the Muslim Brotherhood overseas. The Center for the Study of Islam and Democracy Inc. also supported the Muslim Brotherhood in Egypt.

One of the men at the mosque, an Egyptian American, got aggressive with him. Safi went away, with nothing resolved.

That fall, I filed complaints with the CAIR civil rights division about how the men at my mosque had denied me my civil rights.

I never heard back.

What I didn't realize was that I was enlisting a power structure in our American Muslim community that had a very different agenda than getting women and girls through the front doors of mosques. I was naive. I didn't know I was trying to enlist people who saw me as their enemy.

In the fall of 2004, I walked up to the lectern at the Islamic Society of North America's national conference and presented an "Islamic Bill of Rights for Women in the Mosque." An angry young man confronted me. Days later, I saw a shocking message, "deathtoasra," pop up on my computer screen without warning, written from a fake email address, dta@dtasra@gov.saudi. For my advocacy for women's equality within Islam, the anonymous writer called for my death, as a Muslim feminist, and the death of my fellow Muslim reformers, writing, "may allah remove these terrorist imposter pigs from this earth and destroy them by the Hands of the Believers, *inshaa Allah*" (God willing) in Arabic. After days of cybersleuthing, tracking the writer's internet protocol address and piecing together clues, I discovered the author was Hamdan Yousuf, a Pakistani American student at Penn State University and a Muslim fundamentalist in the school's conservative Muslim Students Association. He didn't respond to queries seeking comment. FBI agents paid him a visit and warned him that future threats could result in his arrest. This attack introduced me to the deadly underbelly of cyber jihad, which puts in its crosshairs Muslim reformers and others who call out Islamic extremism.

CHAPTER 4

Silencing Reformers with Disinformation

As the uncles of the Muslim Brothers network faced arrest and surveillance, a new generation emerged to carry the mantle. The Honor Brigade's operations against American Muslim reformers began in earnest with the new weapons of the internet.

New keyboard warriors took advantage of the new emerging technology platforms to launch anonymous character assassinations on any Muslims who challenged the orthodoxy of the Muslim Brothers. "Sock puppets" describe people who assume false identities on the internet and engage in "sock puppetry," using fake names to further their cause. Their fake identities could also be called "avatars" or "trolls." "Flamethrowers," like the name suggests, throw out controversial ideas to rile people up. By any name, they can be a game changer in public discourse.

In mid-October 2004, several anonymous Muslim writers started a new blog, *Living Tradition*, using a new platform, Blogspot, that made blogging easy. A secret band of bloggers started their own version of the Muslim dark web. Its operatives drew up a hit list of individuals to target. They then collected information from the internet and community gossip—or RUMINT, rumor intelligence, as it's called in information warfare—that they recast in as derogatory a way as possible. Nothing was off limits. Not children. Not illness. Not personal lives. They convinced themselves they were righteous. They were true believers.

One of the cofounders used the fake name "DrMaxtor."

According to people familiar with his ruse, "DrMaxtor" was Javad Hashmi, a student on the campus of UC Berkeley, protesting beside his mentor, Hatem Bazian, and fellow student Wajahat Ali. After arriving at UC Berkeley in August 2000, Hashmi had left the school in December 2002 to enroll a while later in a five-year medical program at Aga Khan University in Karachi, Pakistan.

Now, Hashmi had found a side hustle to challenge progressive Muslims through anonymous blogging. And he had a cadre of like-minded writers who used the cloak of anonymity to target Muslim reformers. The other cofounders used the fake names "IzzyMo," "Living Tradition," and "SunniSister." A few years later, "AJSuhail," a coauthor at a blog, *Madras Muslim*, joined their effort.

"IzzyMo" was a black convert to Islam, Kelly Izdihar Crosby. On LinkedIn, she said she was an artist, arts administrator, administrative assistant, freelance writer, poet, and speaker. Her website, izzymo.myshopify.com, featured her moniker, IzzyMo. Her LinkedIn connections included a rising technology entrepreneur, Shahed Amanullah.

She was part of the post-9/11 generation, earning a BA in fine arts and painting from the University of New Orleans in 2002. Two years later, she cofounded the blogs attacking progressive Muslims. Later, she earned an MA in arts administration in 2007. She started working as an assistant editor at *Azizah Magazine*, a hip Muslim women's magazine in Atlanta, and sold her work online at KellyCrosbyDesign.com. When I asked her about cofounding these fake news sites, she wrote back to me, "I would rather leave my blog in its retirement mode until I can dedicate time to writing it again." She declined further comment.

Meanwhile, the many character assassinations the blogs' writers had launched on progressive Muslims had lives of their own, discrediting Muslim reformers with impunity.

The next year, the blog added the names of four more writers to its roster: "Abdur Rahman Squires," "Kelly Izdihar Crosby (Risama)," "Dr. Max," and "Umm Zaid," which meant "mother of Zaid" in Arabic. Later, "1DrM" emerged and wrote that "Umm Zaid," "AJSuhail," and "IzzyMo" had gotten him into blogging.

They would just be another blog of writers with a dizzying roster of names, to be forgotten, but they had an indemnifying impact on the fledgling progressive Muslim movement that was emerging in America to challenge fundamentalist ideas espoused by followers of the Muslim Brotherhood and other hard-line interpretations of political Islam.

* * *

While CAIR and other leaders from the alphabet soup of Muslim organizations born out of 500 Grove Street stuck to their regressive ideals, a band of progressive American Muslims was emerging with a vision to integrate in the US without importing the sexism, homophobia, anti-Semitism, and orthodoxy of Islamist movements.

Among them, a new kid on the block had emerged as a voice for the Muslims that the establishment ignored. He was an Egyptian American marketing specialist, Ahmed Nassef, who had just launched an edgy new website, Muslim WakeUp. It promoted progressive interpretations of Islam. Nassef was creative and courageous.

Born in Egypt, he was once part of the establishment, as president of the Muslim Students Association at UCLA in the 1980s, before finishing his studies in 1990 with a BA. He was turned off by the rigidity he saw in his fellow students in the Muslim Students Association, especially about men and women hanging out together.

After launching his career, he started Muslim WakeUp with the hopes of reaching the many Muslims, like him, who were secular while also spiritual, opposed to interpretations of Islam that are sexist, intolerant, and rigid. He disagreed with the Muslim Brotherhood vision of Islam in governance. He believed in the separation of mosque and state. From Brooklyn, New York, to Los Angeles, progressive Muslims had started using MeetUp.com, the website popularized by supporters of Democratic presidential candidate Howard Dean.

The followers included Omid Safi, an Islamic studies professor at Colgate University in Hamilton, New York, and editor of an anthology, *Progressive Muslims*. In October 2004, they incorporated a new organization, Progressive Muslim Union.

Nassef said at the time, "Muslim WakeUp gives them the opportunity to be themselves and express their love for who they are and the community without being judged.... It just begins a process."

In December 2003, he republished on Muslim WakeUp a column that I published in the Outlook section of the *Washington Post*, chronicling my family's and my struggle for women's rights at our mosque. I heard from hundreds of Muslims—women and men—all frustrated with the sexism, bigotry, and regressive interpretations of Islam at their mosques and in their communities. Maybe we could transform the community, I dared to tell my mother one day, in my childhood home.

My mother responded, ominously: "Asra, they will never change."

* * *

Indeed, if the character who called himself "1DrM" had his way, none of these calls for reform would succeed. He was another fake name for the former UC Berkeley student Javad Hashmi, according to people familiar with his work.

One day, he wrote disparagingly about Muslim WakeUp.

The "vile website was the launching pad for charlatans," he wrote, including bold voices for Muslim reform in his hit list: Egyptian feminist writer Mona Eltahawy; Canadian Pakistani journalist and activist Raheel Raza; Canadian Pakistani writer and activist Tarek Fatah; American Muslim convert Michael "Muhammad" Knight; black convert and scholar Amina Wadud; Republican Muslim advocate Muhammad Ali Hasan; and Hasan's mother, Seeme Gull Hasan.

"No one had ever heard of these bottom feeders before," he wrote, "as they had nothing to do with the Muslim community on any level."

He targeted Muslim WakeUp editor Ahmed Nassef for special attack for pushing progressive values and "seeking to undermine established Muslim civil rights groups like CAIR whom they branded as 'conservative.'"

Character assassinations in these circles obsessively involved the state of Israel. "1DrM" alleged Nassef was "openly taking tips" from "Zionist Cheryl Bernard," a respected researcher at the think tank, the Rand Corporation. Bernard authored a prescient and cogent 2004 report, "Civil Democratic Islam," that argued "contemporary Islam is in a volatile state, engaged in an internal and external struggle over its values, its identity, and its place in the world. Rival versions are contending for spiritual and political dominance. This conflict has serious costs and economic, social, political, and security implications for the rest of the world." She concluded, "Clearly, the United States, the modern industrialized world, and indeed the international community as a whole would prefer an Islamic world that is compatible with the rest of the system: democratic, economically viable, politically stable, socially progressive, and follows the rules and norms of international conduct."

Clear-eyed, she advised, "It therefore seems judicious to encourage the elements within the Islamic mix that are most compatible with global peace and the international community and that are friendly to democracy and modernity."

In this calculation, Islamist revivalists would lose. And Hashmi, writing as "1DrM," knew it.

He blasted the Muslim "pro-regressives" as an "outsourced Zionist job."

In October 2004, Hashmi started a second blog, *DrMaxtor*, to "deliver the coup de grace to the usual suspects," he wrote to his fans. He also contributed to a third blog, *PMUNADebate*, to critique a new organization, Progressive Muslims Union of North America, or PMUNA, that Ahmed Nassef and others had just launched. The Progressive Muslim Union of North America, he alleged, was a "prototype to future AstroTurf 'Muslim' organizations."

Alleging reform was Astroturf, or, in effect, fake, was a go-to smear Hashmi would repeat in a very telling way years later.

In early March 2005, we triggered "1DrM."

* * *

On March 15, 2005, Ahmed Nassef and I teamed up with a young black Muslim, Saleemah Abdul-Ghafur, and an Egyptian American emerging scholar, Sarah Eltantawi, to organize a remarkable day in our global Muslim community.

The morning of the Ides of March, at the corner of W. 110th Street and Amsterdam Avenue, our team stepped onto the sacred grounds of St. John the Divine, an Episcopal church on the upper West Side. We walked past police officers and bomb-sniffing German shepherds from the New York Police Department. Walking through a final metal detector, we stepped inside a massive hall in the Synod House, and we smiled.

Shortly afterwards, Amina Wadud, a black feminist scholar and convert to Islam, stood before a congregation of about 150 women, men, boys, and girls to lead the Friday prayer. Abdul-Ghafur and I stood in the front row, shoulder to shoulder, in prayer. I didn't wear a headscarf in prayer, for the first time ever, because I had had an epiphany that morning. Since I didn't believe Muslim women have to cover their hair, why should I do so in prayer?

Nassef prayed nearby. Other men prayed behind us and beside us.

The consensus of scholars was that it was *haram*, or illegal, for women to lead men in prayer or even stand in front of men in prayer, but we harkened back to the *sunnah*, or traditions, of the prophet Muhammad, in which he instructed a woman, Umm Waraqa, to lead men and women in prayer. The men's club of clerics had rid that tradition from our practice. We were bringing it back.

* * *

Outside, a young man in a khaki-colored jacket held a sign with a clear message.

MAY ALLAH'S

CURSE BE UPON:

AHMED NASSEF

AMEENA WADOUD

& ASRA NOMANI

Another held a sign, opposed to the prayer.

MIXED-GENDER

PRAYER TODAY

HELLFIRE

TOMORROW

A young man in a cap spread a black banner with the *shahada*, or proclamation of faith. These protesters had printed the sign on 8½" by 11" papers and taped them together on poster board. Another man stood in the background with the sign that read: "HELLFIRE TOMORROW." The photo had a time stamp of 1:18:53 p.m.

These young men said they were part of a new organization, Muslim Thinkers, but they were espousing conventional wisdom, not practicing critical thinking.

* * *

Four days after the historic prayer, writing as "DrMaxtor," the former UC Berkeley student, Javad Hashmi, published a fake interview with me on his blog, headlined "Honest interview with Asra Nomani."

"Imagine if Nomani got some sodium pentothal in her martini and gave an honest interview...," he began. Sodium pentothal is known as a truth serum.

Speaking directly to me, he asked, "You're a bit of a whack job, aren't you?"

The objective was to discredit progressive Muslims to the wider American and Muslim communities, and, with most of us raised in cultures defined by honor and shame, the goal was to intimidate us and make us hide our heads in shame. Many of these tactics worked at silencing individuals. Some activists became less engaged after these attacks against them. For Muslim activists, operatives would look for evidence that they had acted in ways that were anathema in conservative Muslim circles, such as premarital sex, dating, alcohol consumption. In my case, I openly admitted these truths, believing that we had to be honest about our lives if we were to find pathways for faith to uplift us, not suffocate us in rigidity, judgment, and shame.

Years later, writing as "1DrM," Hashmi took credit for destroying the fledgling progressive Muslim movement, with his fellow anonymous bloggers. He wasn't wrong. He had been ruthless in his attacks, and the new community couldn't take hold. "The pro-regressives and their enablers were exposed and refuted at every turn, they were academically and philosophically under siege," he bragged.

"*Alhamdulillah*" [praise be to God]," he wrote, the Progressive Muslim Union of North America collapsed. So did Muslim WakeUp. (But the vision resurrected in a new 501(c)(3) organization, Muslims for Progressive Values, established in 2007.)

* * *

To mark the end of 2005, writing as "DrMaxtor," Hashmi released a "top ten pro-regressive Moslim idiots of 2005."

He reserved his No. 1 pick for Tarek Fatah, a journalist living in Toronto, Canada. Fatah had emigrated from Pakistan decades earlier, and he had grown to be very troubled by the rise of Islamist extremism in Canada. He thought he had left it behind in Pakistan, but what he saw was the same rigid mentality of the orthodoxy imported to his new homeland. "DrMaxtor" called Fatah a "Jerk-in-the-Box" and a "festering boil on the butt cheek of humanity."

Fatah was abrasive, but it was because he was a man in a hurry. He could see the growing aggression of the Muslim establishment to protect its interests in business, governance, and society, and to weaponize a concept they were calling "Islamophobia" to further their interests. The Muslim community has many valuable contributions to make to the West and the US, including values of truth, compassion, and justice, but these important values are lost when our most visible representatives resort to terrorism—and the voices from within our community engage in the cycle of denial. We allow shame and honor to silence us. We must break out and own up to our problems. Fatah was one of those who argued for owning up.

At No. 3, he wrote that Amina Wadud, the scholar who had led our woman-led prayer earlier in the year, needed a "swift kick in the kaboose," when in prostration during prayer.

I made it to the list at No. 4. "A lot of words come to my mind," he wrote, "when I hear the name Asra Nomani : [*sic*] clueless, patronizing, bitter, but above all a LIAR. Already known for her friendship to slain reporter Daniel Pearl, Nomani decided that she wanted to boost her profile even more by making demonstrably false and misleading statements about the Morgantown masjid."

He continued, "The unrepentant adulteress ran for a position on the masjid board and pulled a Nixon when she realized she couldn't win." I actually hadn't run for election, but he feigned authority. I had known I didn't stand a chance against the coalition of Muslim Brotherhood and Hamas supporters.

Using his identity as "DrMaxtor," Hashmi wrote: "Bitter and angry, she starts making claims of inequality at the masjid in addition to citing that her daddy contributed financially to the masjid. Oh I see, so that means that whenever I cant [*sic*] have my way at my local masjid, I can make ridiculous demands, phony claims and even drag a camera crew there because I stuffed a few dollars in the donation box. It's this sort of convoluted logic which places the disgusting Nomani at number four. If only RU-486 was available in Pakistan...."

RU-486 is known as "Plan B" to end unwanted pregnancies.

Hashmi had choice words for his No. 7 pick: Syrian American poet and literature professor Mohja Kahf, a creative writer who had started a "Sex and the Ummah" column at Muslim WakeUp, inspired by the *Sex and the City* series that had opened up conversations in the US around intimacy. He called Kahf a "resident pornographer" on the website.

There is a Quranic verse (4:135), "*Al-Nisa*," or "The Women," that reminds Muslims of our divine imperative to testify to the truths of problems inside our community: "Oh ye who believe! Stand out firmly for justice, as witnesses to God, even if it may be against yourselves, or your parents, or your kin." Instead, Muslim interests were focused on pointing the finger to supposed problems outside the community, starting with cartoonists.

* * *

That year, Islamists in America were in danger of their cover being blown. They were under multiple FBI and US Customs Service investigations for allegedly financing terrorist organizations in Israel and hiding money. One of the cases would end years later with guilty verdicts on all charges against the Holy Land Foundation and five of its officers, including a sixty-five-year sentence for Ghassan Elashi, the founder of CAIR's Dallas chapter, for funneling over $12 million from the Holy Land Foundation, headquartered at 500 Grove Street in Herndon, Virginia, to the Palestinian militant group Hamas.

Years later, the FBI issued a letter in April 2009 to the US House Subcommittee on Terrorism, Technology, and Homeland Security and said that it suspended contact with CAIR because of evidence introduced during the Holy Land Foundation trial, demonstrating that CAIR and its founders were part of a group set up by the Muslim Brotherhood to support Hamas.

For now, the cofounders knew they needed more cover.

The Muslim Brothers huddled in the building they had bought years earlier at 500 Grove Street. They had a crisis on their hands. They were under investigation. Law enforcement was closing in. They needed cover.

The meeting included Jamal Barzinji and other key Muslim Brothers from the founding of the labyrinth of organizations housed at 500 Grove Street. "The new strategy was that if we want as American Muslims to survive, we must engage in interfaith dialogue," recalled Muhammad Shafiq, one of the original cofounders, in a video posted by the International Institute of Islamic Thought. Islamic studies wouldn't be enough. Muslims had to lead interfaith efforts in academic institutions.

With this strategy in place, the Muslim Brothers signed an agreement with the Catholic community in Arlington, Virginia, to forge an "interfaith" relationship. It was to be the first of many agreements.

Daan Braveman, a dean at Nazareth College in Rochester, New York, made the pilgrimage to 500 Grove Street with his team from the college. They had lunch with Barzinji and clicked, beginning a long relationship that would give the Muslim Brothers the perfect outpost to run interference for Islamist regimes worldwide. It helped that Braveman was Jewish. Whenever they got the opportunity, the Muslim Brothers would refer to him as the "Jewish dean" at Nazareth.

In 2004, the International Institute of Islamic Thought established a chair at Nazareth College, which hosted a special inauguration ceremony that key members of the Muslim Brothers joined to celebrate this victory. Through interfaith dialogue, the "Islamization of knowledge" was continuing. They got a contract with Macmillan Press. They ramped up to fight "Islamophobia" with other faith leaders. They planned trainings for health care workers and Syracuse University students.

The Muslim Brothers, connected to the International Institute of Islamic Thought, had bought cover and influence in the United States. Academic institutions in the US were helping to make mainstream very problematic ideas, if you stopped to associate them with any other religious ideology. US academic institutions were supporting the promotion of Islamism, or political Islam, something that would be very unsettling if Christian theocracy and biblical education were being promoted in the modern day by their counterparts in Christianity. It isn't odd that the Muslim Brothers would be trying to spread the word of the Qur'an, but what they were claiming about tolerance didn't match up with the Islamist ideology they embraced.

* * *

The next summer, the number one aim of the Islamists—to destroy Israel—gained new momentum. A young Palestinian, Omar Barghouti, organized a coalition of Palestinian organizations, activists, and community leaders that issued a call on July 9, 2005, for a boycott of Israel and its products, a divestment from any enterprises in the state, and sanctions against the nation—or "BDS," boycott, divestment, and sanctions. They harkened back to the boycotts and divestment movement against South Africa when the country separated blacks, whites, and other minorities in a racial apartheid. The declaration made three demands: an end to Israeli "occupation" of Arab lands, including East Jerusalem; an end to Israel's "institutional, legal and societal discrimination" against Palestinians in "apartheid" conditions; and, significantly, a "return" of Palestinian refugees to their "homes of origin," including in modern-day Israel. According to estimates in 2022, that would amount to a "right of return" for some 5.9 million Palestinians living in the diaspora of the world, or half of the global Palestinian population of about 11.8 million. Meanwhile, the total population of Jews in the world is an estimated 15.2 million, with only about 6.7 million Jews in Israel.

The petition's signatories included groups seeking the "return" of Palestinians from around the world to lands, including Israel, in an effort to outnumber the Israeli Jews. They included Al-Awda: The Palestinian Right to Return Coalition, based in Coral Springs, Florida.

* * *

That fall 2005, Islamists had the grievance they needed to win sympathy with their "woke" allies. Danish newspaper *Jyllands-Posten* published twelve cartoons of the Muslim prophet Muhammad to make a free speech point.

Nobody outside Denmark might have noticed the cartoons except for the shenanigans of a young Lebanese Muslim man, Ahmed Akkari, living in Copenhagen. He worked with a local imam, Ahmad Abu Laban, and assembled the "Akkari-Laban dossier," with all the cartoons and a few other inflammatory images. They headed to the Middle East, landing on December 3, 2005, in Egypt, where they showed the dossier to anyone who would take an interest. They even met the general secretary of the Arab League. Akkari was speaking on behalf of the "European Committee for Prophet Honouring," alleging "Islamophobia" in the West.

A young politician in Copenhagen, Naser Khader, watched the theatrics in horror. Born in Damascus, Syria, in 1963 and raised in a rural town outside the capital, he was the son of a Palestinian father and a Syrian mother. They had named him after the secular president of Egypt, Gamal Abdel Nasser. Unable to find steady work in Lebanon, Khader's father had immigrated to Europe for work, and Khader joined him in Copenhagen in 1974 as a teen. A journalist, he was elected to the Danish parliament, first representing the Danish Social Liberal Party and then later the Conservative People's Party. He didn't subscribe to the narrative of Muslims as victims. The US had legitimate concerns about protecting its ports from terrorism, and the cartoonists had every right to express their views publicly.

* * *

Three days later, on December 6, 2005, the kings, heads of state, and other leaders of the Organization of Islamic Cooperation descended on Mecca for the third "Extraordinary Islamic Summit." There, Egyptian foreign minister Ahmed Aboul Gheit had something to show his colleagues: the dossier.

He passed the dossier around. And, as could be predicted, it riled everyone up. They were already on edge because it looked like distrust of Muslims could kill a proposed deal to give Dubai Ports World, based in the wealthy Gulf nation of the United Arab Emirates, management control over US facilities at the Port of New York and New Jersey, Port of Philadelphia, Port of Baltimore, Port of New Orleans, Port of Miami, and sixteen other ports. The ruler of Dubai, Mohammed bin Rashid Al Maktoum, ran the holding company that controlled Dubai Ports World, and he had asked the Committee on Foreign Investment in the United States to approve his planned purchase of a British company, the Peninsular and Oriental Steam Navigation Company, that managed the US ports. Coast Guard intelligence officials had raised an issue over security risks.

Inspired to act fast, the leaders signed a "Ten-Year Program of Action" that included an influence operations campaign to "protect and defend the true image of Islam" and "combat defamation of Islam." They also committed to "encourage dialogue among civilizations and religions." The ten-year plan called on the Organization of Islamic Cooperation to "emphasize the responsibility of the international community, including all governments, to ensure respect for all religions and combat their defamation." A new website popped up: Islamophobia.com.

Later, Akkari apologized for his role in stoking worldwide protest against Denmark.

* * *

Countering "Islamophobia" fit naturally into the civil rights narrative of the West, protecting minority groups, such as the LGBT, Jews, Hispanics, and blacks, even though Organization of Islamic Cooperation countries were themselves notoriously bad at protecting minority rights.

Muslim leaders were leveraging identity politics to play a very dangerous game and split Muslims from the American majority by convincing them that they were hated by others and needed to band together with the downtrodden against a racist and hate-filled Christian and white nationalist majority. The "Islamophobia" term was also part of a broader effort to delegitimize criticism of Islam by pathologizing criticism as a "phobia." Arguments based in fear and prejudice do not need to be answered but can be dismissed as irrational and bigoted.

The Organization of Islamic Cooperation also sought to get the United Nations to adopt an international resolution to "counter Islamophobia" and call upon states to "enact laws to counter it, including deterrent punishment." They were seeking the kinds of blasphemy laws that nations such as Afghanistan, Pakistan, Saudi Arabia, and Iran enforced, criminalizing speech that offended Muslims.

Their efforts begged several important questions. Was the honor of Islam really threatened, and who were these people claiming the right to "defend" it? What is "Islamophobia" anyway? Where did the idea come from? Is all criticism of the actions of individual Muslims—or even Muslims as a whole—irrational and bigoted? Or are there rational concerns that some people may have with the religion and its followers? This is critical, because if there are reasons, it isn't Islamophobia. A phobia is an irrational fear. How are accusations of Islamophobia abused and, more importantly, why?

At their headquarters in Jeddah, Saudi Arabia, staffers at Organization of Islamic Cooperation started a tally of offenders, including alleged offenses by the cartoonists at a satire magazine, *Charlie Hebdo*, based in Paris.

In Phoenix, Arizona, a Syrian American physician, Zuhdi Jasser, watched in horror. He had just formed a group, American Islamic Forum for Democracy, to challenge the orthodoxy that advocated for political Islam. Here the Organization of Islamic Cooperation was creating a brigade to protect the honor of Islam, the perfect foil to deflect criticism of the controversial ideas and growing influence of Islamist governments and movements. "These countries that run thugocracies launched this honor brigade to protect the image of Islam," he told me. "They are just bullies. They think they own the Muslim community and all interpretations of Islam."

Early the next year, the "Islamophobia" defense even landed on the pages of the conservative *National Review*, where columnist

Larry Kudlow criticized the attack on the Dubai Ports World deal, writing "Call It What It Is: *Islamophobia*." Still, in early March 2006, the US House of Representatives voted 62–2 to block the deal, and Sen. Chuck Schumer (D-NY) added amendments to a Senate bill to block the deal. Dubai Ports World later sold the US operations to a US company, American International Group. United Arab Emirates Sheikh Hamdan bin Rashid Al Maktoum, the founder of Dubai Ports World, had lost the battle, but he was going to see to it that he'd win the war.

* * *

Today, Muslims in the United States number about three million people. It is just a tiny fraction of America's population of about 320 million. Muslims have succeeded academically, professionally, and politically in the United States, despite the typical assimilation challenges that beset any community. But something unique has hamstrung our progress: our knee-jerk inclination to be something that one FBI agent calls being "a couch jihadi," leveling grievance after grievance against the West in a thinly veiled effort to avoid discussing the real crisis of extremism in our communities. The consequence has been the failure of many Muslims to fully assimilate. To fully integrate, we must heal our grievances and contribute positively to solutions that defeat Islamic extremism.

Too many Muslims deny the issue of Islamic extremism with polemics like "Islam is a religion of peace." We deflect from serious truths about Islamic radicalization, argue that Americans and others have an irrational fear of Islamic extremism, and demonize anyone who talks about Islamic terrorism as an "Islamophobe."

It is not "Islamophobia," or an irrational fear of Islam, to be frightened of Islamic extremism, but rather a rational fear of an interpretation of Islam slaying innocent lives from Pakistan to Canada. Instead of saving face, we need to do something that children learn: own up. With honesty and pragmatism, we could then relieve the fears that others have of Muslims and make the world safer for everyone, including Muslims.

* * *

Muslim leaders heard the cue to make a big deal about "Islamophobia" in the West, but they needed money to fund their efforts. That spring, Sheikh Hamdan bin Rashid Al Maktoum of the United Arab Emirates agreed to meet an old friend, former Democratic Rep. Paul Findley, who was leading a delegation of American Muslim leaders to the United Arab Emirates. The delegation included three cofounders of the Council on American-Islamic Relations: executive Nihad Awad, communications chief Ibrahim Hooper, and board chairman Parvez Ahmed. It also included North Carolina General Assembly Democratic state senator Larry Shaw, at the time the highest-ranking Muslim elected official in the US. He later joined the CAIR board, becoming its board chairman. They had a simple goal: to raise $50 million for a PR and advocacy campaign, pushing the "Islamophobia" criticism of the West.

Hamdan had already generously supported CAIR through his Al Maktoum Charity Foundation. Right after the 9/11 attacks, the Al Maktoum Foundation had taken a nearly $1 million stake in CAIR's headquarters on New Jersey Avenue SE, in Washington, DC, just three blocks from the US Capitol. The foundation shared CAIR's anti-Israel position. It had faced criticism as being anti-Israel, and it had held telethons to support families of Palestinian suicide bombers and other so-called "martyrs."

This round, local media reported that Maktoum "endorsed" a plan to build a CAIR endowment. Awad was quoted saying the endowment would be a "source of income" and "further allow us to reinvigorate our media campaign projecting Islam and its principles of tolerance, which is based on promotion of peace, co-existence and dialogue among various religions and cultures." Findley briefed Hamdan on CAIR's strategic plan on "correcting the image of Islam and Muslims among the American public." Awad said CAIR appreciated Hamdan and his Al Maktoum Charity Foundation for supporting CAIR plans to "promote dialogue." One article said CAIR sought to "empower the North American Muslim community through political and social activism."

* * *

The next day, then US Ambassador Michele J. Sison dispatched an unclassified cable, marked "SENSITIVE," from Abu Dhabi to her bosses in Washington, DC, on the high-level visit. The CAIR delegation snagged an audience with Sheikh Sultan bin Muhammad al-Qasimi, ruler of Sharjah, the third-largest city in the United Arab Emirates. Sheikh Ali al-Hashemi, the nation's presidential advisor on Islamic affairs, hosted a reception for the delegation.

The delegation "expressed ideas about countering negative stereotypes about Muslims in the US ('Islamophobia') and addressing anti-Americanism in the Middle East." Don Myers, an executive at the big PR firm, Hill & Knowlton, and former US Defense Department official, provided a "short demonstration of a PR campaign designed to support CAIR's overall organizational objectives defined as: 1) political empowerment of Muslims, 2) grassroots efforts by CAIR to improve community relations with non-Muslims, 3) launching of an effective, long-term (5-year) advertising/outreach campaign to counter negative stereotypes about Muslims." The campaign would be called "Let the Conversation Begin."

* * *

Two days later, the delegation scored an important headline in the *Gulf News*, a popular English language newspaper in the Middle East, reading, "An influential American Muslim group on Monday urged Arab businesses to invest in image-building in the US to secure their long-term interests."

CAIR board chairman Parvez Ahmad was quoted saying, "If the image of Islam and Muslims is not repaired in America, Muslim and Arab business interests will continue to be on a downward slide in the US."

CAIR leveraged another close friendship that former Democratic Rep. Paul Findley had with a rich local businessman, Emirate tycoon Khalaf Ahmad Al Habtoor, cofounder of Al Habtoor Group LLC, to get an invitation from Habtoor for a lunch meeting. The

Gulf News reported that CAIR officials had spoken with Habtoor and other Dubai businessmen about a $50 million public relations campaign in the US to "change negative public perceptions about Islam."

The article quoted CAIR board chairman, Ahmad, bragging, "It is the most ambitious public relations campaign anywhere in the world that the Muslims have thought about to change perceptions about Islam." The *Gulf News* said Ahmad was calling on Arab businesses to contribute to the campaign.

"Do not think about your contributions as donations," Ahmad was quoted as saying. "Think about it from the perspective of rate of return. The investment of $50 million will give you billions of dollars in return for 50 years."

The vision of the Muslim Brothers at CAIR took them to Saudi Arabia later that year to raise funds. The US ambassador to Saudi Arabia sent his bosses in Washington, DC, a cable describing their meetings. He also marked his cable "SENSITIVE."

There was something that CAIR officials wanted to hide behind their multimillion-dollar PR campaign: the actual radicalization of Muslims across the United States from their base in Northern Virginia to Texas.

* * *

When Lyndon Johnson lifted quotas on immigrants to the United States in 1965, a few of the Muslim Brothers found their way to North Texas.

By the late 1970s, there were an estimated five thousand Muslims in Texas, praying at a few prayer spaces. Many were immigrants from India and Pakistan, drawn by the warm weather, jobs, and relatives already settled in the city. In 1989, the Muslim Brothers from Northern Virginia set up an organization, the Holy Land Foundation for Relief and Development, in the sleepy town of Richardson, Texas. In the 1990s, refugees had arrived from war-torn places, including "Palestinians from Kuwait, Kurds from Iraq, Bosnians, Kosavars, and Somalis," wrote a *Texas Monthly* writer. By 2000, there were an estimated forty-eight thousand Muslims in the Dallas area, according to the Association of Religion Data Archives and twenty-eight Muslim congregational spaces.

In late 2001, the US government convicted five leaders of the Holy Land Foundation for using the organization to fund terrorism. The Department of Justice referred to the Holy Land Foundation as "the U.S.-based fundraising arm of the terrorist group Hamas." By 2010, the largest number of Muslims in the United States called Texas home, with 422,000 Muslims statewide.

The next generation, coming of age as adults post-9/11, knew they had to sell Islamist ideas carefully.

* * *

Born in 1975 in Houston, Yasir Qadhi grew up in the local Muslim community, where his parents, immigrants from India, were a fixture.

Qadhi earned his BA in chemical engineering at the University of Houston, graduating in 1995. On campus, he had befriended a young Muslim woman from Pakistan who was a strong personality at their meetings of the Muslim Students Association. Her name was Aafia Siddiqui, and she would one day be known as "Lady Al-Qaeda" for her support of the extremist group. She would return to Texas to be sentenced to eighty-six years in prison after being convicted of seven counts of attempted murder and assault on US military personnel in Afghanistan.

Back then, in the 1990s, Qadhi was like many first-generation American Muslims who wanted to get closer to their Muslim identity. To do that, he went to Saudi Arabia for a decade to study at the orthodox University of Medina, first earning a BA in hadith studies in 2000. Steeped in the Saudi spin on Islam, Qadhi set about to create a business network to disseminate Salafi ideas. The *salaf* were the first generation of Muslims who lived in the seventh century at the time of the prophet Muhammad. The school of Islam called Salafi came out of the strict Hanbali *madhhab*, or school of jurisprudence, that spawned the dogmatic Wahhabi interpretation of Islam. Salafism was like a sister school of thought to Wahhabism. It had a puritanical and rigid interpretation of sharia, ruling for example that men could marry four wives, that women are required to cover their faces with veils and their bodies with shrouds, so as not to tempt men, and that violent jihad is not only permissible but a sacred duty of Muslims. It was the interpretation of Islam that Saudi Arabia had exported to the world since the 1970s.

In 2001, Qadhi helped a friend, Muhammad Alshareef, and others establish a new organization, the AlMaghrib Institute, which sold the rigid interpretation of Islam to young people using seminars, workshops, slick marketing, a cult-like fervor, and a business model that built close-knit communities based on geography. Some AlMaghrib adherents were later tied to terrorism, including Farouk Abdulmutallab, the notorious "Underwear Bomber," who attempted to detonate explosives hidden in his underwear at the age of twenty-three while aboard Northwest Airlines Flight 253 from Amsterdam to Detroit on Christmas Day 2009. The ideas of the AlMaghrib Institute conflicted with secular, progressive ideas of the West.

By early 2003, Alshareef had established himself in American Muslim community, a popular tour guide on the haj pilgrimage, run by the Islamic Society of North America. He had an easy smile and was warm and gregarious. His wife wore a gown and full-face black veil called *niqab*. Soon after, Alshareef taught an AlMaghrib course at George Mason University in Fairfax County, Virginia, off Route 7. It was on *fiqh*, or Islamic law, and could have been called "fatwa school." He taught students how Islamic scholars issue a fatwa, or religious ruling. Some of the women students wore *niqab* with full-face veils, revealing their strict interpretation of Islam. One drove on I-495 with her face covered with a veil.

In 2005, Qadhi earned his MA in theology and theological studies and returned to the United States to spread the gospel. He was fast becoming one of the most dangerous purveyors of Salafism in America.

* * *

By early 2007, face-to-face classes weren't enough to spread the hard-core teachings of AlMaghrib Institute and Yasir Qadhi.

Cryptically, a Muslim blogger, "Amad," announced to readers he was going to expand his personal blog, *Musings of a Muslim Mind*, and establish a new online website, MuslimMatters.org. He openly self-identified as practicing the hard-line ideology of Salafism.

"Amad" thanked a friend, "Dr. M"—the fake name for the former UC Berkeley student Javad Hashmi—for inspiring him, writing, "I wanted to write about USA politics, a departure from the old days of 'politics = haram'. But I was still very much into the Muslim conflict politics. So, my focus was raising the 'orthodox voice' or at the time 'not-salafi but salafi voice' because the blogosphere was dominated by what I preferred to call, 'pro-regressives', a term that may have been coined by the illustrious, in-your-face, Dr. M."

He had pitched the idea of a new blog to his "college-mate, friend, and Shaykh," Yasir Qadhi, to advance Salafi ideology in America. "Amad," or @AmadShk on Twitter, was Amad Shaikh, raised in the United States to immigrant parents from Pakistan, and cofounder of AlMaghrib Institute. He wrote that Qadhi "was quick to latch on to the idea." Shaikh didn't return requests for comment.

In late January 2007, a young student at the Massachusetts Institute of Technology, Sam Ahmad Zamanian, registered MuslimMatters.org, using his Cambridge, Massachusetts, address, to take the teachings online. The new website identified him as the blog's business manager and, later, as one of the site's founders, using the name, "Ahmad al-Farsi," or as it showed up on the blog, "Ahmad AlFarsi." Farsi is the main language of Iran. Zamanian was from the Sugar Land suburb in Katy, Texas, outside Houston. There were so many Pakistanis living there, the nickname for Sugar Land was *Shukur Nagr*, which means "sugar place" in the language of Urdu, spoken by many Muslims in South Asia—and Houston. AlFarsi meant "the Farsi," the language of Iran and parts of Afghanistan. In an online bio, he said he was born in "South Texas" in an Iranian Christian household and embraced Islam in 2003 as a college student. He was part of the post-9/11 generation. He completed his master's degree in electrical engineering and computer science from MIT in 2007, later earning a PhD. On Google+, he posted a photo with a wide smile. After graduating, he started working at Shell, the oil giant, as a geophysicist and worked there in January 2022.

Later, some people accused him of being a writer with the fake name, "SZ," supporting theocratic leaders in Iran. Zamanian didn't respond to a request for comment.

Meanwhile, Shaikh assembled an A-team of writers for the staff of MuslimMatters, publishing dangerous anti-American, anti-Israel, pro-Salafi dogma and propaganda.

* * *

To even the surprise of cofounder Amad Shaikh, the effort caught the attention of a Muslim tech entrepreneur, Shahed Amanullah, who wrote to Shaikh extending his support.

Born in 1968 in Hollywood, California, to parents who had immigrated to the US from India, Amanullah grew up in an upper-middle-class life in Southern California. His family settled into a comfortable life in the US, his father, Saeed, becoming a structural engineer for the Los Angeles County Department of Public Works, with security clearances, and his mother, Naveed, getting a job with the US State Department. As a boy, sitting in a mosque, he met the boxer Muhammad Ali, who was visiting the mosque and did magic tricks with Amanullah and the other children. He grew up going to the Islamic Center of Southern California. He started at the University of California at Berkeley in 1986 and graduated in 1991 with a BS in civil engineering. He was part of the first generation of American Muslims with talents and skills in technology, activism, and protest. By day, starting in 1994, Amanullah was a project engineer for the City and County of San Francisco, working on typical engineering projects on a new Fisherman's Wharf streetcar line, historic office building conversion, and light rail development. By night, he was busy breaking new ground on the emerging technology called the internet. In 1995, he launched mpac.org, a website for a new organization, the Muslim Public Affairs Council, established out of his home mosque in Southern California. He used an Oakland, California, address. He established Halalfire Media LLC, *halal* meaning "legal," the Muslim version of kosher, and set about building an internet empire with numerous websites.

In 1998, Amanullah was recruited to Yack Media Services, an online media company, as principal manager of product design and development, including creating website designs and managing a team of fifteen graphic designers and programmers. The next year, he cofounded a company, Relatia Networks, based in Mountain View, California, in the heart of Silicon Valley, near companies with well-known names including GoDaddy, Twitter, and Facebook. He created a list of halal restaurants in the area for his fellow Muslim colleagues. The next year, Amanullah moved his operations to Washington, DC, where he started studies at Georgetown University. That year, Amanullah launched several websites, using the address for an office building at 2200 Wilson Avenue, Suite 102-26, in Arlington, Virginia. The websites were zabihah.com for restaurant reviews (ritual Muslim butchering is called *zabihah*), muslimparents.com, Shahed.com, and Eat-Halal.com.

In 2000, Amanullah started another set of websites, Amila.com and Amanullah.org, using an Arlington, Virginia, post office box. In early 2001, Amanullah launched AltMuslim.com, a blogging platform for Muslims that published more mainstream content than MuslimMatters. (As of March 2022, muslimparents.com redirected to halalfire.com. Amila.com directed to a Wayback Machine archive. AltMuslim.com directed to Shahed.com.) That summer he started at an architectural and engineering firm back in Northern California, managing 3G upgrade projects for SprintPCS, Verizon, Nextel, and AT&T Wireless.

Back in Fullerton, California, his family had a house on Paseo Dorado, where a car sometimes sat out front with a vanity plate with the Amanullah family name. Paseo translated as "walk" in English, and "Dorado" translated as "golden."

One of the aliases at LoonWatch was "Dorado." Was that just a coincidence?

Shaikh wrote, "Who would have guessed that only a few years later, I would write a piece for altmuslim, and be friends with Shahed Amanullah!"

* * *

In late February 2007, the *Doha Debates* aired a discussion on the question of whether the *niqab*, or face veil, should be banned. The team voting to ban the *niqab* won, 57 percent to 43 percent. At his *AmadDen* blog, Shaikh protested that the team against the *niqab* had no right to weigh in. He wrote disparagingly about the team that debated against *niqab*, attacking Reem Maghribi, founder of *Al Sharq*, an English-language Arab culture and lifestyle magazine in the United Kingdom. Born in London, Maghribi was the daughter of a former Libyan diplomat and a Syrian mother. She had established herself as an editor, publisher, and communications consultant in London. But she had nothing of importance to say, according to her critic. "...What do you expect from this pro-regressive woman, who does not even wear the hijab!" Shaikh wrote, borrowing the "pro-regressive" language coined by "DrMaxtor."

"Check her 'young and energetic' team...does it even look like that she cares about Muslim issues, let alone have any right to discuss the *niqab*??"

At 9:35 a.m., the former UC Berkeley student, Javad Hashmi, wrote from his anonymous "DrMaxtor" account, supporting Shaikh. "Great post Amad," he wrote, "I do not see *niqab* as *wajib*," or mandatory, "but who are these presumptive whitewashed prima donnas anyway? The Doha Debacles have always been a waste of time. What hubris on the part of these sell outs to declare such nonsense on our sisters."

He ended: "What a spineless munafiq," using his classic smear of "hypocrite."

A few hours later, at 12:17 p.m., Shaikh responded, "Dr. M, good to see ur comments on this blog.... I am a fan of your pro-regressive hit-jobs...."

He continued, "I think we need to do even more to expose those who now pretend that 'progressivism is dead' yet are themselves only slightly less progressive. In fact, these new breed [*sic*] is more dangerous since like Qadiyanis, they pretend they are 'just like you' and then bite you when you least expect it."

The "Qadiyanis" are a sect of Islam that Salafis consider heretical.

He ended: "*Wallahu musta'an.*" And Allah is our refuge.

In early March 2007, Shaikh penned an anonymous blog, going after a fiery Syrian American woman, Wafa Sultan, who had just gotten a lot of attention over an Al Jazeera interview criticizing Islam. The article was headlined "Wafa Sultan: The bubble is bursting."

Iranian American academic Reza Aslan despised her as well.

Shaikh added, "See also this scathing post from Dr.M, the master of pro-regressive analysis!" He linked to a fake article published by Dr. Maxtor on his blog, headlined "Oy Vey! The Wafa Sultan fraud EXPOSED," with an image of Sultan in a clown mask with an oversized red nose and white-painted face.

In the comment section, Hashmi, writing as Dr. Maxtor, wrote, "Being that I'm on vacation and have not had the time to keep track of the criminal network, thanks for bringing this to my attention. I always knew Sultan was a liar…nice to see the truth finally surface. With your permission I will add you to my blogroll."

Shaikh responded soon after, writing, "Absolutely, and I have been meaning to add you to my roll as well. Your pro-regressive take is my favorite."

Over the next months and years, Shaikh collected a treasure chest of writers who followed the Salafi doctrine. One was even the cousin of "American Taliban" John Walker Lindh, who was captured as an enemy combatant during US operations in Afghanistan in November 2001.

CHAPTER 5

Weaponizing "Islamophobia"

Flush with cash from their overseas fundraising trips, CAIR and other Muslim leaders were about to launch a major propaganda offensive in the West. For this effort, they needed foot soldiers.

In the summer of 2007, an intern, Muhammad Tauseef Akbar, joined the offices of CAIR in Chicago. Like Northern Virginia, Chicago was another hub for Muslims in the United States.

Born in 1976 to immigrant parents from South Asia, he had just earned a BA in English from North Park University. His CAIR bio identified him as "an active member" of Young Muslims, a Chicago-based youth organization affiliated with the orthodox Islamic Circle of North America. AmericansAgainstHate.org, run by critics of CAIR, included Akbar in its roster of people peddling "hate" against Americans and Jewish people. It used as one point of evidence the fact that he featured the "DrMaxtor" blog on his "blogroll" of websites he recommended.

He was just what his boss, Ahmed Rehab, the executive director of the CAIR chapter in Chicago, needed. Rehab had energized the CAIR office just a few years earlier with his skills in marketing, technology, and business development. Now, he wanted to flex his muscle in the war of ideas.

That summer, Akbar used the byline "M.T. Akbar" to publish articles on a website, MediaMonitors.net, at first attacking conservatives, including TV host Glenn Beck and radio host Don Imus. MediaMonitors.net had been registered seven years earlier in 2000 to "M. Khan" of MMN International Inc., with an address of PO Box 6157, Fullerton, California, outside Los Angeles.

Later, Akbar republished the Islamophobia pieces on a WordPress site, MTAkbar.wordpress.com. (As of March 2022, the website was set to "private.") Following the themes his boss had published earlier in the year, Akbar published a piece on his WordPress site critical of the writer Joe Kaufman. CAIR Chicago then reposted Akbar's articles on its website.

CAIR Chicago's executive director, Ahmed Rehab, published an article in *InFocus*, a Muslim publication, targeting former CNN investigative reporter Steve Emerson, who had stumbled across an anti-Semitic, anti-West Muslim conference years earlier in Oklahoma City and represented a consistent voice criticizing CAIR. "Going many years back," Rehab wrote, "his track record is fraught with well-documented anti-Muslim bias."

* * *

Later that month, M. T. Akbar published an article headlined "Islamophobic Industrial Complex: What Are the Quasi Muslims Really Selling?" on a website, MediaMatters.net, home to Media Matters Network, which described itself as a platform for people who want to know the "whole truth about current affairs." Akbar targeted as "Quasi Muslims" a group of writers and speakers, including Brigitte Gabriel, Walid Shoebat, Nonie Darwish, and Ibn Warraq.

The CAIR community had developed its own "Good Housekeeping Seal of Approval" for Muslims and non-Muslims. The ones who didn't pass muster came under relentless attack.

In 2004, entrepreneur Shahed Amanullah and medical physicist Aziz Poonawalla had created the "Brass Crescent Awards" to publicly arbitrate some of these evaluations. In 2007, they recognized an emerging attorney-columnist, Glenn Greenwald, with an award for his "Unclaimed Territory" column series in *Salon* magazine as "Best Non-Muslim Blog," a category that asked, "Which blog writen [*sic*] by a non-Muslim is most respectful of Islam and seeks genuine dialogue with Muslims?"

Amanullah and Poonawalla wrote: "Glenn's 'sympathy for the Muslim predicament' and his 'dismantling of the excuses' for Iraqi and Palestinian suffering make him a 'friend of Muslims.'" It made sense that Greenwald, an avowed man of the left, cared about Muslim civil liberty issues as an attorney, but, as an openly gay man, it was odd that he didn't seem to have any commentary on the wide swath of Muslim countries that criminalize homosexuality, sometimes even with executions.

In February 2007, *Salon* editor Kerry Lauerman had welcomed Greenwald as a contributing writer. Greenwald would later use backing from PayPal billionaire Pierre Omidyar to start the media website, The Intercept.

* * *

In August 2007, Virginia Governor Tim Kaine, a Democrat, appointed a young Muslim surgeon, Esam Omeish, from Northern Virginia to the Virginia Commission on Immigration. On paper, it seemed like an inspiring immigrant success story. But he was part of the rise of the Muslim Brothers in America.

Born in 1967 in Tripoli, Libya, Omeish had arrived in the US with his family in 1982, when he was fifteen, knowing very little English. Settling in Falls Church, Virginia, Omeish enrolled as a student at J. E. B. Stuart High School in Bailey's Crossroads, Virginia, across Route 7. The next year, in 1983, the doors opened on the Dar Al-Hijrah Islamic Center, an ultraconservative mosque. In 1983, a group of Muslims also started the Muslim American Society, and they were closely affiliated with the work—and controversy—of the organizations not far away on Grove Street in Herndon, Virginia. In high school, Omeish and his brothers started some of the first Friday Muslim prayers at a Washington, DC, area high school. He eventually attended Georgetown University, where he started the Muslim Students Association chapter, chairing the MSA Council for the DC area.

Omeish joined the board of directors at Dar Al-Hijrah Islamic Center, and in 2000 he voted to recommend the board hire Anwar al Awlaki for the job of imam at the mosque. At one point, Omeish got an apartment, 1005N, in the same Skyline apartment complex where two 9/11 hijackers lived, near the Dar Al-Hijrah Islamic Center. Some of the hijackers had prayed at Dar Al-Hijrah. Omeish said he didn't know their deadly plans. After the 9/11 attacks, al-Awlaki ended up in Yemen as an imam for al-Qaeda. In 2011, the US would kill al-Awlaki in a drone strike.

In the fall of 2007, video circulated of Omeish at a Jerusalem Day rally, bellowing into the microphone after a series of "Allahu Akbar," calling for the freedom of "Philistine," the Arabic word for Palestine.

"We the Muslims of the Washington metropolitan area are here in sub-freezing temperatures," he yelled, his protests captured on a video posted on YouTube, "to tell our brothers and sisters in Philistine that you have learned the way, that you have known that the jihad way is the way to liberate your land. And we, by standing here today, despite the weather and despite anything else, we are telling them that we are with you, we are supporting you, and we will do everything inshallah to help your cause." He rallied Muslims to oppose the United States' "unconditional support of the Zionist entity in Philistine."

He had also been filmed at a 2006 rally, opposing the "Israeli war machine" and the "Israeli agenda" in the US Congress. After a caller asked Kaine about Omeish's comments during a radio talk show, Omeish resigned.

* * *

The next day, at a news conference organized by the Muslim American Society's Freedom Foundation, Omeish sat beside Wright Mahdi Bray, the Freedom Foundation's executive director. Omeish declared that the criticism against him came from "the same people" who painted the American Muslim community as a "fifth column, sadistic, dangerous, you can't trust them; they have double faces," who had created a "cottage industry," fomenting fear and distrust of Muslims.

Omeish spoke and said *jihad* meant "struggle" and that he had been taken out of context. He claimed that he was the target of a "smear campaign" that was trying to paint the Muslim American Society as a "front for terrorism" by "Islamophobes and Muslim bashers to intimidate Muslims from playing a broader and more influential role in mainstream American politics and societal affairs."

He said that Muslims would patiently wait for their turn. Little did local residents know that it would be Omeish's daughter, Abrar, then very young, who would be the one tapped to claim the family name in politics. And she would do everything in her power to vindicate her father, even calling upon teens in 2021 to engage in "jihad," as she delivered remarks at her father's high school alma mater, renamed Justice High School, amid social justice protests. After an outcry, she did the "jihad" tap dance, saying it wasn't meant as a conflict but rather a "spiritual struggle."

A reporter asked Omeish about the alleged ties of the Muslim American Society to the Muslim Brotherhood. He answered slowly.

"The referenced relationship with the Muslim Brotherhood is clearly historical and it's clearly obsolete, with no bearing on what MAS is today," he said. He added, "Some people did at some point have relations with the Muslim Brotherhood and that is reality that the documents have shown. The fact is that many mainstream Muslim organizations have had that degree of interaction at some point or another."

Then, he denied any ties currently. Still, he spoke well of them. "We still view them as a good ally that our government engages in different capacities," he said.

* * *

Just about every day meant another day putting out fires in CAIR's brand management problems. In late September 2007, Ahmed Bedier, an up-and-coming leader in the American Muslim community, got his turn to put out a fire. The *St. Petersburg Times* had published an article with a photo of CAIR cofounder Nihad Awad speaking at a rally while standing near a flag of the Shia militant organization, Hezbollah. With a mutual hate of Israel, Hezbollah had common ground with the Sunni militant group, Hamas.

Bedier went ballistic. The Jewish pro-Israel organization, the Anti-Defamation League, had supplied the photo. On a page on its website, marked "Anti-Bias Education," it had declared, "CAIR's stated commitment to 'justice and mutual understanding,' however, is undermined by its anti-Israel agenda," dating back to CAIR's founding. Bedier wrote to *St. Petersburg Times* editor Catriona Stuart, who agreed to change the caption and place the photo lower on the screen. At Bedier's request, she added to the caption that CAIR denies the authenticity of the photo "and contends that Awad never saw the flag or the individuals holding it at the rally."

It would take this kind of pushback to transform CAIR from pariah to patriot.

Bedier was triumphant.

* * *

In November 2007, CAIR saw the realization of the public relations campaign that it had pitched in the United Arab Emirates the year before. Rep. Keith Ellison (D-MN) stepped onto the stage in Arlington, Virginia, for CAIR's thirteenth annual fundraiser with the theme "Let the Conversation Begin."

That first meant getting rid of some inconvenient people in the conversation.

* * *

There was a concept emerging called "white fragility" used by "critical race theory" ideologues to describe whites who resisted the fundamental assumptions of "critical race theory." They were to be mocked, harassed, and excommunicated. But when the criticism flipped and

Muslims exercised something that could be called "Muslim fragility," they were coddled.

Ex-Muslims and Muslim reformers pushed up against this fragility most dramatically. And there was one ex-Muslim who was a trigger for the Islamists and their sympathizers. Her name was Ayaan Hirsi Ali. She was a threat to the Islamist narrative.

Born in Mogadishu, Somalia, in 1969, she grew up in Somalia, where her father, Hirsi Magan Isse, was a prominent member of the Somali Salvation Democratic Front and a leader in the Somali revolution for independence. Soon after Ali was born, the administration of Somali leader Siad Barre imprisoned him for his political activism. He had opposed the tradition of female genital mutilation, but while he was in prison, her grandmother hired a man to perform the brutal operation on Ali when she was five years old, according to her testimonial.

When her father escaped from prison, the family fled Somalia in 1977 for Saudi Arabia, then Ethiopia, and finally Nairobi, Kenya, in 1980. Living comfortably with her family newly settled in Kenya, Ali studied at the Muslim Girls' Secondary School, where a popular teacher indoctrinated Ali and her classmates to the rigid Wahhabi interpretation of Islam that Saudi Arabia was exporting to the world. She believed in the Muslim Brotherhood, its strict rules about women and girls covering their hair with "hijab," and its cruel code of law. She agreed with the fatwa by clerics in Iran against novelist Salman Rushdie for committing blasphemy with his book, *The Satanic Verses*.

She grew up reading Nancy Drew novels and the archetypal girl heroine inspired her. In 1992, aged twenty-two and traveling to Germany to visit family, she escaped being forced into an arranged marriage and won asylum in the Netherlands. She worked many jobs, including as a translator; read new books that expanded her horizons; and joined a think-tank aligned with the center-left Labour Party. After the 9/11 attacks, she was disheartened by how Osama bin Laden had justified the murders with sections of the Qur'an. She became an atheist. She switched to the center-right party, which offered her more security protections than the party on the center-left.

After winning election to Parliament in 2003 at the age of thirty-three, she spoke bluntly about Islam, the prophet Muhammad, and Muslims. "At the very least Islam is facing backward and it has failed to provide a moral framework for our time," she told the *New York Times*. She also was quoted as saying, "If the West wants to help modernize Islam, it should invest in women because they educate the children." It was blunt and more monolithic about "Islam" than what some reformers saw, but she exercised the right to speak freely from a place of pain.

Tragedy struck on November 2, 2004, when a Dutch Moroccan Muslim, Mohammed Bouyeri, twenty-six, shot and killed her friend, the writer and film director Theo van Gogh, as retribution for the work he had done with her in making a short film, *Submission*, which dealt with the treatment of women in Muslim societies. Bouyeri cut van Gogh's throat with a large knife, attempting to cut off his head. He left a letter pinned to van Gogh's body, with a death threat to Ali. For two years, Ali lived in hiding.

In 2006, she found a new home in the United States, at the American Enterprise Institute, a conservative think-tank located near the White House. Controversy followed her to the US. In the spring of 2007, local Muslims in Johnstown, Pennsylvania, protested her planned speech at the University of Pittsburgh. At the Islamic Center of Johnstown, imam and mosque president Fouad ElBayly told a local reporter that Ali deserved the death sentence for her blasphemy and should be tried and judged in an Islamic nation. "She has been identified as one who has defamed the faith," he said. "If you come into the faith, you must abide by the laws, and when you decide to defame it deliberately, the sentence is death." ElBayly was also a prison chaplain.

* * *

By early December 2007, UC Berkeley alumnus Wajahat Ali, now an attorney and playwright with a growing following, targeted Ayaan Hirsi Ali's credibility in a scathing critique laden with sexist innuendo. Wajahat self-published a column, writing that a new "in-fo-tain-ment circus" was supported by the "pros-ti-tute," which he defined as "one who sells one's abilities, talent, or name for an unworthy purpose."

He singled out the "act of employing Muslims, especially but not exclusively Muslim women (with a strong preference to non-practicing, 'enlightened women'), to bash and vilify Muslims, Islam, and 'Islamic' culture certainly constitutes one of the oldest acts in the infotainment circus." He explained that the circus used a "non-threatening, aesthetically pleasing female, like a marionette puppet, to assail and mock those interests and reforms that would benefit that same minority." The reforms were a "plague to the ideological detriment of an elite majority (mostly affluent, influential White men)," so they had to be stopped.

"The most recent anointed ringleader of this ever increasing gallery popularized by right wing think tanks and media pundits, as well as several left-leaning liberals is Ayaan Hirsi Ali," he wrote, continuing with his sexual innuendos. She left her "satisfied customers yearning for more."

He closed: "Let's hope Ali and her ilk learn that once their trick turns stale or too threatening, her respective ringleaders will quickly and mercilessly substitute her position with an upgraded 'act'. After all, they don't call it 'the world's oldest profession' for nothing."

* * *

One hit after the next, the Honor Brigade tried to silence anyone they thought brought shame on Muslims.

In the summer of 2008, Muslim tech entrepreneur Shahed Amanullah heard about a historical fiction novel, *The Jewel of Medina*, set to be published that year by Random House about the life of Aisha, the youngest wife of the prophet Muhammad. Amanullah sent out an alert to his network. It did the trick. Within weeks, the book was dead.

Four days later, MuslimMatters published a link to a column I wrote in the *Wall Street Journal*, adding this commentary: "...if you see what would have been published in this book, you'd totally support Random House's decision, and definitely disagree with this article here."

Amad Shaikh, the antagonistic MuslimMatters cofounder, weighed in on the debate just using the name "Amad," calling me "the loony neo-Muslim *neo-con + Muslim* Asra Nomani."

It was an odd combination of insults. Loony. Neo-Muslim. Neo-con.

He lamented, "Amazing how she works actively on behalf of the right-wingers in her anti-mainstream-Islam agenda."

He added a link to a letter to the editor that an academic, Denise Spellberg, had published in the *Wall Street Journal*, explaining her opposition to the book, and said it was an "excellent response to the lies of Asra Nomani," though Spellberg's letter asserted no corrections.

Meanwhile, he supported a reader's request that MuslimMatters write about the life of Aafia Siddiqui, the Pakistani former MIT student convicted of attempting to kill US Army officers in Afghanistan. The cofounder of MuslimMatters, Yasir Qadhi, had admired Siddiqui when he knew her as a student at the University of Houston. Shaikh expressed sympathy for Siddiqui, saying, "…indeed it is a horrible story" of injustice that she had been sent to jail.

* * *

The Honor Brigade saw another high-level victory in the spring of 2008.

The National Counterterrorism Center, a multiagency center formed after 9/11 to coordinate the US war on terrorism, had developed a guide, "Words that Work and Words that Don't: A Guide for Counterterrorism Communication." The center, based in McLean, Virginia, down the road from CIA headquarters, advised, "Avoid labeling everything 'Muslim.' It reinforces the 'U.S. vs. Islam' framework that al-Qaeda promotes."

Among the new taboo words: "Islamism" and "Islamist."

CAIR featured a United Press International article about the development on its website.

The counterterrorism center's guide said, "Although the al-Qaida network exploits religious sentiments and tries to use religion to justify its actions, we should treat it as an illegitimate political organization, both terrorist and criminal."

The guide recommended words including "totalitarian," "terrorist," and "violent extremist," which were "widely understood terms that define our enemies appropriately and simultaneously deny them any level of legitimacy."

It said, "Never use the terms 'jihadist' or 'mujahideen,'" among others, to describe "the terrorists. A mujahed, a holy warrior, is a positive characterization in the context of a just war," the guide said. "In Arabic, jihad means 'striving in the path of God' and is used in many contexts beyond warfare. Calling our enemies jihadis and their movement a global jihad unintentionally legitimizes their actions."

The guide also banned the word "caliphate" because it had "positive connotations for Muslims.... The best description of what [al-Qaeda] really want to create is a 'global totalitarian state,'" it said.

One of the writers for the guides was Daniel Sutherland, who ran the Department of Homeland Security Office for Civil Rights and Civil Liberties, which produced the guides. He told United Press International, "There are some terms which al-Qaida wants us to use because they are helpful to them." He insisted the effort was "in no way an exercise in political correctness" or the "watering down" of "what we say." (In December 2021, Sutherland joined Meta, the new company name for Facebook, as director and associate general counsel, cybersecurity law and investigations.)

The guide incorporated advice from Muslim community leaders and religious experts in the US about terms to avoid. In a section titled "Terminology to Define the Terrorists: Recommendations from American Muslims," the guide recommended terms such as "death cult," "cult-like," "sectarian cult," and "violent cultists" to describe the "ideology and methodology of al-Qaeda and other terrorist groups."

On "Islamism" and "Islamist," the guide said, "the experts we consulted did not criticize this usage based on accuracy. Nevertheless, they caution that it may not be strategic for [US government officials] to use the term because the general public, including overseas audiences, may not appreciate the academic distinction between Islamism and Islam."

The guide recommended using "Takfirism," which wasn't really a word, but captured the practice of *takfir*, declaring a Muslim to be an apostate, or a non-Muslim, who can be killed. It was more of the same tap dance that the Honor Brigade and its Islamist interests had been attempting to avoid any direct conversation about Islam. "Takfirism" didn't stick in the media.

* * *

Members of the Honor Brigade didn't take well to losing.

In the spring of 2008, author Reza Aslan and others faced off against a team (that included me) in a debate in New York City, organized by Intelligence Squared, a nonprofit organization promoting debates in the US on the motion, "Islam is dominated by radicals."

Aslan's debate team included Edina Lekovic, communications director for the Muslim Public Affairs Council, one of the alphabet soup of organizations that emerged out of 500 Grove Street.

Before the debate, Aslan needled one of his opponents, Daveed Gartenstein-Ross, vice president of research at the Foundation for Defense of Democracies and the author of a book, *My Year Inside Radical Islam*.

"Be prepared to lose," Aslan said.

Gartenstein-Ross smiled politely.

In the debate, Gartenstein-Ross argued that Muslims with a radical interpretation of Islam dominated the way that Islam expresses itself in communities in the US and in Muslim-majority countries, where legal interpretations of sharia, or Islamic law, prevailed, sanctioning criminal punishment for apostasy or sex outside of marriage.

At debate's end, Aslan's team lost. Afterwards, members of the audience said that the sooner we acknowledged the prevailing, intimidating force of hardcore ideology in Muslim communities, the sooner extremism could be defeated. On the way to dinner afterwards, Aslan, angry at losing, attacked Gartenstein-Ross, trying to wrestle him to the ground. Gartenstein-Ross evaded Aslan's attack. With my mother, I watched, shocked.

The effort to undermine Gartenstein-Ross would go more covert. Later, "Ilisha" at LoonWatch republished a *Salon* column by writer Glenn Greenwald smearing Gartenstein-Ross as part of the "sham 'terrorism expert' industry."

* * *

The allegation of "Islamophobia" had become widespread during the Obama presidential campaign, leading up to the 2008 election. Critics, including Donald Trump, promoted the idea that Obama was born outside the United States or in Kenya, his father's home country. Obama also was criticized for his twenty-year-long relationship with a controversial Chicago preacher, Rev. Jeremiah Wright, who was very sympathetic to Palestinians.

The effort to curb national security rules took off in early 2008 when Muslim groups built a coalition, in anticipation of an Obama victory, and they set their sights on various targets from the New York Police Department to the US Armed Forces.

In January 2008, as billionaire George Soros pumped money into Barack Obama's presidential campaign, he launched a new initiative, the National Security and Human Rights Campaign, teaming up with Atlantic Philanthropies to fund nonprofits to "dismantle" Bush-era counterterrorism policies. They pooled their money in a joint account called the Proteus Fund and funneled at least $10 million to the effort. Soon after, Soros agreed to fund a new Security and Rights Collaborative to "restore civil liberties and human rights lost in the name of the 'war on terror.'"

Based out of an ordinary one-story building off Research Drive in Amherst, Massachusetts, the collaborative was run by an American Muslim, Shireen Zaman. She was previously executive director of the Institute for Social Policy and Understanding, which the Muslim Brothers on Grove Street established in 2003 and became home to an Egyptian American researcher, Dalia Mogahed, who supports Islamists. Before that, Zaman led the Middle East program at Vital Voices Global Partnership. A longtime "social justice warrior," she identified four areas of interest: "Secrecy, Oversight and Accountability," "Profiling and Discrimination," "Surveillance and Dissent," and "Torture, Detention and Rendition." After President Obama's election, an Open Society official sent a memo from Muslim Advocates to John Podesta, a key player in Obama's presidential campaign. The memo outlined a list of recommendations for overhauling America's national security policies.

* * *

Starting in late 2008, after Obama's victory, Soros funded a "field-wide Communications Hub" providing some $20 million over the next eight years to Muslim groups, liberal allies, and media outlets, including Media Matters, a propaganda machine run by a former conservative turned Democratic operative, David Brock. The theme of the campaign: Muslims are under attack in the West.

Soros gave millions of dollars to a new nonprofit, ReThink Media Inc., a strategic communications 501(c)(3) nonprofit organization established in 2008, based in Berkeley, California. Later, the *New York Times* described the group as a "progressive advocacy organization." In reality, it was a propaganda channel. By 2019, according to its IRS 990 tax filing, its revenue grew to $3.2 million. At first blush, ReThink Media seemed like any radical left-wing group, founded by two veterans of left-wing politics, Lynn Fahselt and Peter Ferenbach. They were married. Raised in New York, Ferenbach was a graduate of Georgetown University with advanced studies in global media and communications from the University of Melbourne in Australia. Fahselt earned an MA in global media and communications from the University of Melbourne. She graduated from Michigan State. She completed a senior fellowship at Fenton Communications, and she was a communications consultant to Fenton, Ploughshares Fund, Carnegie Corporation, Open Society Institute (later named the Open Society Foundations), Proteus Fund, Piper Fund, Atlantic Philanthropies, and others left-wing groups. Those foundations pumped money into ReThink Media. In their online story describing ReThink Media's origins, the organization's founders said they asked themselves several questions, including: Why do some movements fail, while others succeed? Why did their opponents dominate public conversations and frame debates?

They concluded that media and communication were key to building a movement. "Strategic communications isn't just about sending out a press release or penning an op-ed, it is about driving a powerful narrative," they wrote.

They had a long history working with CAIR and other Muslim groups that promoted anti-Israel activism. They hired a former official from the Council on American-Islamic Relations, Zainab Chaudary, as senior media associate for a program, the Security and Rights Collaborative. They set up a plan to create an echo chamber—calling it just that—for like-minded liberal groups.

Chaudary drafted daily talking points for liberal allies to repeat, most importantly: Muslims were victims. This narrative fed into liberal sympathies for minorities as victims, including defense of "terrorism suspects." The Honor Brigade teamed up with other Soros-funded groups, including Black Lives Matter and MoveOn.org, to promote a victimhood narrative in a "brown-black" alliance.

With funding from Soros paving the way, Muslim special interest groups and their liberal allies convinced President Obama that mentioning Islamic extremism would offend the very Muslim governments whose ideology—and funding—supported it.

CHAPTER 6

Launching a Disinformation Website

At 8:33:38 p.m. on April Fool's Day 2009, a young man used the name "Zuhair Thomas" to register a new account at GoDaddy, one of the many new internet service providers that had emerged in the 1990s. Founded in 1997 in Baltimore by software entrepreneur Bob Parsons, the company got its name when a group of male employees at Parsons's Jomax Technologies suggested Big Daddy as a new company name. It was already taken, so Parsons suggested Go Daddy, which became GoDaddy. The company registered website domain names and hosted websites.

"Zuhair Thomas" was Shopper ID 27179307 in GoDaddy's system, according to hundreds of pages of documents received in response to subpoenas filed as part of a defamation lawsuit. He put his address as 1200 Market Street in Philadelphia—a Loews Hotel in downtown Philadelphia. The phone number he provided, 215-627-1200, was for the hotel's front desk. He used a Muslim first name, an Anglo-Saxon last name.

Had someone read GoDaddy's internal "Shopper Info" files, they would have read, "Verified by Fraud Dept—Customer OK."

He was part of a stealthy network of anonymous cyber hitmen who had decided to expand the Honor Brigade's campaign by targeting the West, Israel, Muslim reformers, and anyone who got in their way using their new secret website. In Order No. 161790480, they bought the domain name LoonWatch.com from GoDaddy and designed the website to look like an online magazine.

What they had in mind was no joke. Research proves that the more lies are believed the more they are repeated. The act of dehumanizing enemies through character assassination also serves an important purpose of denying opponents any moral authority or claim to decency, respect, and civility. The campaign called for LoonWatch operatives to disseminate negative disinformation about Muslim reformers, critics of Islamic extremism, and others in ways that could not be tracked back to their real identities, employers, or organizational affiliations. The goal was to discredit Muslim reformers and shift the discussion away from Islamic extremism. The project's messages were designed to convince Americans that it was more important to discuss the impact of "Islamophobia" on Muslims as victims than to focus on Islamic extremism and the threat of Islamism. They wanted to usurp the attention shown to Jews and blacks in America. A central goal of the LoonWatch operation was to "expose" Muslim reformers and their allies, especially if they supported the state of Israel, in part by alleging they were tools of the Zionist movement.

They had one anonymous "Admin" identity and then unfamiliar fish species as the names for six pseudonymous accounts: "Emperor," "Garibaldi," "Mooneye," "Danios," "Zingel," and "Darter."

Whoever was writing as "Emperor" was apparently the leader. He frequently posted articles about "Islamophobia" and Israel, dishing out grievances several times a week. His sidekick was "Garibaldi." In reality, Garibaldi was actually the name of a nineteenth-century Italian philosopher. But it was also the name of a fish whose color—scarlet—is the same color as the coats that Garibaldi's followers wore. Later, they got contributions from two other anonymous writers, also with the names of fish species, "American Sole" and "Barbel."

That was nine of them, assuming each moniker belonged to a different person.

The email address for Shopper ID 27179307 was mtakbar4983@gmail.com, according to GoDaddy documents.

That was the email address of Muhammad Tauseef Akbar, research director for CAIR Chicago. His birthdate is April 9, 1983—the same as the "4983" in the email address in month, day, and year format. He was one of the keyboard warriors set loose by Ahmed Rehab, the executive director of the CAIR chapter in Chicago. Rehab had decided to turn up the heat in his disinformation war on America.

The creators of LoonWatch recruited a trusted, squirrely band of young American Muslims to adopt the names of fish as their fake names and become an army of keyboard warriors in the soft propaganda campaign of a cyber jihad. They weren't lone wolves, but members of well-known and established Muslim organizations and brands. Muhammad Tauseef Akbar wrote as "Garibaldi." The medical student, Javad Hashmi, became "Danios." His UC Berkeley classmate, Wajahat Ali, a budding columnist, contributed dispatches. They had been groomed by their fiery Palestinian American, anti-Israel activist, and university lecturer, Hatem Bazian, in the days after the 9/11 attacks. Hashmi confided to a friend, Ify Okoye, that he had helped start the new LoonWatch operation, writing hit pieces against everyone from Muslim reformers to politicians as "Danios."

"He wants to stay anonymous," Okoye later told me. "His wife doesn't know what he is doing. He wants to protect her."

* * *

Some courts have established limits to sock puppetry. In 2010, in *People v. Golb*, the courts convicted fifty-year-old lawyer Raphael Golb on thirty criminal charges, including identity theft, criminal impersonation, and aggravated harassment, for using multiple sock puppet accounts to attack and impersonate historians he considered to be rivals of his father, Norman Golb. The New York Court of Appeals affirmed the convictions for nine counts of criminal impersonation in the second degree and all the convictions for forgery and vacated the remainder of the convictions, holding the mere creation of email accounts in others' names, which accounts are not used, does not constitute criminal conduct. Golb defended his actions as "satirical hoaxes" protected by free speech rights. He was disbarred in 2011 under New York's Judiciary Law §90, which requires disbarment for attorneys convicted of a felony.

In 2014, a Florida state court ruled that two defendants, Brian and Kathy Davis, used fake names to publish negative reviews of a business, New Directions for Young Adults Inc., in behavior that "tortiously interfered" with the company's business. In pretrial discovery, Kathy admitted she had used four fake names—Cheyanna, Kayla, Kathy D., and William P.—to publish the negative reviews. The court awarded injunctive relief against New Directions for Young Adults Inc. during the pendency of litigation.

With these rulings, US courts have safeguarded the social contract that exists in the country, just as twentieth-century British philosopher John Locke had said we must do in a civil society, so we don't live in a Hobbesian state of nature that is "nasty, brutish, and short," as seventeenth-century British philosopher Thomas Hobbes warned about.

Section 230 of the Communications Decency Act of 1996 gave immunity to "third party providers" of communication services, such as GoDaddy, Twitter, and Facebook, as platforms, not content providers. They had no legal liability for the content they published. And in this case, it gave folks in the Honor Brigade free reign on the internet.

Their campaign was a dangerous—if not illegal—one.

Character assassinations involve a deliberate and sustained campaign involving pushing defamation, falsehoods, and lies to damage a reputation. Purveyors use open and covert strategies to undermine the credibility of a target's reputation, using false accusations, spreading rumors, and manipulating information. Hiding behind the anonymity of the internet, the Honor Brigade was about to subject its targets to a barrage of exaggeration, half-truths, manipulated facts, ad hominem and personal attacks, and caricatures. This shadowy network was about to make its targets persona non grata.

* * *

From time to time, "Admin" posted updates on LoonWatch. Most websites have an administrator who runs the website behind the scenes. And @Guest would publish articles by a stable of writers, including law professor Khaled Beydoun, lawyer-writer-activist Wajahat Ali, writer-author Reza Aslan, and lawyer-activist-ally Glenn Greenwald, all pushing the thesis of "anti-Muslim racism" and "Islamophobia," borrowing from the rhetorical tricks of "critical race theory."

The operatives took advantage of liberal registration policies on the internet and masked their real identities to publish "name-and-shame" attacks on anyone calling out Islamic extremism, misrepresenting their views, and branding them "loons."

Their masthead featured a stock photo of a frightened man inside their LoonWatch name and a sarcastic message: "the mooslims! they're heeere!" Numerous websites, from film criticism to arachnophobia, used the stock photo, "terrified-21." "LoonWatch" had another stock photo inside the "c," of a woman with arched brows, wide eyes, and open mouth. Coincidentally, quite a few websites, featuring women and vibrators, used the same image.

Just like Russia operated troll farms that employed anonymous internet users to further its propaganda interests, somebody had set up an operation that was a mixture of a troll farm and a fake news operation to target anyone who called out Islamic extremism and launch attacks on the United States, the United Kingdom, and Israel. There was a political dimension to the Honor Brigade's strategy. Hyping Muslims as targets of "Islamophobia," it appealed to moral guilt to buy silence. Its strategy replicated the propaganda of militant Islamic organizations, which declared the West is at war with Islam and that Muslims shouldn't cooperate with law enforcement. In the UK and France, officials questioned their policies on multiculturalism, recognizing the dangers of "non-violent extremism." Importantly, the use of propaganda, enemy image making, and indoctrination provides the fertilizer for the recruitment, radicalization, and terrorist acts of militants. "These e-jihadis stoked grievances to create wound collectors," a retired FBI senior supervisory special agent, Joe Navarro, told me, "and they exploited the wounds to foment anger, hate, and violence."

A name showed up as paying bills for the account, according to the records: Ahmed Rehab, the strategic communications director for CAIR and the executive director of the Chicago chapter of CAIR, known to critics as "Goon."

At one point, Akbar said he was having trouble with his "Garibaldi" account.

On April 24, 2011, at 3:58:49 a.m., the mailing address for the account was for Rehab and his home address in Oak Park, Illinois, 60604, and his email address of arehab@yahoo.com. The name for the Visa credit card used to pay the bill was Rehab's.

Over and over again, Rehab and Akbar were points of contact for LoonWatch in the GoDaddy documents. Akbar even used his wife's credit card once.

CAIR officials at headquarters in Washington, DC, knew about the operation, including executive director Nihad Awad and his communications chief Ibrahim Hooper. Later, so, too, did CAIR government affairs official Robert McCaw and many of its board of directors and legal staff, according to people familiar with the disinformation operation.

On April 3, 2012, 2:07:00 p.m., the billing information was updated by "Mohamed Akbar," with an address on N. Whipple Street in Chicago, Illinois. That was Akbar's home address.

Three days later, on April 6, 2012, at 9:41:03 a.m., the billing information was updated by "Ricky Martinez," using the email address mtakbar4983@gmail.com, to 270 Biscayne Boulevard, Miami, Florida, 33131, the address for a Kimpton hotel.

This was a classic deception operation.

Two years later, on December 29, 2014, at 2:02:00 p.m., GoDaddy got a call from "Zuhair" at 312-212-1520, upset about a technical issue. That was a phone number for the CAIR Chicago office.

On April 6, 2017, at 9:40:55 a.m., "Jehan Gir" updated the billing information, using the email address mtakbar4983@gmail.com. The fake name was a play off the name of Jahangir, a seventeenth-century Mughal emperor whose name means "conqueror of the word." The address was 2086 Allston Way, Berkeley, California, with a phone number of 773-318-7121—the office phone number for Akbar, the CAIR Chicago research director.

The address was for the Hotel Shattuck Plaza in Berkeley, one block away from the offices of ReThink Media, a PR firm that worked with CAIR. There was more. So much more. Hotel addresses were used many times but always tied back to a real phone number, credit card, or email address, linked to CAIR and its offices.

* * *

Early on, "Mooneye" published an article on LoonWatch, trying to argue that "Islamophobia" had many victims, including Muslim-run businesses, such as Dubai Ports, the United Arab Emirates company that was thwarted by US regulators, military officials, politicians, and national security fears in its efforts to manage port operations in the US. "It's well known that Islamophobia effects non-Muslims as well," he wrote. "It hurts those who are perceived to be Muslims or friendly to Muslims, this includes: Sikhs, Hindus, Arab Christians, Turkish Atheists, Norwegian teenagers and others. It also effects economic relationships, remember the Dubai Ports controversy?"

Through the lens of linguistic forensics, or the study of language, it became clear "Mooneye" made grammatical mistakes and typos, used "effects" when he should have written "affects," forgot periods at the end of sentences, and used commas incorrectly.

In modern-day vernacular, anonymous online identities are called avatars, trolls, catfish, and sock puppets. A 2010 documentary spawned an MTV reality show in 2012 of the same name, *Catfish: The TV Show*. Later that year, when news broke that Notre Dame footballer Manti Te'o was ensnared by a person with a false identity pretending to be his girlfriend, the concept of "catfish" became a verb. Nowadays it means a person who creates a fake online profile for nefarious purposes.

In the second month of operations, CAIR Chicago's Muhammad Tauseef Akbar, writing as "Garibaldi," published an article against the Clarion Fund, an organization based in Jerusalem, critical of Islamic extremism. He criticized the group as "anti-Muslim."

In a year-end retrospective, writing as "Garibaldi," Akbar wrote: "The year has been wacky and sad, we witnessed Islamophobic murders, violence, and incitement, the continuing repitition [*sic*] of the double standard of castigating all Islam for the crimes of a few Muslims in the media, we saw crazy conspiracy theories revolving around Barack Obama's supposed 'Mooslimness' increase, and much more and Loonwatch has been in the middle of it all, documenting and breaking it down."

With this fake persona, Akbar itemized the new online site's most popular targets. At the top of his list was Pamela Geller, the creator of the blog *AtlasShrugs*. He called her "The Looniest Blogger Ever." Second was Fathima Rifqa Bary, a young Muslim woman who had alleged her parents had threatened to murder her in an "honor killing" for converting to Christianity. She was just a teen. Third was an article about alleged pedophilia in Islam. Fourth was Geert Wilders, a Dutch filmmaker. Next came Wafa Sultan, the Syrian American who had criticized Muslim extremists on Al Jazeera. After her was author Robert Spencer, the founder of a website, Jihad Watch. Next came Temple University for allowing Wilders to speak on campus. After that was US Army Maj. Nidal Hasan, for his murders of innocents at Fort Hood, Texas. Then, he listed Spencer for a second time for "allegedly creating anti-Islam websites, fuck-allah.com and fuckislam.com." Finally, he targeted Debbie Schlussel, a conservative Jewish freelance columnist who had written pointed criticisms of alleged Muslim extremists.

* * *

One of the ways that the Honor Brigade managed to manipulate public opinion was through the many messages posed on the comment board at the end of LoonWatch articles.

LoonWatch used a comment board platform created and operated by Disqus, a privately held company that powered the comment boards at the bottom of many blogs worldwide. It was founded in the summer of 2007 in San Francisco by two undergraduate students, Daniel Ha and Jason Yan, at the University of California, Davis. It launched that fall. The company has grappled with a lot of criticism about the privacy of its user data, usually from folks who don't want it released. But, in 2013, a Swedish group, Researchgruppen, used some technological jujitsu to unmask a number of anonymous Disqus identities and worked with a Swedish tabloid, *Expressen*, to visit the homes of some of the users and confront them about allegedly racist, sexist, and derogatory statements they had posed. On the popular side of political correctness, Researchgruppen and *Expressen* won an investigative reporting award for their work.

In 2017, Zeta Global purchased the company for an undisclosed amount. "1DrM" used the comment board to hurl vile insults at the targets of his assaults. He had reposted the blog articles by "DrMaxtor," calling me a "Zionist media whore," among other pet names. "Amad" was associated with MuslimMatters, the Salafi blog. Other fake names included "Aspie and Atheist," "Beautiful Muslim Doll," and "Dzalexander."

Other names had direct links with LoonWatch, including @GaribaldiofLoonWatch, @Ilisha, "Ilisha Loon," and "JSpooner" @Disqus_XkXuGZhs1A, all the names of contributors to LoonWatch articles. The rest were a hodgepodge of folks who might have clues to the real names of others: "Abdul-Rehman," @Chameleon_X, @CriticalDragon1777, "Khushboo," "KnowingTheTruth," "Mikael," "Mindy1" @Disqus_E9ZNyz3EC1, "RDS," @SaracenSam, "Senor," "Solid Snake," "Syed," and "Ustadh," an honorific for a respected teacher.

Years later, in response to a subpoena for the identities of twenty-three users, Zeta Global provided me files on seven of the users.

The file for "1DrM" was 1,066 pages. His email was drdriveby@hotmail.com. Zeta Global marked the email address as verified, but the email address didn't appear anywhere online.

Disqus released fifteen IP addresses for "1DrM." Understanding IP addresses, or "internet protocol" addresses, is like learning a foreign language, but there is a way to decipher what they mean—or more specifically, their geolocation. Software platforms, such as IPLocation.net, allow users to plug the numbers of an IP into a search bar, "IP Lookup." IPLocation.net scanned three IP search engines and provided three possible geolocations for an IP.

* * *

A hit list went up against forty-three "Prominent Islamophobes" on an innocuous WordPress website that CAIR's Muhammad Tauseef Akbar set up, writing under the nom de plume, "MTAkbar."

In an article, "Islamophobia Documentation," Akbar divided his list into several categories. The first was straight-up "Racists," including author Robert Spencer, as "No. 1," followed by journalist Steve Emerson and radio host Don Imus. "Self-loathing Muslims/Quasi-Muslims" included a Muslim convert, Stephen Schwartz, and Muslim reformers Zuhdi Jasser, Kamal Nawash, Irshad Manji, Khaled Abu Toameh, and Salim Mansour. "Ex-Muslims/Quasi-Muslims" included Ali Sina, Nonie Darwish, Ibn Warraq, Wafa Sultan, Ayaan Hirsi Ali, and Glen Jenvey. "'Ex-Terrorists'" included Walid Shoebat, Tawfik Hamid, Kamal Saleem, and Zachariah Anani.

"Mainstream Media" covered pundit Anne Coulter; author Christopher Hitchens; radio host Rush Limbaugh; columnist Michelle Malkin; Fox News hosts Bill O'Reilly, Sean Hannity, and Glenn Beck; columnist Jeff Jacoby; ex-Muslim Walid Phares; and author John Loftus.

"Public Officials" listed Colorado Republican Rep. Tom Tancredo, New York Republican Rep. Peter King, Virginia Republican Rep. Virgil Goode, Pennsylvania Republican Rep. Rick Santorum, Arkansas Republican Gov. Mike Huckabee, former Republican Massachusetts Gov. Mitt Romney, Arizona Republican Sen. John McCain, and former Republican New York Mayor Rudy Giuliani.

"Reverends/Priests/Bishops/Rabbis" included Bishop Keith Butler, Reverend Rod Parsley, Reverend O'Neal Dozier, Pastor John Hagee, preacher Pat Robertson, and Rabbi Mordechai Eliyahu.

"Lex, Agent of Chaos," posted a comment of support and said, "Mail me sometime."

At one point, Akbar shared an article by "MTAkbar" on his Facebook page. He also shared the article in a comment on the Facebook page of his CAIR Chicago boss, Ahmed Rehab.

* * *

Following the 9/11 attacks on America, the Council on American-Islamic Relations—touting itself as the largest Muslim civil rights organization in the United States—had created a secret network of Muslim academics, professionals, writers, and activists, which joined forces with progressive and liberal non-Muslims, many of them unsuspecting do-gooders, to target anyone who might raise questions about extremism in Islam. What they doled out again and again on LoonWatch were their grievances against the West: US soldiers raping Afghan prisoners with dogs. (They didn't.) Muslim reformers funded by the government of Israel. (They weren't.) Much of their tenor, defensiveness, and aggressiveness actually fueled more misunderstanding, polarization, and hurt. And that was their plan.

One of the most tragic consequences was the wearing down of Muslim reformers.

The secret network had cast itself as "anti-loons" and their targets "loons." Their tentacles reached into the highest levels of leadership in the American Muslim community.

Trained in information technology, web development, and online platforms, they honed their communications, writing, and social media skills to engage in an "information operations" war, also called "perception management."

The network reveals more than a clash of cultures between Muslims and the West, but a disturbing window into Muslims in the West living with loathing for fellow Americans and other citizens of the West.

A group of older leaders had groomed a band of young American Muslims, born in the 1980s and 1990s, to fiercely oppose US foreign policy on issues from Palestine and Israel and the National Security

Agency to the wars in Iraq and Afghanistan. They roped young American, non-Muslim liberal thinkers to join their cause as well.

Named writers, such as lawyer Glenn Greenwald and author Reza Aslan, worked with this shadowy network. Their activities weren't the kind of stuff typically on the radar of counterterrorism and counterintelligence analysts, but they should be.

The network exploited the new rules of the internet and journalism to create secret blogs, write anonymous comments, and publish commentaries, unedited. Lax internet and media policies allow too many bloggers to hijack public debate, with little public accountability, through anonymous identities, unedited columns and comments, and backdoor self-publishing blogs on websites run by places from Google to *Salon* magazine and the *Huffington Post*.

At 2:10 p.m., on April 26, 2009, CAIR's Muhammad Tauseef Akbar registered SpencerWatch.com at GoDaddy with an email address of info@loonwatch.com, connecting SpencerWatch to LoonWatch.

The registration address was in Chicago, Illinois, 60545. He listed the registrant's name as "Mohamed Akbar."

* * *

The war of ideas waged within the Muslim community is a very real, poignant, and often tragic battle for our bodies and souls. For the Islamists, like theocrats in any religion, one of the most significant battles is for control over the bodies of women and girls.

From reproductive freedoms to marriage, an Islamic state, like any religious state, dominates the personal decisions of women and also girls. For example, in Iran, after the 1979 revolution brought the Ayatollah Khomeini and other religious clerics to power, that Islamic theocracy makes it illegal for women to feel the wind in their hair, forcing all women to cover their hair with scarves. In Saudi Arabia, the clerics wouldn't allow women to drive a car, let alone feel the wind in their hair. In Pakistan, thousands of women were jailed for alleged morality crimes after the military dictator put in place new 1979 religious laws following a strict interpretation of sharia. Even in the United States, Canada, and Europe, where civil rights are more protected, there are de facto restrictions put in place on women by Muslim families who follow the dominant view of clerics that their daughters are forbidden Islamically from marrying men who are not Muslim.

In the spring of 2009, organizers of a debate series called the Doha Debates invited me to fly to Doha, Qatar, and debate the question of whether Muslim women can marry anyone they choose. The Doha Debates was a confusing construct. It was funded by the al-Thani family that ruled the theocracy of Qatar, but they allowed debate on taboo topics. It was one thing to advocate for women's and girls' rights from the relative protection of the United States. It was another thing all together to go into the lion's den of fundamentalist Islam. I knew, however, that I had to overcome my fears to fight on behalf of my younger self and all the Muslim women and girls whose hearts—and bodies—religious clerics were trying to control. By eliminating non-Muslim men from competition, they were certainly eliminating much of the competition for the hearts of Muslim women.

That April, my stomach trembling and queasy, I walked onto the stage of the Doha Debates. Paired with a Syrian Muslim man, I faced off against a Saudi psychologist who described herself as a feminist and the Pakistan American Islam scholar, Yasir Qadhi, who had founded AlMaghrib Institute and MuslimMatters.

By debate's end, my partner had argued on behalf of our opponents, leaving me to advocate for women's rights on my own, but our side won. At a dinner afterwards, I tried to speak cordially with Qadhi, but he responded only with curt answers. I shrugged it off, happy that my argument had prevailed.

* * *

The spin on the debate came a month later. In late May 2009, Qadhi published an article on his website, MuslimMatters, with the headline "The Doha Debates: An Insider's Perspective (Yasir Qadhi, Asra Nomani & Women's Freedom to Marry)." His friend and cofounder of MuslimMatters, Amad Shaikh, supported the article. Shaikh lived in Doha, had a new job as director of business analysis at Qatar

International Petroleum Marketing Company, and wanted to fight back against the vote that Qadhi had lost.

The next day, the former UC Berkeley student, Javad Hashmi, groomed by anti-Israel activist Hatem Bazian, weighed in, writing from behind his mask as "DrM."

"One of the reasons I got into blogging was to expose Nomani and her neocon supported pro-regressive munafiqs. The fact that western media organizations continue to bring on and promote those who aren't part of the Muslim community as representatives (Ed, Hussien Nomani, Sultan, Hirsi Magan etc) is part and parcel of how dishonest and unprofessional they are. It's a set up, and I wish some of us would wake up to that reality."

With his typos, he was targeting emerging critics of Islamic extremism: Ed Husain, a Pakistani-British Muslim reformer and cofounder of Quilliam with fellow Muslim reformer Maajid Nawaz; Somali writer Ayaan Hirsi Ali; and Syrian American atheist Wafa Sultan, who had made a splash on Al Jazeera challenging Islamic extremism in a video that went viral.

The editor noted: "Comment edited by moderator for language."

A day later, writing only as "Amad," MuslimMatters cofounder Amad Shaikh wrote, "I think there is a certain level of debate decorum that would not be befitting of such a personal inquisition. It would quickly spin out of control."

He added: "By the way, here is Asra's own writing," quoting from my *Washington Post* article arguing against capital punishment for sex outside of marriage: "Shibli [Asra's son out of wedlock] is proof that I, an unmarried Muslim woman, am guilty of zina, or 'illegal sex.'" He added the phrase in brackets, "Asra's son out of wedlock."

He continued, "If that's not flaunting the laws of Allah, I don't know what is. It is one thing to be guilty of sin, which we all are, but quite another to openly display them. As we know from one of the statements of the Prophet (S), publicized sins are far worse than secret sins. I can't locate the exact hadith so if someone can add it, it would be great. Regardless, let's not waste time on this charlatan, but instead focus on the debate itself inshallah."

The "(S)" after "Prophet" was shorthand in Arabic for *salallahu alayhi wasallam*, or "peace be upon him."

Writing only as "Zaytoon," a contributor responded: "I also really wish (I have a lot of wishes!) that the Sheikh would do a lecture or write a paper on how to deal with munafiqs on a social/political level. As far as I know, the sheikh has only dealt with the topic of nifaq at an aqeeda level (Allah Knows Best)."

Again, a *munafiq* is a "hypocrite" in Arabic, equal to an apostate, punishable by death. *Nifaq* means "hypocrisy." *Aqeeda* is Arabic for "creed."

Then, "Khalid" continued the mudslinging, adding, "a cursory perusing thru Ms. Nomani's background should tell you that this is kufr of the RAND variety that is being promoted by neo-cons from the top. It is absolutely sheer coincidence that the 'pro-regressive' Muslim individuals such as the 'Muslim lesbian' Irshad Manji and the proud adulteress Nomani were heavily promoted by U.S. media and govt. types after 9/11 and right around the time of the Iraq war."

A *kufr* is a nonbeliever, punishable by death. The RAND Corporation, based in Santa Monica, California, is a thinktank established in 1948 to do "research and development" on national security issues.

He used the "pro-regressive" term coined by "DrMaxtor."

He published a 2005 letter in *Dawn*, "Asra Nomani no kin of Allama Shibli," and said that "she has to lie about her background to gain any currency or fiction of any standing among Muslims." The letter came from the family of a scholar, Allama Shibli Nomani, who was in my paternal ancestry, but some of his descendants wanted to disown me because of my progressive views.

A kind soul "AsimG" tried to restrain Javad Hashmi's "DrM" alter ego, saying, "We gain nothing by name-calling. In fact, we are the ones that look like fools when we insult people rather than their arguments." He ended, "Even if the stage is riddled with screaming lesbians and munafiqs we have to speak up. [*sic*] (but there are limits...)."

Unfortunately, Hashmi, writing as "DrM," had to have the last word. He wrote, "I called Nomani a lying, manipulative woman and I stand behind that assessment. I calls it as I sees [*sic*] it."

He continued, "I'm quite familiar with Asra Nomani and the fitna she's been promoting for years."

Fitna is a strong accusation. It means conflict. Chaos. When women don't cover their hair, clerics allege we are creating *fitna* by sexually distracting men.

"Now I really do not care about Nomani or what she does in her personal life but the fact remains is that she has led a promiscuous life (read her bio in detail and you'll see she's had no shortage of boyfriends) and sees nothing wrong with it. On top of that she wants to teach Islam to you and I as some sort of 'Muslim reformer.' Fat chance of that happening. How many people (including the 2 idiots above) know that : [cq] Nomani was for years the mascot of neocon supported pro-regressive munafiqs."

It is the crime of hypocrisy. The comment board also contained information that surprised me. Somehow, "DrMaxtor" raised the issue of my candidacy for leadership at my mosque.

"Go look at her website. Nomani came with the idea of 'woman lead salah' after pulling shenanigans at her local Morgantown masjid, after failing to win a place on the masjid's board of directors. She made sure to bring a camera crew there to show what a poor little oppressed gal she was (by those nasty immigrant men who followed a cultural Islam while only her own articulate self knew the true essence of Islam). Yeah right. No better way to get free publicity then to create a controversy. Nomani defended the publication of a 'historical fiction' novel slandering Aisha(r.a.) and her marriage of the Prophet (s.a.w)."

He ended: "Now if a guy with that sort of track record showed up out of nowhere and started calling himself a 'Muslim reformer,' he'd be laughed out of the room. This woman is a disgraceful fraud and has nothing to do with the Muslim community. And yet for media outlets to promote charlatans like this should be all you need to see what the real agenda is. To call that irresponsible journalism would be an understatement."

The moderator responded, "Edited. Can you pls instead provide the actual links to what you are charging Asra with? There is some vocabulary we just don't like to use on these pages, even if you feel they are accurate descriptors."

The day after, Hashmi reappeared again as "DrM," this time with links to interviews I had done with Jacques Berlinerblau, a professor at Georgetown University at the Center for Jewish Civilization.

"Notice the softball questions (Jewish interviewer, 'israeli' flag and all)," he wrote.

"She proves her knowledge is non-existent when she calls Hajar a 'single mother' when in fact she was the second wife of Ibrahim(a.s.)," he added, using the "a.s.," shorthand for *alayhi al-salaam*, which means, "peace be upon him."

"She also calls her one of the 'original bad girls of Islam' whatever that means," he wrote. "Then there's the recycled lies she's been repeating for years. The Jewish interviewer then suggests that it might be a good idea for Islam to be broken into denominations along the lines of Judaism to entertain interpretations, to which Nomani the bug eyed [*sic*] sycophant that she is agrees to ('we need the same evolution that Christianity and Judaism went through' and 'eventually we'll be at the pulpit'). She's way too old and media savvy to be that much of an airhead, I believe that she is very aware of the fitna that she's promoting.

"Apparently PBS has nothing better do and is making a documentary about her antics at the Morgantown Masjid. Be ready to hear the hype and fictitious 'death threats' which will be used to sell the 'propumentary.' Think I'll have to blog and expose this munafiqa all over again."

Munafiqa is the feminine version of a *munafiq*, or a hypocrite.

In response, "Zaytoon," a female name, wrote, "Subhanallah... how does the Ummah expect to go unpunished when we do not confront these traitors."

Subhanallah means "God is perfect."

The *ummah* is the community of Muslims. "Zaytoon" capitalized the word.

Writing as "AnonyMouse," "Zainab bint Younus" answered, "Honestly, I wonder how anyone can consider her an intellectual of any sort—all her arguments were based upon emotional manipulation, intellectual dishonesty, and when all else failed, interrupting loudly and accusing others of 'twisting Islam.' If she were in any high school debate team, she'd be disqualified immediately." Her moniker translated as Zainab "daughter of Younus," and her real name was Zainab Kathrada. A contributor to the Salafi MuslimMatters website, she was the daughter of a controversial Salafi preacher from Victoria in British Columbia, Canada, Younus Kathrada. In 2004, B'nai Brith Canada filed a police complaint for a hate crime after the older Kathrada called Jews "brothers of monkeys and swine." In the spring of 2020, he would go on to call on Allah to "humiliate the unbelievers and polytheists" and "grant victory to those waging jihad on your path in every place." Right before Christmas 2021, he delivered a sermon with this message in Arabic: "Oh Allah, give strength to Islam and the Muslims, humiliate the infidels and the polytheists, destroy the enemies of [our] religion, annihilate the heretics and the atheists. Oh Allah, support those who wage jihad for Your sake everywhere."

* * *

Weeks later, using the alias "Mujahideen Ryder," the young IT professional, Amir Sahib, posted a video of the debate on his blog with the headline "Yasir Qadhi Dominates Asra Nomani."

Qadhi had lost the debate.

Facts didn't matter with "Mujahideen Ryder," who wrote: "May Allah preserve Sh. Yasir!"

"Sh." was abbreviation for Sheikh.

Buried deep inside his blog, someone referred to him as "Amir" and mentioned that he went to Stony Brook University, where Amir Sahib was a member of the Muslim Students Association.

Many years earlier, Sahib had posted a message on AlMaghrib Institute's online forum, expressing gratitude for the condolences he had received on his father's death. (He also wrote on MuslimMatters as "Amir.") On Geni.com, a family genealogy website, Amir Sahib's father's name was Percy, making Sahib "ibn Percy," or "son of Percy."

He was another post-9/11 Muslim college student, like his counterparts at UC Berkeley, angry, impressionable, and driven. He had started at Stony Brook University in the fall of 2003. He was a research aide with the Research Foundation at State University of New York during his first year of college, offering research and technical assistance. For three years, starting in January 2005, he was a technical assistant, maintaining three computer labs at Stony Brook University, assisting faculty, staff, and students with technical questions. He made the dean's list in the fall of 2006.

In late March 2006, he wrote that he was quitting AlMaghrib Institute.

He wrote: "Anything you want to discuss with Jinnzaman, please visit his blog!"

Jinn is an Urdu word referring to a spirit.

He recommended visiting "Yursil's Blog in support of Jinnzaman's boycott." The link to www.yursil.com:80 was listed as "restricted files." In March 2022, the blog wasn't visible online.

On seekersdigest.org, "Shaykh Faraz" linked to a recent post by Yursil on a blog, but that link led to a dead URL. (In March 2022, seekersdigest.org wasn't connected any longer to Islam.)

Another link to "Sidi Salman" and his blog, alchishti.wordpress.com, led to a live article with the headline "Muslim Bloggers Urging Boycott of Salafi Institute."

What was the Salafi Institute?

It was none other than AlMaghrib Institute. Slick in its marketing, it didn't easily label itself publicly as Salafi, but clearly students considered it a "Salafi Institute."

AlMaghrib Institute's theological leader, Yasir Qadhi, had declared a revered Sufi scholar, Shaykh Sayyid Muhammad ibn 'Alawi, guilty of an Islamic concept called *shirk*. Among Salafis and other rigid interpreters of Islam, *shirk* means equating a being equal to God. To some, it amounts to polytheism.

* * *

Around then, Ahmed Rehab, the executive director of CAIR Chicago, went after another target: Robert Spencer, the founder of the Jihad Watch website that he had registered six years earlier in late 2003 to challenge extremism in Islam.

By mid-July 2009, publishing in the *Huffington Post*, started by liberal businesswoman Arianna Huffington, Rehab wrote an article criticizing the American Library Association for inviting Spencer to speak to members. The headline: "The Islam-Basher and the Librarian Kerfuffle."

Ten days later, his trusty staffer, Muhammad Tauseef Akbar, published an article on LoonWatch as "Garibaldi" attacking Spencer's speaking gig with the American Library Association.

Later that summer on LoonWatch, "Mooneye" published a piece against blogger Pamela Geller, a Jewish American critic of Islamic extremism. Born in 1958, the third of four daughters, Geller grew up in Hewlett Harbor, New York, one of Long Island's "Five Towns," where affluent Jewish families were prominent. Her father, Reuben, or "Ruby," owned a textile mill in Brooklyn, working long hours. He died in 1996. She once wrote: "Right or wrong—he backed me (and would take me aside later and admonish me if he thought I got it wrong). He got me—and I was not an easy kid." She attended Lynbrook High School and Hofstra University. She didn't finish her degree. She became associate publisher of the *New York Observer*. On 9/11, she was on the beach on Long Island's South Shore. The *Village Voice* described her as the "quintessential New York trophy wife." Then, she saw a skyscraper burning in the distance in the Manhattan skyline. She ran inside and saw the news of the attack. She ran back outside, cursing at the attackers when she saw it: the second plane hitting the World Trade Center tower. She had not heard of Osama bin Laden, and from that day on, she became a student of Islam. In 2004, Geller started her blog, *AtlasShrugs*, after Ayn Rand's book. She became friends with fellow blogger Robert Spencer, published the Danish cartoons of the prophet Muhammad, and teamed up with Spencer to close Khalil Gibran International Academy, a private middle school that planned to teach Arabic. The school didn't close, but they forced the principal, Debbie Almontaser, a Yemeni-born Muslim woman, to step down.

Geller had secured a place as an enemy of the "anti-loon" network.

* * *

The anti-Israel theme remained a constant in the disinformation campaign of the Honor Brigade.

In mid-July 2009, MuslimMatters published a three-part series, "Islamic Jerusalem: We Will Drive the Jews into the Sea," only describing the writer as "our latest associate author, Dr. J. Hashmi."

He was none other than Javad Hashmi, writing under the name "J. Hashmi."

"Dr. Hashmi has worked for the Cooperative Office for da'wah in Rawdah and various Islamic websites. His areas of interest include aqeedah, da'wah, interfaith dialogue, and combatting the twin evils of Islamophobia and Islamic extremism."

Dawah means proselytizing. The city of Rawdah was in Saudi Arabia. *Aqeedah* means belief and faith. Many Arabic terms have multiple spellings when anglicized.

Another bio provided more information, "Dr. Hashmi was born and raised in California."

The MuslimMatters bio continued: "Apart from medicine, he enjoys writing about Islamic topics, which he does under a number of online aliases. Dr. Hashmi is proud to be one of MM's more liberal-leaning writers, providing controversial and highly opinionated views."

"Dr. Hashmi."

Hashmi was also writing as "Jayshullah" and "Salahuddeen" at an extremist online forum, IslamicAwakening.com, defunct in March 2022.

A short profile said he had "a number of online aliases."

I did a Google search of the two names.

On IslamicAwakening.com, "Wild West" had connected the dots and told others that the contributor they knew as "Jayshullah" and "Salahuddeen" was J. Hashmi with a new writing gig.

Jayshullah.

In Urdu, *jaysh* means "army." One of the militant groups in Pakistan is Jaysh-e-Muhammad, or "Army of Muhammad." It's also spelled *jaish.*

Salahuddeen was a twelfth-century Muslim military officer who defeated Christian crusaders. To many Muslims, he was a military hero.

Hashmi joined IslamicAwakening.com as "JayshAllah" on April 23, 2007, defending a white convert to Islam, Aukai Collins, before leaving the forum in June 2008.

Collins was an American of Irish descent who had written a memoir about how he had joined the Pakistani militancy and trained at the same militant camp as Omar Sheikh, the young London School of Economics dropout who had orchestrated the kidnapping and murder of former *Wall Street Journal* reporter Daniel Pearl in Karachi, Pakistan, in 2002. The two annoyed Pakistani militants by playing cops and robbers with stick guns. In an interview with me, he said, "We were losers." (Collins died in July 2016 of sepsis at the age of forty-one.)

On IslamicAwakening.com, "JayshAllah" fiercely supported Collins. "It is altogether *amazing* how the Muslims can sit here and *slander* not only another Muslim brother, but a white convert to Islam who risked his life defending the lives of Muslims of another country to whom he has absolutely no blood relation with at all! How *dare* you claim that he turned into a Christian? I seek refuge in the Lord of the Worlds from the slander with which you so callously say! Brother Aukai Collins is *still* very much a Muslim, no thanks to the ingratitude of so many immigrant Muslims towards him."

He added: "Is this how you people view the Mujahideen? This is the praise they get from you? On the one hand, you all praise the people who blow up little kids, but when it comes to a real Mujahid then it is all scorn? Anyways, if you have nothing good to say about brother Aukai Collins, then Insha-Allah remain quiet/silent. Is that not the Sunnah? Is it or is it not? I still haven't gotten a response to that. Instead, I get side arguments."

When a commentator accused "JayshAllah" of shaming others, he took offense. "Please tell me which of them I have named and shamed? I talk about them in general terms, as is the Sunnah for sinners. On the other hand, you have violated the Sunnah by specifically mentioning one person by name and shaming him. There is a difference between saying something generally without naming names, and with pointing to one specific person and saying they are this or that. Do you understand the difference or should I produce daleel to back my position up? Additionally, even if I was wrong (though I am not), then does this somehow justify your position? Do two wrongs make a right?"

He concluded, "Can you please stick to the topic at hand. Is it Islamically right to attack a brother's character when he is not here to defend himself? Please I beg you to answer with a simple yes or no."

Auki Collins arrived on the site to set the record straight under a fake name, "Abu Saifudeen," or "father of Saifudeen," he later told me in an interview.

When a commentator called "JayshAllah" "naive" and "gullible," he responded: "I'm not some 16 year old kid. Within a year I will be a doctor Insha-Allah, and I think it's frankly annoying of you to use such a term for me."

He continued: "Salam, Your choice of words were poor. There is a dramatic difference between saying: 'You are naive and gullible.' [insulting] And: 'Brother, there are some facts that you may not know about which would actually make you think otherwise. We shouldn't be naive about this...' [not insulting]."

He certainly had a thin skin for a troll.

He continued, "You were saying I was naive and gullible, full-stop. This is insulting. If you can't figure this out, then you are stupid. There is a difference between saying you are being naive about one issue, and you are naive full-stop. Perhaps I initially accorded you too much respect due to the fact that I liked some of your posts, but it seems that your head has gotten too big that you refer to me in condescending and patronizing terms. You have no right to call me naive or gullible, because you don't even know me."

In another post, he blasted "Web Warriors." In another, he wrote, "You sound like one of those fob uncles with conspiracy theories about everything," using the slur for immigrants "fresh off the boat."

* * *

Two days later, on his Blogspot website, Javad Hashmi, using the "DrMaxtor" again, published another hit piece on me, writing: "Five years later, Asra Nomani is still a lying and manipulative Zionist media whore."

He called me a "munafiqa," or a "female hypocrite," a death sentence to extremists who consider apostasy and blasphemy punishable by death.

"Why does he hate me so much?" I asked my mother.

"You helped Danny," my mother said, without a pause. "You helped a Jew."

My mother told me that helping Danny, trying to find him after he was kidnapped by Pakistani militants, had sealed my fate as a traitor to those Muslims who hated Jews and the state of Israel.

* * *

In less than six months, Ikhwanweb.com, the official website of the Muslim Brotherhood, started picking up articles from LoonWatch.

In September, Ikhwanweb reposted an article by "Garibaldi," the pen name for CAIR's Muhammad Tauseef Akbar, headlined "Geert Wilders wants to tax women who wear hijab." It included a photo of Wilders with bloggers Robert Spencer and Pamela Geller, sworn enemies of LoonWatch.

And the effort to cast "Islamophobia" as the No. 1 problem facing Muslims continued to expand by anonymous forces, exploiting privacy capabilities on the internet to hide themselves. On October 29, 2009, at 4:17 p.m., GoDaddy Shopper ID 27179307 put in orders for new websites with private registrations. The first website ordered was IslamophobiaToday.com. The order went through without a hitch. It was Order No. 1116348718. The "about" page said the website was a "one-stop Islamophobia news clearing house on the web" and an "awareness project by Americans Against Islamophobia." The administrator spelled clearinghouse incorrectly as two words.

In a section labeled "links," the website's creators recommended viewers also visit LoonWatch.com and SpencerWatch.com.

Ten seconds later, GoDaddy Shopper ID 27179307 bought IslamophobiaSucks.com and IslamophobiaSucks.org, according to GoDaddy's records.

* * *

Its first postings, starting in April 2009, included republishing LoonWatch.com articles. The list of contributors, with "exclusive guest editorials," included "key academics, religious leaders, and writers on contemporary and current Islamophobic matters."

The list included only names and headlines of articles they had written. Scott C. Alexander had written, "Response to Hatchet Job on Turkish Scholar, M. Fethullah Gülen." Craig Considine published, "One Film 9/11 can make a difference," and "Founding Fathers rolling in their graves with Gingrich."

Daniel Tutt wrote, "Four Myths that Led to the NYPD's Attack on Muslim Civil Liberties." Chicago freelance writer Anya Cordell published, "Muslims and Lowes Are Both Integral To Our Society," "Hate Speech Against Muslims Incites Violence," and "Where the Anti-Muslim Path Leads." Emily Kianka wrote, "Islamophobia and the Social Consequences of Social Media."

The writers and their work with "Islamophobia" intersected consistently with one organization, CAIR.

* * *

Somebody using the fake name, "Jacob Hausner," targeted Zuhdi Jasser with an article, "Contradiction in Terms: Zuhdi Jasser Appointed as a US Commissioner on International Religious Freedom."

He blasted "well paid Islamophobe" Frank Gaffney, founder of the Center for Security Policy, and his organization's "crusade against American Muslims." He went after "hate blogger" Robert Spencer.

There was a "Jacob M. Haunser "on Facebook.

His profile picture had a graphic for Islamophobia Today. He featured the URL for islamophobiatoday.com on his page. His "likes" included Facebook pages for Muslim activist Irshad Manji, the UC Student Regent, "The Modern Muslim Project," "Australians Against Islamophobia," Collectif Contre l'Islamophobie en France, Loon-Watch, "The Christian Left," Altmuslimah, Aslan Media, "Pamela Geller Gives Me the Heebie-Jeebies," "Europeans Against Islamophobia," "Americans Against Islamophobia," Muslimah Media Watch, and "Peter King: Resign from Homeland Security Committee now."

In his "About" section he wrote that he went to Adlai E. Stevenson High School. There was a school by that name in Lincolnshire, Illinois. A "Jacob Hausner," from Pasadena, California, had posted a Change.org petition that Jasser and a Christian leader, Robert George, "do not belong" on the US Commission on International Religious Freedom." Sponsored by IslamphobiaToday.com, it had 2,517 supporters.

Among the first supporters: Ahmed Rehab, the executive director of CAIR Chicago.

CHAPTER 7

Living with the Reality of Jihadis

While CAIR, its foreign patrons, and its cadres were frenetically trying to cast all criticism of Muslims as "Islamophobia," the world was learning the hard way that radicalized Islamists were still a threat.

In March 2010, the "Caucasus Emirate" claimed credit for bombings in the Moscow metro, killing forty. Two months later, the Tehrik-i-Taliban Pakistan, an extremist Muslim group, took responsibility for attacks on two mosques belonging to a minority sect of Islam, Ahmadiyya Muslims, killing eighty-six people. By the end of the year, a Muslim female suicide bomber blew herself up in the middle of a crowd at a United Nations food center in the Bajaur region of Afghanistan.

But such incidents didn't stop the anti-"Islamophobia" propaganda machine. The Islamophobia Observatory made a series of recommendations "to address Islamophobia in the West," including the idea that nations in the West "should prohibit by law, publishing or uttering of matters that grossly abuse or insult matters held sacred by any religion or stereotype its followers."

This year's report included one reference to a LoonWatch article by "Mooneye," about a Christmas display by Dove World Outreach

Center in Florida, where fundamentalist Christian preacher Terry Jones later threatened to burn the Qur'an. The display said: "Islam Is Of The Devil." Born in Cape Girardeau, Missouri, Jones graduated from high school in 1969, studying for two years at Southeast Missouri State University before leaving early. He earned an honorary degree from California Graduate School of Theology. A traveling missionary for many years, he had run-ins with other leaders at a church he had started in Germany, Christliche Gemeinde Köln. He returned to the US, starting Dove World Outreach Center.

By now, the Organization of Islamic Cooperation widely quoted work by John Esposito, the executive director of the Saudi-funded Bin Talal Center at Georgetown University. In one of its regular reports on "Islamophobia," the Organization of Islamic Cooperation wrote that it had "borrowed" from Esposito, according to footnote No. 55. In fact, the quote had been reprinted exactly as Esposito had originally written it, republished in the *Huffington Post*.

* * *

Two days later, the State Department's Office of the Special Representative for Muslim Communities announced Shahed Amanullah would be a senior advisor for technology. It cited his work on "Generation Change" and "Viral Peace." Calling him "a serial entrepreneur," it noted he worked with the White House and other US government departments on "social entrepreneurship, social media policy, combatting online extremism and fostering innovation."

It also noted he had been named one of the five hundred most influential Muslims in the world in 2009, 2010, and 2011 by Georgetown University and the Royal Islamic Strategic Studies Centre in Jordan. This was the list released by the Georgetown University Prince Alwaleed bin Talal Center for Muslim-Christian Understanding, led by John Esposito.

* * *

The next day, in an article published on Iran's government-run PressTV.ir media website, Hamid Mowlana, an advisor to Iranian president Mahmoud Ahmadinejad, warned the country's leaders about the West's "soft war" against Iran and the importance of protecting Iran's "soft power infrastructure."

At a conference in Tehran on "soft warfare," Mowlana said Iranian officials and organizations don't have "enough knowledge" about the tactics of the West, using companies, academia, and the media "to put into practice its policies in the world."

For decades, Mowlana was professor of international communications at American University's School of International Service, founding the international communications program in 1967. He had become a professor emeritus. (When I started my graduate studies at American University in 1986, he was my advisor, teaching my class about the coming "new information order" that would usurp the monopoly of "the North," code for the West, against "the South," shorthand for developing countries.)

Later that month, the American University student newspaper, the *Eagle*, reported on an editorial, headlined "Mowlana's treason," at TribLive.com, a conservative media site, that "questions former SIS professor Hamid Mowlana's loyalty to the U.S." According to the article, Mowlana held dual citizenship in the US and Iran.

* * *

Across the border, Turkey's emerging leader, Recep Tayyip Erdoğan, was learning how to exercise "soft power" in the West. Born in 1954, he had been a semiprofessional soccer player before becoming the young charismatic mayor of Istanbul in the 1990s and before establishing the religiously conservative Justice and Development Party in 2001. Known as AKP for its Turkish name, the party rose to national power with Erdoğan's election as prime minister in 2003, and over almost two decades of continuous rule, Erdoğan moved the country in an Islamist direction.

The year before, George Mason University launched the Ali Vural Ak Center for Global Islamic Studies with Ahmet Tekelioglu, a Turkish academic, leading the center. That spring, the center joined Twitter using the name @AVACGIS. George Mason named the center for its principal donor, Ali Vural Ak, a businessman in Istanbul, Turkey, who was the founder and CEO of Intercity Rental Car Company, the biggest car-leasing company in Turkey. On its official website, the center said its "strategic location" would allow the center to "draw on unparalleled resources to advance its mission in research, education, and professional opportunities for current and future scholars of Islamic studies." Its mission was to "advance a sound and nuanced understanding of Muslim societies and the Islamic faith, its role in world history, and its current patterns of globalization." The center "recognizes that Islam is a universal faith and a world civilization with a global community." Oddly, it wrote the center provides a "global, rather than regional, framework for exploring Islam."

* * *

The campaign to censor debate on Islam was working. That spring, the producers of *South Park*, the bitingly satirical animated TV show, announced they would modify programming that some Muslims thought concerned "Islamophobia." In response, Robert Spencer and Pamela Geller announced an initiative for May 20, "Draw Muhammad Day."

Soon after, operating as "Danios," former UC Berkeley student Javad Hashmi posted a column on LoonWatch with the rare byline of a real person: Shahed Amanullah, the Obama administration's technical advisor.

In his article, Amanullah claimed the "Draw Muhammad Day" was "collectively punishing" American Muslims. Amanullah had first self-published the op-ed at his altMuslim website. The *Huffington Post* reprinted the piece. And then LoonWatch reprinted the op-ed.

Amanullah carefully defended free speech, saying the "Draw Muhammad Day" organizers had "every right" to their day "without threat of violence or coercion from Muslims." He'd stated his thoughts in an op-ed published "all over the Muslim world." But the organizers occupied no "moral high ground," but were rather "hypocrites that apply collective punishment to a vast majority that did them no harm and wished no ill on *South Park*, and are letting their thinly-veiled hatred show in the process."

There was that "hypocrites" allegation again.

As "Danios," Hashmi added a note to the op-ed: "But it doesn't absolve people from being assholes. And with Draw Muhammad Day, the participating artists are proving themselves to be just that."

On May 20, the *Chicago Tribune* published a column by CAIR Chicago's executive director, Ahmed Rehab, arguing it "was not about rights."

"It's about what's right," he wrote.

He made virtually the same argument as Amanullah.

The next day, Rehab, writing as "Emperor," published his own column on LoonWatch, claiming the day had devolved into a "hate fest criticizing LoonWatch's arch-enemies, Spencer and Geller."

He lauded Amanullah's column and hyperlinked the words "collective punishment" back to LoonWatch's reprint of the original AltMuslim op-ed.

On LoonWatch, CAIR's Rehab wrote as "Emperor," saying, "As Shahed Amanullah said, this is pretty much collective punishment on the whole Muslim community for the actions of a few. The inspiration for this event was the threats that the South Park creators received from a group called Revolution Muslim."

On the comment board, former UC Berkeley student Javad Hashmi used his "1DrM" persona to blast the day as a "childish admission of defeat" by "cowardly spineless hypocrites, haters, and racist provocateurs who wouldn't dare pick a fight with a Muslim in real life. They want to play 'free speech' martyrs online to get some attention, but have no interest whatsoever in the real meaning of free speech or peoples [*sic*] civil rights."

* * *

That year, Shahed Amanullah and his business partner, Aziz Poonawalla, at Brass Crescent Awards announced that "Danios" and LoonWatch had won special recognition in their "best blog" category. MuslimMatters won the prize, but Amanullah and Poonawalla said about LoonWatch: "Finding its way into the blogosphere at just the right time, Loonwatch makes this list 'because it is awesome' and because of spectacular analysis by writer Danios."

In intelligence, a "false flag operation" is when someone pretends to work for someone other than their real identity to throw people off their tracks. Amanullah and Poonawalla perpetuated a myth about LoonWatch as run by non-Muslims, by making it a winner in their best "non-Muslim" blog category. They wrote, "Relatively new on the scene, Loonwatch has made a splash in the fight against Islamophobia, taking on the big names and deconstructing the lies about Muslims they tell."

The other noteworthy blogs in that category: one by Glenn Greenwald and Islamophobia Watch.

Writing under his fake name of "Danios," former UC Berkeley student Javad Hashmi won "honorable mention" in the "best blogger" category. Amanullah and Poonawalla noted: "One of Loonwatch's most proficient writers, Danios consistently gets under the skin of bigots seeking to tar all Muslims with the crimes of a few."

* * *

The former UC Berkeley student, Javad Hashmi, had been moving along with his career. He graduated from the five-year medical program at Aga Khan University in Karachi, Pakistan, with a bachelor of medicine, bachelor of surgery, or MBBS, on December 12, 2009, according to a university announcement.

In late May 2010, writing as "JHashmi," Hashmi wrote a controversial article, headlined "Declassified: Israel offered to sell nukes to apartheid-era South Africa." He quoted *Guardian* articles that alleged then-Israeli president Shimon Peres proposed a nuclear sale to South Africa. Peres denied the charges, and it was never independently verified.

"Perhaps the reason why Israel saw no problem in giving nuclear weapons to an apartheid state is because Israel itself is one," he wrote.

He called Israel an "apartheid state."

* * *

In the spring of 2010, a new young writer, going by the moniker "Muslim Apple," was emerging at MuslimMatters.

Unlike most of the contributors at MuslimMatters, she revealed her real name: Ify Okoye. As a young woman, she converted to Islam, moving to College Park, Maryland, to be part of an orthodox Salafi community at Al-Huda, studying at AlMaghrib Institute courses. She wore the tight *hijab* and baggy *abaya*, or gown, of ultraconservative Islam, but she couldn't keep her inquiring spirit and sense of critical thinking under wraps. In early 2007, she had started a blog, *Muslim Apple*, eventually joining MuslimMatters as a writer in late December 2009. There, she met the former UC Berkeley student Javad Hashmi, as he wrote under his fake name "Jhashmi" at MuslimMatters and "Danios" at LoonWatch. She openly challenged gender segregation in mosques, writing about walking through the front door of the Islamic Center of Washington on Massachusetts Avenue, into the stunning main hall, with Turkish tiles on the dome ceiling. The men there scolded her and told her to pray in the "women's section" in the corner, divided from the main hall by office partitions.

In mid-May 2010, Ify organized a pray-in at the Islamic Center of Washington with other women (including me). She posted photos from the pray-in on her Facebook page with no shame. She then organized another pray-in for the last Saturday of May at 5:00 p.m., with another Muslim convert, Fatima Thompson, announced on a Facebook page, "Pray-In." They met at the Dar Al-Hijrah Islamic Center, right off Route 7, where the 9/11 hijackers had prayed. So had Anwar al-Awlaki and Maj. Nidal Hasan. The Egyptian American imam, Shaker Elsayed, called Fairfax County police officers to throw us out for trespassing.

The crime? Praying in the main hall behind the men.

A few weeks later, Thompson, ever persistent, organized a town hall meeting on the issue of women's rights at mosques at the Woodbridge Neighborhood Library in Southeast DC. The imam at the Dar Al-Hijrah Islamic Center, Shaker Elsayed, agreed to participate if I was disinvited from speaking on the panel. I consented to sit in the audience, so that we could include conservative voices at the town hall. Elsayed arrived with dozens of supporters. Elsayed did a beeline to my son, then seven years old, playing a Pokémon game on his Nintendo DS gaming system. He murmured something, pressing on Shibli's chest and giving him an awkward kiss on the forehead. During the town hall, the imam proceeded to wave my book, *Standing Alone in Mecca: An American Woman's Struggle for the Soul of Islam*, and ridicule my feminist views of Hajar, the single mother of Ishmael, and mock my honesty as an unwed mother, accusing me of promoting hypersexuality among women. I listened silently to the verbal assault, sick to my stomach, glancing backwards to see if Shibli could hear this shaming of his mother. He seemed buried in his game. On the way home, as I nosed our Ford Escape along the Potomac River, my son complained that his stomach hurt. All night long, he vomited. After that, I never again took my son to any events of the Muslim community.

CHAPTER 8

Exploiting the Ground Zero Mosque

The perfect storm to implement the new strategy of flipping the narrative for Muslims in America arrived in 2010. An imam, Feisal Abdul Rauf, launched a plan to build an Islamic center and mosque a few blocks from Ground Zero in Lower Manhattan. A coalition of critics opposed its construction.

American flags flapped in the wind where the World Trade Center had once stood, the space now eerily empty except for the construction beams traversing the sky. Blocks away, at an abandoned building at 51 Park Place, the faded letters of Burlington Coat Factory above the steel doors still advertised "Coats and more…for less!" This was where Imam Rauf and his wife, Daisy Khan, wanted to build an Islamic center that some folks called the "Ground Zero mosque."

Years earlier, at a retreat on the bucolic banks of the Hudson River, Imam Rauf had led women and men in prayer in parallel sections divided by gender, unlike typical Muslim prayer arrangements. Imam Rauf wouldn't go on record supporting parallel prayer lines for women and men. "It wouldn't be politically expedient," he said.

Two blocks north at 20 Warren Street, beside a wine store, New York Vintners, below a gay bar, the 2020 Club, an open door marked

"MASJID" in red stick-on lettering stood propped open, beckoning the way to another mosque, missed in the hoopla over the "Ground Zero mosque." The MASJID Manhattan was known in the Muslim community as "the Salafi mosque," embracing the rigid interpretation of Islam parallel to Wahhabism.

It was very close to the wound. Ashes had been strewn from the carnage of the 9/11 attacks to the street where this mosque would stand. The memory of Islamic extremism was still too fresh for many New Yorkers. Faisal Shahzad had just attempted to detonate bombs at Times Square on May 1, 2010.

Liberal and progressive Americans and their organizations had dropped the ball in having a nuanced, intelligent critique of extremist Islamic ideology, currying pluralism points instead in the name of interfaith relations. In their PR campaign to defend the name of Islam, mainstream American Muslim organizations such as the Council on American-Islamic Relations had failed to acknowledge there is an interpretation of Islam that preaches violent *jihad* against the West. Their mantra had become: "Islam is a religion of peace," and they explained away men such as the alleged Fort Hood gunman, Major Nidal Hasan, by saying, "He isn't Muslim." Now they were jumping onto the Ground Zero bandwagon in the name of religious freedom, tone-deaf to the feelings of fellow Americans.

* * *

Imam Feisal Abdul Rauf had arrived in Manhattan from his native Egypt in 1983. Local Muslims asked him to lead prayers at a small mosque, Masjid al-Farah, in Lower Manhattan, twelve blocks from the World Trade Center. A Sufi order, Nur Ashki Jerrahi, or the Order of Light and Love, ran the mosque, which hosted prayers led by a woman imam, making it one of the most progressive mosques in the world. Sufism is a mystical interpretation of Islam that emphasizes a direct and personal experience of God through devotion and is known for adapting to local culture. It's found in Sunni and Shia sects of Islam.

Rauf had branded himself as an interfaith leader, working to build bridges between American society, the American Muslim community, and Muslim countries. In 1997, he founded the American Sufi Muslim Association, a civil society organization aimed at promoting positive engagement between American society and American Muslims. In the late 1990s, he married his third wife, Daisy Khan, an Indian American Muslim from the northern state of Jammu and Kashmir and a progressive Muslim. They changed the name of the organization to the acronym ASMA when Sufism went out of vogue among Muslim philanthropists.

One of the congregants at the mosque was a Muslim property developer, Sharif El-Gamal. He had bought the building at 51 Park Place, near the former site of the World Trade Centers. He had a pitch he brought Rauf: transforming the building into a mosque.

Rauf's wife, Daisy Khan, had ambitious plans for a bigger progressive mosque than the one they ran nearby in the Tribeca neighborhood of Manhattan. She had been trying to expand her vision for an Islam of feminism. Four years earlier, she had assembled Muslim women from twenty-five countries to strategize plans for a council of female Islamic jurists, or *muftias*. These women jurists would be able to issue fatwas, or religious rulings. Their idea was "to ensure that women's perspectives on Islamic law become part of religious deliberation in the Muslim world—particularly on issues such as domestic violence, divorce, and inheritance."

Khan said at the time that it was "important to express the principles of social justice within the framework of Islamic law," she said, adding: "This is why we need muftias, in order to do that. Otherwise, it falls on deaf ears."

If you bought into Khan's publicly stated view, the Muslim viewpoint was that a progressive mosque near Ground Zero would be an affirmative response—an antidote—to the beliefs of the Islamic terrorists who carried out the attack. Khan, however, seemed to have little patience for a contrary view: that a mosque of any kind rising even near the now hallowed ground of innocent Americans slaughtered by terrorists was at best an insensitive gesture.

* * *

Tensions heated up with temperatures in the late summer of 2010.

A young man slipped into a taxi and said to his driver, Ahmed Sharif, then forty-three, "*As-salam-alaikum*. Are you a Muslim?"

"Yes," the driver responded. An immigrant to the United States from Bangladesh, he was proud to be American and Muslim.

"Welcome to a checkpoint!" the young man responded, pulling a knife out of his pocket and stabbing the driver across the face. As the cabbie screeched his taxi to a halt, the young man fled, soon to be picked up by the NYPD.

The attack underscored the deep tensions that lay at the heart of the intense battle that had broken out in America about the place of Islam in the nation, as the country waged a war thousands of miles away in Afghanistan against Taliban fighting the US in the name of Islam.

In the seventh century, the Muslim community was torn apart by its first civil war between the extremists, called Kharijites, and others. The war was called *fitna*, or "conflict." It was a loaded term in the community, akin to blasphemy and betrayal. In Toronto, Pakistani Canadian writer Raheel Raza penned a column with Pakistani Canadian colleague Tarek Fatah, accusing the "Ground Zero mosque" organizers of causing *fitna* in America. Raza flew to New York City and met with the families of 9/11 victims. Neda Bolourchi, an Iranian American mother of a 9/11 victim, fled the 1979 Iranian Revolution in Iran, and she opposed the building of the mosque.

Before the meeting, Raza stopped at a TV studio for an interview with a lightning rod to the Muslim community: then-FOX News personality Bill O'Reilly.

On the show, she criticized the organizers of the mosque plan for being insensitive.

There were others who refused the narrative of the United State as "Islamophobic." A black former imam, Abdur-Rahman Muhammad, penned an op-ed, published in the *New York Daily News* on September 5, 2010, headlined "Whether or not Ground

Zero mosque is built, U.S. Muslims have access to the American Dream." He wrote that "the question of whether America is 'Islamophobic'—now bandied about so casually, as though opposition to the mosque has revealed a nasty strain in the American psyche, akin to the terrible racism or anti-Semitism that once ran wild—is so deeply offensive.

"This loathsome term is nothing more than a thought-terminating cliche," he said, "conceived in the bowels of Muslim think tanks for the purpose of beating down critics."

* * *

On the anniversary of the 9/11 attacks, at a corner in Lower Manhattan just blocks from the site of the tragedy, bloggers Pamela Geller and Robert Spencer rallied a crowd to oppose the mosque. They stood on a stage in the middle of a blocked-off street as protesters held signs that read, "Go back home, Muslims!" and "No sharia in America!"

One man walked around with a toilet seat, feigning using pages of the Qur'an as toilet paper. On the other side of the street, American Muslims stood with placards that read, "We're American too!" and "Don't judge us because of the actions of 19 lunatics."

Muslim reformers differed from campaigners such as Geller and Spencer in the lack of hope by the bloggers for Muslims and the potential for a reform of Islam in the world. There are people on the right who are monolithic in their analysis of Muslims. They sometimes have legitimate points in their criticisms, and their concerns are understandable even if expressed in ways that may seem bigoted. The trouble is that these people ultimately play into the hands of the alliance between political American liberals and hard-line Muslims in their struggle for the hearts and minds of mainstream Muslims.

The bar for "Islamophobia" has been lowered to the point that even legitimate criticism of certain antiquated views that are incompatible with Western culture—not to mention the infiltration of mosques and prisons by radical Islamists in the pay of foreign powers—is wrongly dismissed as bigotry versus a healthy concern with fostering pluralism in the context of an open society.

Some of the purveyors of the new strategy weaponizing "Islamophobia" to silence critics now gained mainstream audiences. That included the fake news site LoonWatch.

In a *New York Times* profile that fall, headlined "Pamela Geller: Outraged, and Outrageous," LoonWatch even earned a mention and hyperlink. The reporters wrote, "She inspires laughs at sites like LoonWatch…." LoonWatch shared the article with its readers, saying, "We won't let it get to our collective head."

* * *

Days after the 9/11 attacks, Imam Rauf had sat down for an interview with CBS *60 Minutes* host Ed Bradley. Rauf said that fanaticism and terrorism have no place in Islam. Bradley asked him if the US deserved the attacks.

Rauf answered, "I wouldn't say that the United States deserved what happened. But the United States' policies were an accessory to the crime that happened."

When Bradley asked Rauf how the US was an accessory, he replied, "Because we have been accessory to a lot of innocent lives dying in the world. In fact, in the most direct sense, Osama bin Laden is made in the USA."

A child of colonialism, Rauf expressed views many uncles in the American Muslim community expressed in living rooms during heated political debates. America had indeed funded the Afghan fighters, or mujahideen, who had fought the Soviets. They later became the Taliban, and their foreign counterparts, including bin Laden, created al-Qaeda.

But it was a callous analysis for many Americans to hear just days after the 9/11 attacks.

Now, *60 Minutes* interviewed him again. Why not just move the mosque?

"Because it's the right thing to do," Rauf said emphatically. "It's the right thing to do. Our community wants it, and now America *needs* it."

* * *

Fox news host Eric Bolling played the *60 Minutes* interview that week, on the set with Geller, whom he introduced as "my good friend." Geller called the *60 Minutes* segment a "big wet kiss" to the mosque effort.

In the segment, CAIR Chicago executive director Ahmed Rehab appeared via a remote studio and went after Geller and blasted *AtlasShrugs* as an "anti-Muslim blog." He alleged that she had "implied" in a video that "Muslims have sex with goats" and Muslims should wear "Mohammed condoms."

"Okay, that's a lie!" Geller shouted. She said it was "farcical."

"You are one of the most anti-Muslim bigots out on the internet," Rehab continued. He was stern, moralistic, and unsmiling.

"No, you are an anti-non-Muslim and Muslim supremacist. And all you do is hate."

"Pam also said we should nuke Mecca," Rehab continued.

"I did not say that."

He continued with his criticism of Geller, with the dénouement: "She is a certified *loon*...."

There was that word again: loon.

* * *

The Honor Brigade jumped into the debate over the mosque project, also called "Park 51" because of the proposed mosque's address at 51 Park Avenue.

Writing as "Danios," former UC Berkeley student Javad Hashmi chronicled "opposition to a new mosque, without the Ground Zero excuse." Headlined "On the Not Mosque at Not Ground Zero," Muhammad Tauseef Akbar, the research director at CAIR Chicago, used his "Garibaldi" account to describe the "anti-Muslim movement" as a "curious blend of old-fashioned racism, naive nativism, fear, and the brute, thuggish rage that infects a diseased minority in every generation and finds its scapegoat in every culture."

Ikhwanweb.com, the official website of the Muslim Brotherhood, reposted the article immediately.

In another piece on LoonWatch, Hashmi, writing as "Danios," claimed "right wing radio host" Michael Barry wanted the New York mosque "blown up."

Ikhwanweb reprinted another piece by CAIR's Muhammad Tauseef Akbar, masquerading as "Garibaldi," claiming to lay bare, "The Connection Between Zionism & Organized Islamophobia—The Facts."

Behind his fake identity, Akbar wrote, "Now we learn that there is more to that claim than unfounded conspiracy theories. It turns out the main funder of anti-Muslim blogger/anti-Park51 [*sic*] organizer Robert Spencer and his hate site JihadWatch are husband and wife duo Aubrey and Joyce Chernick."

* * *

In late September 2010, IslamophobiaToday.com published an op-ed on the "Park 51 controversy" by Scott Alexander, professor of Islam and director of the Catholic-Muslim Studies program at the Catholic Theological Union in Chicago. He called the controversy a "moral fallacy," arguing the "sensitivities of some of the families of 9/11 victims and first-responders, as well as other intensely hurt and angry U.S. Americans" were "deeply flawed" since "hardworking, deeply patriotic, and peace-loving U.S. American Muslims," like Imam Feisal Rauf and Daisy Khan, weren't responsible for the 9/11 attacks and, in fact, "courageously and effectively struggle to stand up to a small but dangerous minority of extremists who would pervert their faith into a medium for hate."

For then, the opponents of the "Ground Zero mosque" won the battle. The mosque wasn't going to be built, but there was a new weapon that the Honor Brigade had successfully launched: the word "Islamophobia" had now made it into modern-day lexicon. And the "Ground Zero mosque" would become code for "anti-Muslim racism."

CHAPTER 9

Battling for the Narrative: One-Two Punch

By the middle of the Obama administration, the battle for the narrative of Muslims in America was in full gear.

In October 2010, the American Islamic College hosted a two-day conference on "Islam and Muslims in America" with some important connections. At the grand opening of the American Islamic College, CAIR Chicago's executive director, Ahmed Rehab, a member of the college's advisory board, had mingled with Organization of Islamic Cooperation Secretary General Ekmeleddin İhsanoğlu, a Turk. He arrived with ambassador to the United Nations, Ufuk Gokcen, also a Turk. The board of advisors included CAIR ally Scott Alexander, a professor at the Catholic Theological Union, and John Esposito, director of the Prince Alwaleed bin Talal Center for Muslim-Christian Understanding at Georgetown University. The Obama administration sent its envoy to the Organization of Islamic Cooperation, Rashad Hussain, and the first special envoy of the White House to the Organization of Islamic Cooperation, Sada Cumber, to the conference.

While these high-level meetings conveyed a sense of stature to the fight over the narrative, a lot of the action was taking place in the gutter.

* * *

The success of the fake news accounts established to press the "Islamophobia" narrative was that its spin often made it into mainstream media coverage.

Earlier that year, Zahra Billoo, the executive director of the CAIR San Francisco Bay Area chapter, had taken on a symbol of American fashion, Abercrombie & Fitch, for allegedly firing a nineteen-year-old Muslim woman who wore a headscarf, because the headscarf didn't fit its "Look Policy," which spelled out how its employees could style themselves. Mooneye republished a *Salon* article with a headline that would be a nightmare for any corporate PR team: "Abercrombie Hates Your Hijab." Billoo loved this fight. She was born in the United States to parents who had immigrated to the US from Pakistan. Raised in San Jose, she said she remembers being bullied as a girl for being Muslim, one time in fifth grade having her headscarf pulled off. She started working for CAIR as a college intern. One of her first jobs was to study a security watch list being compiled by the Transportation Security Administration. After she graduated with a JD from the University of California Hastings College of the Law, she joined the CAIR San Francisco Bay Area chapter as acting executive director. A year later, CAIR named her executive director. Billoo's CAIR chapter later defeated Abercrombie & Fitch in court, after scoring slam dunks in the court of public opinion.

She kept on finding new cases. In October 2010, "KhaledTheGypsy" posted a message on Reddit, sharing photos of a GPS tracking device a friend had found on his vehicle and wondering: "Does this mean the FBI is after us?"

Days later, IslamphobiaToday.com published an article by Jesse Emspak, "Muslim Student Finds FBI's GPS Device On His Car," about Yasir Afifi, a local college student who said he found an FBI tracking device on his car.

The article quoted Zahra Billoo at CAIR saying she was investigating if legal action could be taken.

It made it seem as if the article was written exclusively for IslamophobiaToday.com.

In fact, Emspak wrote the article for a website, International Business Times. On its own, that wasn't a big deal but, with this cross-fertilization with real media outlets, known as "cross-posting" in the jargon of new media rules, these fake websites won themselves the appearance of credibility and original content.

Two days later, CAIR's Muhammad Tauseef Akbar, writing as "Garibaldi," reprinted the article on LoonWatch with the headline "The Hazards of Driving While Muslim: FBI GPS Tracking Devices."

Three days after the LoonWatch article, *Washington Post* reporter Jeff Stein wrote about the case, saying that CAIR, an "advocacy group," was representing the student.

That day, the Islamic Organizations of Greater Chicago and the Muslim Public Affairs Council hosted a one-day conference in Chicago on civic engagement. The workshop on Islamophobia had two familiar names: UC Berkeley lecturer Hatem Bazian and CAIR Chicago executive director Ahmed Rehab.

* * *

Two enemies faced each other in early October 2010.

Iranian American author Reza Aslan appeared with Jihad Watch blogger Robert Spencer for a town hall taping on ABC News *This Week*, with journalist Christiane Amanpour. Behind the scenes, Aslan was speaking regularly with members of the Honor Brigade, spinning everyone up to make the mosque debate a case study for "Islamophobia" in America.

Amanpour turned to Spencer and asked, "Let me ask you Robert Spencer, should America fear Islam and why?"

Spencer answered, "Well, Islamic jihadis point frequently—they actually consistently explain and justify their actions and try to make recruits among peaceful Muslims by pointing to texts of the Qur'an, the actions of Muhammad, and the teachings of Islamic law. And so, this is something that moderate and peaceful Muslims have to confront. But instead, they always just displace responsibility and blame the people who are calling attention to these things. And in—and then, of course, you have even peaceful Muslims like the Imam

Rauf, advocating for sharia, which does deny equality of rights to women. It does deny the freedom of speech, even cultural restrictions on the freedom of speech in his book, *What's Right with Islam*. And, you know, you talk about that Islam doesn't allow for wife beating. Well, it's in the Qur'an, to beat your wife. And also, there's a television show in Saudi Arabia where they discuss the right implements to beat your wife with."

Amanpour turned to Daisy Khan. "What do you answer to what Robert Spencer has just said?"

Khan answered, "Well, let me assure all Americans that the vast majority of Muslims around the world and in the United States—are living a peaceful life. We are law-abiding citizens. We have people in the armed forces. My own niece, who's in her early twenties, went to Iraq for two years and just came back from there—young, Arab American, born in this country, served the nation to keep it secure. We have a thousand police officers just in the New York Police Department keeping the city secure."

She didn't address Spencer's legitimate points about violent interpretations of Islam.

Amanpour turned to Iranian American novelist Azar Nafisi, author of *Reading Lolita in Tehran*, "Should people fear Islam?"

Nafisi answered, "I came here to America because I expected that that image which those people had imposed on us would not be imposed on us again. And look at my surprise. From both sides of the aisle, what you hear is that there is one Islam. If we think there is only one Islam, then we have to take sides. Either it's evil or it's good. But there are as many interpretations of Islam as there are Muslims."

She threaded the needle correctly.

Amanpour turned to Aslan, filmed in Amsterdam. "Reza, you have heard just right now several points raised. One is that Muslims in this country are trying to bring Sharia law. Is there a shred of evidence for that?"

Aslan responded, "No, not a single shred whatsoever. I think somebody needs to remind Franklin Graham that we don't judge our values in the United States by comparing them to what the Saudis do. This is a common refrain that you hear from a lot of anti-Muslim activists in the United States, including Robert Spencer, that, well, if, in Saudi Arabia, you can't have a church, then, therefore, in the United States, you shouldn't be allowed to have mosques. This is an appalling and laughable argument."

* * *

Three days later, writing as "Emperor," CAIR Chicago's executive director, Ahmed Rehab, published a dispatch on Aslan's debate, headlined "Reza Aslan Serves Robert Spencer Overdose of Truth."

As "Emperor," Rehab wrote, "There seemed to be too many people on the show and not enough time, but at the end of the day the result was a positive one: Robert Spencer got roasted for being the anti-Muslim bigot that we have always known him to be."

Aslan "took him to task for promoting nonsense about Islam and Muslims and then trying to evade responsibility for his rhetoric on his fanatical followers," the article continued. He also "called out" a new group Spencer had started, "Stop the Islamization of America," as a "bigoted anti-Islamic organization imported from Europe."

In the LoonWatch comments section, writing as "DrM," former UC Berkeley student Javad Hashmi promptly responded with a slam against Muslim reformers, writing, "I have no desire to be a 'moderate Muslim' by the West's bogus standards, ever."

Addressing another reader, he later ridiculed as fake even openly public Muslim extremists, like a British Muslim preacher, Anjem Choudary, whom he mocked called "Andy," writing: "I think its [*sic*] rather sad how ignorant, and naive jokers like you are, completely unconnected to reality that governments lie and conduct psyops. Just last [*sic*] we had the FBI harassing antiwar activists by raiding their homes for simply protesting. Andy isn't an irhabi(terrorist) [*sic*] as you insist, but he is no different then [*sic*] the 'Revolution Muslim' rabble rousers trying to scare non-Muslims. If these guys were the real deal, they would be behind bars, not on shows presented as legitimate spokespersons for Islam."

He later continued with typos, "Pro-regressive Muslims(secular Arabs and desis with no interest in Islam pre-911) had their heyday on the RAND bandwagon in the early 2000s, trying to make a fast buck, discredit genuine Muslim organizations and secularize Islamic spirituality. These same called pro-regressive 'Muslims' today babbling neocon rubbish on FOX. Raheel raza, [*sic*] Tarek Fatah, Asra Nomani, Ahmed Nassef, Mona Eltahawy are a few who come to mind. Get back to me when you've done your homework."

* * *

By October 2010, LoonWatch announced that it was looking for "gems of talent" to write for its site, as well as two other sites that it proudly announced it had started: SpencerWatch.com and WhatIfTheyWereMuslim.com.

LoonWatch solicited writing samples at info@loonwatch.com.

Later in the month, WNYC aired a segment, "Muslims Try to Get Media-Savvy," with radio host Arun Venugopal, featuring two "media-savvy" American Muslims: Reza Aslan and Shahed Amanullah.

Venugopal even put in a plug for LoonWatch, with a hyperlink to the fake news website. "More serious, but equally edgy is LoonWatch, a relatively new Web site whose editors want to remain anonymous," he wrote, in an article accompanying the radio segment.

He continued, "The people behind LoonWatch (which bears the faux-alarmist tagline, 'The Mooslims! They're Heeere!') said their mission is to expose 'anti-Muslim loons, wackos, and conspiracy theorists' on the Internet. One of their most widely-circulated articles was 'All Terrorists are Muslims…except the 94% who Aren't,' and was based on FBI statistics showing that only 6 percent of terrorists since 1980 have been Muslim."

He interviewed a friend of CAIR Chicago's Ahmed Rehab, writing, "DePaul University professor Laith Saud said LoonWatch is not only funny and incisive, but much better at addressing Islam and critics of Islam than the mainstream media." He quoted Saud saying, "In terms of the intellectual claims being made by Islamophobes, those really go unchallenged. What the mainstream media is really concerned with is how Islamophobia is playing out politically in this country, in terms of Republicans and Democrats, in terms of voter registration and voter drives."

* * *

Meanwhile, the fight between CAIR leaders and their arch critics—notably Robert Spencer—devolved deeply into mudslinging, with LoonWatch playing a central role. This got very little attention in the mainstream media, but it highlighted several issues.

People like Spencer are provocateurs whose confrontational style makes them easy targets for the term "Islamophobe." But they are armed with significant knowledge and aren't always wrong. While CAIR and its proxies profess to be above the fray and an only-the-facts kind of an organization, they do propaganda quite well—and seethe with rage when people like Spencer dispute their spin.

* * *

A network of American Muslim leaders used a private Google Group, Muslim American Leaders Network, or "mlnet," to share information, a read of the Google Group emails reveals.

One evening, Ahmed Rehab sent his friends an email with the subject line: "Robert Spencer Challenges me to a Debate."

The message went out to leaders at the Muslim Public Affairs Council, among others, including communications director Edina Lekovic, founder Salam Al-Marayati, and Washington, DC, government affairs director Haris Tarin.

Rehab groused, "Robert Spencer did a hit piece on me."

Spencer had written an article on Jihad Watch, saying, "CAIR's brave Ahmed Rehab who ran from debate with me claims never to have run from a debate."

Rehab wrote to his friends, "The strategy to respond to that is tricky. Do you officially respond via your organization and legitimize a nobody and help publicize his attack on you? Do you ignore it and allow him to frame you? Seems like a lose."

He explained his media strategy: "That's where the importance of a personal blog comes in. It gives you the chance to pushback on something like this as a personable human being with character, humor, and a regular voice that is accessible to the people and that they can relate to. Of course the language (laid back but factual) and angle taken (dismissive) is key."

He continued, "I am sharing this in the context of the anti-hate strategy we have been talking about on this list knowing that many of you here face the same attacks and the same dilemma."

He had replied earlier that day on his personal blog with a column, headlined "Internet Sociopath Robert Spencer Wants to Debate Me."

"These days," Rehab wrote, "the internet is booming with shady characters raking up big bucks in the Bash-and-Cash Islamophobia business."

He singled out Spencer and his "amateurish" website, Jihad Watch. Spencer "claims to be a scholar of Islam, Islamic Law, and Theology but holds no degrees in any of those subjects and has never even published a single peer-reviewed paper. Actual scholars see him as something of a joke."

Rehab wrote, "And now for some irony. Spencer, you are claiming you are ready to debate anyone but that alas no one wants to debate you because no one can. But, is this actually true? Does the name Danios of Loonwatch ring a bell Spencer? You may be burying your head in the sand hoping no one will notice, but a simple Google search on 'Robert Spencer debate' reveals your hypocrisy."

He linked to a LoonWatch column by "Danios," headlined "Robert Spencer is a chicken."

In it, writing under his fake name of "Danios," former UC Berkeley student Javad Hashmi had written, "How come you are ignoring an invitation from another blogger who has challenged you numerous times and whose articles shredding your arguments to pieces are all over the web without a peep of a rebuttal from you? Are you conceding defeat? Are you 'running away?'"

The LoonWatch column had a note to readers: "For the full monty on this sociopath, visit Spencerwatch.com," with a link to the website that Rehab and his staffer, Muhammad Tauseef Akbar, had actually purchased and created through their GoDaddy account, according to GoDaddy records.

On his blog, Rehab had published a photo of Spencer next to Dutch filmmaker Geert Wilders and written the caption: "Spencer is the small one on the right."

Later, Iranian American author Reza Aslan weighed in: "Robert Spencer is a clown and the only legitimate response to clowns is laughter. Debating him would be like debating a child. It is a useless enterprise."

* * *

As the Honor Brigade attempted to distract Americans from the serious issues in the Muslim community, al-Qaeda in the Arabian Peninsula planned an attack to blow up cargo jets.

CAIR Chicago executive director Ahmed Rehab went on with Fox News host Eric Bolling, who asked him about the "radical Islamists" who recently tried to kill innocents, from the "Underwear Bomber" to the "Times Square Bomber." Born in 1963, Bolling was a conservative former commodities trader who had lost friends in the 9/11 attack.

Rehab immediately pivoted. "Here's also a pattern that you need to be aware of...," he said. The Muslim father of the "Underwear Bomber" turned him in. A Muslim saw the smoke from the car the "Times Square Bomber" attempted to blow up. "Muslims are our greatest ally in the war on terror," Rehab insisted.

Bolling and the other guests tried to get Rehab to acknowledge the issue of Islamist radicalization. He refused.

* * *

Sophisticated threat assessment is a key part of a successful national security policy. That includes assessing the threat people pose based on a number of factors from behavior, of course, to race, religion, ethnic identity, political ideology, and other factors that can motivate a person to violence.

By late 2010, the question of profiling had become an animated debate. Again, I went on the debate series, Intelligence Squared, and argued this time in favor of religious profiling at airports. I explicitly stated that "profiling" had become a dirty word but that it really amounted to strategic threat assessment and should *never* include harassment or discrimination. I said I understood, too, if such a threat assessment singled out my father or me. The audience agreed with my team, and we won the debate. But any nuance that I offered in the debate was lost on my critics after the debate.

Within a day, a Wikipedia contributor, "ASRAHASNOEYE-LIDS" professed that my critics "don't object to Nomani's views," but they "do have a problem with Nomani herself." "ASRAHASNO-EYELIDS" wrote, "Clearly this woman has anger/daddy/self-hatred issues that require a therapist, not another book publisher, or another soap box podium, to air her idiotic, uninformed, and self-hating views, as a real or legitimate opinion from a Muslim scholar/thinker."

"Edgar181" blocked the user. I didn't know him, but I was grateful that there was a grown-up in the room.

Two days later, in late November 2010, I made my argument on a CNN Headline News segment hosted by Joy Behar.

Quickly enough, using his "Danios" moniker, former UC Berkeley student Javad Hashmi published a column, attacking me on LoonWatch. It was shared instantly on Twitter by "Hussamee" who wrote: "Danios of loonwatch dismantles the 'colonial liberalism' of house Muslim Asra Nomani. An excellent read." He linked to the LoonWatch article and tagged "Ikhras."

The profile picture "Hussamee" included the image of a flag with "Palestine" above it. The handle often retweeted Electronic Intifada and its founder, Ali Abunimah.

That day, UC Berkeley alumnus Wajahat Ali published a column at the far-left British newspaper, the *Guardian*, headlined "Time for FBI to stop spying on American Muslims."

Like clockwork, CAIR Chicago executive director Ahmed Rehab used his "Emperor" moniker to republish the article the next day on LoonWatch with a near-identical headline: "FBI: Stop Spying on American Muslims."

Through "Emperor," Rehab wrote, "Wajahat Ali writes piercingly on the topic."

Now using his "DrM" handle, former UC Berkeley's Javad Hashmi immediately weighed in on the comment board: "The FBI is a terrorist organization, and should not be trusted."

Rehab also attacked a Pakistani Canadian, Mubin Shaikh, who had written a book, *Undercover Jihadi*, about his life as an undercover informant in a case that led to the arrest of eighteen Muslims in Canada for terrorism. Shaikh had branded himself to the US State Department, Canadian law enforcement, and others as a subject matter expert on violent Islamic extremism.

Shaikh responded to Hashmi, using "DrM," and said: "Dr. M—stop sympathizing with terrorists—it'll just get you in trouble. ;)"

Hashmi, using "DrM," said Shaikh "cannot be trusted." He "may not be as large a con artist, as Irshad Manji or Tarek 'T-Fat' Fatah, but he's still guilty of partaking in a bogus fishing expedition."

He added, "I suspect we haven't heard the last of Mubin Sheikh [*sic*], he's a young guy and will no doubt figure out ways of earning fast money at someone else's expense. Cocaine isn't cheap."

From behind his mask, "DrM" rebuked his detractors, saying, "I'm a TRUTH first kind of guy with ZERO tolerance for liars." He railed against "intelligence services waging war on the Muslim community," calling Sheikh a "filthy munafiq," the slur that means hypocrite.

He continued, acting self-righteous and dropping Arabic script into his insults: "I'll speak the truth no matter where I am and regardless of the price I have to pay. Enjoy the fame and money while it lasts, bastard. Just remember that one day you'll be in another court, in front of another judge, and on that day اهَرَابَخْأَ ثُدِّحَتُ ٍذِئَمَوْيَ those who lined your pockets won't be able to help you."

In an interview, Shaikh said he had tried to address some of the issues "DrM" had raised, but he eventually dropped it, concluding the effort would be fruitless. He had no idea who he was and why he hated him so much.

CHAPTER 10

Discrediting "House Muslims"

In this new age, disinformation is rewarded.

In 2011, LoonWatch won some important recognition while it went about trying to harass folks. At Brass Crescent, technology entrepreneur Shahed Amanullah and medical physicist Aziz Poonawalla gave "Danios" their "best writer" award in its annual honors, saying, "Powerful and poignant, bringing the fight to the Islamophobes." They hid his true identity: former UC Berkeley student Javad Hashmi.

In early January 2011, CAIR Chicago's Muhammad Tauseef Akbar used his "Garibaldi" fake name to attack me on LoonWatch with the tags, "LoonPeople." That month, "Mooneye" went after Syrian American Wafa Sultan, calling me out for writing a neutral—and not condemning—profile of Wafa for *TIME* magazine.

In a ramp-up to a new campaign on "Islamophobia," CAIR's Corey Saylor and ThinkProgress editor Faiz Shakir took to the stage for an all-male panel at Busboys and Poets in Washington, DC, with attorney-turned-playwright Wajahat Ali and two other speakers. Drawing laughs, Wajahat joked that he was sitting next to the "only white man on the panel," Saylor, holding on to him "like a life vest."

"Corey, you're our savior," he said.

* * *

There were constantly two tracks running in the information warfare campaign of the Honor Brigade, giving cover to hardcore Islamists and those attacking Israel.

In late January, "Dorado" arrived on SpencerWatch.com, as "our newest reporter on Spencer." Meanwhile, from late January to mid-February 2011, UC Berkeley's Hatem Bazian launched a national speaking tour, "Never Again for Anyone," the week of International Holocaust Remembrance Day. One of his talking points: "Islamophobia."

He recruited a Nazi Holocaust survivor, Hajo Meyer, who went on the road with him, equating the Holocaust to Israel's occupation of Palestinian territories. Meyer was born in Bielefeld, Germany, in 1924, fleeing alone to Holland to escape the Nazis in 1939, at the age of fourteen. When Germany occupied Holland, the Gestapo captured him in 1944, and he survived ten months in Auschwitz.

In early February 2011, Bazian and Meyer hit Chicago. There, aggressive Palestinian American blogger Ali Abunimah joined them. A pro-Israeli group, "Stand With Us," called the event "dangerous" for suggesting "Zionists collaborated with the Nazis."

Born in the US to Palestinian parents, Abunimah had graduated from Princeton University with a BA and the University of Chicago with an MA, and had published the book *One Country: A Bold Proposal to End the Israeli-Palestinian Conflict.*

The three spoke at Room 314A, in the student center at DePaul University. The event was sponsored by a network of groups: the organization that Bazian started at UC Berkeley years earlier, Students for Justice in Palestine; International Jewish Anti-Zionist Network; and Middle East Children's Alliance.

Set to speak at the SALAM Center, a mosque in Sacramento, California, Meyer received backlash from local Jewish leaders, including a rabbi, Reuven H. Taff, who told the *Sacramento Bee* in a February 16, 2011, article that the evening was a "program of hate."

One of the speakers: Bazian.

The next day, writing as "Emperor," CAIR Chicago's Ahmed Rehab republished the article under the headline "Holocaust Survivor's Planned Talk Angers Jewish Leaders."

He posed the rhetorical question: "Does a Holocaust survivor have the right to speak his mind and say, 'what happened to me during the Holocaust, I see it happening again to Palestinians, Never Again for Anyone.' Should he be labeled an anti-Semite for such statements?"

In February 2011, using the fake name of "Garibaldi," CAIR Chicago's Muhammad Tauseef Akbar wrote attacking conservative TV personality Glenn Beck and, later an initiative by Robert Spencer called "Stop the Islamization of America." The character assassination was part of a long campaign. Four years earlier, "M.T. Akbar" had written against Beck on USA.mediamoniters.net.

* * *

Meanwhile, Javad Hashmi was successfully moving along in his day job.

According to an online bio, he had passed the US medical exam for foreign-educated doctors, saying, "He will be applying for a residency position in the fall of this year, insha-Allah," using the Arabic phrase for "God willing."

In January 2011, the newly minted physician married a young Pakistani American woman, Farrah Hassan, at Fort Gordon in Augusta, Georgia. An announcement in the *Columbia County News-Times* reported their wedding. One Facebook album was filled with happy, celebratory photos from her *mehndi* celebration, a prewedding ritual in South Asia when a bride's hands are painted with henna in intricate designs. Another album, "Javad and Farrah Hashmi Wedding," was filled with photos from their wedding.

For his Facebook profile picture, Hashmi had uploaded a photo of himself with his wife, her hair falling freely over her shoulders, a wide smile across her face. He told a friend his wife didn't know about her husband's double life. At first, Hashmi was a resident physician with United Health Services. In the summer of 2011, the alumni magazine of his alma mater, Aga Khan University, announced Hashmi had landed a residency at State University of New York, and he started a new job in July of that year, working at a community free clinic in Binghamton, New York. In the fall of 2011, SUNY's Upstate Medical University published its in-house magazine, *Residency Report*, with a feature headlined "Welcome New Residents," and naming Hashmi as its emergency medicine resident. In Hashmi's profile, the SUNY website listed UC Berkeley as his undergraduate school, but Hashmi had never finished his BA, according to the UC Berkeley registrar's office.

* * *

In the predawn darkness of a cold, rainy morning in early March 2011, folks lined up in the marble and limestone threshold to Cannon House Office Building at the corner of Independence Avenue SE and New Jersey Avenue SE, waiting for the building's doors to open for the first hearing of the US House of Representatives Committee on Homeland Security on a critically important topic: "The Extent of Radicalization in the American Muslim Community and That Community's Response."

Three days earlier, I had published an article for the *Daily Beast* supporting the hearing. The editors had splashed a provocative headline, "Peter King's Hearings on American Muslims Are No Witch Hunt," but I argued simply that we had a radicalization problem that Muslim communities needed to acknowledge to defeat it. I also argued that rational profiling is a necessary part of law enforcement and intelligence, as long as it steered 100 percent clear of harassment or discrimination.

Allies of the Honor Brigade didn't agree. Before the hearing's start, the Southern Poverty Law Center published an article on its *Hate Watch* blog headlined "Why Are Peter King's Hearings So Loathsome? Let Us Count the Ways." It was written by Mark Potok, a journalist and editor of its *Intelligence Report* who was going to clock twenty years at the SPLC before unceremoniously leaving his job in 2017. For now, he quoted statistics from the Triangle Center on Terrorism and Homeland Security that "48 of the 120 Muslims suspected of plotting terror attacks in the United States since 9/11 were turned in by fellow Muslims," conveniently ignoring the fact that the simple math made it so the majority of cases were not reported by "fellow Muslims." He pivoted instead to "anti-Muslim hate crimes," the "demonization" of Muslims, and "a renewed bout of Islamophobia," making the unsubstantiated claim that, to Rep. Peter King, "Islam is the enemy."

This approach earned SPLC grant money. That year, the Foundation to Promote Open Society, based in New York City, one of the two major grantmaking foundations funded by billionaire George Soros, gave SPLC $25,000 to "support" the "Table to Combat Anti-Muslim Sentiment." Really, Potok later admitted, "We see this as a political struggle, right?... I mean, we're not trying to change anybody's mind. We're trying to wreck the groups, and we're very clear in our heart.... We are trying to destroy them.... As a political matter to destroy them...." He brought up CNN host Lou Dobbs and admitted SPLC was trying to "shame" him.

* * *

Inside the hearing, liberal Democrat representatives showed the hearing's three main witnesses' "disrespect" during tense exchanges. The witnesses include two Muslims—Syrian American former US Navy Lt. Commander Zuhdi Jasser and Somali American Abdirizak Bihi—who had been working tirelessly in the trenches to defeat Islamic extremism in US communities. The third witness was Melvin Bledsoe, a black father, whose son had taken the name Abdulhakim Muhammad after converting to Islam and then ending up in jail for terrorism in the deadly shooting at a military recruiting center in Arkansas.

These were men who had started extremism in the face. They knew it. If we didn't listen to them, who would we hear?

* * *

At hearing's end, CNN asked me to speak on-air about the hearings. We walked down the hall to the majestic rotunda of the House Cannon Building, light pouring through large windows onto the wide marble spiral staircase cascading through the rotunda. I slipped an earpiece into my right ear. The cameraman handed me a microphone I snaked through my *kurta*. I didn't know whom I'd be debating.

Soon enough, I learned I'd be facing Nihad Awad, the executive director of CAIR.

I caught my breath.

The idea of challenging the institutional megaphone for what claimed to represent the American Muslim community was intimidating, but I had to do it. I had clarity of thought, made precise around the dining table in Karachi, hunting for the men who had kidnapped my friend, Danny Pearl, and made clear in long conversations in the kitchen with my mother.

"Three, two, one," a producer said in my ear.

I spoke my mind, saying that mainstream Muslim organizations like CAIR hadn't done enough to police our communities so it was only appropriate for lawmakers and law enforcement to investigate the issue of extremism in our communities.

On the drive home, I told my mother about the interview. "I don't know why CAIR lets me get away with challenging them," I told my mother.

"They don't," she said, presciently.

* * *

CAIR Chicago's Ahmed Rehab used his "Emperor" cover to publish an attack on the witnesses immediately on LoonWatch.

"Peter King's 'Muslim Hearings' Theater to Target Muslims," he wrote.

Rehab attacked Jasser, Bihi, and Bledsoe as "non-experts" who were "bereft of any credentials or expertise in the field of radicalization, terrorism or extremism."

Then in the light of day, Rehab walked into the local studio of WGN-TV to criticize the hearing. He also held a press conference, excerpts airing on the local ABC 7 station and uploaded to CAIR Chicago's YouTube channel, featuring Rehab, with the headline "ABC 7: CAIR Chicago responds to King hearings on radicalization of Muslim Americans."

Three days after hearing's end, someone anonymously started a new Facebook page called "Zuhdi Jasser is a Clown and an Uncle Tom Muslim."

Over the months, posts were published, again anonymously, alternatively calling Jasser "a lapdog," "shameless," one of many "fools," and "a well-behaved pet."

* * *

While one part of the Honor Brigade's strategy was to go directly after the witnesses, another element of the strategy was to attack anyone who supported the viewpoint that Islamic extremism had to be challenged.

In the Midwest, CAIR Chicago's Ahmed Rehab called liberal HBO comedian Bill Maher the "Islamophobe of the day." This effort to oppose the Rep. Peter King hearings got funding from none other than George Soros's Open Society Foundations network. According to an internal brag sheet, Open Society funded "an organized force of opposition" by the Islamic Society of North America (ISNA) to the hearings. ISNA was one of the legacy organizations created by the Muslim Brothers at 500 Grove Street. The internal document bragged: "National Security and Human Rights Campaign grantees remain at the forefront of coordinated efforts to counter the tide of anti-Muslim sentiment in the U.S. Last year, with a seed grant from the Campaign, the Islamic Society of North America united religious leaders from an array of faiths and launched a high-level campaign, 'Shoulder-to-Shoulder: Standing with American Muslims; Upholding American Values.' The group featured prominently as an organized force of opposition to Rep. Peter King's (R-NY) controversial congressional hearing challenging the loyalties of American Muslims." Congressional Black Caucus representatives had also blocked any substantive discussion of Muslim extremists as "profiling." Meanwhile, ISNA regularly ran matrimonial ads in which applicants spelled out their bigotry and discrimination against darker-skinned women, setting credentials for women of "wheat" or "fair" complexions.

* * *

In Phoenix, CAIR Arizona executive director Imraan Siddiqi published an article on a blog, *Stop Islamophobia Now*, with the headline "The Rise of the Muslim Agent-Provocateur: Asra Nomani."

Siddiqi called me a "self-styled former Wall Street Journal writer" who had "gained a cart blanche within the media—right and left alike." He took issue with my alleged "near-reflexive tendency to defend any actions against mainstream Muslims."

I wrote back on his comment board. Addressing "friends," I wrote that I understood the issues that some folks had with the King hearings, but I supported the conversation about radicalization of Islam in our communities because I rejected the assumption that having the conversation was an indictment of *all* Muslims or *all* of Islam. Muslims and Islam would be better served by recognizing the very serious issues in our community, rather than trying to deflect the conversation. I left my email address. No one responded.

Siddiqi was part of a wider effort that didn't seem interested in dialogue. He was a founding member of CAIR's Arizona chapter in 2002. The son of immigrants from Pakistan, he'd grown up in Roswell, Georgia, before leaving to get his BA in marketing from the University of Texas at Arlington. He got his MBA from Arizona State University and sold gold in mall kiosks with a business he'd established, Sell Us Your Gold LLC. Later, he started another company, WhereUBean Coffee LLC, while launching CAIR Arizona, but he'd been using his blog for years to launch personal attacks on people he perceived as foes. He'd been after me for years, once calling me an "agent provocateur." He was also very anti-Israel, one time attacking a rabbi, Shmuley Boteach, for contributing to the "Israeli war and propaganda machine."

In fact, hard-line Muslims were gaining credibility in the mainstream media as they denied the extremism issue among Muslims. A reporter for the *New York Times*, Andrea Elliott, profiled Yasir Qadhi for the *New York Times Magazine*, and the profile was so softball, it shocked Muslim reformers. Elliott had made a name for herself with a profile of an imam in New York City. She had covered our women-led prayer. She should have known better. The cover story vaulted Qadhi to the national stage.

* * *

That month, another anonymous website—Ikhras.com—joined the bandwagon, targeting anyone who supported the Peter King hearings.

In an article headlined "House Muslim Asra Nomani Supports Islamophobic Witch Hunt," it published a photo of me with the caption: "House Muslim Asra Nomani." The tags included: "Asra Nomani, House Muslims."

It read, "She shamelessly uses verses from the Qur'an to justify her House Muslim stance. She goes on to list the grievances she has against the Muslim American community. All religion obviously requires updated interpretation. We're not objecting to that. We are objecting to Nomani's approach; she completely disregards Muslims' First Amendment rights by inviting a lawmaker of a racist, genocidal, islamophobic empire to approach the community with a scalpel. Ask thousands of dead Iraqis and Afghanis just how friendly the US is to Muslims."

It continued, "Just like Mona Eltahawy had encouraged racist state power to regulate the *niqab* in Europe, Nomani invites racist state power to profile an already-traumatized community that has put up with the USA Patriot Act, summary deportations, NSEERS special registration, secret evidence and no-fly lists. That is not to mention the hundreds of wars on thousands of Muslims in Iraq, Afghanistan and Palestine, which Peter King has supported and voted for as congressman. While state power should obviously never be utilized to profile people on the basis of religion or ethnicity, King is a politician we should be particularly alarmed about."

* * *

A few days later, CAIR Arizona's Imran Siddiqi started a new blog on WordPress, *Stop Islamophobia Now*!

Across the country, two days later, the State Department named Shahed Amanullah its senior advisor for technology.

That month, in the dynamic of the parallel tracks, "Mooneye" lauded CAIR Chicago's civil rights director, Christina Abraham, for her work against Robert Spencer. Abraham cited the value of Loon-Watch and SpencerWatch.

* * *

The old CNN Headline News interview I'd done the fall before with host Joy Behar suddenly reemerged. Behar had invited me on air to talk about "profiling" at airports. The other guest was Marc Lamont Hill, then a professor of anthropology at Columbia University.

I explained my position: that "profiling" is a critical element of threat assessment.

Hill spoke from the talking points of the Islamists. "Yes it's true," he said, "that all the people who support al Qaeda are Muslim but that makes less in one in one thousand of the people who were actually—one in one million for the people who are actually passing into airports or who subscribe to its plan."

I argued what the data revealed: "We understand really clearly that religiosity does influence terrorism."

Hill interrupted: "No, it doesn't. No, it doesn't."

He insisted on the position of CAIR and the Muslim Brothers: "The Muslim community is policing itself."

I disagreed passionately, and Behar noted my "courage" in speaking out from within my community.

Now, someone at the Facebook page, "Zuhdi Jasser is a Clown and an Uncle Tom Muslim," posted a link to the CNN interview, with a biting comment, "Zuhdi is not the only Uncle Tom Muslim out there who is serving the anti-Muslim agenda. This video here shows Asra Nomani arguing IN FAVOR of profiling Muslims at airports despite being Muslim herself. As much as watching this video boils my blood, it is still worth it to see Marc Lamont Hill make short work of Asra's flawed logic."

There was a dizzying revolving door of disinformation. CAIR Chicago's Ahmed Rehab used his "Emperor" fake name to reprint an article on LoonWatch headlined "King Witness' Story Undermined by Reality" by *Religion Dispatches* journalist Sarah Posner. She had exposed the Christian Right but seemed to turn a blind eye to the hard-line Muslim Right. She went after the father who had been a hearing witness. The "Zuhdi Jasser is a Clown and Uncle Tom Muslim" Facebook page reposted the LoonWatch article with the message, "Yet another of Peter King's witnesses exposed by LoonWatch."

The echo chamber of character assassinations seemed to get louder and louder.

These guys had no shortage of melodrama. Their go-to tactic involved naming and shaming their opponent. There was no civil debate of ideas. It was a strategy of slash-and-burn that they were unleashing on their enemies.

If they couldn't win in the court of public opinion, this wing of the Woke Army had to declare victory in the gutter.

* * *

Four days later, a new article went up on the fake Facebook page. The post said, "From Ahmed Rehab," and it linked to an article from Rehab's blog, headlined "Yaser Tabbara Eviscerates Rep Peter King Star Witness Zuhdi Jasser."

There was so much showmanship to this propaganda effort. It wasn't enough to have a debate. Jasser had to be eviscerated.

Tabbara went back a long way with Rehab. In his CAIR Chicago biography, Rehab had credited "long-time friend" Tabbara with revitalizing CAIR Chicago with him in 2004. Born in Chicago in 1975 to Syrian parents, Tabbara grew up in Damascus, returning to Chicago in 1993 to earn a BA in political science and economics from the University of Illinois. He earned a JD from the DePaul

University College of Law, where he was a research assistant to the well-respected and revered human rights lawyer M. Cherif Bassiouni. After graduating in 2002, he launched the Post 9/11 Immigrant Legal Rights Project at the Midwest Immigrant and Human Rights Center. He established Project Mobilize to support political candidates in Chicago. In 2004, Tabbara and Rehab cofounded the CAIR Chicago chapter. He was its first executive director before moving back to Damascus. There he taught at the University of Kalamoon. He launched the Syrian American Council, and he was its executive director. He also cofounded the Syrian Forum. He is also spokesman and legal advisor to the president of the Syrian interim government, the National Coalition of Syrian Revolution and Opposition Forces, and the Syrian National Council. And, since 2008, he had been a partner at the law firm, Zarzour, Khalil, and Tabbara.

He was associated with Zaher Sahloul, president of the Syrian American Medical Society and an associate clinical professor at the University of Illinois. (Sahloul would later be named to the Illinois Muslim Advisory Council, launched in August 2011 to advise the governor on Muslim issues and trade with Muslim-majority countries.)

* * *

Meanwhile, LoonWatch kept growing. In late March 2011, LoonWatch announced a new writer had joined its roster: "Amago."

"Amago" apologized for a first post he had published, not explaining what it was about. He said he had used "images which were as many of you pointed out, 'needlessly offensive' and in fact prejudiced."

"Emperor" had told him of "my error."

It wasn't clear what his "error" was, and he didn't explain.

He hoped his mistake would not "put me out of favor with the loonwatch family."

In the comments, "RDS" responded: "Welcome to the family!"

* * *

Writing as "DrM," former UC Berkeley student Javad Hashmi took another shot at me. Years earlier, I had posted a comment on the article alleging I was a "Zionist media whore."

"Hello, this is Asra Nomani," I wrote, rather naively. "So you get a good laugh calling someone a 'lying and manipulative Zionist media whore.' But I'm curious: Who are you Dr. M? You seem to have made it your hobby to mock others. Why don't you have the courage to identify who you are? Are you ashamed of your work that you don't reveal your true identity? Seems only someone ashamed of themselves would hide. Thanks, Asra."

That summer, Hashmi responded as "DrM," mocking me even further in a new blog post, "Reply to Asra 'zionist media whore' Nomani."

"Now I don't know whether this is the wild eyed bimbo herself, but lets [*sic*] humor her shall we?" he wrote.

"I was one of the earliest voices who exposed Nomani back during the hey day [*sic*] of the pro-regressive bowel movement," he bragged. "Notice that Nomani's comment does NOT address any of the criticisms against her, instead whining about the red herring of internet anonymity.

"Who's the coward, now?

"Of course you wouldn't be concerned about my identity if I was showering you with praise would you?" he continued. "We're not playing hide and seek here, granny.

"Let me also state that I have no interest in you, your politics, what you eat, who you sleep with, your trendy assortment of STDs, or how many times you've broken a leg or two attempting to float on a broom stick. I really don't," he insisted.

"You chose to make this about yourself. What DOES concern me is your decade long campaign of lies and slander against the Muslim community, all the while marketing yourself as a legitimate Mooslim voice. Your repeated support for Islamophobia over the years is well known, so don't pretend you don't understand why Muslims dislike you.

"There's really nothing special about you being 'mocked' since I regularly perform circumcisions on Judeofascists, shabbos goyim, and pro-regressive Uncle Tom Mooslims with the rusty tetanus inducing axe of truth. I despise *fasiqs* like you."

Shabbos goy is a Yiddish term that means a non Jew who performs certain types of work that Jewish religious law doesn't allow Jews to do on the Sabbath.

A *fasiq* refers to someone who violates sharia law.

He continued with more taunts: "Any wonder why so many Muslim haters cite your rubbish as a validation of their Islamophobia? Now I'm not into *takfir* but it would be an understatement to say that you're not a member of the Muslim community. You're not a Muslim, but a media savvy, Islam hating opportunist. I don't expect you to change, so don't expect critique and mockery of your religious illiteracy and political BS to go away anytime soon."

Takfir is as close as Muslims have in Islam to excommunication. It means calling a Muslim a non-Muslim.

He ended, "I'll leave you with words of wisdom I imparted to one mindless troll: Islam doesn't come from YOU or me, it comes from Allah(swt) through his Messenger(saw), if you like it keep it, if you don't, leave it but don't try to change it. Enjoy the red carpet."

He posted a stock image of a red carpet with the names of sexually transmitted diseases on the carpet, velvet movie theater ropes on both sides of the carpet.

"HPV. HIV. AIDS. HEP-C. GENITAL WARTS. GENITAL HERPES."

His tags to help readers find the post: "Asra Nomani, fraud, liar, media, shabbos goyim, whore, zionist."

* * *

In early May 2011, a fake Facebook page, "Americans Against Islamophobia," posted a TV segment from Fox News with CAIR Chicago executive director Ahmed Rehab debating Zuhdi Jasser.

It linked to IslamophobiaToday.com.

The comments were explicit. "Omar Saleh" wrote, "I doubt Zuhdi Jasser is even a muslim [*sic*]."

CHAPTER 11

Building a Propaganda Machine

"If anything, they're really just hate mongers," said Faiz Shakir, a Pakistani American rising star in Democratic Party politics, speaking into the Al Jazeera camera as video clips of Robert Spencer, Steve Emerson, Pamela Geller, and others on the LoonWatch hit list flashed across the screen.

In the late summer of 2011, the Center for American Progress, a liberal sidekick of the Democratic Party, dropped a blockbuster report called *Fear Inc.*, and it went after most of the men and women that LoonWatch had put on its hit list years earlier.

How had a liberal activist group created by John Podesta, a former Clinton administration official and a Democratic operative, become a platform for the Honor Brigade? Billionaire George Soros's Open Society Foundations had given $225,000 to the Center for American Progress to do "opposition research" in an "Examining Anti-Muslim Bigotry Project."

As editor of ThinkProgress, the propaganda arm of the Center for American Progress, Shakir led the report's writing, along with his friend, UC Berkeley alumnus Wajahat Ali.

Al Jazeera aired the nine-minute segment on its show *The Listening Post*, featuring the new crop of experts on "Islamophobia" in America. "The people who are being invited aren't experts, and they're making money off of being Islamophobes," said Palestinian American Linda Sarsour on the segment, punctuating her comment with a little laugh.

Shakir did the rounds, including liberal host Amy Goodman's *Democracy Now!* show. He was a critical voice from within the Democratic establishment. In 1979, Shakir played baseball for Harvard University before graduating with a BA in government. He earned a JD from Georgetown University before working as a communications aide in the White House Office of National Drug Control Policy. He moved to work on Capitol Hill as a legislative aide to Sen. Bob Graham. He joined Sen. John Kerry's presidential campaign in 2004. When Kerry lost, Shakir started working as a policy advisor at Clinton aide John Podesta's Center for American Progress. He launched ThinkProgress in 2005 and became its editor in 2007.

Some days later, his coauthor hit the airwaves with an interview with Al Jazeera English on the report.

* * *

Zuhdi Jasser, the Muslim reformer and a target of the report, wasn't impressed. "Wajahat Ali has made an industry out of Islamophobia," he said.

Irate, Jasser called Ali and said: "You have three pages on AIFD, and you never called me." Two days later, a website, CIFWatch.com, monitoring the "Comment is Free" section at the *Guardian* newspaper, ran the headline "Meet CiF's Wajahat Ali: Anti-Islamophobia crusader with a soft spot for anti-Semites."

* * *

Two days before the tenth anniversary of the 9/11 attacks, Wajahat Ali published a petition on his GoatMilkBlog.com, "'By Us, For Everyone': A Muslim American Declaration," pledging loyalty to the US.

They committed to creating a network of "anti-loons," the same language used by the creators of LoonWatch.

He was the first signer.

The second was Hussein Rashid, a contributing editor at Religion Dispatches and professor at Hofstra University.

The third name was Iranian American author Reza Aslan.

Other familiar names jumped out.

Other signatories were some stalwarts in the Honor Brigade: Aziz Poonawalla, founder of the *City of Brass* blog and cofounder of the Brass Crescent Awards; Haroon Moghul, executive director of the Maydan Institute; Fatemeh Fakhraie, founder and editor of Muslimah Media Watch; Haris Tarin, Washington, DC, director at Muslim Public Affairs Council; Willow Wilson, a novelist; and Zahed Amanullah, editor of AltMuslim.com and brother of technology entrepreneur Shahed Amanullah.

* * *

Two days after the anniversary of the 9/11 attacks, ThinkProgress posted an article, "U.K. Parliament Invites Former IRA Supporter Peter King to Testify About Muslim Radicalization."

Manafi Mutualo, the young Mozambique staffer running the Islamophobia Observatory for the Organization of Islamic Cooperation, shared the article, writing, "Islamophobia at the service of institutional mechanisms of UK with the help of US, which proves the world is sick and is going after ghosts...."

* * *

In early October 2011, Chicago freelance writer Anya Cordell published an article at TheRoot.com, a website operated at the time by the *Washington Post*, "Hate speech against Muslims incites violence."

A Jewish American, Cordell was a staple in CAIR's circles in Chicago. She advertised workshops on "anti-bias issues," "allying with the other," and "appearance-ism," among other trendy topics. She had once spoken at the American Islamic College, where CAIR

Chicago executive director Ahmed Rehab was a regular speaker, on the topic, "An Ally's Journey: Standing Up to Stereotyping, Islamophobia, Xenophobia and 'Appearance-ism.'" Her opening slide promoted an article of hers published at IslamophobiaToday.com, another blog run anonymously.

The next day, "Emperor" republished TheRoot.com piece on LoonWatch with the exact same headline.

Three days later, "Admin" republished the article on IslamophobiaToday.com.

They'd created the perfect echo chamber.

The next month, "Amago" published an article on LoonWatch against atheist scientist Richard Dawkins with the headline "Another Anti-Muslim Rant from Dawkins."

"Amago" didn't write with proper grammar, separating two independent sentences with a comma instead of a period.

* * *

The alliance between leftists and Islamists kept getting stronger.

For four days starting in mid-November 2011, Students for Justice in Palestine and other groups hosted an event at UC Berkeley, "Bring Down the Walls Week!" In it, they argued that the security fence installed by Israel was similar to the US fence at its border with Mexico.

As Occupy Wall Street protests took off that year, anti-Israel activism also became interwoven with the protest of agitators. The month before, Jewish Women for Justice in Israel/Palestine organized an "Occupy Boston, not Palestine" march. Then, Young, Jewish, and Proud, the youth chapter of Jewish Voice for Peace, called on young Jews to "occupy Jewish institutions" that "actively obstruct human rights for Palestinians," including the American Israel Public Affairs Committee (AIPAC), the Jewish Federations, Birthright, the Jewish National Fund, Hillel, and the "foundations of right-wing philanthropists." Then, Young, Jewish, and Proud activists used the "human mic," a protest trick in which demonstrators echo a speaker's words en masse, to disrupt a lecture on Jewish achievement organized by the Birthright Israel Alumni Community. At Occupy Oakland protests in Northern California, protesters held signs that read "Occupy Oakland Not Palestine!" quoting Jewish Voice for Peace. In New York and Boston, a group called "Existence is Resistance" rallied to release Palestinian prisoners held in Israel, including convicted terrorists. In early November, some ten protesters marched from their Occupy Boston encampment to the Israeli consulate.

In early November, somebody from the unofficial New York City Occupy Wall Street Twitter account expressed solidarity with the Freedom Waves mini-flotilla, which tried to break an Israeli blockade of Gaza. The tweet was deleted hours later.

* * *

For Thanksgiving that year, LoonWatch published one of its few articles with a real name in the byline.

The article, "The Stealth Halal Jihadist Turkey: Or, How I Learned to Stop Worrying and Love the Muslim Trojan Horse," was a satire about a story that blogger Pamela Geller had shared, that Muslims were selling *halal* turkey to Americans.

It was a "guest article" by the UC Berkeley alum Wajahat Ali.

Sharing the article with friends, Ali wrote in a note, "In honor of the parody that is Pam Geller and her current hysteria/fear/obsession with 'halal turkey,' I wrote this piece for Loonwatch."

Kamran Bokhari, an analyst at a security firm, Stratfor, shared the article with friends, writing, "The author is a friend and should be a standup comedian as opposed to the other hats he wears." In 2012, Stratfor would become notorious as a target of Julian Assange's WikiLeaks operation, noting that in its posting of several million emails WikiLeaks exposed "Stratfor's web of informers, pay-off structure, payment-laundering techniques and psychological methods."

* * *

And the Honor Brigade kept using its fake awards to promote its network.

For its 2011 awards, "Admin" at LoonWatch announced Jewish American writer Richard Silverstein was one of its "Profiles in Courage," an "ally and a friend of Loonwatch." His work "detailing the hate amongst extremist Zionists in Israel and their American counterparts has been significant and vital." He is "continuing the Jihad of Tikun Olam, 'repairing the world.'" LoonWatch had a link to his blog on its "Blogroll" of recommendations.

The other winners essentially made the casting call for the rogue's gallery of the Honor Brigade. "Admin" lauded attorney Glenn Greenwald, UC Berkeley alumnus Wajahat Ali, *The American Muslim* blogger Sheila Musaji, CAIR Chicago executive director Ahmed Rehab, author Reza Aslan, journalist Sarah Posner, and NYU alumnus Haroon Mughal. Turkish American Young Turks host Cenk Uygur earned special comments as "another perennial favorite of ours at LoonWatch" with "much material in exposing the fallacies of right-wing loons."

There were rising celebrities in their midst, including fashion designer Russell Simmons, who was "out in front fighting bigotry against all people especially Muslims," and Indian American Muslim comedian and actor Aasif Mandvi, who appeared regularly on comedian Jon Stewart's *Daily Show* on Comedy Central. He was one of the "shining lights of Muslim comedy in...America today."

Other "heroes" were Democratic Rep. Keith Ellison and Lesley Hazleton, a "friend and ally" and "erudite scholar."

Honorable mentions included Bob Pitt, a British blogger and former researcher to one-time London Mayor Ken Livingstone, known in British tabloids as "Red Ken." Pitt edited Islamophobia Watch. Another honoree was liberal *Democracy Now!* host Amy Goodman.

Keeping the moment alive, somebody started an anonymous Facebook account, "StopIslamophobiaNow," connected online to StopIslamophobia.com. It liked the Facebook page of hip-hop mogul Russell Simmons and the anonymous account Americans Against Islamophobia.

* * *

Behind the scenes, Iranian American author Reza Aslan was supporting LoonWatch to change the media narrative on Muslims, but things weren't going as he hoped. He was stressed. He had scored a victory in his vision to create a multimedia empire through the company he had cofounded, BoomGen Studios. The Learning Channel had bought a reality series he had created, titled *All-American Muslim.*

But, in December 2011, the Florida Family Association, an ultraconservative Christian evangelical organization, launched a boycott campaign of the program. Days later, home improvement superstore Lowe's announced it was withdrawing its advertisement of the program. "We based our decision to pull the advertising on this research after hearing the concerns we received through emails, calls, through social media and in news reports," Lowe's said in a statement.

A campaign kicked in to counter the protest, with CAIR at the helm. Melissa Ramoso, a staffer for Democratic California state senator Ted Lieu in Redondo Beach, California, reached out to local CAIR executive director Hussam Ayloush, asking for a list of organizations and public figures that supported Lieu's demand that Lowe's apologize to American Muslims for withdrawing its advertising. (In December 2021, city council members in Artesia, California, outside Los Angeles, elected Ramoso the city's first Filipino female mayor.)

Defending the program, CAIR Chicago's Ahmed Rehab posted a column on his personal website against the "loons" who opposed the show. Writing in the headline "Let's Face it: It's the Radical Right, not Islam, that is the Greatest Threat to the American Way," he featured a stock image of a man in a suit with a yellow Jewish star of David on his lapel, reminiscent of the star of David that Nazis forced Jews to wear during the Holocaust, only this star had the word "MUSLIM" across it and a crescent moon, symbol of Islam, beside the Jewish star.

That same day, "Admin" reprinted the article on IslamophobiaToday.com, with the same headline and image of the man with the Jewish star with "MUSLIM" and the crescent moon.

The next day, writing as "Emperor," Rehab posted the same column on LoonWatch, with the same exact headline and graphic, as well as a positive endorsement: "One of the most thorough and insightful pieces regarding the Lowe's fiasco and the Muslim reality show, All-American Muslim."

Rehab had literally created an echo chamber.

The next day, in a media phone call with Aslan and cast members, a reporter for the Christian progressive magazine, *Sojourners*, noted that some critics had called the show "propaganda."

"I wondered if the cast members could explain how is this not propaganda? How is this just real life?" she asked.

A Muslim high school football coach said, "This is our lives. This is what we do. There is no propaganda behind it."

Aslan stepped in and said, "What they mean by propaganda is that it does not jive with their ideas about Muslims."

I wrote a column for the *Daily Beast* that I understood why Lowe's had pulled its advertising. It wasn't about "Islamophobia." The show simply wasn't that interesting.

At 6:33 that evening, I got an email from Aslan. He wrote, "Another truly pathetic example of your desperate contrarianism and need for sensationalism." He said I'd "aligned" myself with the "most despicable hate groups in America." He added, "Oh but certainly you know better than they what is and what is not Islamophobia. I hope you get a little thrill every time that Pamela Geller quotes you now in her email blasts. You've become her favorite Muslim. Truly pathetic, Asra."

I responded politely.

The show was soon cancelled.

* * *

The NYPD was under attack by Linda Sarsour and other activists trying to curtail their surveillance capabilities.

I wrote a piece for the *Daily Beast*, with a provocative title that my editors had put onto the story, "Why NYPD Monitoring Should Be Welcome News to U.S. Muslims," but with nuance in the piece, arguing that of course we cannot tolerate harassment, intimidation, or discrimination by law enforcement or intelligence, but something called surveillance against any extremist threat was necessary.

Days later, in early March 2012, an emerging academic, Haroon Moghul, published a critique of my work. Then, "Admin" posted the story at IslamophobiaToday.com with the headline "Asra Nomani in the Daily Beast: Spy on White People."

Muslim reformers interfered with the lucrative narrative of victimhood that the Honor Brigade perpetuated to win important grants. Around then, Soros gave new funds to New America, a liberal outfit established in 1999 with an annual revenue of about $37.9 million in 2016. New America's second president was Steve Coll, a journalist and Columbia University professor who had written the book, *Ghost Wars*, documenting in painstaking detail the twists and turns of Muslim radicalization during the war against the Soviet Union in Afghanistan. New America took the money and much more later, even though its foreign policy chief, Peter Bergen, knew better. After the 9/11 attacks, Bergen had actually interviewed Osama bin Laden. Bergen understood the ideological imperative for radicals.

According to publicly leaked documents from his philanthropy, Open Society Foundations, Soros spent at least $750,000 to challenge a supposedly disproportionate counterterror focus on Muslims in a new initiative, "Rights-Based Counterterrorism." The project including hiring Rabia Chaudry, an attorney, as a fellow. She was supposed to represent Arabs, Middle Easterners, Muslims, and South Asians, a community that earned the clunky acronym "AMEMSA."

At one event, she advised policymakers to ignore progressives and listen instead to fundamentalist Muslims with more credibility with radicals. New York University School of Law's Brennan Center for Justice received at least $112,000 from George Soros and his Open Society Foundations to challenge the "anti-mosque movement" and "fight against Sharia and foreign law bans."

* * *

Meanwhile, activists like Linda Sarsour and Khaled Beydoun used their propaganda channels to press their arguments, assigning Muslims to a race assaulted by "racism," with columns like one they published on Al Jazeera headlined "Trayvon Martin: The myth of US post-racialism."

Martin was a seventeen-year-old whose life was cut short by George Zimmerman, a zealous neighborhood watch vigilante in Sanford, Florida. Martin became a weapon in their demonization of a racist America. In response, three "radical black organizers," as a sympathetic profile later described them—Alicia Garza, Patrisse Cullors, and Opal Tometi—established a "black-centered political will and movement building project," called #BlackLivesMatter.

Islamists long had a close relationship with Marxists. For the "new paradigm" to take place, Marxism had to establish firmer roots in the capitalist West. Billionaire George Soros pumped money into supporting their cause, both on race and economics, establishing in 2010 the Institute for New Economic Thinking based in New York with Soros as a cofounder.

Later, Black Lives Matter founder Cullors was installed as an "expert."

Cullors explained, "We actually do have an ideological frame. Myself and Alicia in particular, we're trained organizers. We are trained Marxists. We are super versed on ideological theories."

In their piece, Sarsour and Beydoun wrote that Martin's "rush for safe haven was intercepted by Zimmerman." They blamed "the structurally entrenched demonisation of Black men codified in our laws, perpetuated by our police forces and subscribed to by our friends and colleagues, classmates and family members."

Their talking points were now well-tested, as they said the same thing many different ways, blaming "the structural racism" that is "embedded in police departments and penal systems nationwide," the country's "institutional racism," racism as a "salient core of the US' history and present," "American racism" that is "interwoven into the country's narrative, codified in its law and entrenched in its institutions," its "authors and gatekeepers...still largely white." Ironically, Zimmerman was Hispanic not white.

Quick with their simplicity, Sarsour and Beydoun asserted whites "seldom experience racism," but they used the opportunity to extend the grievance of racism to Muslims. A "racism-free utopia" was a delusion, they wrote, with "citizenship to this colour-blind state" denied to "African Americans, Muslim Americans and Latinos" because of a "virtue of a triumvirate of suspicions: crime, terrorism and illegal immigration."

And Sarsour and Beydoun drew the argument back to their core issue: the destruction of the state of Israel, lamenting the declining "value of Arab life—whether nameless Palestinian children bombed by American-funded fighter jets or American youth profiled."

They claimed Arab and Muslim Americans in New York were "connecting the dots."

Soon after their column ran on Al Jazeera's website, their piece was republished word for word on LoonWatch with the tags "Loon Violence," "Loon Politics," and "Loon-at-large."

* * *

Traveling in the Netherlands, young Palestinian American Ahmad Abuznaid heard the news of Trayvon Martin's killing and was angry. Born in East Jerusalem, Abuznaid had moved to the US with his family when he was one. His parents came from Hebron, where his father, Nabil Abuznaid, an American citizen, was a professor at Hebron University, and when Abuznaid was seven, the family returned to the West Bank. His father was an advisor to Yasser Arafat, founder of the Palestinian Liberation Organization. He had a photo of himself as a boy with Arafat bending down beside him, embracing him, smiling broadly with his cheek pressed against Abuznaid.

He later claimed in an interview, "The day we moved back, I flew into Ben Gurion Airport and was escorted through a separate process whereby my mother and I were taken to a back room and strip searched. As a seven-year-old boy being strip searched next to your mother...that obviously has a lasting effect."

He claimed that the experience generated "some form of self-hatred." When he returned home, he saw "parallels in different oppressions," hanging out with "all the Black and Latino kids," listening to rapper Tupac Shakur, and learning to be "unapologetic."

Armed with a law degree the year earlier from Florida Coastal School of Law, he got on a conference call with friends Phillip "Umi Selah" Agnew, a black activist, and Gabriel Pendas from Florida State University, where they were studying.

In 2019, Agnew would become one of the newest members of the Democratic Socialists of America. He'd get trained by the Rockwood Leadership Institute, a feeder program to liberal activism, including Agnew's future buddy, Andrew Gillum. The next year, he would announce on Twitter through his handle @iPhilSomething that he had joined the Bernie Sanders campaign as a "senior advisor."

At the first conference call, about 150 people joined them. Not long after, they marched for three days from Daytona Beach to Sanford, Florida.

In February 2012, they cofounded a new nonprofit, Dream Defenders, to train youth about Palestinian campaign strategy, "power mapping," mass incarceration, and the "school to prison pipeline." Later, they'd establish the Dream Defenders Action Fund, a 501(c)(4) lobbying organization. Abuznaid was the legal and policy director. In 2014, he attended the Students for Justice in Palestine national conference

In early January 2015, Dream Defenders would tour the West Bank. The roster would include five Dream Defenders: original cofounders Phillip "Umi Selah" Agnew, Abuznaid, Clara Taylor (then Abuznaid's girlfriend), and Steven Pargett (director of communications and culture), as well as Sherika Shaw (field organizer). Tef Poe and Tara Thompson, activists who organized the "Hands Up United" campaign in Ferguson, Missouri, joined. So, too, did a CNN celebrity: Marc Lamont Hill. Justice League NYC's Cherrell Brown and Carmen Perez took the trip, along with Black Youth Project's national director, Charlene Carruthers; poet and artist Aja Monet; Black Lives Matter cofounder Patrisse Cullors; and Syrian American journalist Maytha Alhassen.

In Nazareth, Cullors participated in a "flash mob" to support the BDS campaign. "From Ferguson to Palestine the struggle for freedom will continue," said one of the activists as the group slipped into the *debke*, a traditional Palestinian folk dance, as Carruthers and Agnew melodiously sang "Ella's Song." As they sang, the group danced hauntingly behind them, breaking into chants and jumping up and down, as locals watched arms crossed, ending with an embrace. "Group hug! Group hug!" one yelled.

That year, Abuznaid paid tribute on Instagram to controversial Palestinian activist Rasmea Odeh, convicted in the 1969 murder of two Israeli college students by the Popular Front for the Liberation of Palestine, or PFLP. He also posted a selfie with Odeh, calling her a "revolutionary, bad ass." He added the hashtags #JusticeForRasmea #FreeAllPoliticalPrisoners #Free Palestine.

Tweeting under the handle @YezzirArafat in 2016, Abuznaid launched a social media strategy against Israel. In March 2016, he promoted an educational curriculum series by Dream Defenders for sixth graders through eleventh graders, stating that Popular Front for the Liberation of Palestine leaders had built a "Palestinian Marxist-Leninist" organization, and they "want to be free from global imperialism," to build a "democratic socialist Palestinian state." It said, "They want equal rights, just like the Dream Defenders." In May, he posted an image of convicted Palestinian fighter Leila Khaled holding an AK-47 rifle, writing that "she taught us how to fight." Khaled was a leader in the Popular Front for the Liberation of Palestine and the hijacking of TWA Flight 840 in 1969 and El Al Flight 219 in 1970. That summer, he wrote on Facebook, "Stop Genocide in Gaza."

That year, he met his future wife, Shahd Abu Ishak, on the campus of Florida International University, when she spoke as part of a "Right to Education" tour of students from Birzeit University, outside Ramallah in the West Bank. The next year, they met again in the lobby of a hotel in Ramallah, when Abuznaid arrived as part of a Dream Defenders delegation to the West Bank.

The next year, in February 2017, he started working as director of the National Network of Arab American Communities, based in the Detroit area. That was the same place where Linda Sarsour had been the advocacy and civic engagement coordinator before her rise to the national stage.

Abuznaid's father was an advisor to the Palestinian Liberation Organization, and now the new generation had their eyes trained on US politicians to deliver Israel. Abuznaid endorsed Sanders because, he said, the Vermont senator was the "only candidate that is willing to take on Israel's racist government and its US lobbies."

CHAPTER 12

Hunting Masked Keyboard Warriors

In 2013, the Boston Marathon bombers accomplished something that Islamist powers and CAIR officials hoped would never happen: a mainstream Muslim actually acknowledging that radical Islamic preachers could sway Muslims to terrorism. It's exactly what a lot of progressive Muslims like Zuhdi Jasser, Raheel Raza, Naser Khader, and others had been saying for years. Of course, the vast majority of Muslims were peace-loving and live-and-let-live types. But it is patently dishonest—and dangerous—to pretend as CAIR and its apologists did that a murderous strain of Islam didn't exist in the world.

In the spring of 2013, Ruslan Tsarnaev was that mainstream Muslim. Fit and clean-shaven, wearing a polo shirt over jeans and flip-flops, Tsarnaev strode from the front door of his home in Gaithersburg, Maryland, a manicured suburb of Washington, DC, to the end of his driveway. Visibly angry, the muscles in his neck inflamed with just about every word he spoke.

His nephews had "shamed" their family by killing innocents at the Boston Marathon that past weekend. They had been "radicalized" as Muslims. And they needed to turn themselves in to the police.

Tsarnaev refused the defensive posture of denial from so many Muslim community leaders. The uncle had a completely different demeanor.

A reporter asked him what had motivated his nephews.

In words heard around the world in live coverage, he shouted, "They're losers!"

To his left, I asked a question: "Is your family Muslim?"

He paused for the slightest beat before answering. Yes, his family was Muslim. His nephews had been radicalized.

Tsarnaev offered the kind of honest acknowledgment that so many had wanted to hear from a Muslim, rather than PR sound bites like: "Islam is a religion of peace," "No Muslim would be violent," and "He may claim to be a Muslim, but he isn't a Muslim."

I published a *Washington Post* column headlined "Muslims have a problem. Uncle Ruslan may have the answer," calling on Muslims to "own up" to issues of extremism and follow the example of "Uncle Ruslan."

In just a few minutes, "Uncle Ruslan" had accomplished something that eleven years of post-9/11 press releases, news conferences, and sound bites by too many American Muslim leaders from the organizations spawned from 500 Grove Street had failed to do. With raw, unfettered emotion, he publicly owned up to the problem within. On the issue of radicalization and terrorism, he rejected denial and deflections.

"Uncle Ruslan" had said he realized his nephew, Tamerlan, had gone through some kind of transformation when Tamerlan started saying "Insha'allah" (God willing) regularly. The Chechnyan equivalent is "*Dalamuklah*," using the Chechnyan word for God, "*Dala*." Uncle Ruslan told me the use of the Arabic language made him wonder what was going on with his nephew.

I wrote: "What 'Uncle Ruslan' was admitting is something true but politically incorrect to talk about: the increasing use of these phrases of religiosity are code inside the community for someone who is becoming hardcore. It doesn't mean that they're becoming violent or criminal, but it's a red flag." I wrote "hardcore" intentionally.

The piece was well received by readers, who agreed with the need for a conversation based on acknowledgment of extremism. A reader with the ID "nuanced" wrote: "beautifully told story—thanks." Another reader wrote: "Ms. Nomani—wow. What a well-written, sensitive and informative piece. Your voice is a rare journalistic expression of plain honesty."

A professor of Islam in North Carolina was about to twist a few words in my 1,834-word column.

* * *

In the of wake innocents murdered in Boston, American Muslim leaders continued debating semantics. UC Berkeley alumnus Wajahat Ali wrote a *New York Times* essay about *The Rise of Al Qaeda*, a film that referred to the terrorists as "Islamists who viewed their mission as a jihad."

He shared it on social media, tagging Palestinian American activist Linda Sarsour and Pakistani American professor Hussein Rashid and asking for their thoughts.

Sarsour responded: "Yo—its mad wack. A regular John Doe ain't gonna know the difference. Smh," an acronym for "shaking my head."

"Couldn't they just say violent extremism? I don't know. I ain't feeling it but I am trying not to be a troublemaker. I am laying low. LOL," Sarsour continued.

Yet in that climate of laying low, Uncle Ruslan had dared to step forward.

* * *

Caner Dagli, a professor of Islam at the College of the Holy Cross in Worcester, Massachusetts, scolded me via email. "I am very disheartened by your repeated public stance on the Muslim community's responsibilities when it comes to the violent acts of some of its members," he wrote.

He recommended I read *The American Muslim* by editor Sheila Musaji and follow the #MyJihad social media campaign started by Ahmed Rehab, executive director of CAIR Chicago. "Read Scott

Atran," an American French cultural anthropologist who started his career as an assistant to anthropologist Margaret Mead, an icon in the field, Dagli advised. Rehab lauded Atran's recent testimony to the US Senate, saying, "Jihad is an egalitarian, equal-opportunity, employer: fraternal, fast-breaking, thrilling, glorious, cool—and persuasive."

The attacking confluence of rudderless social media journalism and extremism began the early morning of the next day. Hena Zuberi, editor in chief of MuslimMatters and a reporter at *Muslim Link*, a community newspaper in College Park, Maryland, misrepresented my article in a posting on Facebook.

"Asra Nomani—taking all that was amazing about Uncle Ruslan and sopping it yucky. Readers beware if you have started saying inshaAllah or giving salawat on the Prophet it could be a sign that you are 'radicalized'. I am not going to post her article whoever wants to read it can find it themselves," wrote Zuberi, who studied at AlMaghrib and contributed to MuslimMatters, both known to espouse the hard-line Salafi interpretation of Islam.

At 4:08 a.m., conservative MuslimMatters contributor Zainab Kathrada, popularly known as "AnonyMouse," wrote this time as "Zainab bint Younus," and said, "*Gag* *Vomit* I can't let myself look for it or I'll spend the whole day in red-eyed rage." She was the writer who was the daughter of the controversial preacher Younus Kathrada.

Later that day, Imraan Siddiqi, the CAIR Arizona staffer who had devoted an "Islamophobia" blog to attacking Muslim reformers and the state of Israel, twisted my words on "Inshallah." The truth didn't matter. It was the best of "RUMINT," or "rumor intelligence." It can be a strong vehicle for propaganda—and smear campaigns.

* * *

That weekend, Omid Safi, a professor of Islam at the University of North Carolina at Chapel Hill, pushed the publish button on a snarky blog at Religion News Service, headlined "5 dumbest things said about the Boston Marathon: Fox News, Asra Nomani, (some) Republicans." He alleged I had used special "access" to the media to publish my articles, claimed I was in "alliances with the most vicious of Islamophobes," and misquoted my *Washington Post* column in ways that made my argument seem quite laughable even to me. Misidentifying me as a "Muslim journalist for Washington Post," he claimed I was asserting that "use of phrases like 'God-willing' is a sign of radicalization."

Born in Jacksonville, Florida, in 1971, Safi had grown up in an immigrant family from Iran. After his father, a graduate of Tehran University of Medical Sciences in Tehran, served a residency at Howard University in Washington, DC, Omid's family moved to Iran. In 1979, he was in third grade when the Iranian Revolution's Ayatollah Khomeini brought a hard-line theocracy to Iran, throwing out a military dictator, Shah Reza Pahlavi. Years later, in a profile in the *Charlotte Observer*, journalist Yonat Shimron wrote that "like his classmates," Safi "was thrust into the streets shouting, 'Death to the Shah.'"

Many of Safi's classmates volunteered as child soldiers and died during the Iran-Iraq War. When Safi was fifteen, in 1986, his father, then a pediatrician, returned his family to the US. Safi went to Duke University in Raleigh, North Carolina, for his undergraduate degree, launching the local chapter of the Muslim Students Association.

Safi wrote to "ridicule" his targets, including me, for our "idiotic ignorance," and he was getting important attention. Religion News Service was affiliated with the highly respected University of Missouri Journalism School and funded by the Lily Foundation. Safi had a blog, *What Would the Prophet Muhammad Do?*, on the site.

Attacks against me followed on the comment board: "House nigger.... Enemy of American Muslims."

That night, Safi published another column, "Open Letter to Asra Nomani: Enabling Islamophobia," alleging I had forged "alliances" with "Islamophobes." He told me to read the work of a professor at Columbia University, Hamid Dabashi, to understand how I had become "a native informant."

"Read up on the history of the civil rights era, and see what people like Malcolm X said about people who enable this type of oppression. I won't use those words here, but I trust you know where to find them," Safi wrote.

One of his readers used the "words" in the comment board: "House Muslim."

Another, "JGandhi," alleged my son was the "bastard son to Daniel Pearl, again an extremist jewish zionist."

* * *

Born in Iran, Hamid Dabashi was friends with Safi. In 2006, he had published a scathing assault of Azar Nafisi, the Iranian American author of a profound book, *Reading Lolita in Tehran*, about a bold book club she had led with her students in Tehran. Dabashi had placed it in *Al-Ahram*, a large government-owned Egyptian daily newspaper founded in 1875. He wrote about "native informers turned comprador intellectuals," who provided "public consent to imperial hubris." Dabashi called Nafisi "the personification of that native informer and colonial agent."

Originally a term in anthropology, a "native informant" refers to someone who speaks about their own community. These academics had turned it into a smear akin to "traitor." Dabashi continued his attack on Nafisi. "If Edward Said dismantled the edifice of Orientalism, Azar Nafisi is recruited to re-accredit it."

* * *

Safi and others took advantage of the new rules of journalism and the internet, where there are virtually no rules, to stage their attacks.

Religion News Service editor Kevin Eckstrom admitted he exerted no control. "I've had to explain journalism to Omid," he told me, but allowed Safi to self-publish without an editor's review. "When they get edited, they don't want to write for us, so we let them publish their blogs without editing," he explained.

Activists and academics, such as Safi, had discovered a back door to publishing on the internet where the professional rules of journalism, like avoiding defamation and seeking comment from an article's subject, simply did not matter.

And this aberration of journalistic ethics wasn't because Religion News Service was a shoestring fly-by-night operation. Based at the prestigious University of Missouri Journalism School in Columbia, Missouri, Religion News Service was founded in 1934 by journalist Louis Minsky as an independent, nonprofit affiliate of the National Conference of Christians and Jews. And, over the years, Religion News Foundation operations have received about $16 million in funding from foundations. Its biggest donor is Lilly Endowment Inc., which has given it $13.3 million.

* * *

Soon enough, CAIR shared the Safi column on Twitter from its official account. It served its strategy to discredit Muslim reformers.

Safi's followers responded, calling me an "enemy of the Muslim community," "a Jewish Zionist," and "munafiq" (the Arabic term that means "hypocrite"). When I asked for evidence of the allegations against me, Religion News Service provided none and deleted the blog. But the damage was done.

* * *

The next evening, behind the wheel of our 2005 Ford Escape, heading east on Elden Street in nearby Herndon, Virginia, my stomach clenched in anguish as I drove my son home from basketball practice. We passed the buildings at 500 Grove Street in Herndon, where the International Institution of Islamic Thought was based, doling out millions of dollars since the 1980s to a labyrinth of organizations promoting the illiberal Islamist narrative here and around the world.

"They're terrorists of the mind," said my son, now ten years old, putting his hand on my shoulder, trying to comfort me.

* * *

CAIR posted a link to Omid Safi's column on its Facebook page. Hamdan Azhar, the Penn State alumnus who had posted a death threat against me on Muslim WakeUp, "liked" the CAIR post.

Amid the backlash, Religion News Service news editor Kevin Eckstrom deleted the "Open Letter to Asra Nomani" on his website.

But the Honor Brigade wasn't going to let the campaign die. The next day, CAIR Chicago's Ahmed Rehab used his "Emperor" fake name to repost the "Open Letter" on LoonWatch.

The slurs shot out one after the other. *Munafiq*. "Pretender scum." One of the "Uncle Toms of the American Muslim community." One of the "complete tools of the Islamophobia Hate Industry."

The next day on Twitter, College of the Holy Cross professor Caner Dagli wrote, "@AsraNomani is such an ambulance-chaser. She doesn't even realize Ruslan's denial of Islam as a cause totally undercuts her own argument."

Huma Yasin, a Muslim attorney in Oklahoma City, @Humie924, wrote, "@Caner_K_Dagli as a lawyer I'm offended by charac as 'ambulance chaser.' I'd happily embrace AC's over her—she's much worse. #15minoffame."

Brandeis professor Joseph Lumbard responded by calling me a "presstitute."

Then, RizwanX @caringsoul786 tweeted the Safi "Open Letter" with the message: "stop being a #HATER of #ISLAM #MUSLIMS." He described himself as "a liberal Muslim who is intolerant of Haters...if you dare mess with Islam, I will BUST U UP FOOL :) You have been warned."

Early the next morning at 8:45, Lumbard tweeted, "Thorough accounting by Omid Safi on the ways of @AsraNomani."

Three minutes later, a young Pakistan American man, Zaid Jilani, ridiculed my protests over being misquoted, tweeting out, "Asra Nomani claims that people are criticizing her because she's a woman." I had debated Jilani years earlier on RTV, Russia's propaganda channel in the United States, over my support of the New York Police Department's surveillance program of Muslim organizations, mosques, and individuals. He later apologized for his thoughtlessness as an oversight of his youth.

At 11:27 a.m., the young IT specialist Amir Sahib, Yasir Qadhi's devoted disciple at MuslimMatters and AlMaghrib Institute, turned to his fake "Ibn Percy" avatar to share the column on Twitter.

By evening at 8:58, Safi shared the "open letter" on Twitter writing, "This is what happens to those gullible in politics."

At 9:30 p.m., UC Berkeley graduate Wajahat Ali, the emerging writer, shared the link on Twitter.

A little while later, at 10:15 p.m., CAIR Arizona's Imraan Siddiqi shared the "Open Letter" with the message, "This Retweet = Endorsement." He was the blogger who had once disparaged me as an "agent provocateur" when I defended the hearings on Muslim radicalization chaired by Rep. Peter King.

Moments later, at 10:23 p.m., Ruth Nasrullah, a convert and one of the cofounders of MuslimMatters, shared the "Open Letter" with the message, "Right on."

* * *

The next day, the drumbeat of taunts continued. On Twitter, Imraan Siddiqi used his @CAIR-AZ handle on Twitter to share Safi's article, "5 dumbest things said...."

At 11:43 a.m., Zahra Billoo, the executive director of the CAIR San Francisco Bay Area chapter, shared the link from her Twitter account, writing (with a typo), "Powerfule: Open letter to Asra Nomani: Stop Enabling Islamophobia."

Joe Bradford, an American convert, suggested folks tweet me with their activities and an addendum, "Inshallah." He had studied at the University of Medina in Saudi Arabia, where AlMaghrib Institute and MuslimMatters cofounder Yasir Qadhi had studied, and he promoted scholars from the Hanbali school of jurisprudence.

The backlash spoke to two areas of serious concern: the deterioration of public discourse in America and our inability to have a conversation with critical thinking about Islam without being labeled an "Islamophobe."

* * *

Early the next morning, Yasir Qadhi acolyte Amir Sahib anonymously shared Safi's "Open Letter to Asra Nomani: Stop Enabling Islamophobia," this time on his Facebook page for "Ibn Percy."

A Facebook user, Asma Manejwala, responded, "She is a disgrace...."

That day, Amad Shaikh, the cofounder of MuslimMatters, posted a snarky comment on my Facebook page, attacking me.

On cue, in May 2013, Hatem Bazian published a list of Islamophobes with my name on it. He didn't return numerous calls seeking comment.

* * *

By the summer of 2013, former UC Berkeley student Hashmi had settled into a home with his wife on Westbrook Hills Drive in Syracuse. One day, he went on the website for IndieGoGo. He plugged in his email contact: Danios@LoonWatch.com. He used a fake name, "Danios from LoonWatch," to share big news on IndieGoGo, the web-based platform for raising money. He was going to write a book!

This time, he added a first name to his fake name, claiming he was "Steven Danios (aka Danios of LoonWatch)."

"I write for LoonWatch.com, a website that monitors Islamophobia," he wrote. "For the past few years, LoonWatch (LW) has been taking the fight to the Islamophobes, but we can't do it without YOUR help. The Islamophobes are heavily funded by right-wing millionaires and billionaires, BUT with the power of social media—and YOUR help—we can raise funds of our own. Take a stand against Islamophobia and CONTRIBUTE to our IndieGoGo campaign." He promised donors an advanced copy of his "upcoming" book, *The J Word: Jihad, Between Hype and Reality.*

"Who is Danios of LoonWatch?" he asked.

He mentioned his Brass Crescent Awards from former Obama administration official Shahed Amanullah and acknowledged, "Due to a busy schedule, I 'disappeared' from LoonWatch in 2012 (much to the delight of the Islamophobes)...but, now I'm back and ready to pick up where I left off."

He continued with his deceit until it came time for his "disbursement_account_name," according to IndieGoGo documents. Hashmi wrote the information down fully, including his middle initial: Javad T. Hashmi. He added Bank of America as the disbursement bank, plugging in a bank account number in his name. The phone number for the disbursement was registered to Hashmi. The account holder's date of birth was July 16, 1982, Hashmi's birthday. The "disbursement account address" was Hashmi's address on Westbrook Hills Drive.

The year before, in the fall of 2012, Hashmi had also launched a company, Jinn Systems LLC, using the same Westbrook Hills Drive address. In Muslim culture, a *jinn* is a word for a spirit that can be either good or evil. It's the word that is the inspiration for the English word "genie." Later, Hashmi registered jinnsystems.com, using an address on Crenshaw Court in Camillus, New York.

The "About Us" page said Jinn Systems LLC was a "Silicon Valley start-up comprised of a small group of physicians and computer hackers.

"They banded together to create Jinn," it said. According to the vision statement, physicians would use a voice-activated technology to file medical orders at a patient's bedside. "Jinn will revolutionize" the health information industry, the website promised. The founder and CEO of Jinn Systems was a "practicing physician," and while the company had the "best computer hackers helping us," the website pitch noted that Jinn was "physician-created."

Hashmi never got his business off the ground, just as he never published the book for which he raised money, but he was soon to pull off another jinn-like disappearing act.

* * *

To solicit donations for his fake persona, Hashmi got references from people who didn't care that they were vouching for someone hiding behind a fake identity.

One was Lesley Hazleton, a former journalist born in 1935 in England, based in Jerusalem from 1966 to 1979, when she moved to the US, settling in Seattle. She once described herself as "a Jew who once seriously considered becoming a rabbi, a former convent schoolgirl who daydreamed about being a nun, an agnostic with a deep sense of religious mystery though no affinity for organized religion." She has given numerous TED talks on Islam and written a book on the life of prophet Muhammad, also penning a blog, *The Accidental Theologist*. In 2010, the masked men behind LoonWatch had given her "honorable mention" recognition for its annual "Anti-Loons of the Year" award.

Hazleton had once noted: "Everything is paradox."

In the case of "Danios," she later told me, she allowed his identity to remain a paradox.

"I didn't know who he was," she said, in an interview. "I didn't ask."

Later that month, in late July 2013, the Muslim Matters sycophant Amir Sahib, writing as "Ibn Percy," circulated the LoonWatch IndieGoGo fundraiser details on his blog in an article headlined "Ever felt helpless when hearing certain individuals insult Islam & Muslims? Now you can do something about it!"

He wrote: "LoonWatch is probably the only site on the web that has single handedly defended Islam and Muslims against bigotry and hatred from individuals. These individuals are not different than the Osama Bin Ladens of the world. They both agree on almost everything regarding their ideological views on Islam. One of the famous writers of LoonWatch, Danios, has started a campaign to raise funds for his new book that will dispel myths about Islam being the most violent religion." Among his tags: "Islamophobia," "Islamophobe," and "Robert Spencer."

The next month, using its anonymous account on YouTube, a platform operated by Google, @LoonWatchTV posted a selfie video by author Reza Aslan endorsing the LoonWatch website and urging people to donate to the IndieGoGo campaign. In the video, "Reza Aslan: 'I love LoonWatch'" Aslan sat in the driver's seat of a vehicle with a black interior. He wore a dark-collared button-down shirt with white polka dots. His dark hair lined with silver, he looked into the camera with a slight smile and said, "Hey folks, Reza Aslan here…."

"If you know anything about me, you know I *love* me those Islamophobes."

He broke into a wide smile now, seemingly amusing himself.

"And I *love* LoonWatch, which tends to really bring out the crazy in the crazies on the far, far, far fringes of the right."

They went after much more than the "far, far, far fringes of the right," not that that would be appropriate anyway from fake accounts.

"So if you support LoonWatch, I suggest you go to IndieGoGo.com and help them with their campaign. They are doing a valuable service to all of us by bringing to light these roaches hiding in the dark corners."

The video cut to dramatic sound and "The time to act is now" across the screen, a man reading the words in booming voice-over.

The description of the video read, "Reza Aslan loves and supports LoonWatch. Do you? Contribute NOW to LoonWatch's IndieGoGo campaign…."

Within days, "Danios" raised $8,100. But he never wrote the book. Until now, nobody has ever known who was behind the fundraising.

* * *

Javad Hashmi had another cover he used: "1DrM."

That year, according to company documents, Disqus recorded an IP address of 173.51.158.104 for "1DrM," assigning it to him five times from December 10, 2012, through December 19, 2012, when he signed on at 8:30 p.m. The time was recorded precisely to the slightest fraction of a second: 2012-12-19 20:30:10.626741. Time stamps are often recorded to a fraction of a second so that they provide unique identifiers for events in which multiple users may be using a platform around the same time for activities like posting comments.

On LoonWatch, a reader said she was a former Muslim on the comment board. From behind the anonymity of his fake identity, "1DrM" would have none of it, calling the reader "scum" and one of many "losers suffering from an identity crisis and deeply seated inferiority complex raised by deadbeat parents who let the degenerate society raise them."

He revealed his homophobia, asking, "I mean, really, since when has homosexuality become the yardstick for the authenticity of religions anyway? What demented Eurocentric cultural rubbish!"

He railed against "Zionist Jews," "Yanks," and "Eurocentric trash" Iranians, sparing hardly anyone in his demagoguery and slurs.

A few days later, on December 23, 2012, Verizon assigned "1DrM" a new IP address, 71.118.209.21, he used 396 times over the next eight months. That day, he logged into his account at 2:02 p.m. and defended his anti-American views, writing, "Anti-Americanism is a fairly rational response to decades of American terrorism around the world."

This IP traced back to a Verizon subscriber located in either Chicago, New York City, or Ontario, California, in Southern California, east of Los Angeles. It was a geographically disparate set of possibilities, but "1DrM" now had a possible link to the West Coast.

He repeated the talking points of CAIR and the Honor Brigade, calling atheist scientist Richard Dawkins a "psychotic, empty, deeply pained man." For these dogmatic Muslims, the increasingly sharp critiques of atheist thinkers, such as Dawkins, toward Islam was like a fatal blow to their egos. They couldn't process the fact that the rebuke wasn't personal and atheists reject *all* religions.

Engaging in the dark social media tool of deceit called "sock-puppetry," Hashmi defended his own alter ego—"Danios"—saying that the blogger Robert Spencer would never have the courage to debate "Danios." As "1DrM," Hashmi attacked an Egyptian Coptic Christian, Usama Dakdok, who founded the Straight Way of Grace Ministry in Marble Hill, Missouri, after immigrating to the US in 1992. Once a student of Islamic law, he was now on a mission to "warn all Americans about the deceptive methods being used by Muslims that lead so many into the cult of Islam."

"1DrM" slammed him as "another Coptic crook making a fast buck."

He even ventured, "Some serious immigration reform is necessary to keep foreign con artists out of the country."

CAIR officials had Dakdok in their sights. On a website they would create—Islamobophia.org—CAIR officials would put him in their "U.S. Islamophobia Network" database, bragging that in October 2013, a Minnesota high school "rescinded approval" for a speech by Dakdok after "learning about his bias speech regarding

Islam and Muslims." The year before, CAIR had just protested a talk, "Infiltration of Islam in America?" that Dakdok was scheduled to give at Mansfield High School in Mansfield, Ohio, sponsored by the Mansfield North Central Ohio Tea Party.

In other posts, "1DrM" talked about "HasbaRat rubbish," a derogatory reference to *hasbara*, a Hebrew word for "explaining" something; *hasbara* has become a sarcastic term that's even made it to Urban Dictionary to describe a pro-Israel "Zionist" who is a propagandist. Hashmi went off on many tirades about "chauvinist Jews," degrading someone as a "typical Zionist liar" and calling someone else "another Zionist lunatic." At one point, he had argued that "Zionism is incompatible with life."

* * *

That Halloween—and 216 more times—Javad Hashmi logged into his "1DrM" fake account on Disqus from IP address 173.51.151.217. A reverse IP address placed the IP in either New York City, Newark, or Pomona, California, again on the West Coast, this time again between Los Angeles and Ontario. This time, he blasted the French as "gutter snipes," writing, "French 'culture' is disgusting, intolerant, primitive and deeply racist." In 2003, the equivalent of the Muslim Brothers in France had established an organization called Collectif contre l'islamophobie en France, or the Collective Against Islamophobia in France, and had been documenting alleged attacks against Muslims for years, raising the ire of American Muslims like Hashmi.

That night, Hashmi also slipped and revealed his profession, telling the story of a female patient, "back when I was a medical student," requesting a female physician. He wasn't offended.

Two months later, in January 2014, Hashmi used the IP address 71.118.209.179, associated with addresses in either Chicago, New York City, or Ontario, California, again. Later that month, he signed in using 71.189.229.102 in either New York City, Newark, or Pomona, California.

One time that month, he signed in using 71.104.228.209 in Los Angeles, Pomona, or New York City.

There was a pattern. He was either in the New York City area or the Los Angeles area. He wasn't using virtual private networks—or VPNs—that allowed users to use fake IP addresses, and he wasn't using technology that had his IP hopscotching around the world.

One evening in October 2014, about 6:45, "1DrM" signed in using the IP address of 172.249.179.166. Charter Communications Inc. assigned him this IP many times that he used his Disqus account to comment on blog posts online. In fact, 542 times. This time, the geolocation only traced this IP back to Los Angeles.

The next year, on March 30, 2015, "1DrM" used the IP address 76.172.82.76 right before midnight. He'd used it some 425 times. This time the geolocation of the IP address placed him in San Diego, just a few hours south of Los Angeles, close to the Mexico border.

He dropped another clue about being a physician, writing just past midnight on November 19 of that year, "You're talking to a medical doctor, fool…."

With the next breath, he typed out his hate for the "terrorist outpost" Israel.

Later that year, on December 15, "1DrM" was assigned the IP address 205.197.242.174, either in Chicago, New York City, or, in a turn of events, New Orleans, Louisiana. Sometimes, the IP geolocations threw a curve into the equation and only a subpoena of the records from the internet service provider could resolve the conflicts.

In 2016, "1DrM" was switched to a new IP address with a different series of numbers at the beginning than before. This one, 216.4.56,167, he used just once on April 6, 2016, at 11:04 a.m., located again either in Chicago, New York City, or San Diego. Again, one more time that day, he was assigned a similar IP address. By July 15, Charter Communications Inc. had given him a more stable IP address of 108.185.34.10, which the geolocator search engine said he used 431 times from only one place: Temecula, California, southeast of Los Angeles. He slipped and released another detail about his real identity, telling readers he had graduated from medical school.

Twice that month, his IP switched to 107.178.45.65 in either New York City or Cupertino, California, but the internet service provider wasn't the usual Verizon services. It was a local company,

Hurricane Electric LLC, a unit of CloudMosa Inc., based in Fremont, California—Hashmi's hometown (and also the hometown of his former fellow UC Berkeley classmate, Pakistani American writer Wajahat Ali).

* * *

Javad Hashmi was deep into his double life—and a makeover.

As an attending emergency physician at Athol Memorial Hospital outside Boston, he had not only continued his secret life as a troll and member of the Honor Brigade, but he had also been a fellow of medical ethics at Harvard Medical School's Center for Bioethics from 2014 through 2015. Then, he enrolled as a graduate student in theological studies at Harvard. In his bio, he stated he was interested in the "intersection between ethics, theology, and human rights"—an unbelievable combination considering the unethical life he was leading as a closet agent of disinformation. He said he was interested in "Islamic bioethics" and "believes Muslim physicians like himself must play a role in advocating for human and women's rights in the Islamic world." This was the same man who had spent the last decade targeting Muslim reformers advocating for human rights and women's rights. He claimed he was writing his first book, *Flogging for God: A Muslim's Call to Abolish Corporal and Capital Punishments.*

But the staff at Harvard Divinity School perpetuated his rebranding, publishing an article about how a "doctor's passion" led him to the school.

His new persona was in complete contradiction to the hard-line Salafi ideology he had been pumping out for years behind his anonymous accounts.

In his Harvard bio, he now inserted "Jay" as his middle name, and the bio stated, "In addition to his medical training, Dr. Hashmi holds bachelor's and master's degrees in Arabic & Islamic Studies from U.C. Berkeley and Harvard respectively."

He won a scholarship from the Islamic Scholarship Fund, in part funded by the network of Muslim nonprofits created by scholars affiliated with Muslim Brotherhood sympathizers in Northern

Virginia. Academic activist Hatem Bazian, Hashmi's former mentor at UC Berkeley, was a leader at the scholarship fund.

As "1DrM," he wrote a smear against someone as a "Zionism worshipping white christofascist high on armageddonist rapture fantasties."

By the time the summer rolled around the next year, "1DrM" had logged into Disqus from the IP address 172.115.77.39 some 222 times, with only one likely city for his location: Ontario, California, outside Los Angeles. His position hadn't shifted. He was still staunchly against Israel, gays, same-sex marriage, and Muslim reformers.

His last log in was on September 9, 2017, going into the Disqus portal at 7:02 in the evening, wearing his mask.

CHAPTER 13

Going After Ayaan Hirsi Ali

There was one woman the Honor Brigade truly despised: Ayaan Hirsi Ali, the Somali-born activist and author of a new book, *Heretic*.

In late March 2014, Brandeis University announced five recipients of honorary degrees that year. One caught the eye of the Honor Brigade: Ayaan Hirsi Ali, honored in part for her activism for women's rights as a survivor of female genital mutilation.

A few days later, a Jewish American writer, Richard Silverstein, published an article at a blog he edited, *Tikun Olam*, with the mission, "Exposing secrets of Israel's national security state," and he took issue with Brandeis University awarding "Islamophobe Ayan [*sic*] Hirsi Ali" an honorary degree.

He railed against Ali's "unfettered almost genocidal hate" and "murderous murmurings on Islam." He lamented that Brandeis president Fred Lawrence was "very close" to the American-Israeli Political Action Committee (AIPAC) and "the pro-Israel right," and placed Ali among "raging Islamophobes," "Muslim haters," and "pro-Israel hasbara," the smear for a "Zionist propagandist."

Based in Seattle and armed with a blog, Silverstein was a trusted ally of the Honor Brigade. He called himself a "progressive (critical) Zionist." Born in 1952 in New York City, Silverstein earned a bachelor's degree in Hebrew literature from the Jewish Theological Seminary, another bachelor's degree from Columbia University in Jewish comparative literature, and an MA in Hebrew literature from UCLA. In 2003, he left his job as a fundraiser at the University of Seattle to start blogging, with the intention of "exposing the excesses of the Israeli national security state." At the beginning, he wrote about Seattle restaurants, music, and culture. After Israel's 2006 war in Lebanon, he saw an increase in readers and started focusing on Israel in his writings. He befriended writers such as Philip Weiss of *Mondoweiss* and writer Max Blumenthal of The Electronic Intifada. In 2011, "Admin" at LoonWatch announced Silverstein was one of its "Profiles in Courage," an "ally and a friend of Loonwatch." His work "detailing the hate amongst extremist Zionists in Israel and their American counterparts has been significant and vital." He is "continuing the Jihad of Tikun Olam, 'repairing the world.'" LoonWatch had a link to his blog on its "blogroll" of recommendations.

Within hours, CAIR Chicago's Ahmed Rehab again took to his "Emperor" fake identity to republish the article on LoonWatch. On the comment board, physician Javad Hashmi chimed in as "1DrM" with his trademark slurs: "Big surprise. Brandeis was trying to promote con artist Asra Nomani several years ago as well. More evidence that Zionism is the main pillar of Islamophobia." (On my book tour in 2005, I had spoken at Brandeis, which hosts a serious investigative reporting center, and led a prayer of a small group of women and men.)

Four days later, CAIR dispatched one of its pro forma letters of complaint, this one to the Brandeis president. Like clockwork, Sarah Fahmy, a Brandeis senior and member of the Muslim Students Association, posted a petition on Change.org to demand Brandeis rescind Ali's honorary degree because of her "extreme Islamophobic beliefs" and "pure hate speech." The Honor Brigade machine kicked in, with the petition racking up 6,745 signatures.

The next day, Brandeis announced big news. It was rescinding Ali's honorary degree. "We cannot overlook that certain of her past statements are inconsistent with Brandeis University's core values," it said in a statement.

Within hours, CAIR communications official Ibrahim Hooper issued a press release cheering the news as "victory over hate" by a "unified community response." He alleged Ali "seemed" to "express sympathy" for Anders Breivik, the Norwegian right-wing extremist convicted for a 2011 mass shooting. She didn't.

CAIR's executive director, Nihad Awad, thanked the de facto deputized lieutenants in the Honor Brigade: the Brandeis Muslim Students Association; the Brandeis student newspaper, the *Justice*; blogger Richard Silverstein; Islamic Society of Boston imam Suhaib Webb; the Islamic Council of New England; and Brandeis professor Joseph Lumbard.

On LoonWatch, "Mooneye" reported the triumphant news that Brandeis had rescinded "Islamophobe Ayaan Hirsi Ali's honorary degree."

"Mooneye" wrote, "After a veritable social media storm, complaints from students at Brandeis University and a petition that quickly gathered 6,000 signatures, Brandeis has withdrawn its honorary degree offer to extreme Islamophobe, Ayaan Hirsi Ali."

LoonWatch hyperlinked to the Change.org petition.

While Ali's comments about Islam hadn't always been nuanced, she had said in her latest book she was "wrong" and moved to a more moderate place. As a victim of female genital mutilation and the target of death threats for her views, it seemed appropriate she had a process of reconciliation to go through to settle her thoughts on Islam.

Al Jazeera reported the victory, quoting CAIR's Hooper, representing "the nation's largest Muslim advocacy group," saying, "It is unconscionable that such a prestigious university would honor someone with such openly hateful views."

* * *

The next month, Ayaan Hirsi Ali had a project about to be released on an issue close to her heart: women and girls. She had narrated a powerful documentary, *Honor Diaries*, with interviews with leading women's voices, including Raheel Raza, the Canadian Pakistani writer, challenging crimes like female genital mutilation and forced marriage.

The producers were optimistic, but CAIR officials again used the tactics of "cancel culture" to deplatform the discussion of issues considered offensive to the Honor Brigade. At the University of Michigan, administrators cancelled a screening of *Honor Diaries* after protests from the Muslim Students Association and the Council on American-Islamic Relations.

The protesters used a social media hashtag campaign, #Dishonor-Diaries, to discredit the film. In early April 2014, they targeted a screening at the University of Illinois Women's Resource Center that Zainab Zeb Khan, a dynamic Afghan American clinical psychologist interviewed in the film, had spent weeks organizing. Born and raised in Chicago, she was a clinical therapist with a PhD in psychology, working with survivors of domestic violence. An artist, she was creating a new organization, MALA: Muslim American Leadership Alliance, to advocate for a humanist, creative expression of Islam. For now, she hoped to educate people about crimes against Muslim women, but orthodox Muslims in Chicago were blocking the documentary's airing.

Word got around among orthodox Muslims that Fox News host Megyn Kelly was doing a related segment. A like-minded Jewish American writer, Richard Silverstein, and Linda Sarsour declined invitations to go on the show. This time, Arsalan Bukhari, executive director of the CAIR Washington State chapter, advised keeping the CAIR name out of publicity for getting the movie showing cancelled. It wouldn't be good optics for a so-called civil rights group. The week before, CAIR Detroit chapter executive director Dawud Walid had similarly kept a low profile when *Honor Diaries* had been cancelled the week before in Dearborn.

Still, CAIR Chicago senior communications coordinator Agnieszka Karoluk went on Kelly's show to advocate for the cancelling of *Honor Diaries*. She dispatched a letter to the film organizers to put pressure on them.

She had one objective: Inshallah ("God willing") to stop the film.

Within a day, she had good news. The Women's Resource Center was cancelling the premiere.

"It was a nightmare," said Khan, who organized a successful substitute screening at a downtown Chicago theater. "They are using the same tactics of shame used to silence people in our traditional cultures. We can't allow it."

* * *

Meanwhile, across town, George Soros and his Open Society Foundations funded an effort to amplify the voices of apologists in the Boston Marathon tragedy. On the second anniversary of the marathon bombings, Open Society gave the Muslim American Society money to secure positive media. An ultraconservative group, it has seen five of its young congregants from Alexandria, Virginia, flee to Pakistan to join the jihad.

Within the Soros network, Shireen Zaman, director of a Soros funding intermediary, Proteus Fund, also assigned at least $150,000 to her former employer, the Institute for Social Policy and Understanding, whose policy director, Dalia Mogahed, an Egyptian American Muslim, argued violence by "white male Christians" was more threatening than Muslim "radicalization."

* * *

UC Berkeley instructor Hatem Bazian's organization, American Muslims for Palestine, launched an ad campaign on Washington, DC, Metro buses attacking "Israel's occupation" in the West Bank.

Blogger Pamela Geller responded with a new ad campaign that declared, "Islamic Jew-Hatred: It's in the Quran."

It wasn't subtle. It didn't account for historical context. But it was technically true: there were verses in the Qur'an that cast Jews as enemies of Muslims. On LoonWatch, "Amago" published another article, lamenting that Geller was "back" with a new "anti-Muslim" Metro advertising campaign.

* * *

That summer, "Jacob Hausner" published another article in the cause of the Honor Brigade, headlined "Racist Debbie Schlussel Smears Arab Environmentalist Known as the 'Green Sheikh,'" on the IslamophobiaToday website. He called Schlussel a "racist and anti-Muslim bigot." He defended the "green sheikh," Sheikh Abdul Aziz bin Ali Nuaimi.

Schlussel was born in Detroit to parents of Polish Jewish ancestry. She earned a BA from the University of Michigan and a JD and MBA from the University of Wisconsin-Madison. A columnist, she had written a *New York Post* column in 2003 detailing how the FBI was about to give an award to Imad Hamad, a Palestinian American previously targeted for deportation because of alleged ties to the terrorist group, the Popular Front for the Liberation of Palestine. In 1999, a federal judge had ruled that the allegations against Hamad were vague and uncorroborated. In 2007, Robert Mustaq John, a Muslim immigrant living in the Bronx, pled guilty to intimidation against Schlussel and was sentenced to four months in prison for sending her an anti-Semitic death threat and a photo of Daniel Pearl being beheaded.

He warned she would be next.

The next year, Mohamad Fouad Abdallah, a resident of Dearborn Heights, Michigan, pled guilty to sending Schlussel obscene anti-Semitic death, rape, and torture threats in the name of Hezbollah. He was sentenced to eight months in jail.

Now, the Honor Brigade had Schlussel in its sights.

The next day, writing as "Emperor," CAIR's Ahmed Rehab reprinted the article in its entirety on LoonWatch.

CAIR was running the two websites in lockstep with each other.

* * *

The strategy was clear—isolate detractors as "racists" to be discredited—but up-and-coming activist Linda Sarsour needed to establish her street credentials. Tragedy struck in August 2014 on the streets of Ferguson, Missouri, and extremist Muslims seized the moment. At MuslimMatters, the orthodox Salafi website, the editor, Hena Zuberi, jumped onto her soapbox to draw parallels between the lives of blacks in Ferguson and Palestinians in Gaza. She wrote that journalists were "arrested and tear-gassed—coincidentally, the same American-made tear gas used by the Israeli army."

"It was extremely twilight zone-ish seeing folks in Gaza sending Ferguson protesters tips and tricks on teargas via Twitter, but started making sense when according to a St. Louis County Police department press release the former Chief Timothy Fitch, along with law enforcement officials from across the United States, visited Israel to 'learn how Israel's police, intelligence and security forces prevent terror attacks,'" she wrote.

In the midst of riots, Phillip Agnew, one of the cofounders of Dream Defenders, wrote a Facebook post saying, "yes, #thankyouferguson for your Molotov," in support of protesters throwing Molotov cocktails during violent face-offs with police. Later that year, he said on Facebook, "I am not an activist. I am a militant."

Sarsour kicked into action, traveling to Missouri in October to speak with Arab and South Asian business owners. She arrived in St. Louis and was on the streets, one day in skinny jeans tucked into boots, a bright red blazer pulled over a white T-shirt, topped off with a black-and-white keffiyeh scarf, signifying support for the Palestinian intifada.

Later she claimed that "young black kids" were chanting "From Ferguson to Palestine, occupation is a crime."

She was writing her script precisely. Later, the Iowa State University "Archives of Women's Political Communication" wrote that Sarsour "helped organize the Muslim community response and Black Lives Matter protests, and has worked extensively with BLM since." She shouted into a microphone, fist thrown into the air, as a march staffer carried the microphone pack for her. She later provided the photo to Religion News Service, the website that had published the first allegations of "Islamophobia" against me the year earlier. Religion News Service had received a grant from Google and, ironically, an accompanying article it published on Sarsour was part of a series on "religious tolerance and combatting hate speech online, brought to you with support from Google." The reporter mentioned in the article that Sarsour was "chased down the street in September by a man who was later arrested for threatening to behead her," linking to the *Daily News* article that wrote about the white homeless man in her neighborhood who everyone knew as a drunk.

"It was the most beautiful thing," she later said in a Facebook Live video. "They were like, 'Where is Palestine?'

"It was one of the most beautiful moments of my life," she said, "to share the struggle of one people with the struggle of another people right here in the United States of America."

In a Facebook Live event, "Ferguson & Palestine," interviewing Sarsour, Andom Ghebreghiorgis, a candidate for Congress in New York's Sixteenth District, praised Sarsour's testimonial on how "power and hegemony" are "manifested across the world," with "intersections between them," raising issues about the "military industry complex" and its intersection with "forces around the world," from the Ferguson Police Department to the Israel Defense Forces.

* * *

For many decades, Muslim reformers have long known that there are "no-go zones" in most European capitals if you dare to be a progressive or a feminist, your hair uncovered or your legs bare. But this was a reality that Islamist sympathizers didn't want discussed.

Former CNN reporter Steve Emerson broke that rule in early January 2015 when he went on Fox News with host Jeanine Pirro and spoke about "no-go zones," saying, "They're sort of amorphous. They're not contiguous necessarily, but they're sort of safe havens. And they're places where the governments, like France, Britain, Sweden, Germany—they don't exercise any sovereignty, so you basically have zones where sharia courts are set up, where Muslim density is very intense, where police don't go in."

He continued: "There are actual cities like Birmingham that are totally Muslim, where non-Muslims just simply don't go in."

The Honor Brigade launched a campaign to mock Emerson. British Prime Minister David Cameron tore into Emerson, saying, "This guy's clearly a complete idiot."

But Emerson wasn't a "complete idiot." He was one of the world's experts on Islamic extremism in the West. He had erred with an overreach. Emerson's analysis conflicted with Cameron's appeasement of Islamists and Muslim extremists in the UK.

The damage was done. By Saturday morning, a host on *Fox & Friends* issued a correction. Pirro followed up with another correction. Certainly, as Pirro stated, census data from 2011 showed that only 22 percent of Birmingham citizens self-identified as Muslim, but the pockets where they lived were known among locals and Muslim reformers as "no-go zones." Later, in its "Fighting Hate Intelligence Report," the now-discredited SPLC published an article headlined "'No-Go Zones': The Myth That Just Won't Quit."

It wasn't enough to destroy just Emerson.

Anyone of "color" who got in the way also had to be smeared. For example, Republican politician Bobby Jindal subverted the narrative of the cult of "critical race theory." Born to parents of descent from India, he had risen in Republican politics to become governor of Louisiana. In early 2015, he spoke out against "no-go zones" in Europe, where Muslims dominated, threatening and bullying outsiders. That comment put Jindal in the crosshairs of the Honor Brigade, which wanted as little scrutiny as possible on these dangerous communities. The hit went to Arsalan Iftikhar, an attorney who had worked for years at CAIR as a staff lawyer before leaving to start a blog, branding himself as "The Muslim Guy." Iftikhar appeared on MSNBC's *Now with Alex Wagner* and said Jindal "might be trying to scrub some of the brown off his skin."

Jindal, followed by other conservatives, condemned the remark.

A spokeswoman for MSNBC told CNN, "We found this guest's comments offensive and unacceptable, and we don't plan on inviting him back."

* * *

That next year, "critical race theory" specialist Khaled Beydoun published an open letter headlined "Why Ferguson Is Our Issue: A Letter to Muslim America" in a religiously conservative Muslim publication, *Islamic Monthly*, and it was reprinted in a Nation of Islam website, Nation of Islam Research Group, promoting the controversial Louis Farrakhan. He argued Muslims needed to stand against "state-sponsored" and "structural" violence against "Black America."

"Dear Muslim America," he opened, "Ferguson is your issue. Ferguson is our issue. For a range of reasons that go well beyond passive commitment to civil rights or symbolic solidarity, Muslim-Americans are bound to Ferguson—and the shrill demand calling for an end to state-sponsored and structural violence against Black America—that reverberates from its embattled streets." The next year the article was published in the *Harvard Journal on Racial & Ethnic Justice*.

* * *

The Woke Army isn't without its detractors, especially among people concerned about the violence and divisions it stokes. One key tactic it has in buttressing the groups and people in its ranks is to use proxies to out-shame anyone who tries to call it out.

That's what happened in the fall of 2015 when the United Arab Emirates, concerned about growing Islamist influence potentially overthrowing its feudal heads of state, designated the Council on American-Islamic Relations and its sister organization, the Muslim American Society, "terrorist organizations."

CAIR turned to law professor Khaled Beydoun to publish a column in Al Jazeera, lauding CAIR as a "vital and vocal opponent" of "state-sponsored discrimination against Muslim-Americans," with "unapologetic" programs "eroding Islamophobia and defending Muslim-American individuals and institutions," post-9/11. The "terrorist" designation amounted to a "full-fledged assault" against CAIR by a "native state informant...deepening the stereotype" that Muslim civil rights groups were "subversive and anti-American," he wrote.

Of course, that's not what the United Arab Emirates alleged.

But facts didn't matter. The trump card was to play the victim. The terrorist designation would "embolden Islamophobic elements" in the US to express their "hateful rhetoric, and expedite draconian policies against Muslim-Americans."

He quoted Egyptian American Hussam Ayloush, director of the CAIR Greater Los Angeles chapter, alleging the designation would "fuel Islamophobia, and undermine the safety and well being [*sic*] of Muslim communities [in the United States] and around the world." Beydoun added the bracketed clause for emphasis.

Right on cue, that day, behind his fake name of "Emperor," CAIR's Ahmed Rehab posted the column on LoonWatch.

* * *

That fall, CAIR Chicago's Muhammad Tauseef Akbar, writing as "Garibaldi," reprinted a Canadian Broadcasting Corporation account on LoonWatch about a woman, Inas Kadri, in Mississauga, Ontario, from the Greater Toronto Area, or GTA, who had her *niqab*, or face veil, pulled off at a mall. The story was headlined "GTA woman has niqab pulled off in assault." In the comment section, another anonymous writer, "Ilisha," remembered a Muslim mother, Alia Ansari, murdered in Fremont, California, while wearing a headscarf. Police did not identify the murder by a Hispanic man as a hate crime.

An increasingly popular network of atheist thinkers represented one of the strongest challenges to the Honor Brigade's strategy of deflection and denial. They included neuroscientist Sam Harris, HBO comedian Bill Maher, writer Christopher Hitchens, and scientist Richard Dawkins.

As the Honor Brigade and its well-intentioned liberal allies undermined Muslim reformers as bigots, racists, and "Islamophobes," this small posse of key liberals challenged their fellow liberals to have the courage to oppose the illiberal ideas of Islamic theocracies and support the reformers. This was even more reason for the Honor Brigade to try to demonize the atheists.

At one point, "Guest" posted "original guest article" on LoonWatch by two writers, "Michael Ellwood" and "Tarik Abdallah," with little paper trail online related to these names. The headline read, "Strange Bedfellows: Extremists, Bigots, and the Quran." It featured a photo of Sam Harris with his eyes half closed, looking demonic. The writers equated Harris to the extremist group ISIS, saying both unfairly quoted verses in the Qur'an that sanctioned violence.

Writing as "Garibaldi," CAIR Chicago staffer Muhammad Tauseef Akbar posted the first comment, thanking the two writers for their contribution, writing, "Great article Michael and Tarik."

Elwood was a frequent commenter. There was little trace of "Tarik Abdallah" online, just @TarikAbdallah.

CHAPTER 14

Killing *Charlie Hebdo*

In the West, character assassination against critics of Muslim supremacy is only one tactic of attack. CAIR and its LoonWatch allies chased Robert Spencer from speaking engagement to speaking engagement to lobby event planners, Catholic archdiocese, and others to cancel the appearances of "an Islamophobe," usually with success.

Then, an attack in January 2015 gave fresh impetus to those who knew it was dangerous to not only call out Islamic terrorism by its name but also to refuse their cries of "Islamophobia."

One early day in January, two brothers rushed up the stairs of an ordinary office building on a quiet street in Paris. They leveled their submachine guns at the heads of cartoonists and staff members at the French satirical magazine *Charlie Hebdo*, slaying them in pools of blood.

"We have avenged the Prophet Muhammad," one of the men shouted.

Two days later, a gunman connected to the brothers killed four hostages, including Jewish clients, at Hyper Cacher, or "Super Kosher," a kosher supermarket in the Porte de Vincennes suburb of Paris. That week, many of the world's leaders, including controversial

Israeli prime minister Benjamin Netanyahu marched through Paris to chants of "*Je suis Charlie.*" Then-US president Barack Obama did not attend or send a high-level official.

That week, Brian Greenspun, a Hillary Clinton friend, wrote a column, "The time is now to root out Islamic extremism." He had asked her why she wasn't meeting the Israeli ambassador in the fall of 2009. He wrote, "I was just a bit reluctant to use the word Islamic when describing the radical terrorists who, as best I can tell, were brought to justice Friday morning by French authorities. The idea of tarnishing the name of one of the world's oldest religions by associating it with murdering thugs is not particularly fair or American. But, it is hard to ignore the fact that the people who are killing innocent people by blowing them up or gunning them down are Islamist fundamentalists. And that is what this world can no longer afford to do. Ignoring this problem will not make it go away."

The next week, I wrote a widely circulated essay for the Outlook section of the *Washington Post* titled "Meet the Honor Brigade: Silencing the Debate on Islam," about a group of academics, bloggers, community leaders, politicians, and others who attack anyone they believe criticizes any aspect of Islamic theology.

The "Honor Brigade" acted like a paramilitary force, engaged in not only the dark arts of propaganda and disinformation but also character assassination. "Garibaldi" responded to a query for comment, sent via the LoonWatch online form. He refused to reveal his true identity.

The Honor Brigade shamed its targets by overhyping "Islamophobia" with "Islamo-*faux*bia," while denying the seriousness of the radical threat of Islamism, or political Islam, and its ties to extremism. It weaved a cult of victimization into a narrative that blamed the ills of Islam on the West and asserted that efforts to reform Islam were plots by its enemies—particularly Israel and the Jews—to attack the faith. Its strategy was to scream loud enough to silence debate and demonize the other side.

* * *

As if Muslim extremists hadn't shocked the world enough, the Islamic State released a shocking twenty-two-minute video of Lt. Muath al-Kasasbeh, a Jordanian pilot, being burned alive in a cage.

The video proved the theology of the Islamic State was very much Islamic, despite protestations from the Honor Brigade. For Americans, soldiers in the Cyber Caliphate were close to home. The Salafi student of AlMaghrib Institute, Tarek Mehanna, was in prison for conspiracy to provide material support to al-Qaeda, providing material support to terrorists and conspiracy to do so, conspiracy to commit murder in a foreign country, conspiracy to make false statements to the FBI, and two counts of making false statements. His boyhood friend, Ahmad Abousamra, was still on the job as an Islamic State propagandist. Qatar-based Al Jazeera's footage in the United States was eerily similar in its anti-West mantra to that of the Islamic State propagandists. The soft propaganda of the Honor Brigade merged with the Cyber Caliphate of the Islamic State, putting Muslims on a conveyer belt to radicalization.

For months, President Barack Obama had been repeating the mantra of the Organization of Islamic Cooperation, CAIR, and the misguided American Muslims in his administration. He had made a point of saying the Islamic State was "not Islamic." Even allies in Europe weren't making that mistake. Obama had said "whatever ideology" fueled the group's barbarity. And later, at the National Prayer Breakfast, the president said Americans need to get off their "high horse" about religious extremism, invoking the Crusades, the Catholic Inquisition, and US slavery. He kept trying to argue that the Islamic State wasn't religiously inspired.

The twenty-two-minute propaganda film of the Jordanian pilot's murder told a different story.

The militants leveraged symbols from three sources—the Qur'an, the holy book of Islam; the hadith, or sayings and traditions of the prophet Muhammad; and historical fatwas, or Islamic rulings—and blended them with historical grievances and highly produced sequences incorporating battle scenes from Hollywood war movies to legitimize themselves as Rambo Muslims for jihad.

In the video, the Islamic State fighters were young men with runny noses that smear their ski masks, exploiting centuries-old grudges to justify their violence. They were, as former FBI agent Joe Navarro had told me, "wound collectors."

CAIR had issued a statement advocating for "separating the brutal actions of ISIS from the faith of Islam," but the Islamic State squarely planted itself within Islam, with fighters as *mu'mineen*, or "believers," a Qur'anic concept (23:1).

The answer to defeating the Islamic State, particularly in its propaganda and recruitment, rested not with denying the Islam in "Islamic State," but rather addressing and rejecting the interpretation of Islam propagated by the terrorist organization and other Muslim militant groups and promoting a culture of productive solutions and healing.

The video's themes moved from protesting "apostasy and treason" to promoting "the application of sharia," or Islamic laws. Protesting "the Jewish state," the video invoked the divine value of the land of "Philistine," or Palestine, with a reference to a mystical Qur'anic story in which the prophet Muhammad supposedly flew on a winged horse from Mecca to the now-contested Dome of the Rock in Jerusalem.

The video referred to the killing of Muslims "displaced from their homes" (Palestinians), "secret prisons" with "rotten smell" ("black sites"), "tracking the mujahideen" (drone attacks), and "assassinating their leaders" (Osama bin Laden, among others). It griped about the "invaders' troops on Muslim lands," like Afghanistan, and the "international coalition" to "stop the spread of the caliphate state," "raining the fire of death on people of Islam."

After almost four minutes of the diatribe, Lt. Muath al-Kasasbeh appeared in an orange jumpsuit, symbolic of another grievance: the detaining of prisoners in Guantanamo Bay, Cuba.

The mosque symbol alternated with the image of a flapping black flag, reminiscent of a dubious *hadith* of the prophet Muhammad that says an army of "the Mahdi," or "messiah," will come from Khurasan, a region in northern Afghanistan and eastern Iran, to claim Jerusalem. It's a key vision in Islamic eschatology, or the study of the apocalypse.

In the video, the flag of Israel was simply labeled "Jews." And the Islamic State invoked the grievance to "defend Al-Aqsa mosque," the mosque beside the Dome of the Rock, "and what belongs to the Muslims in Philistine."

Images flashed of burned children, followed by a fatwa by a fourteenth-century Islamic scholar, Ibn Taymiyyah—a rock star for extremist Muslims—who declared it "legitimate" for Muslims to fight Mongol Muslims on the grounds that they did not follow sharia.

After Muslim fighters "pray for them to become believers or call upon them to stop their aggression," they quoted Taymiyyah saying, it is "lawful jihad" to fight them.

As the young pilot was horribly, tragically, cruelly burned alive, a song broke out: "Inside your own home, the wars will be waged, only for your destruction and suffering, my sword is sharpened."

* * *

In Florida, CAIR executive director Hassan Shibly used his outside communications firm, Advocate Marketing PR, to write an op-ed that it was offering to place. The argument in the op-ed was that the media had to stop using Islamic State to describe the "ISIS death cult."

Center for American Progress released a second version of its "Islamophobia" report, this one called *Fear, Inc. 2.0*, financed by funding earmarked by George Soros's Open Society. Wajahat Ali had moved on to hosting a show on Qatar's propaganda network, Al Jazeera America.

* * *

As the Islamic State rose, the White House sponsored a summit on "countering violent extremism," without mentioning Islam. Muslim special-interest groups convinced President Obama to avoid mentioning Islamic extremism for fear of "offending" the very Muslim governments whose ideology supported extremism. The West's response to the threat of Islamic extremism had been a failure.

Inside the auditorium in the Old Executive Office Building, next door to the White House, the leaders of failed American Muslim organizations assembled: Muslim Public Affairs Council, the Islamic Society of North America, the Muslim Students Association. A young woman relayed updates to CAIR officials outside. Shahed Amanullah, the technology advisor at the State Department, sat near attorney-turned-playwright Wajahat Ali.

When Obama spoke at the end of the day, the event resembled a pep rally by the Honor Brigade.

* * *

Muslim reformers challenged the talking points of those who did apologetics for the Islamists.

After day three of the summit on countering violent extremism, I sat in front of the camera at the studio of CNN, near the US Capitol, wearing a bright red kurta, or tunic, to talk with CNN host Erin Burnett. The other guest was James Zogby, friends with Hatem Bazian at UC Berkeley and cofounder of the Arab Anti-Discrimination Committee. Across the TV screen read the headline, "NEARLY 100 CHRISTIANS ABDUCTED BY TERROR GROUP."

"Asra, the president of the United States says ISIS is a death cult, a criminal group. He is very specific to say that ISIS is not in any way Islamic. You say that is wrong. ISIS is Islamic. I know you have analyzed two of the most recent ISIS videos. In what way can you show us?"

"The sad truth is that the Islamic State is very much Islamic," I said, noting: "They are not just a death cult. They are an Islamic death cult."

Zogby shook his head in disagreement. "They are a death cult that uses Islamic language...." He winced and continued: "The question was should the president have called them Islamic? And the answer is no...."

* * *

On Electronic Intifada, activist Rania Malek published an article in early February 2015 with the headline "Israeli man describes Muslims as Nazis at far-right rally in Frankfurt."

The next day, writing under his fake name, "Emperor," CAIR Chicago executive director Ahmed Rehab reprinted the article on LoonWatch with a photo of the Israeli flag.

Rehab wrote that "for quite some time" LoonWatch had noticed the "prominent and intentional use of the Israeli flag by Islamophobes, mostly, but not limited to the Far-Right wing," including—he alleged—the English Defence League, Danish politician Geert Wilders, "rowdy anti-Muslim Texans," and the Pegida political movement in Germany, making the Israeli flag an "ubiquitous feature of many anti-Muslim/Islam rallies."

Among his tags: "Anti-semitism," "Israeli Flag," "Islamophobia," "Israel," and "Pegida."

* * *

In early February 2015, the Honor Brigade found just the tragedy to exploit when newlywed Deah Shaddy Barakat, twenty-three, a Syrian American dental student, answered the doorbell at the condo he had bought in the Finley Forest Apartments complex in Chapel Hill, North Carolina.

It was about 5:11 on the evening of February 10. An irate neighbor, Craig Stephen Hicks, forty-six, stood at the door. Hicks was known as a parking vigilante, flying off the handle when he couldn't find a parking spot.

Hicks complained, "You've got three cars in the lot, and I don't have a parking spot."

Barakat kept videotaping.

Hicks continued, "If you're going to be disrespectful towards me, I am going to be disrespectful of you."

Barakat asked him to leave.

Instead, Hicks pulled out a gun and shot and killed Barakat from the porch.

Behind him, his Palestinian American wife, Yusor Abu-Salha, twenty-one, also a dental student, and her sister, Razan Abu-Salha, nineteen, a college student, shrieked and begged for mercy. Hicks kept shooting, killing them.

Outside, a woman walking through the apartment complex dialed 911 and told the dispatcher, "I just heard gunshots...I heard kids screaming."

Hicks turned himself in to the Chatham County Sheriff's Office in nearby Pittsboro, North Carolina.

The murders were a tragedy. HumanizePalestine.com profiled their young lives. The site had started in July 2014 after the murder of a Palestinian boy, Mohammed Abu Khdeir, by three Israeli teenagers. Its site was designed to "honor the deceased as martyrs by bringing them back to life through their pictures, stories, art, and poetry," because "contrary to Western bias, a Palestinian life is no less valuable than the life of another." (In March 2022, the domain name was for sale $1,795.)

Barakat was a dental student at the University of North Carolina, a basketball fan, and a volunteer and fundraiser for Refugee Smiles, a nonprofit that provided dental aid to Syrian refugees in Turkey. Yusor had just graduated with a degree in human biology from North Carolina State University the year before and was planning to join her husband as a dental student at the University of North Carolina. The couple had just married in December 2014, and the family called them "lovebirds." Razan had started studying architecture and environmental design at North Carolina State University the summer before.

Deah's brother broke the news to Ahmed Al-Shehab, a member of the CAIR national board of directors, and he alerted his CAIR colleagues.

Quickly, Nihad Awad, CAIR's executive director, got on the road to North Carolina. His eldest son, Haithem Hammad, a budding photographer, took photos at a vigil.

Within hours, Muslim activists politicized the tragedy, seizing upon a statement by the father of the two sisters calling the murders "a hate crime." It was completely understandable for a family to reach for any answers to the inexplicable act of murder. But the anti-"Islamophobia" machine that kicked into operation in the hours following the murder revealed the troubling reality of the network of organizations, academics, and activists that had emerged over the past decade to reactively allege racism—and "Islamophobia."

Just a little over twenty-four hours later, ReThink Media, based in Berkeley, California, with offices in Washington, DC, and generously funded by liberal donor George Soros's Open Society, circulated "talking points," including a social media graphic for clients and others to post, with the message, "END Hate Speech. END Hate Crimes," above the profiles of two women in headscarves and a man, depicting the three North Carolina victims.

A Facebook post noted: "Please use this image, approved by the family, if you are going to a vigil."

ReThink Media staffers scoured Hicks's Facebook page, looking for hate. They pointed to posts he had made on Facebook, calling himself an "anti-theist" and supporting "Atheists for Equality" and "Freedom from Religion Foundation." On one post that they highlighted, he wrote, "Praying is pointless, useless, narcissistic, arrogant, and lazy; just like the imaginary god you pray to."

With the jury still out on the Chapel Hill murders, the anti-"Islamophobia" machine had already reached its own verdict, employing the hashtags #MuslimLivesMatter and #ChapelHillMurders to punctuate a campaign that called the alleged murderer a "White Terrorist." It added more fuel to the debate on Islam and Muslims. President Obama had just harkened back to the Christian Crusades of the eleventh century at the National Prayer Breakfast the week before to argue extremism isn't the monopoly of any faith.

A little after 7:00 the next morning, CAIR spokesman Ibrahim Hooper sent me an email with a thinly veiled accusation against me for hate against Muslims writing, "You give ammunition to Islam-haters..." with a link to an article about the murders.

* * *

In the hours that followed, writers, bloggers, leaders, activists, and ordinary Muslims vested in the anti-"Islamophobia" machine scrambled to speak to this narrative of "hate" against Muslims in a day of frenzied, frenetic activity. In a corner of NBC News studios in

Washington, DC, being interviewed for a web show, *Road Map*, I listened through my earpiece as Muslim American comedian Dean Obeidallah asserted the media was engaging in "a double standard" for not calling the murders an act of terrorism.

Twitter user @iBinThaleth, claiming to be in Dubai, called the murders "an act of terror."

With some writers, including one at Muslim Matters noting Hicks espoused atheism on social media, Muqtedar Khan, a professor of Islam at the University of Delaware, published an essay, "New Atheists and the Same Old Islamophobia."

Ali Abunimah, the Chicago-based editor of Electronic Intifada, the website that promotes the cause of Palestinians while dubbing critics "Islamophobes," wrote: "Relentless hate, suspicion & collective scapegoating that's NORMAL in US & getting worse takes its toll. Hit home today. #ChapelHillShooting."

Not long after, Hatem Bazian, director of the UC Berkeley's Islamophobia Research and Documentation Center, shared a link to the 2011 report, *Fear Inc.*, written by UC Berkeley alumnus Wajahat Ali and published by the Center for American Progress.

The Honor Brigade's disinformation machine kicked into gear despite evidence presented all day long against the murders being a "hate crime," albeit a truly tragic and horrific travesty. A man with a history of mental instability in the community, Hicks had shot and killed the three young adults after a year of obsessive campaigning against neighbors who took parking spots not assigned to them.

A neighbor told the *Los Angeles Times* that Hicks made "everyone feel uncomfortable and unsafe," noting, "He had equal opportunity anger toward all the residents."

Even Abdullah Antepli, the Muslim chaplain at Duke University, said at a press conference "this may or may not be a hate crime," and the US Attorney Ripley Rand said police and prosecutors didn't believe the murder was part of "a targeted campaign against Muslims."

* * *

This was the perfect moment for the new enterprise that John Esposito and the Muslim Brothers at 500 Grove Street had been cooking up at Georgetown University. On the third floor of Healy Hall in the President's Room, Esposito welcomed guests for the launch of the Bridge Initiative.

"Born out of recognition that the age of the Internet—with its democratization of communications—presents unique challenges and opportunities for those seeking to educate the public and inform popular culture," The Bridge Initiative assembled "faculty, subject-matter experts, and researchers" to "examine attitudes and behaviors towards Muslims," "dissect public discourses on Islam," "uncover the operational mechanisms of engineered Islamophobia," and "develop and disseminate alternative narratives that raise public awareness and enrich public discourse on this dangerous form of prejudice."

They also assembled propagandists.

At the inaugural "Conversation on Islamophobia," a new man on the scene in America held court. He was Al Jazeera host Mehdi Hasan, newly based at the Qatar propaganda channel's Washington, DC, offices. Born in 1979 in the UK, to parents from India, he enjoyed an exclusive educational path, graduating from the University of Oxford in 2000. From the minority Shia sect of Islam, he held regressive views, once calling non-Muslims "cattle," later only saying his comments were "ill-judged." Rising in British media to a position at the BBC, he got a job as a host on Al Jazeera in May 2012. The next year, putting on his trademark snarky, feisty front, he helped his team win a debate at the Oxford Union that Islam is a "religion of peace." He'd just moved to the United States, and he had arrived just in time for the next stage in the fight. Donald Trump was running for president of the United States. And they needed someone to challenge him without mercy.

Inaugurating the Bridge Initiative, he acknowledged his "good friend," Nathan Lean, sitting in the back of the room, and lauded him for combating "Islamophobia" in "tweet form." They were united in the cause of apologetics for Qatar and its brand of dogmatic Islamism.

The challenge was monumental: the ideas of Islamism were admittedly regressive. How would Mehdi Hasan and Nathan Lean craft their messages to win sympathies in America?

Also on the panel were Anne Norton, a professor of "Muslim political thought" at the University of Pennsylvania with a research interest in "colonialism" and "post-colonialism," and Roland Schatz, founder of Media Tenor International, a global communications firm that touted itself as a "leading media institute," established in 1993 with a specialty in "applied Agenda Setting Research." A longtime pal of Esposito, Schatz worked in lockstep with his friend over the next years to spread his message from the campus of Georgetown to rented space at the Newseum. Now, he declared he was angry that the world's politicians had marched in support of the slain cartoonists at *Charlie Hebdo*.

"*Je ne suis pas* Charlie Hebdo!" he proclaimed, to a burst of applause.

The answer to the question lay in using the rhetorical language of "colonialism" to guilt the West, especially liberals in the West, about their "structural," "anti-Muslim racism." They weren't there yet, but they were on their way.

* * *

A journalist for ThinkProgress, the propaganda arm of the Center for American Progress, which published the *Fear Inc.* report, interviewed Muslim mothers about fears they felt and warnings they were giving their children. I told the reporter I wasn't feeling any fear for my son for "hate crimes," but I warned him about facing off against anybody with the parking equivalent to road rage.

After finishing the interview, I boarded a Vamoose bus for New York City with my son behind a Muslim mother, her hair covered in a tight headscarf, and her two young children, for a quiet, uneventful ride to Manhattan.

CHAPTER 15

Waging Character Assassination

A critical tactic of the Woke Army and its subset, the Honor Brigade, is silencing debate—most often by coordinating AstroTurf outrage with character assassination.

In the spring of 2015, the University of Michigan was about to host the film *American Sniper*, about US Army sniper Chris Kyle. Suddenly, an Arab American Muslim student complained that the film "offended" her. The Muslim Students Association said that the movie was "hurtful" to Muslims and Arabs. The University of Michigan football coach, Jim Harbaugh, was one of the few people with the courage to push back. With his dissent, the University of Michigan reversed its position and said it would allow the film's viewing and show the animated children's film *Paddington* at the same time elsewhere on campus.

In early April, organizers of a conference on women and gender at the University of South Dakota defied pitched protests to screen the documentary *Honor Diaries*. The controversy has been "very upsetting," wrote Miglena Sternadori and Cindy Struckman-Johnson, the event organizers, and the controversy underscores the battle over whose voices are "authentic," they said.

* * *

Across the country, I experienced a similar flip-flop by officials at Duke University. After a South Asian group, Diya, invited me to speak at Duke on "The Paradox of Women in Islam," I got a call that my speech had been cancelled. The Muslim Students Association president, Shajuti Hossain, a Duke economics senior, had spoken with Omid Safi, by then director of the Center for Islamic Studies at Duke, and Adeel Zeb, Muslim chaplain at Duke, and she sent an email to the Diya organizers: "Thanks for sharing the upcoming event you are hosting with Asra Nomani. We are uncomfortable with directing people to this event because of Asra Nomani's straightforward alliance with many Islamophobic speakers (Robert Spencer, Ayan [*sic*] Hirsi, Bill Maher, Sam Harris), as condemned by Omid Safi, the Director of Duke Islamic Studies Center, in an open letter."

She was referencing the "open letter" Safi had written two years earlier at Religion News Service, ordering me to "stop enabling Islamophobes." He alleged I had "alliances," the same word the MSA president was now repeating, "with the most vicious of Islamo-phobes."

The Diya organizers were stunned. They told the assistant director in the Duke Center Activities and Events; she recommended that they cancel the event. The group's internal affairs president said, "We were exhausted and didn't feel like we could handle a confrontation. We know we did the wrong thing, and we apologize."

That weekend, as if on cue, I was smeared on Facebook as "a native informant" by Amad Shaikh, the Pakistani American cofounder of MuslimMatters, working in Doha, Qatar. On Twitter, he said that he would "go after" folks like me. He posted a link to a reprint of Safi's attack on me from two years earlier.

After I protested and sent Duke officials a copy of my *Washington Post* op-ed on the Honor Brigade, Duke reversed its position and reinvited me to speak. When I arrived, the student organizers were welcoming and humble, but I received a cold shoulder from Duke. There were twelve people in attendance, including my parents and son.

As I stood on the stage, a wireless microphone clipped onto my pink kurta, no barrier between the audience and me, I looked out past the stage lights and said, "There are many who want to make us invisible. But I am standing here today because I believe that, if we try, we can be invincible."

My Duke experience went beyond feminism to a broader debate over American Muslims responding to critical conversations on Islam with snubs, boycotts, and calls for censorship, exploiting feelings of conflict avoidance and political correctness in event organizers and prompting event cancellations.

We had to stand up for America's principles of free speech and have critical conversations, especially if they make people feel uncomfortable.

By standing on stage, I was standing up to the forces in our Muslim communities that were increasingly using tactics of intimidation and smears like "Islamophobe," "House Muslim," "Uncle Tom," "native informant," "racist," and "bigot" to cancel events with which they disagreed.

* * *

Meanwhile, the Duke School of Law began offering course No. 504, "Critical Race Theory," with a "heavy focus" on "storytelling," "interest convergence theory," the "social construction of race," the "black-white paradigm," the "myth of the model minority," "intersectionality," "essentialism," "working identity," "covering whiteness" and "white privilege," "colorblindness," "microaggressions," and "implicit bias."

Duke law professor Trina Jones taught the course. A founding member of the UC Irvine School of Law, she established the Center on Law, Equality and Race. She is the author of "Shades of Brown: The Law of Skin Color" (*Duke Law Journal* 49, 2000), described as explaining the "past and continuing significance of colorism" in the US, and "Aggressive Encounters & White Fragility: Deconstructing the Trope of the Angry Black Woman" (coauthored with Kimberley Jade Norwood, *Iowa Law Review* 102, 2017), about "how negative stereotypes render black women vulnerable in a myriad of social and economic circumstances."

* * *

In early May 2015 the Brooklyn Academy of Music organized a conversation on "Islamophobia." I was one of the scheduled speakers, along with ex-Muslim author Ayaan Hirsi Ali, the by-then notorious Linda Sarsour, and Pakistani American blogger Wajahat Ali.

Days before the talk, the Brooklyn Academy of Music's Facebook RSVP list included a familiar name: Hamdan Azhar, the student at Penn State University who had published a death threat against me, using the subject line "deathtoasra." He had graduated from Penn State University and made himself over as a senior data scientist at Facebook, later landing a job as the head of data science in the global marketing at BlackRock Inc., an investment management company based in New York City.

I alerted the event organizers so they would warn the NYPD.

That night, my parents and son walked by a phalanx of NYPD officers.

Also speaking that night were Douglas Murray, a conservative from the UK, and Faisal Al Mutar, an Iraqi. Born in the city of Babylon in Iraq to a well-educated family, he grew up in Baghdad, where his father was a physician and his mother was trained as an attorney.

In the green room, I extended my hand to Sarsour. She took my hand, limp-wristed, and muttered a greeting in response, evading eye contact.

During the debate, I raised the point that Wajahat Ali had engaged in "slut shaming" Ayaan Hirsi Ali.

He didn't answer me, but a woman yelled at the end: "What about the slut shaming?"

Afterwards, Wajahat Ali walked over to me and said that he'd deleted the reference to Ayaan as a "prostitute" at his site, since he could control it.

"If she had come, I had planned to apologize," he said, weakly.

A few days later, a new website, MuslimGirl.com, published a wildly inaccurate account of the debate, claiming that Douglas Murray, Faisal Al Mutar, and I argued that Islam was violent. That was irresponsible. The editor was Amani Al-Khatahtbeh, a Palestinian American recent Rutgers graduate whose parents immigrated to the US from Jordan. A young girl on 9/11, she called Sarsour a figurative "auntie." She shared a passion with Sarsour to destroy the state of Israel, at one protest leading Rutgers's activists with the popular anti-Israel chant to destroy Israel: "From the river to the sea!" In 2009, as Muslims were creating an online presence, she cofounded MuslimGirl.com as a seventeen-year-old high school senior. She started wearing a sloppy, oversized headscarf as her trademark, burying her face in yards of fabric. She was a 2014 graduate of Rutgers University, where she had earned quite the controversial reputation as anti-Semitic and wildly anti-Israel.

Now, her new website claimed it was a place where "Muslim women talk back" to correct "misconceptions surrounding Islam." After much delay, she edited the piece to delete the claim that Murray and I had said Islam was violent. But it was just one bump in the road for her. This young woman was about to rise to the highest ranks of naïve American feminism.

CHAPTER 16

Mounting a Muslim Reform Resistance

In August 2015, a group of young men assembled at the Comfort Inn in Springfield, Virginia, for a meeting of Hizb ut-Tahrir America. Inside, they covered artwork of greyhounds with a black flag, the *shahada*, or proclamation of faith, on it in white Arabic script. The young men railed against the "American Raj," a play off the British Raj, which described the British empire.

Jesse Morton, a convert to Islam who had changed his name to Younes Abdullah Muhammad, stood in the back of the room, watching the presentation. He was just out of federal prison for conspiring to solicit murder, making threatening communications, and using the internet to place others in fear. He had run a website, Revolution Muslim, which had published death threats in 2010 against the creators of *South Park* for caricatures of the prophet Muhammad.

He knew the men at Islamic Thinkers who had called for the death of organizers of the woman-led prayer a decade earlier. Meanwhile, the Islamic State kept drawing more recruits, including a young Mississippi Muslim man and his fiancée, a former cheerleader and convert. In December 2007, Morton had cofounded

Revolution Muslim and exploited many of the internet platforms available at the time, including Blogspot, Google Groups, Blip.TV, Paltalk, YouTube, Scribd, SlideShare, Facebook, and multiple website addresses.

Morton and his friends at Revolution Muslim followed cleric Abdullah Faisal. The US government alleged they used the organization's websites to "encourage Muslims to support Usama bin Laden, Anwar Al-Awlaki, al-Qaida, the Taliban, and other Muslims engaged in or espousing jihad. They encouraged Muslims to prepare for and engage in jihad against those they believed to be enemies of Islam."

The leaders and members of Hizb ut-Tahrir were honest about their goals: a global Islamic caliphate. Others had more deceptive ways.

* * *

That October, a new Facebook page, "Black-Palestinian Solidarity" was launched, releasing one product: a slick video with sixty-some black and Palestinian celebrity activists evoking parallels between the two movements. They include singer Lauryn Hill; actor Danny Glover; popular Palestinian hip-hop group, DAM, based in Israel; Boycott, Divestment, Sanctions founder Omar Barghouti, and writer Alice Walker.

At 1:02 p.m., radical 1960s activist Angela Davis, seated on a comfortable sofa, held up a sign, "Racism is systemic. Its outbursts are not isolated incidents." *Systemic* was going to be an underpinning of this movement. Anyone who denied that racism was "systemic" was declared a racist.

Also in the video were Palestinian American Yousef Erakat, a longtime YouTube personality under the name of @fouseyTUBE, and the younger brother of "critical race theory" legal academic-activist Noura Erakat; Palestinian American filmmaker Annemarie Jacir; hip-hop artist Raymond Lawrence "Boots" Riley, a leader in the Occupy Oakland movement in 2011; academic activist Cornel West; and polarizing activist Linda Sarsour. The organizations now working together were Dream Defenders, Black Youth Project 100, the DC Palestinian Film and Arts Festival, and Jewish Voice for Peace, among others.

One of the first comments was illustrative of the audience: "9/11 was an inside job."

By the summer of 2020, the video had 270,000 views.

* * *

Others, like Dalia Mogahed, ran cover for the talking points spun out of 500 Grove Street.

She had made a home for herself at Georgetown University, cozy with John Esposito, the founder of the Prince Alwaleed bin Talal Center for Muslim-Christian Understanding. She was also policy director at the Institute for Social Policy and Understanding, a place with an innocuous, forgettable name, but its viewpoints were dangerous, supporting Islamism.

In recent years, Shireen Zaman, director of a funding intermediary, Proteus Fund, in the billionaire George Soros's funding empire, had allocated at least $150,000 to her former employer, the Institute for Social Policy and Understanding.

One weekend, on *Meet the Press*, Mogahed stuck to the talking points of the Honor Brigade: that white extremists outnumbered Muslim extremists, and Muslim extremists didn't radicalize in mosques but rather away from the positive influence of mosques.

The physician and former UC Berkeley student Javad Hashmi had made that assertion in a 2012 LoonWatch article by "Danios." In the fall 2015 edition of the *Barry Law Review*, published by the Barry University School of Law in Orlando, Florida, Khaled Beydoun, assistant professor of law and proponent of "critical race theory," also made the argument. In a defense of sharia law, "War, Violence, and Punishment: A Media-Centric Approach of Sharia and American Legal Doctrines," Beydoun's research assistant, Yazen Abdin, a law student, asserted, "In comparison," to Muslim battles at the birth of Islam in the seventh century, "the United States has engaged in warfare since its inception."

His footnote, No. 126, led to none other than a 2011 LoonWatch article by the anonymous writer "Danios," headlined "We're at War!—and We Have Been Since 1776: 214 Years of American War-Making."

* * *

In late November 2015, Palestinian American activist Linda Sarsour stepped into a small amphitheater on the campus of Georgetown University. It was an evening cosponsored by Unity Production Foundation.

She took her seat at the dais with John Esposito to her right and Dalia Mogahed beside him. "Islamophobia in an Election Year" was the topic. Sarsour said she refused to apologize for ISIS. She went to vigils not as a Muslim but as a human being. "You should be apologizing to me that you expect me to apologize for my faith that I believe doesn't condone those things," she said.

Alex Kronheimer, cofounder of Unity Production Foundation, was on stage, too. A convert to Islam, he had stumbled upon a lucrative operation: making positive films about Muslims and Islam. The International Institute of Islamic Thought had doled out $525,000 to Unity Productions Foundation in 2015 for program assistance, including "peace through the media." Sterling Charitable Gift Fund in Herndon, Virginia, gave it $450,000 that year. In 2016, it got another $200,000 from Sterling Charitable Gift Fund, and in 2019, the fund gave Unity Productions another $25,000.

* * *

Moderates in all communities have a moral imperative to speak up about extremism. One afternoon, in early December, @LoonWatchers attacked me on Twitter. There was something more important distracting me. Journalists were reporting that gunmen had laid siege to the Bataclan, a music venue in Paris, and other locations, ultimately killing 130 people throughout the city.

That evening, I stepped into the offices of CBS Studios to film an episode of HBO's *Real Time with Bill Maher*. The year before, actor Ben Affleck had attacked Maher and neuroscientist and atheist Sam Harris for their views on the dangers of extremist Islam. UC Berkeley students protested a scheduled appearance by Maher on campus. It was part of an assault by the Honor Brigade to tag atheists, like Maher, Harris, and biologist Richard Dawkins, as "Islamophobes."

Just weeks earlier, "Guest" at LoonWatch.com had posted an article by an Iraqi American writer, Laith Saud, then a religious studies professor at DePaul University in Chicago and a friend of CAIR Chicago's Ahmed Rehab. Saud was angry at Hawaii Democratic Rep. Tulsi Gabbard, then vice chair of the Democratic National Committee. Gabbard, an Army veteran who had served a tour of duty in Iraq, had told Maher that the extremism issue among Muslims is a real issue, saying socioeconomic conditions weren't to blame for Islamist violence.

And the people behind LoonWatch were clearly irked.

In the piece headlined "The Failure of Progressive Thought," Saud (who also spelled his name Al-Saud) tapped the gibberish constructed by the emerging scholars in "critical race theory," blasting "the Left" for its "white privilege," "Eurocentrism," and "racism," which "is a product of inequity as well." Saud would later say that, after immigrating to the US as a boy, he felt as if he made a shift in the 1990s, after the US invaded Iraq in the first Gulf War, from an "exotic kid from the East that was seen through a white orientalist lens as this blended Muslim, Hindu, or Buddhist identity to that of a distinct Iraqi, Arab, Muslim enemy."

For patriotism day at school, he says he drew an Iraqi flag on a white T-shirt as an "official 'fuck you' to America on behalf of all the dehumanized Iraqis in the conflict." (His parents wouldn't let him wear the shirt.) He didn't mention that back on Halloween 1992, according to court records, Saud, then fourteen, had ended up in juvenile delinquent court after pointing a revolver at the heads and body of several peers at various house parties.

Two years earlier, CAIR Chicago executive director Ahmed Rehab had raised $25,530 on the fundraising platform Kickstarter for a film project, *Beyond Tahrir*, about the protests in the Arab Spring, coproduced by two companies including Alef Lam Mim, a "media group based in Chicago," started a year before by Rehab, Saud, and another friend, M. Yaser Tabbara. They promised to "glean into the world of the Muslim Brotherhood and get a sense of their roots in Egypt and the diversity of their members." A year earlier, Rehab had shared another similar article by Saud, whom he described as "my friend." They had known each other for years as Saud established his career after a troubled youth. In 2012, they had promoted a Chicago bus ad campaign, "My Jihad," with Muslims talking about their struggles in life. Along with Rehab, Saud was also affiliated with Georgetown University's Bridge Initiative. He also became podcast executive editor at the *Chicago Monitor*, a local publication, where Rehab was the founder and publisher and one of his staffers, Muhammad Tauseef Akbar, was editor-at-large.

Now, on Twitter, @LoonWatchers sent white writer and ally C. J. Werleman a direct message asking him to share the "important guest feature."

"Great piece. Shared," Werleman responded. (In 2018, ironically, a former DePaul University student sued Saud for battery and violation of the Illinois Gender Violence Act for allegedly coercing her into sexual intercourse twice, noting Saud was the subject of many complaints for sexual harassment, unwanted touching, and obnoxious behavior during work hours. Saud was dismissed from his job, the university settled with the student, a judge dismissed the case against Saud, and he sued for racial discrimination.)

* * *

Within hours, the Islamic State issued a statement taking credit for the Bataclan attack titled "A Statement on the Blessed Onslaught in Paris against the Crusader Nation of France."

On cue, CAIR called a press conference to deny the Islam in Islamic State.

"Let's not legitimize ISIS and help them in their propaganda by calling them the Islamic State," CAIR executive director Nihad Awad told reporters. "They're not Islamic. They're not state. They're anti-Islamic. Let's not call them jihadis. They have nothing to do with jihad. Jihad is a legitimate self-defense in Islam. Let's not give them this legitimizing title. They are brutal killers. They have no legitimacy.

"And I urge media, politicians, analysts to be very careful with the choice of their words. ISIS is appealing to the marginalized, disenfranchised and alienated young people in the Middle East and in the West. Let's not help ISIS recruit more disenfranchised and alienated young people."

* * *

News rang out about another attack days later on Wednesday, December 2, 2015. A husband-and-wife team had murdered fourteen people and wounded at least seventeen people at a holiday party at a social services center in San Bernardino, California. They had pledged their allegiance to ISIS.

Within hours, Linda Sarsour dispatched orders to fellow activists on a private listserv. "Stay coordinated," she warned. "Join the larger chorus for gun control." She reminded readers that there had just been a shooting of a Planned Parenthood clinic.

At CAIR, Awad agreed with Sarsour.

CAIR's government affairs director, Robert McCaw, returned to the tried-and-true complaint that Muslims were unfairly held responsible for the actions of other Muslims, while Christians weren't being blamed for the Planned Parenthood shooting.

There was no discussion of condemning the actual interpretation of Islam, sponsored by states from Saudi to Qatar, that fueled the violence. That's what Christians had done. That's what McCaw seemed to miss.

And, sure enough, the next night, CAIR's executive director Hussam Ayloush used money from a "rapid response" grant from billionaire George Soros's philanthropic network to hold a press conference in Los Angeles, where speakers did not own up to the role of radicalization in motivating the husband and wife to become murderers. Soros paid ReThink Media to do media spin for CAIR, speculating the killers were motivated by work, rage, and mental illness, even though they left a manifesto attributing their murder to their allegiance to ISIS and its murderous interpretation of Islam.

The night after, just two nights after the murderous rampage, local Muslim leaders led an interfaith peace rally. NPR's *This American Life* did a feature, headlining their segment "Confronting Islamophobia after the San Bernardino Shooting." A speaker at the rally was Muhammad Shafiq, who had arrived in the US in the 1970s as a young Muslim student from Tora Bora, Pakistan. He was one of the Muslim Brothers who had driven from Philadelphia to Herndon, Virginia, to eye the new building at 500 Grove Street that would be a headquarters for the Muslim Brothers in America. He was still executive director at the Hickey Center for Interfaith Studies and Dialogue at Nazareth College in Rochester. And he was now pushing forward the pivot to the "Islamophobia" backlash.

In fact, from New York state to Berkeley, the International Institute of Islamic Thought, founded at 500 Grove Street in the 1980s by the Muslim Brothers in America, had made sure that there would be diverse voices making "Islamophobia" an issue front and center at moments like this.

In 2015, it doled out $100,000 to the Union Theological Seminary in New York City. Seven days after the San Bernardino attack, the seminary president, Rev. Dr. Serene Jones, and four colleagues issued, "A Statement on Anti-Muslim Rhetoric," railing against "fear mongering based on anti-Muslim hatred," without once acknowledging the victims in San Bernardino who had lost their lives because of hate *by* Muslims.

* * *

On the campus of University of California at Berkeley, "Islamophobia" studies architect Hatem Bazian said he wanted to say no to an invitation to a panel on the Paris attacks. Instead, he relented and launched into an academic, emotionally detached response to the tragedy. Between the Bataclan attack and the *Charlie Hebdo* attack, he lamented attacks in Muslim-majority countries that he claimed received little attention.

A CNN article on a bomb attack in Lebanon amounted to an "erasure" of victims. He quoted Edward Said and his notion of an "imagined geography" of violence. Politicians inserted a "heavy dose of Islamophobia" and a call for a "civilizational war," he complained.

* * *

Meanwhile, Muslim reformers had a very different response. After the San Bernardino attacks, a phalanx of Muslim reformers from the US, Europe, and Canada stood at the National Press Club in Washington, DC. They included Zuhdi Jasser and Raheel Raza. I was among them, my son, then thirteen, sitting in the front row.

We announced the founding of the Muslim Reform Movement, with three principles: peace, human rights, and secular governance. Then, we went to the Islamic Center of Washington, run by Saudi Arabia. Raheel Reza's husband, Sohail, took the declaration and taped it to the front door.

The Muslim community has many valuable contributions to make to the US and Western society, including values of truth, compassion, and justice, but these important values are lost when our most visible representatives resort to terrorism—and the voices from within our community engage in the cycle of denial.

Islamic extremism is causing massive problems worldwide, and even many "moderate" Muslim beliefs—like apostasy laws—are appropriately considered backward and regressive by those in the West on both sides of the political aisle. What can Muslims do? To transform our culture of denial, we need to own up to the internal problems within our community, from female genital mutilation to gender apartheid and terrorism. We have Islamic values of forgiveness, truth telling, and honesty to take personal and societal responsibility for acknowledging, challenging, and ultimately defeating radicalization within the community from an Islam of grace.

* * *

Larycia Hawkins, a black Christian professor at Wheaton College, the granddaughter of a pastor, called CAIR Chicago's Ahmed Rehab with an idea. Religious faith was important to her. Her grandfather had died two days after he doused her in water, baptizing her.

She was thinking of wearing a headscarf in solidarity with Muslim women. Would that be okay?

Would it be offensive?

Rehab loved the idea. He gave her CAIR's blessing.

Soon enough, Hawkins posted a photo of herself with a scarf on Facebook. "I stand in religious solidarity with Muslims because they, like me, a Christian, are people of the book. And as Pope Francis stated last week, we worship the same God."

Her college sent her a notice of termination.

To many Muslim women, the action wasn't a sign of solidarity with a positive philosophy. The headscarf was a symbol of an interpretation of Islam that judged women's hair as too sexy for public viewing and denied women equal rights.

* * *

Days later, I coauthored a *Washington Post* op-ed with my Egyptian American friend, Hala Arafa, with whom I'd dissected ISIS propaganda earlier in the year. We argued that Muslim women and girls aren't Islamically required to cover their hair. By definitions of liberal thought, this was purity culture. In fact, alas, the headscarf is a symbol of rape culture, telling women and girls that we have to cover our hair to avoid losing our "honor."

On Facebook, Brooklyn activist Linda Sarsour called me "fringe" and attacked "white-washed feminism," adding: "Proud of my hijab and my faith and don't need Asra Nomani to tell me what to think. She has an agenda, and she is bankrolling on it." (I received $200 for writing the article.) Earlier, when I had debated a friend of Sarsour's, Dalia Mogahed, who also wears headscarves, Sarsour wrote: "I wanted to punch my TV every time Asra opened her mouth." Sarsour didn't respond to requests for comment. On Facebook, Ahmed Rehab, the executive director of the CAIR Chicago chapter and CAIR National's strategic communications director, called me "delusional." When I asked Rehab about his comment, he said, "Listen, you need to stop being a hypocrite." CAIR and Rehab didn't return queries seeking comment. Others called us "leeches" and "*dajjal*," the Muslim equivalent of the proverbial anti-Christ.

At LoonWatch, Rehab used his fake "Emperor" account to repost an article that misrepresented my analysis on how militant groups require women and girls to wear the headscarf. On the comment board, the physician Javad Hashmi used his fake account, "DrM," to call me a "Zionist media whore," and "Jekyll" mocked me as "Whorenami."

By late December 2015, UC Berkeley's Hatem Bazian was deep into his mission to racialize Islamist agenda with the Woke Army's philosophy of "critical race theory."

On the campus of UC Berkeley, he opened a conference on "Islamophobia" by saying that if anyone had a problem with the "Islamophobia" term, it was too late to complain.

"...Islamophia right now is a codified term, academically already established with a journal in its behalf, an academic program at UC Berkeley and other places. The train has left the station," he said, waving his hands for emphasis.

For all the Honor Brigade tried to allege that an "Islamophobia industry" doled out hate against Muslims, it had put in place a lucrative enterprise that would generate millions of dollars in funding for their efforts to "counter Islamophobia" by hosting academic conferences, publishing books, and booking speeches and media appearances. Often, the older Muslim Brothers groomed younger activists and writers to churn out products.

One of those young writer-activists was a young white man from North Carolina, Nathan Lean, born into a Christian home. The Iranian American author Reza Aslan gave Lean one of his first breaks, hiring him to be a writer at an online platform he had created, Aslan Media. There, Lean established a name for himself as a pit bull who not only barked but landed ferocious bites on the targets of his assaults. To his critics, he was a smear merchant.

Two summers earlier, he had published a column on *Salon* headlined "Bill Maher and Fox News's Muslim feminism: How Ayaan Hirsi Ali and Asra Nomani embrace the soft Islamophobia of Western expectations." He was using the "Islamophobia" smear to discredit Ali and me. He used a photo of me with my lips pursed angrily and my eyes wide. It scared even me. In the article, Lean left many sexual innuendos about Ali and me, both of us "worn by matrimonial woes," and patronizingly lamented, "Pain must surely plague Ayaan Hirsi Ali and Asra Nomani." He documented me being abandoned by my "lover" in Pakistan and published several inaccuracies, not the least of which was that he claimed I had "married a US Army officer." I had once written about being engaged to a US Army officer, but I hadn't gotten married. *Salon* editor David Talbot ignored my numerous requests for a correction. Later, he said in an interview that *Salon* was a "smart tabloid." In the scramble for content, it had become a go-to platform for hit pieces by the Woke Army.

The next month, Lean wrote a tweet, tagging @SamHarrisOrg, the popular atheist author, in a conversation about a new book Harris had written with British Muslim Maajid Nawaz. Lean complained that Harris's "lapdog Maajid" had blocked him. Another time, he tagged @DrZuhdiJasser, calling him "America's 'credentials free' trophy Muslim," and promoting an article he'd written for author Reza Aslan's Aslan Media, claiming Jasser's "father-in-law hates him," as if that were even relevant. Jasser's father-in-law had been a leader at the CAIR Ohio chapter.

Lean wasn't just a random troll. He was director of research at Georgetown University's Prince Alwaleed bin Talal Center for Muslim-Christian Understanding, funded by the Islamist sympathizers in the building at Grover Street in Herndon, Virginia. In February 2016, a place in Washington, DC, called the Rumi Forum hosted a conversation with Lean, moderated by Asma Uddin, legal counsel at the Becket Fund and editor of AltMuslimah.org, an online blog that tech guru Shahed Amanullah had helped set up. Controversial Turkish Muslim preacher Fethullah Gülen had established the Rumi Forum. It was a strange place for Lean to be speaking. Rumi is an inspiration for Sufi Muslims, who are more spiritual, not as dogmatic as the Muslims in the Honor Brigade.

During his talk, Lean ticked off from memory the many agents of hate, including "pernicious, nasty attacks," against Muslims that he'd documented in his book.

When Uddin opened the floor for questions, I stood up and said, "So I'm thrilled that you have an opposition to 'pernicious, nasty attacks.' My question is: why do you engage in them? If the audience isn't familiar, you are very well known now for your attacks on Muslim reformers. You call them 'lap dogs,' 'trophy Muslims.' Against me, just a couple weeks ago, you said when I talked about the grief that I felt over the murder of my friend Danny Pearl, you said that they were 'crocodile tears.' So why do think that it's okay—which is rightfully so to defend Muslims against attack—but why do *you* participate in that? And my other question to you is are you also Muslim?"

Lean paused and responded, "We'll take another question."

I stood up again, "So you're not going to answer that question?"

Lean said again, "We'll take another question."

"No, I'd like to know, is he not answering that question then?"

Lean continued, "We'll take another question. This, this, this comment comes from someone who has written in the *Wall Street Journal* before that Muslims should be profiled, that one of the indicators that we have of someone who is Muslim being on a path towards extremism...."

He was repeating Duke University professor Omid Safi's smear.

I interrupted, "...so you want to just misrepresent my writings again, but you don't want to answer the question: why do you engage in the nasty attacks?"

He wouldn't respond.

* * *

That summer, the boxer Muhammad Ali died. A convert to Islam, he was a prize for the Islamists and their evangelical dream. They rushed to be his pallbearers.

Omid Safi, the academic who put a target on my back, lifted the idea of being "unapologetically black" from "critical race theory" and told PRI, the National Public Radio outlet, that Ali was "unapologetically Muslim," as well as "unapologetically black and unapologetically radical."

There were now even T-shirts for sale online with "Unapologetically Muslim" across the front.

* * *

Eight months later, the Honor Brigade wing of the Woke Army launched a calculated attack on some of its biggest targets.

From its headquarters on Washington Avenue in downtown Montgomery, Alabama, where it became a champion for civil rights, the Southern Poverty Law Center named and shamed liberal British Muslim Maajid Nawaz, singling him out in its *Field Guide to Anti-Muslim Extremists*. The SPLC cited Nawaz's criticism of Islamism, sharing of a "blasphemous" cartoon of prophet Muhammed, and a stag night he had with a "naked lap dancer." The scurrilous report also disparaged Muslim-raised author and activist Ayaan Hirsi Ali, but missing was mention of the donor. There were four coauthors on the report: the SPLC, the liberal propaganda machine Media Matters, the liberal propaganda machine ReThink Media, and the liberal community organizing nonprofit Center for New Community. They each received funding regularly and significantly from one donor: billionaire George Soros. Heidi Beirich, director of the Intelligence Project at the Southern Poverty Law Center, responded to a request for comment by the Open Society Foundations, saying her group had received a grant that year from Open Society to do the anti-Muslim bigotry project.

She wanted to dispel the idea Soros money influenced the report. "We would do this work with or without the grant," she said.

Soros financing was becoming pivotal to hijacking the debate on Islam. The money funded Islamists who lashed out at Muslim reformers (and others). In turn, the Islamists convinced Democratic Party leaders and even socially liberal activists that it was "Islamophobic" to challenge anything about Islam, including extremist views on governance. The caution left the field clear for exploitation by conservative populists like Donald Trump. ReThink Media pocketed at least $2.1 million for communications work that included messaging the idea of "Islamophobia" in the US, while the Center for New Community in Chicago got strategy money to "define and marginalize the organized Islamophobia movement."

Georgetown University's Bridge Initiative at the Prince Alwaleed bin Talal Center for Muslim-Christian Understanding, CAIR, and LoonWatch all republished news of the *Field Guide to Anti-Muslim Extremists*.

A combative Nawaz later went on air with HBO comedian Bill Maher and vowed to sue for defamation. But could he challenge the Woke Army and win?

* * *

Linda Sarsour was committed to making sure that no one defeat her vision for America.

In 2016, she cofounded a new 501(c)(3) she called "MPower Change," meaning Muslim Power. Importantly, Sarsour created MPower Change Action, a 501(c)(4) that could lobby as its main activity. Her cofounders were Mark Crain, a black Muslim convert and digital expert, and Mustafa Dustin Craun. In a profile, SapeloSquare.com, a website that says it "intervenes in the marginalization and erasure of Black Muslims in the public square," wrote that Craun had become interested in "Black-Brown solidarity" in high school and converted to Islam as a student at Northwestern University in Chicago. An intern at "Friends of Hillary" [Clinton] as a student in 2006, he worked as outreach and communications coordinator at Inner-City Muslim Action Network, a nonprofit in Chicago, then digital constituency manager for Obama for America in 2012 before becoming an online campaigner at MoveOn.org, dedicated to expanding access to health care and "dismantling racism."

Sarsour scored a $25,000 grant from her friends at Open Society's Proteus Fund toward "public engagement and education," "systems reform," and "online engagement" through a new "Muslim Digital Organizing Platform." The Proteus Fund shuffled the money through its Solidaire Fund. The Benjamin Fund provided her another $5,000 grant for "general support." The next year, she would nab another $46,975 from the Proteus Fund and $170,000 shuffled through her fiscal sponsor, NEO Philanthropy, for "general support." In 2018, she'd get $20,000 from a New York City donor, North Star Fund.

By now, Muslim activists had figured out how to appropriate the language of "critical race theory" for their own agenda. "Implicit bias" was one catch-22 term of art used to assume racism in societal dynamics where there wasn't obvious racism, so that no matter how you looked at a situation, you could conclude racism. In Canada, Nakita Valerio, a Muslim self-described "academic, activist, and writer" with the Alberta Muslim Public Affairs Council, wrote a piece on "implicit Islamophobia," with "implicit associations" and "implicit biases." She quoted "research on implicit bias," compiled by the Open Society Foundations revealing—not so surprisingly—that "negative associations can affect people's decisions and their behavior toward people of other demographics than themselves."

What was fundamentally flawed with this approach was that it was myopic. "Implicit bias" can be a two-way street, for example, by Muslims about white people, leading to not only prejudice but terrorism. Instead, this researcher, like so many in the field of "critical race theory," demonized only one group of people—whites—writing, "In spite of their conscious feelings, white people with high levels of implicit racial bias show less warmth and welcoming behavior toward black people." Like the original "critical race theory" ideologues, the new Muslim adherents, like Valerio, argued that "'color blindness' actually produces greater implicit bias than strategies that acknowledge race."

She linked to a seven-day "bias cleanse" created by @LookDifferent with The Ohio State University Kirwan Institute for the Study of Race and Ethnicity. In the summer of 2020, its website homepage featured a banner, "Statement in Solidarity with Black Lives Matter." Established in 2015, the Kirwan Institute was setting itself up as a hub for "implicit bias training," selling the "Foundational Implicit Bias Session" and the "INCASE of Bias Training."

That year, the Ford Foundation and Borealis Philanthropy announced the latter had started the Black-Led Movement Fund, a six-year pooled donor campaign to raise $100 million for a coalition for the "Movement for Black Lives." George Soros and his Open

Society Foundations had already provided $33 million in grants, along with grants from the Center for American Progress.

* * *

None of it was enough to keep Donald Trump from winning the 2016 election. With the success of the Women's March against Trump, the Honor Brigade was committed to waging a political movement against the new president that would keep it front and center in the Woke Army's response.

Two days after the Women's March, the story was all about Linda Sarsour.

That afternoon, a Brooklyn leader, Murad Awawdeh, thirty, rallied fellow Muslims to Sarsour's side. The son of Palestinian immigrants who arrived in the US in the 1970s, he was born and raised in Brooklyn, growing up with Sarsour as a mentor. He recalled a childhood in which police regularly stopped and frisked him and neighbors harangued his family because of their religion. Still a boy during the 9/11 attacks, he recalled youth in the neighborhood throwing rocks at his mother. The family hung an America flag in front of their home to show their patriotism. He rose to become executive vice president of advocacy and strategy at the New York Immigration Coalition. Some years earlier, the Brooklyn Community Foundation named him among six "do-gooders," along with Sarsour, in a contest with a $5,000 cash prize. Now, he was rallying fellow Muslims to "defend Sister Linda" by posting messages of support with the hashtag #IMarchWithLinda. The immigration coalition was established in 2008 with more than two hundred member organizations. He was also president of the New York State Immigrant Action Fund, established in 2011, and would go on to start Yalla Brooklyn in August 2018 to reach Arab and Muslim voters. Yalla means "let's go" in Arabic. Sarsour would be part of the Yalla Brooklyn effort.

"...With all success comes people who are envious, hateful, and disgusting," he told his friends. "Before and after the March, Linda has been meticulously attacked personally and professionally.

A few from within our community but the vast majority from white supremacists and Islamophobes."

A couple hours later, comedian-turned-writer Dean Obeidallah also seized the moment. Raised in Lodi, New Jersey, he was a contributor to the *Daily Beast* and CNN. His mother was Sicilian Italian, and his father was Palestinian Muslim. Later that afternoon, he wrote to fellow Muslims that conservative host Glenn Beck and "Trump supporting Muslim 'reformer' Asra Nomani" were "coming after Linda." He shared my column for Women in the World on the ties of billionaire George Soros to the Women's March.

The "goals of Beck and others like him" are to "marginalize every Muslim American voice from politics and the media except for those Muslims who work with him. We can't let that happen," he implored.

In a Google Group, Muslim Leadership Forum of NY, a Muslim activist, Debbie Almontaser, thanked Obeidallah. She still resented the way the community had let her down when she had come under attack as the head of a Muslim school. She wrote that it was "very important" for "our community" to "mobilize around Linda, not take a back seat as was done in 2007 in my case."

She asked for a conference call the next day.

New York Muslim leader Abdul Aziz Bhuiyan responded that it was "urgent" to have the call. He was a leader at the mosque where the family of Yasmin Seiwald prayed. She was the girl who had filed a false report against "three white racists."

That night, just before midnight, Sarsour thanked the group. "I am humbled by the outpouring of love," she wrote. Her email listed the bold-faced names that had supported her: Vermont Sen. Bernie Sanders. Hip-hop mogul Russell Simmons. CNN analyst Van Jones. Actress Susan Sarandon. Sheikh Yasir Qadhi, a Salafi ideologue who cofounded MuslimMatters and AlMaghrib Institute. Boston imam Zaid Shakir. Imam Omar Suleiman. Amnesty International. SPLC. ACLU. Center for Constitutional Rights. Environmental group 350.org. CAIR. *Huffington Post*. *Elle*. MuslimMatters. Muslim blog *IlmFeed*.

* * *

On cue, @BernieSanders, @WomensMarch, and @BlkLivesMatter posted their messages. And the next day, AJ+, the social media arm of Qatar funded Al Jazeera, posted a flashy one-minute, twenty-eight-second video with its signature bold yellow text, this time of Sarsour pumping her fist in the air, rallying protesters. The video featured her template pronouncements from the protests. "I stand here before you unapologetically Muslim American. Sisters and brothers, you are what democracy looks like." The video got 161,000 views on Twitter.

Over the next few days, activists kept posting messages. This circular echo chamber was critical in the narrative of pitching the movement as the myth of marching millions. Women's March cofounder Tamika Mallory told her thousands of followers to "keep lifting our sister @LSarsour in prayer. She's tough as a nail, but she's still a mom & daughter. We love you, Linda!" The Democratic political lobbying operatives at @MoveOn posted a message that "when @RealDonaldTrump trolls come for one of us, they come for all of us." They included a link to a petition on the MoveOn website. It got 23,294 signatures.

Tariq Ramadan, the grandson of the founder of the Muslim Brotherhood, joined the hashtag campaign with the message, "Solidarity with @LSarsour."

* * *

Four days after his inauguration, President Trump gave his enemies just what they wanted.

He issued Executive Order 13769, restricting immigration and refugees to the US. It underscored his dual emphasis on immigration and its potential impact on national security. Trump was clumsy and overbroad in his rhetoric and needlessly alarmed and alienated many Muslims. On the other hand, the issue was seized on by the red-green alliance to drive an immediate wedge between Muslims and the GOP.

Rather than forcing attention away from the problem of Islamic extremism, Muslim reformers like Zuhdi Jasser—and other well-intentioned folks—continued to direct their outrage at the real enemy, the ideologues that promote Islamic extremism. Defeating them would save lives everywhere, including the lives of Muslims.

Instead, activist Linda Sarsour and the Honor Brigade kicked into action.

From San Francisco to New York City, protesters stormed the airports. They flooded Terminal 4 at John F. Kennedy International Airport to protest the executive order, chanting, "Hey! Hey! Ho! Ho! Muslim ban has got to go!"

A protester held up a sign: "Trump is the terrorist!"

Across town, the ACLU declared: "We filed suit against @Real-DonalTrump's #MuslimBan." In San Francisco, Muslim Advocates issued a statement: "We reaffirm our commitment to working with allies and using every legal tool to challenge discriminatory laws. #MuslimBan #NoBanNoWall," referring to the US-Mexico border.

#MuslimBan and #NoBanNoWall emerged as early battle cries for anti-Trump #resistance protests. Media outlets from the *New York Times* to Qatar's Al Jazeera media channel and liberal outlets *Slate*, MSNBC, Vox, and BuzzFeed repeated the term "Muslim ban."

This was carefully orchestrated hysteria. There was no "Muslim ban." There was a ban on immigrants from certain predominately Muslim countries, but it was the result of an extremism problem we had failed to curb. The Honor Brigade was working in overdrive to co-opt the Woke Army with its priorities and exploit this moment to take nationwide—and also global—its political propaganda that America is hostile to Muslims.

The new order, inherited from the Obama administration, first through the Visa Waiver Program and Terrorist Travel Prevention Act of 2015, identified Iran, Iraq, Sudan, and Syria as "countries of concern," and then through the May 2016 Obama administration decision to include the "addition of Libya, Somalia, and Yemen." The new order removed Iraq from restrictions and made other important revisions to the first executive order. Nowhere on the list were the countries with the world's largest Muslim populations—Indonesia, Pakistan, and India—making the claim of a "Muslim ban" false.

The new order was a necessary first step, and Muslim reformers hoped it was only the first of many measures to stifle state sponsors of extremism. "We are also taking strong measures to protect our nation from radical Islamic terrorism," said Trump at a joint session of Congress. The message was long overdue.

* * *

The hysteria around a "Muslim ban" was irresponsible and dangerous, acting as soft propaganda for extremists, fomenting hate, anger, and, potentially, violence against the US.

It was a strategic campaign, fomented by Democrat and Democrat-leaning nonprofits, activists, and politicians, most of whom Muslim reformers had battled for years, as they systematically shifted the conversation away from Islamic terrorism to "Islamophobia."

The campaign was designed to overlook the horror of Muslims exporting to the world an ideology of political Islam that had metastasized into Islamic terrorism. It was intended to paper over the fact that Muslims had indeed failed to destroy Muslim supremacy, Muslim nationalism, and Islamic extremism.

Now, past and present grantees of the National Security and Human Rights Campaign targeted Trump—inflaming fears with the myth of the "Muslim ban." ReThink Media wrote an anti-Trump message soon after the president's inauguration: "What a difference two weeks makes. Remember, we are stronger when stand together. #NoBanNoWall."

When the first executive order came out, an Open Society Foundations spokesperson said in an email, "OSF's National Security and Human Rights Campaign is an effort to support organizations that stand up for human rights, government accountability and the rule of law. Mr. Trump campaigned on calls for a Muslim ban." She said "the order casts a wide and prejudicial ban on a large class of people, defined by place of origin and religion. This goes against our values and our laws, as evidenced by the concerns voiced by elected officials across the ideological spectrum, and the actions of several federal courts."

Asked if Open Society funds were being used to oppose the executive order, the spokeswoman said: "I would be surprised if organizations working on national security and civil and human rights were not using any available resources to address the extraordinary challenges presented by the executive order."

In an analysis of thirty-eight documents that discuss the operations and funding of the National Security and Human Rights Campaign, the names of many individuals and groups now stoking fear about the nonexistent "Muslim ban" emerged including former host of the Qatar-owned Al Jazeera TV channel, Wajahat Ali, hired to write a 2011 "anti-Muslim hate" report by the Center for American Progress; a left-leaning think tank founded by former chairman of the Hillary Clinton 2016 campaign, John Podesta; and the Brennan Center for Justice at New York University, which tweeted out earlier this year, "#MuslimBan tarnishes American image as land of optimism & opportunity. The fight continues." Ali and the Center for American Progress didn't return queries for comment.

In this battle, like others galvanizing around anti-Trump hate, the American left was aligning with groups that are on the Muslim right. Imraan Siddiqi, executive director of the Arizona chapter of CAIR, took credit for being "ground zero" for #NoBanNoWall.

* * *

CAIR sued Trump over the "Muslim ban." CAIR lawyers named Linda Sarsour as the lead plaintiff for her name recognition, giving the lawsuit the name of *Linda Sarsour, et al., Plaintiffs, v. Donald J. Trump, et al., Defendants.* She was very proud to be the first name on the lawsuit.

MPower Change filed an amicus brief that they turned into a petition that people around the country could sign. CAIR launched another campaign that stoked hysteria, #RegisterMeFirst, to oppose the nonexistent "Muslim registry."

While Obama was a believer in the "Islamophobia" narrative of the left and empowered Muslim radicals, Trump was a walking stereotype of an "Islamophobe." His rhetoric on terrorism and proposed immigration restrictions on certain Muslim countries had infuriated liberals and undoubtedly compounded a sense of alienation and vulnerability among some Muslims.

CAIR and its allies dispatched their staff to flip the narrative on their history of extremism. In a speech at Benedictine University, CAIR Chicago's executive director, Ahmed Rehab, wanted to speak to youth about navigating America between "belonging and vilification." In a jacket and collared shirt without a tie, he was now wearing a "soul patch," or bit of hair below his lower lip. A bare wall and glass window behind him, he argued he could be a "better American" than someone like conservative TV host Bill O'Reilly. "I don't contribute hate. I don't contribute divisiveness. I don't contribute polemics," he said from behind the lectern.

"It's very important for us," he said, "*not* to have a chip on our shoulder."

* * *

In New York, Albert Cahn, CAIR New York's legal director, had great news: an anonymous donor, well known in the CAIR C-suite, would pay for a top-notch website for CAIR to raise funds and build a database of supporters. Cahn was an unlikely person to be on CAIR's payroll. A white American with a BA in politics and philosophy from Brandeis University, he earned a law degree from Harvard. He joined the large law firm Weil, Gotshal & Manges in Manhattan, as an associate, specializing in antitrust. He joined CAIR New York in 2016.

Cahn told Corey Saylor, director of the CAIR "Department to Monitor and Combat Islamophobia," the good news. Saylor contacted CAIR's partners at ReThink Media to see if CAIR could use the #RegisterMeFirst hashtag that ReThink Media had promoted to oppose Trump. ReThink Media gave CAIR the nod.

Within a few weeks, designers at Use All Five, a design and technology studio in Los Angeles, had developed a website, RegisterMeFirst.com. In early March 2017, CAIR officials stood at a press conference, unveiling the website to oppose Trump's "Islamophobic policies." After signing up at the website, registrants got updates so they could "express their solidarity with American Muslims." They also got CAIR email updates. Not only did CAIR gain a megaphone, but new names for its distribution list.

* * *

While some were marching on the streets, others were planning to wage a battle at the ballot box.

In one effort, three days after Trump's inauguration, four "Bernie Bros" from the staff of former Democratic presidential candidate Bernie Sanders put a parallel strategy in place to seize political power—from the inside: establishment of a new political action committee, or PAC, called Justice Democrats.

One of the men—Cenk Uygur—was the brash host of an increasingly popular leftist YouTube channel, The Young Turks, and a brainchild for this next chapter in radical progressive politics that was about to hijack the Democratic Party.

Born in 1970 in Istanbul to a Turkish Muslim family, he moved to East Brunswick, New Jersey, with his family when he was eight, graduating from East Brunswick High School, near the campus of Rutgers University. Raised as a secular Muslim, he later said he was agnostic, but he became a fiery apologist for extremist Muslims, following the talking points of the Muslim Brothers. Uygur graduated from two elite Ivy League schools, earning a BS in management from the Wharton School at the University of Pennsylvania in 1993 and a JD from Columbia University School of Law. After practicing law briefly, he joined MSNBC as a political commentator, before hosting a weeknight commentary show on MSNBC. The fiery black preacher Al Sharpton replaced him. Not long after the 9/11 attacks, he started *The Young Turks* as a liberal politics and entertainment show on the Sirius Satellite Radio network, moving later to Air America and then YouTube in 2015. By April 2022, it had 5.17 million subscribers.

But media influence wasn't enough for Uygur. He wanted political power. Kyle Kulinski, host of the podcast *Secular Talk*, was in. So, too, was Zack Exley, a former Sanders organizer. Also in: Saikat

Chakrabarti, a Harvard University computer science graduate who grew up in Fort Worth, Texas, in a Bengali family from India. After working at some Silicon Valley start-ups, he joined the Sanders campaign in 2015, rising to become the campaign's director of organizing technology, engineering important tools that let volunteers coordinate with each other. After Trump's election, Chakrabarti agreed with his friends that they needed another branding vehicle. They settled on "Justice Democrats."

They were about to get four hundred nominations, selected twelve candidates to run for office. Four of them had names few knew at the time but were going to get to know *very* well. They were Rashida Tlaib, Ilhan Omar, Ayanna Pressley, and Alexandria Ocasio-Cortez.

* * *

In another effort, a young Syrian American man had emerged from the UC Berkeley campus to penetrate the highest levels of US military and diplomatic circles. His name is Wa'el Alzayat.

Born and raised in Damascus, he arrived in the United States, graduating from UC Berkeley in 1997 with a degree in political science and Middle East history. After stints in Silicon Valley, he entered politics in Washington, DC, emerging as an influential policy advisor from the first year of the Obama administration, working with US military officials, diplomats, and ambassadors on Syria, Iraq, and other parts of the Middle East, rising to become senior policy advisor to then-US ambassador to the United Nations, Samantha Powers. He left with Trump's inauguration, and he was ready to pounce back into politics a month later.

He became CEO of a 501(c)(3) nonprofit, Emgage Foundation Inc., established in 2007 in Lakeland, Florida, by its founder, Amin Mitha. It claimed to be a "non-partisan organization" that "aspires to ensure that under-represented communities have the same constitutional rights, social privileges, and political opportunities afforded to all Americans," but soon enough its mission would become singularly focused on protecting Muslim interests—specifically, the interests of radical Muslims with Islamist sympathies. Muslims with names like Rashida Tlaib, Ilhan Omar, and Linda Sarsour.

He'd later tell his friends on Facebook, "When I walked out of the State Department's door back in January 2017, my angst regarding the outcome of the presidential elections was tempered by the knowledge that I was joining an effort that was dedicated to addressing the structural causes that contributed to that outcome."

He had inherited a solid track record with liberal donors. The year before, Emgage Action Inc., established in 2006 with an EIN number 465499822, had gotten $85,000 from the Foundation to Promote Open Society in New York City for its 2016 American Muslim "get out the vote project." It claimed to be a "bi-partisan national political action committee," complete with a website that would one day declare three missions: "building a Muslim American political foundation," "fighting Islamophobia," and "holding elected officials accountable."

"For far too long American Muslims have been on the menu," it declared, "and not at the table." Now was the time to "plant the seeds for generations to come."

That year, Emgage would file its IRS 990 form as "Emgage Action Inc.," a 501(c)(4) political lobbying organization, based in Lakeland, Florida, with about $101,000 in revenue.

Over the next two years, he'd exploit the politics of the Trump administration to create a political machine. He'd increased revenue to $902,524 in 2017 from $740,752 the year before.

The Greater Washington Community Foundation would increase its grant to $81,000 in 2017 from $10,000 the year before. Neo Philanthropy Inc., in New York, the fiscal sponsor for the Women's March, would give the group $75,000 for general operating support. Virginia Civic Engagement Table, based in Richmond, would provide Emgage $50,000 that year for "civic engagement."

Proteus Fund Inc., in Amherst, Massachusetts, would allocate Emgage $30,000 in 2017 to "expand their advocacy capacity," and then it would provide a new entity, Emgage Foundation Inc., based also in Lakeland, Florida, with a new EIN number 26144103, another $30,000 in 2018 for the "expansion of the local communication capacity" for the Florida and Michigan chapters, including to "support marketing and communications professionals" to help the chapters communicate their "nonpartisan civic education and engagement work to the public and partner organizations."

In 2018, Emgage Foundation would score a new $50,000 grant from the Foundation to Promote Open Society to "encourage civic engagement in the American Muslim community." The Greater Washington Community Foundation would give the group another $60,000 for general support.

By 2019, Emgage Foundation would have made it to the big leagues. It would get $50,000 from the Ford Foundation to "build the political awareness and capacity of Muslim American and other AAPI communities in Florida on key local and statewide policy issues."

This group would be anything but nonpartisan.

* * *

In February 2017, at the building at 500 Grove Street in Herndon, Virginia, outside Washington, DC, the International Institute of Islamic Thought hosted a special event: Georgetown University professor of Islam Jonathan Brown teaching a lecture on slavery in Islam. Shockingly, he said that it is not "morally evil to own somebody." He added, "I don't think you can talk about slavery in Islam until you realize that there is no such thing as slavery."

Umar Lee, a white convert to Islam from St. Louis, sat in the audience, stunned.

He challenged Brown, who replied, "If you're a Muslim, the prophet of God...had slaves. He had slaves. There's no denying that. Are you more morally mature than the prophet of God? No, you're not."

Brown insisted "consent isn't necessary for lawful sex" and "slave women do not have agency over their sexual access, so their owner can have sex with them."

Lee protested the talk. It landed on the pages of the *Washington Post.* And then disappeared.

* * *

In March 2017, the Trump administration issued a revised executive order, and a new hyperbole emerged, #MuslimBan2. The ACLU had already used the hashtag hours before the new executive order's announcement.

In the coming months, magazines from *Vogue* to *Vanity Fair* splashed the images of the march's four cochairs on their pages. The four walked the stage to accept *Glamour* magazine's award for Women of the Year.

That year, there were at least three enterprises created to absorb donations: Women's March Inc., Women's March Network, and Women's March Foundation. Total revenues added up to at least an estimated $3 million in the first year and two months of operation—merchandise sales racking up about $1.5 million through today. In 2017, IRS filings show that cochairs from the Women's March made as much $150,000 in salaries from various organizations, including two salaries by one cochair for eighty hours of work a week, while state officials dipped into their savings to support their work for the Women's March.

By the time the Women's March was over, nerves had been frayed. Team Supreme needed to meet. They stepped into a conference room off the entrance lobby, where unacknowledged cofounder Vanessa Wruble reminded Perez what she had told her at their first meeting.

"Jews were behind the slave trade."

"Jews have made money off the backs of brown and black people."

And then what she told her later.

"The Jewish issue doesn't play well with Black Lives Matter."

Mallory was ready for the fight. She flung back at Wruble, "You're toxic!"

"You could hear a pin drop in that room," Evvie wrote on Facebook almost two years later. She didn't say a word. "I was terrified they'd turn on me. Not my proudest moment. I regret my silence to this day."

* * *

On the Slack sharing website, state volunteers listened in as leaders for "Women's March national" spoke freely, unaware that folks could hear them. They lamented that they had to protect the Women's March brand from the states.

The overheard remarks didn't engender trust at a time of fading allegiances. On the morning of the second Thursday of February, state leaders started a poll to see if the states supported a call by the march cochairs to strike on March 8, 2017, the International Day of Women.

Action #4 in the "10 Actions" over "100 Days" would be a "Day Without a Woman."

In early February, a radical sorority of Women's March academic-activists emerged to coauthor a manifesto that declared, "Women of America: We're going on strike." Linda Martín Alcoff, a philosophy professor at Hunter College, had written about the "phenomenology of racial embodiment" as part of "critical race" studies, and she authored *The Future of Whiteness*, just two years earlier. Cinzia Arruzza taught at the New School for Social Research in New York City. Tithi Bhattacharya, a PhD graduate of the University of London specializing in "class formation and colonialism" and Marxist theory, was a professor of South Asian history at Purdue University, teaching Marxism, gender, and the "politics of Islamophobia," writing at the anti-Israel Electronic Intifada, and sitting on the board of the *International Socialist Review*.

Nancy Fraser was a white "critical theorist," teaching philosophy at The New School in New York City, putting forth ideas like the notion that capitalism manifests a "structural basis for racial oppression." Barbara Ransby was a professor of history and African American studies at the University of Illinois at Chicago and author of a book on 1960s activist Ella Baker and her socialist views. Keeanga-Yamahtta Taylor, an assistant professor of African American studies at Princeton University, had written the book *From #BlackLivesMatter to Black Liberation* the year before. That year, she would call Trump a "racist, sexist, megalomaniac" and speak at the Socialism 2017 conference in Chicago.

Among the most controversial coauthors, among many controversial academics, was Rasmea Yousef Odeh, convicted in Israel for the 1969 grocery store bombing that led to the murder of two young students. She was still fighting in court to stay in the United States. In December 2016, a judge in Detroit had granted Odeh a new trial, which had just begun in early January. Finally, the 1960s black radical Angela Davis also coauthored the piece.

* * *

All day, the votes rolled in. New Jersey: No. Pennsylvania: No. Cali fornia: No.

The final vote on Slack was 28–1: No.

On the call, a staffer from the national office told the state volunteers that the national leaders were under "pressure" to strike. She spun the argument: they would give "strike" new meaning.

The women didn't buy it.

That night, an Oregon state volunteer wrote, "(exasperated sigh)," putting her frustration in parentheses.

A week later, Mrinalini Chakraborty, then-head of state operations/coordination and the chair of Women's March Illinois, sent the state leaders the details on the "major action items" that "national" had decided to pursue: "The ultimate ask and the grand finale will be the March 8th General Strike!"

The call went out for protesters to assemble at 59th Street and Fifth Avenue near the Trump International Hotel to form a human chain around the building. NYPD police officers pulled out white plastic ties and started arresting protesters, including four cochairs of the Women's March.

@JusticeLeague posted a two-exclamation point tweet: "They just arrested the National chairs of @womensmarch !! @msladyjustice1 @MalloryDMallory @lsarsour @bobblanddesign." Michael Skolnick also bragged on Twitter his wife had been arrested.

Police led the four into an NYPD paddy wagon.

Click.

Mission accomplished.

Inside the paddy wagon, one of the women took a photo of Sarsour smiling beside Mallory and other protesters.

Eight minutes later, they took a selfie, now with Women's March organizers Mari Lynn Foulger, Carmen Perez in oversized red sunglasses, Paola Mendez, and others.

At 9:59 p.m., @WomensMarch told followers, "We've all been released. Thank you for all your support. #DayWithoutAWoman."

State leaders watched, aghast at the photo from the police van photo shoot. They set up a new account on another networking platform to share work, Base Camp, to circumvent the control of the Women's March Inc. cochairs.

From San Jose, California, a state organizer messaged her fellow organizers on Slack, "Some of the mistrust of WM actually may come from the leaders themselves...." She added, "...it is extremely important for the movement to bring people together. Can we do this by calling white women out for not showing up then also calling white women out for showing up?"

* * *

CAIR was under attack on many fronts.

Historian Daniel Pipes targeted CAIR funders. A staffer at Middle East Forum contacted Silicon Valley Community Foundation to ask them how its leaders could fund an organization as problematic as CAIR. If they thought they were going to cause them to bolt, they didn't realize that supporting Muslim interests was a source of revenue for the Silicon Valley Community Foundation. The Herndon, Virginia, epicenter of funding, the International Institute of Islamic Thought, set up by the cadre of Muslim Brothers almost four decades earlier, was bankrolling the foundation. It had doled out $500,000 in grants to the Silicon Valley Community Foundation in 2015 for its global policy fund. Indeed, upon receiving the query from the Middle East Forum, foundation officials immediately reached out to Zahra Billoo, executive director of the CAIR

San Francisco Bay Area chapter. She responded with a link to their work on Islamophobia.org, along with the report by the Center for American Progress and the Southern Poverty Law Center.

Not only did the Silicon Valley Community Foundation not withdraw their support, but they invited Billoo to speak to their internal staff and a panel for their donors. Then later, they posted a blog article calling CAIR "reliable" and a nonprofit in "good standing."

* * *

In Congress, Sen. Ted Cruz (R-Texas) introduced S68, the "Muslim Brotherhood Terrorist Designation Act," to request that the Muslim Brotherhood be designated a foreign terrorist organization.

CAIR's government affairs chief, Robert McCaw, questioned the authenticity of the early document that chronicled the ambitions of the Muslim Brotherhood in a report titled "How a Discredited Memo Attributed to the Muslim Brotherhood Could Trigger an Anti-Islam Witch Hunt in America."

He released a second document on the dangers of the Muslim Brotherhood Terrorist Designation Act and a third document targeted former FBI agent John Guandolo, titled "CAIR Reveals Disgraced Former FBI Agent Drafted Original 'Muslim Brotherhood' Bill," respectively.

* * *

CAIR had to also destroy the influence of its critics with its proven strategy to discredit. Call a person a racist and "Islamophobe." Call their employer. Have friends call their employer. Celebrate the "good news."

In early March, CAIR's Ibrahim Hooper got news that terrorism expert Patrick Dunleavy was scheduled to teach US Air Force students about Islamic radicalization. He asked senior staffer Corey Saylor to draft a letter to send to the US Air Force.

Dunleavy was a senior fellow at former CNN investigative reporter Steve Emerson's Investigative Project on Terrorism. His course was called "The Dynamics of International Terrorism."

Within eight hours, Saylor had the draft ready. Dunleavy was associated with an "anti-Muslim propaganda mouthpiece." The Investigative Project on Terrorism was a "hate group."

Two weeks later, Hooper pushed out a "Good News Alert" to announce "Air Force to review Islamophobic instructor's course content."

* * *

Early into Sunday morning, news of a murder shook the neighborhood of Northern Virginia the Muslim Brothers had founded in the early 1980s

At about 3:00 a.m., off Route 7 in the town of Sterling, Virginia, Nabra Hassanen, seventeen, was walking with a group of other young Muslims, returning to the mosque after finishing their predawn morning meal at the local twenty-four-hour IHOP. A few rambunctious boys in her group saw a beat-up car at the intersection and threw one of their used drink cups at it in jest. The driver wasn't amused. He pulled his car to a sudden stop and started chasing the crew with a baseball bat. The boys ran. So did the girls, including Hassanen.

When the other young people caught their breath at the mosque, just a mile away, they realized Hassanen wasn't with them.

That night, she had been wearing her mother's flowing black abaya, or gown, for the first time, her hair also covered with a dark scarf. She had tripped on the sidewalk, not far from the Bowl America, where so many parents, like me, had taken their children for birthday parties. There, the driver caught up with her and dragged her, screaming, back to his car. The rest became the evening news. He raped and then murdered the girl, dumping her body in a local man-made pond.

In the coming days, Palestinian American activist Linda Sarsour blasted the murder as "Islamopobia." CAIR issued a statement, calling for a hate crime investigation. They ignored the illegal immigration status of the alleged killer.

It was a tragedy of infinite proportions, but it wasn't Islamophobia.

* * *

The Honor Brigade was obsessed with slapping the "Islamopobia" label everywhere.

Writing as "Emperor" on LoonWatch, CAIR Chicago's Ahmed Rehab shared the video from a TV roundtable discussion with a Pakistani Canadian Muslim reformer, Farzana Hassan.

On the comment board, the physician Javad Hashmi used his fake "1DrM" account to attack Hassan as a "muppet," "ignoramus," "fraud," and "Zionist sock puppet."

It was a tag team effort in assassinating Hassan's character.

In the spring of 2017, academic Craig Considine, a Muslim convert, published an article, "The Racialization of Islam in the United States: Islamophobia, Hate Crimes, and 'Flying while Brown.'" Even though Considine was white, he articulated the thesis of the Muslim activists trying to use the obsession of "critical race theory" with race to elevate their grievances. The paper sympathetically documented the unholy alliance that sat at the "intersectionality of race and Islamophobia."

Examining the "experiences of American Muslims and non-Muslims in the United States," Considine wrote that he used a "multi-tiered methodology" to reveal "how racialization processes interact with Islamophobic discourses and actions in American society." He argued, "Specifically, the dataset is anchored in U.S. public perceptions of American Muslims, hate crime incidents against Muslims and non-Muslims, and the institutionalization of Islamophobia."

He exploited allegations of "Islamophobia" to land Muslims dead center in the racial justice debate. "This kind of 'subliminal racism,' or 'racism without race,' lacks a formal system of segregation and other forms of overt racism, but it does suggest a system of inequality, injustice and racial differentiation," he argued. "Islam and American Muslims play a dominant role in these kinds of racist discourses. The contemporary tropes of Muslims as 'uncivilized,' 'barbarian,' 'primitive,' 'authoritarian,' and 'terrorist' depicts Islam as an inferior set of beliefs and cultural practices. These tropes are a repetition of older biological racist discourses."

* * *

By the summer of 2017, Muslim activists had succeeded in being accepted by mainstream philanthropies and think tanks, reading the talking points of "critical race theory."

The year before, in November 2016, Scripps College professor Lara Deeb reached out to colleagues around the country to see if they'd participate in a joint effort to create a new syllabus with one goal: the conversation had to be about Islamophobia "as a form of racism."

In Washington, DC, Georgetown University's controversial Bridge Initiative at the Prince Alwaleed bin Talal Center for Muslim-Christian Understanding announced that a "collective of scholars" had published a "groundbreaking syllabus" at the Center for Muslim-Christian Understanding called "Islamophobia Is Racism." The syllabus provided a reading list of 130 books, articles and essays, and multimedia products.

The center said that inspired by #FergusonSyllabus about the riots by blacks in Ferguson, Missouri, following the killing of a black man, the new #IslamophobiaIsRacism syllabus "reframes" the concept of "Islamophobia" as "anti-Muslim racism."

"In so doing," the Bridge Initiative said, "the authors seek to convey the process by which Islamophobia functions as not only religious-based discrimination, but discrimination animated by racism as well. The syllabus underscores the institutionalized and structural nature of Islamophobia racism, which begets long-term and systematic inequalities, stigmatization and exclusion."

It was right out of "critical race theory."

And no surprise that law professor and UCLA Law School alum Khaled Beydoun was among the "collective" of ten scholars who had brainstormed to create the syllabus. Some of the scholars were new to me, such as University of Michigan professor Evelyn Alsultany.

One of the goals of the syllabus was to "understand the relationship of race and religion to white supremacy through the racialized figure of the Muslim" and "provide an intersectional and comparative analysis to anti-Muslim racism."

The lexicon of "white supremacy" was becoming normative. And it was the perfect way to deflect from Islamist extremism, using "critical race theory" as the perfect foil.

That year, Caroline Mala Corbin, a law professor at the University of Miami School of Law, published an article, "Terrorists Are Always Muslim but Never White: At the Intersection of Critical Race Theory and Propaganda," in *Fordham Law Review*, arguing, "When you hear the word 'terrorist,' who do you picture? Chances are, it is not a white person. In the United States, two common though false narratives about terrorists who attack America abound. We see them on television, in the movies, on the news, and, currently, in the Trump administration. The first is that 'terrorists are always (brown) Muslims.' The second is that 'white people are never terrorists.'"

She continued, "Different strands of critical race theory can help us understand these two narratives. One strand examines the role of unconscious cognitive biases in the production of stereotypes, such as the stereotype of the 'Muslim terrorist.'"

"Another strand," she wrote, "focuses on white privilege, such as the privilege of avoiding the terrorist label," quoting Peggy McIntosh's 1989 book, *White Privilege: Unpacking the Invisible Knapsack*, and work by Kimberlé Crenshaw.

What she failed to acknowledge anywhere in the paper: Muslim terrorists exist.

* * *

That summer, lawyer-writer-activist Wajahat Ali was in Aspen, Colorado, as a speaker at a retreat of the Aspen Institute, where policy makers rubbed elbows with celebrities. It called itself nonpartisan and invited Republican leaders as speakers, but it was decidedly Democratic. The ambitious young man had emerged as a thought leader now among progressives in America.

He wanted to send them a simple message: they had obligations to support each other. He was going to exploit every bit of "critical race theory" to leverage more power in progressive Democratic politics.

"Finally," he told the crowd, "we all have to carry each other's water. Hate has gone intersectional. The forces of anti-Muslim bigotry also have their targets on women, LGBT, black communities, Latinos, and the undocumented. That means love must go intersectional and be just as audacious and replace miserliness with generosity. Muslims are stepping up for black lives, climate change, living wages, women's rights, and so forth. It has to be reciprocal, and it is."

* * *

The opportunity came weeks later when dueling protests in Charlottesville, Virginia, exploded into a race war.

Retired from the University of California, Berkeley, Judith Butler sat in front of a camera to blame the "Zionists" and the "state of Israel" for stoking anti-Semitism by "white supremacists, neo-Nazis, and fascists," in Charlottesville, rather than activists for the Boycott, Divestment, and Sanctions movement.

* * *

CAIR had worked hard to use this political moment to get folks to forget its dark past as an unindicted coconspirator in the Holy Land trial. By midsummer 2017, it had gotten the bulk of money received by Muslim organizations from Open Society Foundations.

CAIR California had won $140,000 to complete eighty-five "rapid response community safety workshops" at mosques, college campuses, and community centers across California. CAIR Florida snagged $100,000 to add a staff member to provide youth leadership training "focused on bullying prevention" and "help shift the narrative surrounding the American Muslim community through multi-media digital storytelling." CAIR New York grabbed $52,400 to launch a "hate crimes reporting initiative" in New York. CAIR Texas secured $73,610 to develop a "Report Hate Campaign" with mosques in north Texas. In total, CAIR pocketed $376,010.

A Soros favorite, Muslim Advocates, received $100,000 to provide legal services to "survivors of hate crimes and school bullying." In Tennessee, Faith & Culture Center got $25,000 to "engage people of multiple faiths" in two projects to "build understanding and tolerance" about Muslims in middle Tennessee. They were creating a retreat. Global Deaf Muslim received $20,000 to help deaf Muslim communities respond to hate crimes and discrimination through trainings and public education. The WISE initiative by Daisy Khan, who had tried to build the "Ground Zero mosque," got $74,995 to provide self-defense, mentorship, and leadership workshops in New York City and Texas to "equip young Muslim women to overcome violence and become advocates for social change."

* * *

By October 2017, Palestinian American activist Linda Sarsour had another opportunity to use her perch at the Women's March to expand her reach. The group was now organizing a Women's Convention in Detroit with Sarsour as a featured speaker, even charging its state organizers fees, annoying them. "It was a shit show," a former organizer said. The Women's March Inc. said it spent $300,000 on just catering. It sold "Platinum" packages for $100,000, offering a panel discussion, "media opportunities," and tickets to the "Sistahs" party.

In its 2018 annual report, Women's March Inc. reported $288,918 in convention sponsorships with donor restrictions. It said it got $308,022 in additional revenue from the convention, generating a total of $596,940.

They were sealing their narrative. In early October 2017, HarperCollins Publishers sealed a deal with the Women's March Foundation to publish a book, *Together We Rise*. Front and center: Sarsour.

* * *

There are some women who were just considered part of the "Sistahs" party. Asmi Fathelbab was one of them. An Egyptian American Muslim born and raised in Brooklyn, she worked for Linda Sarsour at the Arab American Association of New York when she alleged that a local Arab man would regularly come into the office and sexually harass her. When she publicly spoke about her #MeToo experience in late 2017, Sarsour told her side of the story to an American Muslim friend, Hannah Alam, a journalist at Buzz Feed, portraying Asmi as not believable and mentally unwell. I reported out every detail of the story and found Asmi's allegations credible. Alam wrote skeptically about Asmi's allegations, quoting Sarsour.

So much for Sarsour practicing what the Women's March preached: "Believe Women."

* * *

This Woke work was a moneymaker.

For the four leaders of Women's March Inc., protest had become a job while state organizers were running up bills on their personal credit cards. According to the Women's March Inc. 2017 IRS 990 filing, Mari Lynn Foulger ("Bob Bland") made $73,404 that year as co-president. Tamika Mallory had earned $70,570 as co-president, plus she received "fees paid" of $19,600 from The Gathering for Justice, totaling at least $90,170. Linda Sarsour got $69,927 as assistant secretary. Women's March Inc. reported paying Carmen Perez a salary of $47,710 for forty hours of work per week, while The Gathering for Justice said she earned $90,769, also for forty hours per week, and "fees paid" of $19,600, for a total of $158,079. Women's March, The Gathering for Justice, and the cochairs didn't return repeated requests for comment.

Two salaries didn't make sense. Breanne Butler received $26,400 for forty hours of work as a board of director. Janaya Ingram earned $26,400 for forty hours of work as secretary.

In its 2018 annual report, Women's March said it spent $703,864. The salaries to the board members totaled $314,411.

Women's March Inc. was just one money stream. A receipt for donations came from NEO Philanthropy, a liberal funder and fiscal sponsor based in Manhattan, for Women's March Network. Neo Philanthropy and its spokesman refused to reveal any details about Women's March Network financials.

In 2017, The Gathering for Justice reported again to the IRS that board chairman Michael Skolnik "did the production logistics."

The fiscal sponsorship with Women's March Inc. continued and, while The Gathering for Justice raised $1,536, 787, it only designated $55,270 "due to" the Women's March.

Net merchandise sales for the year totaled $1,166,705.

Women's March Inc. paid $255,747 to consultants and contractors.

* * *

The George Soros philanthropy empire continued to hand out grants to CAIR and affiliates around the country to respond to the Hawaii court ruling on the "Muslim ban." This included $4,000 to OneAmerica in Seattle, Washington, to develop "community action" on the day of the ruling, including "organizing and mobilizing toward a large press event" within twenty-four hours of the ruling and holding an educational event in partnership with CAIR's Washington State chapter and MAPS AMEN, "focused on Islamophobia and the Muslim Ban."

The money went toward paying poets to recite their anti-Trump poetry in front of the US Supreme Court and elsewhere.

Corey Saylor, director of CAIR's Department to Monitor and Combat Islamophobia, could finally push the button on a project he'd been circulating internally since the beginning of the year.

The report was called *The Islamophobia Network's Surrogates* and alleged, "The U.S. Islamophobia Network's ninja-like efforts to promote its AstroTurf Muslim pawns."

The report was Saylor's swan song at CAIR. His last day there was November 30. But not to worry. The next week, December 4, he started work at ReThink Media.

* * *

Trump was a godsend for the "critical race theory" evangelists. On the first-year anniversary of the 2016 election, twelve "social justice" leaders met online for a virtual town hall, "Social Justice SOS," sponsored by the mother of "intersectionality," Kimberlé Crenshaw, and her African American Policy Forum.

They discussed a "Racial Resentment Index," the crisis of "white women" voting for Trump, and "the politics of post-racialism."

The network included just about every slice of identity politics: law professor Khaled Beydoun on Muslim issues; Rosa Clemente; William Darity Jr.; Cornell faculty member Zillah Eisenstein on "intersectional" feminism; playwright Eve Ensler; Laura Flanders; Heidi Hartmann; Saru Jayaraman; Hiroshi Motomura; and Dennis Parker.

Also among the speakers: Alicia Garza, cofounder of Black Lives Matter and director of special projects at the National Domestic Workers Alliance. She challenged the "narrative of identity politics as divisive," FBI's categorization of "black identity extremists," often opposing the police.

Crenshaw turned to her former student, Beydoun, the Egyptian American lawyer who applied "critical race theory" to Muslims, and asked, "A year out now, what's the picture of state-sponsored Islamophobia that's come to view over the past year?"

As Beydoun started to speak, a page of @realDonaldTrump tweets from over the past months flashed on the screen, including, "SEE YOU IN COURT. THE SECURITY OF OUR NATION IS AT STAKE!"

Beydoun took his moment to warn that Trump's "state-sponsored Islamophobia" went beyond the "Muslim ban" to include "counter radicalization policing," including Muslim "informants" who report on "suspicious Muslims" to authorities, "infringing on a range of First Amendment rights," including free speech.

He emphasized the importance to "coalition build" with Muslims to protect black activists from policing.

Crenshaw agreed, reminding listeners of the threat of the FBI and law enforcement officials to their activists.

One by one the scholar-activists ticked off their field of expertise with the fundamental assumption in "critical race theory" that racial issues were a systemic outgrowth of "whiteness."

From Ithaca College, Zillah Eisenstein said, "Okay, well, the fight against feminism against racism and particularly white supremacy is always a feminist issue, but at this moment at a much greater intensity."

A protest sign flashed on the screen: "IT'S NOT FEMINISM IF IT'S NOT INTERSECTIONAL."

Garza, the cofounder of Black Lives Matter, closed by describing her vision of "effective, strategic resistance." It meant tapping the "unique moment" they found themselves by "continuing to link issues, right, that are able to tell a bigger story about who we are."

"We need a symphony," she said.

* * *

Khaled Beydoun reached into "critical race theory" to borrow a phrase—"words that wound"—to publish a new article, "'Muslim Bans' and the (Re)Making of Political Islamophobia," in the *Illinois Law Review*, arguing, "The convergence of structural and private Islamophobia inflicts enhanced injury upon Muslim American bodies, communities and geographies." One of the early ideologues of "critical race theory," Mari Matsuda had written a book, published in 1993, titled *Words That Wound: Critical Race Theory, Assaultive Speech, and the First Amendment (New Perspectives on Law, Culture, & Society)*. It was the perfect argument for Islamist sympathizers to now exploit.

* * *

By the end of 2017, CAIR officials were thrilled about the future.

They were a growing enterprise and had raised $19.5 million over the previous five years. After Trump's election, its revenue increased to $6.5 million in 2017 from $5.1 million the year earlier. That was almost triple since its $2.4 million from 2013.

In 2017, CAIR paid its executive director, Nihad Awad, $258,236 and $21,531 in additional compensation, and Ibrahim Hooper $177,244 plus $23,332. The board included attorney Roula Allouch, the chairperson; Masoud Nassimi, the vice chairman; James Jones, secretary; Ahmed Al-Shehab, treasurer; Sarwat Husain, board member since April 2017; Tahera Mamdani; Arlene Nu'man El-Amin; Manal Fakhoury; Nihad Awad; and Ibrahim Hooper. Corey Saylor, director of the Department to Monitor and Combat Islamophobia, received $116,788, and Lena Masri, national litigation director, earned $111,902.

It gave $950,000 to a little-known nonprofit, Together We Serve Inc., based in Falls Church, Virginia, off Route 7, run by none other than Esam Omeish, the controversial and ambitious leader of Dar Al-Hijrah Islamic Center, the mosque where he hired future al-Qaeda leader Anwar al-Awlaki as the mosque's imam.

* * *

On its first anniversary, in January 2018, the Women's March summoned women to Las Vegas for a "Power to the Polls" rally.

Wearing a tight pink headscarf and pink-tinted eyeglasses over a leather coat and pants, Linda Sarsour stood front and center, applauding enthusiastically, tight-lipped, as black march cofounder, Tamika Mallory, launched into a seven-minute, forty-one-second tirade, railing against the "white woman." Punctuating the air with her finger, Mallory shouted, "Don't come to this rally today with your pink hat on, saying you're with us when black people ask you to show up and ask you to defend our lives. Our job in 2018 is to make good on all the times that you left us out here in the cold."

Sarsour spun her hands overheard and applauded.

"Stand up for me, white woman! Come to my aid! You say you want to be my friend? I don't want to hear it from your mouth! I want to see it when you go to the polls in the mid-term election," Mallory continued.

Sarsour applauded.

Sarsour and the Women's March now had "white woman" in their scopes.

* * *

Soon after, Women's March communications chief Sophie Ellman-Golan and two cocreators launched a website, ConfrontWhite-Womanhood.com, with the mantra, "Challenging white women to do better." They sold T-shirts ($24.99) and pink hoodies ($37.99) that said, "White Womanhood Is White Supremacy." And they also hawked a three-week, six-session "Deep Dive" that examined "white saviorism," "white woman's innocence," and "how white women's safety is used as a tool for racial violence." (At some point after November 2020, the site was deleted.)

The summer before, someone had already anonymously started a Facebook page, @WhiteNonsenseRoundup with a Twitter handle @NoWhiteNonsense, supposedly "created by white people for white people, to address our inherently racist society." By the summer of 2020, it would have 177,825 Facebook followers. Among the folks recommended to follow on Twitter was *New York Times* creator of the 1619 project, Ida Bae Wells @NhannahJones; *New Yorker* writer Jelani Cobb; and author Ijeoma Oluo, who had written the book *So You Want to Talk About Race.*

Sarsour did an interview, published soon after, with *Quartz* reporter Leah Fessler, who wrote, "In profound yet accessible language, she articulates why liberation and safety for Muslim Americans is not complementary to, but rather essential to, liberation and safety for all Americans."

It was language right out of the script of "critical race theory," quoting its godmother, Kimberlé Crenshaw.

"We cannot win if we do not organize across communities, issues, and movements," she told the *Quartz* reporter. "Intersectionality is a term introduced to us by Dr. Kimberley [*sic*] Crenshaw, and now the implementation of her vision is the key to winning elections in 2018 and long-term, systemic changes."

This change was filled with its own rhetorical gobbledygook and preconceived notions. In January 2018, the oddly named Critical Race Studies Education Association issued a call for papers with the theme "Land and Knowledge: Indigeneity, Survivance and Healing." It asked "researchers, activists, educators, practitioners, community members, and youth" to "situate" their work within the "historical and current sociopolitical realities of colonization being endemic in society and its connections to anti-indigeneity, anti-blackness, anti-brownness, anti-immigration, anti-LGTBQ and anti-dis/ability rhetoric." It wanted work that explains how education works to "disrupt and/or maintain various types of oppression," including "racialization, patriarchy, heteronormativity, ableism, islamophobia, linguicism, capitalism, nationalism, and other forms of systematic oppression rampant in society."

Radical Muslims had succeeded in embedding "Islamophobia" inside the many other "-isms" of the Woke insurgency.

The agenda was trickling down to K-12 students.

The questions were bizarre: "What ways does/has globalization and imperialism impact(ed) students in K-12 spaces? With this question, the committee is excited about a critical race analysis of the K–12 curricula, and connections to TribalCrit: the neoliberal/colonial K–12 agenda and who benefits and/or does not benefit from this agenda." Then this tongue twister: "What ways are researchers, community activists and practitioners engaging in pedagogies that employ a decolonizing methodological approach to teaching, learning, research and organizing?"

The 2018 program chair was Cleveland Hayes, a faculty member at Indiana University, where the Muslim Brothers had put down their roots in the 1960s and 1970s.

* * *

There was no better partner for this effort at calling out "white supremacy" than a man named Louis Farrakhan. He was the leader of the quasi-Muslim organization, the Nation of Islam, founded on July 4, 1930, long before Muslim immigrants, like Linda Sarsour's parents, arrived on America's shores. And he brought another critical element to the cause: anti-Semitism.

Wallace D. Fard Muhammad felt he had a sacred duty. In Arabic, his name, *fard*, meant a sacred duty. His goal was to uplift blacks. In June 1934, he disappeared and was succeeded by Elijah Muhammad. In the late 1940s and early 1950s, a convict in jail in Boston for burglary—Malcolm Little—joined the Nation of Islam, becoming a successful preacher for the group when he left prison. Elijah Muhammad ordered him to change his last name from Little to "X," a symbol used by Nation of Islam followers to reject the names white slaveholders had given them. Malcolm X left the group and joined traditional Sunni Islam, after he did the haj, or pilgrimage, to Mecca, as a guest of the Saudi royal family. In 1965, Malcolm X was murdered. After Elijah Muhammad died in 1975, his son, Warith Deen Mohammed, changed the name of the Nation of Islam a few times and tried to move it toward mainstream Sunni Islam. In 1977, Louis Farrakhan—a charismatic, fiery young man who had joined the Nation of Islam years earlier as Louis Wolcott—reestablished the Nation of Islam with its original mission. He took control of Mosque Maryam, or Mosque No. 2, in Chicago, as his headquarters. In 1995, Farrakhan organized the Million Man March in Washington, DC, to advance black men.

* * *

Every year, Farrakhan and his followers in the Nation of Islam celebrated Saviours' Day. That winter, Tamika Mallory, the black cofounder of the Women's March, sat on the dais of the annual Saviours' Day celebration. Louis Farrakhan stood at the lectern and talked about Jews as "Satanic," LGBTQ people as "chemically imbalanced," whites as the "devil," and women as unworthy if they didn't cook for their husbands.

Mercy Morganfield, president of Women's March DC, couldn't believe Mallory just sat there without saying a word of protest. She picked up the phone and called the white American Women's March cofounder, Mari Lynn Foulger ("Bob Bland").

"What the fuck?" she said.

Morganfield didn't mince words. She had grown up in poverty in Mississippi, raised first by her single mother and then by her grandmother. Her mother died by suicide when Mercy was thirteen. She only started getting to know her father, the blues singer and songwriter known as "Muddy Waters," as a teen. She went on to earn a master's degree in organizational development.

Morganfield insisted the Women's March had to disavow Farrakhan.

Foulger balked. The Women's March would be attacking a black man. The other cochairs, including Linda Sarsour, refused.

"I'm a black woman," Morganfield said.

"What would it look like if one black woman attacked another black woman?" asked Foulger.

"I don't care. Right is right. Wrong is wrong," responded Morganfield.

Morganfield issued a statement condemning Farrakhan as a hate preacher. The social media manager for the Women's March, who had shot a selfie in the police van during the Women's March "strike," quit.

The Women's March leaders finally issued a statement disavowing Farrakhan's statements but expressly supported him as a leader.

At their Capitol Hill headquarters, CAIR officials debated whether they should respond to the anti-Semitism of Farrakhan. They decided to stay silent.

Sarsour needed their support.

* * *

Back with the Honor Brigade, the Muslim establishment had slipped into a convenient alliance with Democrats and liberals. How far were they willing to go?

In Seattle, the Minority Veterans of America reached out to Sarah Stuteville, media and outreach director of CAIR Washington State, to partner over opposition to the "Muslim ban" and the Trump administration's proposed ban on transgender people in the military.

No way, protested Karen Dabdoub, a white American convert to Islam. Supporting transgender Americans would infuriate too many people in the Muslim community. Dabdoub had grown up in a cul-de-sac in Cincinnati and went to college at Ohio University in Athens, Ohio, where she met her husband and converted to Islam. In 2004, she had launched the CAIR Cincinnati office. Early on, she and other CAIR staffers realized they were facing a "smear and fear campaign, spreading misinformation" about CAIR to "marginalize us and sideline us completely." They launched a campaign to correct the record. The next year, a small pipe bomb exploded near a two-story brick house with an attached mosque, just a year into Dabdoub's tenure as executive director of CAIR Cincinnati.

* * *

Now, CAIR executive director Nihad Awad nipped the transgender debate in the bud. CAIR national had decided to sit out the debate over same-sex marriage. It wouldn't support the transgender ban, but it also wouldn't join its liberal allies in opposing it.

* * *

By mid-June 2018, the new Women's March COO Rachel Carmona told chapter leaders that the Women's March national office was now working with DC Action Lab, a professional protest company. Liberal activist Robert Diesu had opened DC Action Lab LLC four years earlier in April 2013. Women's March had also hired Megaphone Strategies, a DC political PR company. PowerLabs, which "helps organizations design and run people-powered campaigns," was also now working for Women's March. Former Change.org staffer Randall Smith had launched PowerLabs. Zainab Chaudry, who had orchestrated social media campaigns like #UnpresidentedTweets as a communications specialist at ReThink Media, had moved to Megaphone Strategies. It was her job that ex-CAIR official Corey Saylor had taken.

The Women's March national team switched Women's March Network calls from biweekly to weekly "with the added capacity of DC Action Lab and the large number of forthcoming actions."

Linda Sarsour was now embedded in the professional protest industry of Washington, DC, and so, too, was CAIR. They were gaining benefit from this relationship.

Noor Mir, an activist born and raised in Islamabad, Pakistan, started running weekly meetings with state coordinators for the Women's March. A young activist, Mir was just a girl when the 9/11 attacks happened. That year, she had marched in Brooklyn with Sarsour and hundreds of others, advocating for human rights and dedicating their march to Akai Gurley, Eric Garner, and Shereese Francis. At the march, Sarsour said, "We are in a movement, sisters and brothers, not just here in New York City, but in Ferguson, Oakland,

Mexico, Brazil, Palestine and Hong Kong. We are all connected. Our struggles are connected, our movements are connected and our power is connected." Also that year, she joined Sarsour in a petition against the Muslim Leadership Initiative, a Jewish initiative that paid for trips to Israel for building awareness about the country. "Say no to faithwashing," the petition read.

She became a partner at her new employer, DC Action Lab, which boasted of creating many "direct action" protests, all out of their townhome headquarters, not far from the Capitol.

* * *

Early one morning at 6:47 on June 11, 2018, an alert went out to the "MASA-Organizing Google Group" that the Supreme Court ruling might be out that day. "MASA" was an acronym for "Muslim, Arab, South Asian."

ReThink staffer Gracie Farese had prepared for the "Muslim ban" ruling. Farese was a white American woman and a digital media fellow at ReThink in Berkeley, writing and editing content for a "Millennials and New Media Guide." Earlier in the year, she became a media associate, getting the account on Muslim rights.

She laid out her guidelines.

"It is a Muslim ban; always call it that."

"The waivers are window dressing; call them that."

No matter what the Supreme Court rules, she told coalition members to stick to the talking points. She spelled it out, "This [great/terrible] decision does not change the fact that Donald Trump expresses hate for a great many minorities. We are not going anywhere. We will not be banned."

Also: "We stand for religious freedom for all."

* * *

It was a busy summer. On a bright day in late June, CAIR executive director Nihad Awad stepped forward from a crowd on the sidewalk in front of the US Supreme Court and grabbed the microphone.

"I am a proud refugee," he said, in his trademark dark suit and tie, cheers breaking out around him, as beautiful, preprinted signs danced in the air in the hands of protesters. The fine print said Americans United.

He was a US citizen, of course, settled in the comfortable suburb of Annandale in Northern Virginia.

He railed against the "white supremacist administration."

Someone in the crowd replied: "Yes!"

"Shame on you!" he yelled to the US Supreme Courts for taking America "back to the Dark Ages."

"It appears to be the target is Muslims," he yelled some more. "We are the visible target but the main target is to create a white nationalist state, is to go back to the dark ages of racism, discrimination against people of color. We Americans should not allow this to happen again, and it is up to us, and the mic is in our hand, and the votes are in our hand, and the midterm election should be the signal that shows that we are committed to kick out this administration and defeat white supremacy. Repeat after me. No ban. No wall. No ban. No wall."

That afternoon, CAIR uploaded the clip to YouTube.

* * *

Across the river, at 500 Grove Street, the International Institute of Islamic Thought had started funding a scholarship program, the Islamic Scholarship Fund. One of its early recipients was none other than Javad Hashmi, the physician who led a double life as "Danios" on LoonWatch. He was studying as a student at Harvard University now.

* * *

Labor Day weekend 2018, the Islamic Society of North America hosted its annual conference in Houston, themed "In Allah We Trust." A graphic replicating the US dollar bill, only with the image of a mosque with its minarets instead of the eagle, loomed over the Houston skyline.

In a park on Avenida de las Americas, opposite the entrance of the George R. Brown Convention Center, protesters faced off against counterprotesters.

On one side, men stood ominously with AK-47 submachine guns strapped over their shoulders. One of them waved a flag with the silhouette of a shooter above the words, "An American Infidel." Another man carried a neon green sign: "Islam: 'Religion of peace'? We're awake now!" His sign listed a string of unfortunate truths in Muslim communities: honor killings, stonings, beheadings, rape gangs, acid attacks, female genital mutilation, suicide bombers, jihad, torture, child "brides," genocide, forced conversions, grooming gangs, death to America, death to Israel, slavery, polygamy, and trafficking.

"I don't hate Muslims," the man told a TV journalist.

But the protesters were there to send an unwelcome message to Muslims attending the ISNA conference.

Behind Houston police barriers, counterprotesters responded. A scuffle ensued as police officers pinned three counterprotesters to the ground before hauling them away.

Someone unfurled a red banner over a police barricade. It read, "Houston Democratic Socialists of America." People representing Antifa, the militant leftist protest group, arrived. Men and women with New Black Panther Party patches, black bandanas over their faces, black shirts, black pants, submachine guns in their arms, menacingly stared at the protesters.

They threw their fists in the air and shouted, "Power to the people!"

One of the counterprotesters' signs read, "Stop Islamophobia."

Another said, "No Platform for Fascism."

As someone beat a drum, a woman shouted into a megaphone, "From Palestine to Mexico, all the walls have got to go!"

A poster read, "We Indict the Trump/Pence Regime for Crimes Against Muslims."

At the barricade, a white-haired man talked to the protesters. One tattooed man with a megaphone responded, "Leave sharia law out of Texas!"

"Do you know CAIR?" the protester continued. "Your friends fund Islamic terrorism!"

Meanwhile, the counterprotesters chanted, "Whose streets? Our streets!"

The protesters and counterprotesters captured the polarization that defined America and, like on so many issues, the truth in this debate lay in the middle.

The protesters were correct that there are serious issues that define Muslim communities, in large part because of problematic interpretations of Islam incompatible with Western values—and enlightened Muslim beliefs. The counterprotesters were correct that "Islam" is not the problem. The problem is an interpretation of Islam that promotes sexism, intolerance, and religious governance, or *political* Islam and Islamism.

Some critics legitimately argue Islam has historically been political. That's true. But, just like interpretations of Christianity evolved to advocate a separation of church and state in societies we today call secular, the only pathway forward for Muslim progress—and compatibility with the West—is a *secular* interpretation of Islam that is compatible with values of enlightenment and modernity.

The problem is that there are governments, organizations, leaders, lobbyists, and millionaires in a powerful network of Muslims who oppose an interpretation of Islam that is secular. The heirs of the original Muslim Brothers were in Houston, and so, too, were the Muslim Sisters. They included the leaders of Islamic Society of North America; CAIR; the Islamic Council of North America, or ICNA; the Muslim Students Association, or MSA; and other groups from the alphabet soup of organizations founded over the past six decades of Muslims in America. And they run a disturbing propaganda campaign.

They were the bold-faced names of Islam in America.

The A-list: Linda Sarsour, the Palestinian American "Brooklyn homegirl in a hijab," as the *New York Times* called her; Mehdi Hassan, the Indian British host for the government of Qatar's Al Jazeera TV network; Nihad Awad, the Palestinian American founder of CAIR; Dahlia Mogahed, the Egyptian American pollster who converted

Comedy Central host Trevor Noah to the merits of Muslim headscarves.

It had been decades in the making.

* * *

Inside, it was like Comic Con for Muslims, completely insulated from the mayhem outside.

To the right, in the main convention hall, it was a festive scene with balloons, chatter, and children dashing between vendors' booths. In a far corner, a young man flirted with a younger woman. Many of the young people were members of the Muslim Students Association. Or the Matrimonial Students Association, as it's called, because it's one of the *halal*, or "Islamically legal," places where young single Muslims meet on college campuses. The after-hours at the ISNA convention, like many conventions, is notorious for hookups. Here, among "aunties" and "uncles," as elders are called, the interactions are PG.

A man told one of the ISNA staffers that he recommended they give the protesters bottles of water as a sign of goodwill. "We've taken direction from our security team," she told him. "They have it under control."

In the media room, an ISNA staff handed out a one-page sheet, "Media Guidelines." It included: "Inappropriate behavior, abusive language, and threats of any kind will not be tolerated."

In the bazaar, booth after booth was filled with books, clothes, and religious tracts. Mishkah University, founded in 2004 in Wesley Chapel, Florida, promoted its Islamic studies curriculum for Islamic high schools. "During these challenging times, this is a unique opportunity for youth in the West to hold fast to the rope of Allah through authentic Islamic education." *The rope of Allah.* It's a common refrain, quoting from a verse of the Qur'an.

The Islamic Education Institute of Texas Inc. passed out a slick brochure for its six full-time Muslim schools in the Houston area, teaching "high Islamic values and moral standards." One of the schools, Darul Arqam Southwest, in Sugar Land, Texas, has a strict school uniform policy that includes "white scarf with green trim or PLAIN white scarves with NO pattern or design," strictly "mandatory" starting in fourth grade, when girls turn about nine. Its philosophy is: "To reach the mind of a child, we must capture the heart." Its employee handbook had a special section on "Women Employees' Dress Code," stipulating that female employees must "follow the Islamic code of dress that conforms to the Islamic jurisprudence, based on Quran and Sunnah." That means: "The head cover should really cover. It is to be drawn over the head, ears and neck with an extension to cover the bosom. Slippery head covers are not permissible." The dress should "be loose enough so as not to describe the shape of the body," "should not be sheer," and must have "sufficient thickness" to "conceal the color of the skin it covers and the shape of the body." The fabric should not be "loud, shiny," or have any "glitter, sequins," or "beady decorations that attract the eye." Furthermore, "Golden bangles, flashy rings and necklaces should be concealed."

Finally: "The Muslim Woman's dress should reflect her unique personality. Therefore, it should not be similar to the prevailing fashions of the non-Muslim women." As if that weren't enough, "It should not be similar to men's fashions that are in style. If men wear slacks, women should not. If men wear ties, women should not... and so forth."

Sarsour's new organization, MPower Change, rented a booth in the main hallway. A stack of postcards and stickers sat on a ledge. "#MyMuslimVote," they read. The postcards included a box checked with the message, "I pledge to vote on Tuesday, November 6th."

Nearby was a booth for Soho Properties, founded in 2003. It was the business that bought the former Burlington Coat Factory building on Park Place, a few blocks from the site of the World Trade Center towers, with the plan to build a mosque—the infamous "Ground Zero mosque." A new slick brochure featured a glass tower reaching into the sky. "Tribeca Living. Driven by Design," the brochure bragged.

The contact was Sammy El-Gamal, the investor with a criminal record. He had failed to raise substantial funds for the mosque project. Now, the brochure said the Soho Properties Real Estate Fund was "actively raising capital for a $500M Sharia-compliant Real Estate Investment Fund," the "first of its kind in New York City."

At another booth, a glossy green folder was emblazoned with "North American Islamic Trust" across the front, with the tagline: "Committed to Serving the Muslim Community." This was one of the organizations begun by the first generation of immigrant Muslim Brothers in America, basing their headquarters in Oak Brook, Illinois, outside Chicago. Inside, the public relations material promoted the Islamic Centers Cooperative Fund, established in 1979. "An investment of kindness brings a harvest of duas and good wishes." Dua means "prayer." For Islamic nonprofits, it said it had thirty-six years of "Sharia compliant" 5.6 percent growth. As of December 31, 2016, the fund's pool was about $40 million, the material said, with up to 12 percent of the fund's pool used to "extend no-interest loans to build new or upgrade existing Islamic centers and institutions." About three hundred Islamic centers, schools, "relief and civic organizations" were participating in the Islamic fund. "Nearly" half of the centers have their properties "entrusted" to the "NAIT Waqf family." Funds were invested in "Iman Fund stocks," a sharia-compliant fund and other investments, such as real estate properties and leases. In the past, they had been invested in equipment and car leasing and home financing.

At another booth, the Islamophobia Studies Center had fundraising envelopes out, touting four projects. "Islamophobia on the Campaign Trail" featured an image of President Trump with "TRUMP" across the front. It would "monitor and document the use of Islamophobia on the campaign trail" during the 2018 midterm election and the 2020 presidential election and "provide regular materials for the media and the public." The "Islamophobia Reporting App" was developed, and the center said it was raising funds for "data collection & analysis," "producing monthly reports to media, policy makers & the community."

"Data impacts policy!" the fundraising pitch exclaimed.

The "K-12 Project" was aimed at "countering Islamophobia in public schools," with "training programs directed at teachers and administrators."

Another brochure promoted Shariawiz, an online legal portal based in Hasbrouck Heights, New Jersey, with software that "makes a cutting edge Sharia Compliant Will in minutes!" ISNA distributed its Green Masjid Project and Green Masjid Task Force, formed in 2015, promoting water conservation, recycling, biodegradable products, energy conservation, and solar energy. It has a flyer out for its Shoulder to Shoulder campaign, "Standing with American Muslims; Upholding American Values." It said it was founded in 2010 "by over 20 national faith groups, denominations and interfaith organizations."

The El-Hibri Foundation, based in Washington, DC, was there, promoting its "Collective Action Leadership Incubator."

Dar El Salam pitched a flyer for its haj trip, featuring photos of thirty "experienced religious scholars & leaders"—all men. They included Yasir Qadhi. A note said, "Each program is accompanied by qualified female leaders."

Near the center of the bazaar, Dar-us-Salam Publications, a publishing house based in Houston, sold its carefully curated collection of books with regressive interpretations of Islam.

* * *

An important session was beginning at 2:30 p.m. on a strategic theme: "The Impact of Public Islamophobia." Inside Room 371 ABDE, key colonels in the Honor Brigade held court.

Zahra Billoo, executive director of the CAIR San Francisco Bay Area chapter, was on the dais. So, too, was Khaled Beydoun, associate professor of law at the University of Detroit Mercy School of Law and senior affiliated faculty member at the UC Berkeley Islamophobia Research and Documentation Project. Earlier in the year, the University of California Press had published a book by Beydoun, *American Islamophobia: The Roots and Rise of Fear*, with the image of a Muslim girl with an American flag headscarf. Born in Cairo to parents from Lebanon and Egypt, he grew up in Egypt, returning there for the Arab Spring protests. He launched a "Free Egypt Now" project.

In the acknowledgments he thanked the godparents of "critical race theory," including Kimberlé Crenshaw, Devon Carbado, Ediberto Roman, Hisham Aidi, and Luke Harris. "Through Kim Crenshaw...," he wrote, "I learned what I wanted to do with my life," discovering from her that "innovative scholarship" should be "activated to bring about change, on the ground, during times of great crisis and mass action."

At that time, they could have little imagined that in just over a decade what "mass action" would mean.

Beydoun also thanked the "intellectual community" at the University of California at Berkeley Islamophobia Research and Documentation Project and "most notably" its founder, the controversial Hatem Bazian. He also thanked Open Society bigwig Alvin Starks and the roster of headliners in the Honor Brigade, including Palestinian American activist Linda Sarsour, Iranian American professor Omid Safi, CAIR officials Abbas Barzegar and Dawud Walid, researcher Dalia Mogahed, and Chicago activist Laith Saud. They'd worked in the trenches of many battles. He'd sat in a meeting room of the Office of Management and Budget with Sarsour to advocate for a new "Middle East and North Africa" racial-ethnic category with the US Census Bureau that was really based on geography. Her bottom line in that argument was federal funds. She alleged that "we lose out dramatically because we don't have a separated category... because we are quote 'white.'" Taking a page out of "critical race theory," she added: "At the end of the day it's self-identification, so I'm Palestinian if I want to say I'm black, I'm black, that's on me. I can check whatever box I'd like.... We need to understand the benefits of being white and not white and understand—maybe it's because I'm an activist—privilege that comes with being white and not having white privilege."

In the room, Beydoun encouraged the new "MENA" category.

Also at ISNA, Imam Khalid Griggs, a convert to Islam and associate chaplain for Muslim life at Wake Forest University in Winston-Salem, North Carolina, also sat on the panel. A Wake Forest alumnus rallied fellow alums to protest Griggs's hiring because Griggs had acknowledged being involved in the 1970s with a controversial organization, the "Islamic Party in North America," dedicated to evangelizing blacks.

I swept past families picking their children up from the daycare to join the crowd heading over to Hall A and B for a session, "Unapologetically Muslim," with Dalia Mogahed and Linda Sarsour.

The interpretation of Islam promoted at ISNA wasn't healthy. It didn't teach Muslims to assimilate and integrate. Instead, Muslim leaders, like Linda Sarsour, stoked young people to be angry and so "unapologetically Muslim" they were antagonistic.

* * *

Across the hall, activist Linda Sarsour sat with UC Berkeley's virulently anti-Israel Hatem Bazian, nicknamed "Hate 'em" Bazian by his detractors. Sarsour spoke at session after session at the Islamic Society of North America Conference.

She didn't mince her words. She believed in a "one-state solution" for Israel. Her one-state solution means Palestinians returning to Israel with equal representation to Jewish citizens, demographics that would lead to the destruction of Israel as a Jewish state. She told the crowd there that she refuses to "humanize" the Israeli who is her "oppressor." From Houston, this A-list of Muslims in the Honor Brigade returned to their battlefronts. Berkeley, California. New York City. Detroit. Washington, DC. Boston. My return ticket took me back to my home in Northern Virginia, off Route 7. Sarsour also headed out, armed with a carefully crafted plan for some high-profile shenanigans that would make the nightly news.

CHAPTER 17

Fighting a Political Campaign

Linda Sarsour stepped inside room 226 of the Dirksen Office Building. Inside, US senators on the Senate Judiciary Committee were set to pepper Judge Brett Kavanaugh, whom President Trump had nominated to the US Supreme Court, with questions. Democratic lawmakers were fighting against the nomination. To them, Judge Kavanaugh represented a threat to abortion rights and other Democratic platform issues. Sarsour was geared for a fight.

The Kavanaugh hearings—in which the reconstructed, unsupported allegations of a woman with little credibility almost cost Kavanaugh his nomination to the US Supreme Court—was a preview of what Woke Army "justice" actually looks like.

Sarsour was the second person to be arrested, shouting as US Capitol Police officers dragged her out. The protest was a failure. Women's March had again hired its professional protest team at DC Action Lab to pack hearing rooms, storm congressional offices, corner lawmakers, and interrupt the administration of democracy, but it was to no avail. The votes were there.

By Friday, on the eve of Kavanaugh's expected confirmation, Sarsour stood on the steps of the US Capitol with the other

Women's March cochairs, lamenting the "white women" who had voted for Trump.

The next day, protesters descended on the Capitol grounds, where a professional protest organizer handed out Women's March T-shirts that said "Believe Her" to anyone who volunteered to get arrested and handed over a form with information to get bailed out of jail.

"Watch your step," a woman said, guiding about two hundred people to the Capitol steps. She was Samantha Miller, the DC Action Lab professional protest organizer hired to be the field marshal for this protest.

On the front steps, smiling widely, taking selfies was Women's March cofounder Mari Lynn Foulger ("Bob Bland").

The selling of the Women's March brand continued, even amid controversy, and Linda Sarsour was successfully branding herself with symbols of liberal America. Ben & Jerry's ice cream, a wholly owned subsidiary of the multinational corporation Unilever, released a Pecan Resist flavor, with Sarsour front and center at the unveiling. Marketing activist Michael Skolnick tweeted that he was "humbled" that Ben & Jerry's asked his company, The Soze Agency, to work on the release of the new flavor. A Ben & Jerry's spokesman wouldn't release the terms of the contract.

Meanwhile, when black women leaders tried to ask Mallory to support a march they were organizing, she texted them back, cursing them out.

Sarsour was learning how to monetize a movement. By mid-October 2018, the Women's March national team dispatched a new lineup of sponsorship benefits. For $25,000, "popular options" for benefits for becoming a "presenting partner" for "DC mobilizations" included a "guaranteed spot on the 2019 program for your chosen representative to speak." In addition, "Quotes from your spokesperson will be placed in select media announcements." Also, a $25,000 sponsor would get "shout-outs" on @WomensMarch social media accounts. For $7,500, a "unity sponsor" would get "priority consideration" for a speaking slot on the 2019 program.

The PowerPoint file they used that outlined the benefits was last saved by Noor Mir, the Pakistani American professional protest organizer at DC Action Lab.

* * *

As Muslim activism took a new dimension, an era ended. One of the original Muslim Brothers of the modern day said he was stepping down.

In Istanbul, at a new de facto headquarters for the Brothers, Youssef Qaradawi, now ninety-three, announced his resignation as head of the International Union of Muslim Scholars. About 1,500 scholars had descended on the city for its general assembly meeting.

He accused the West of plotting against the rise of Turkey.

* * *

Two months later, the US Senate voted to end US support of Saudi Arabia in its war with Yemen. Bedier wrote on Facebook, "Thank you Jamal Khashoggi, you continue to make an impact on our world even after you departed. #yemencantwait." He shared an article by ThinkProgress, the propaganda arm of the Center for American Progress.

* * *

News of a great hoax spread through academic circles that fall.

A young American mathematician, James Lindsay, had teamed up with a British cultural critic, Helen Pluckrose, and an American philosopher, Peter Boghossian, to write fake outlandish research papers they submitted to academic journals in the business of publishing "grievance culture" think pieces. They rewrote Hitler's manifesto, *Mein Kampf*, as a work of "intersectional feminism" and found a home for their work in *Social Work*, a journal. They wrote on "whiteness" and the "white gaze" and the "rape culture" in dog parks, also as part of their hoax academic work.

Orthodox Muslim scholar Mohamed Ghilan watched with horror. Not because he was vested in "critical race theory" but for exactly the opposite reason. It was "nonsense," he wrote, for anyone to follow its ideology. "The problem is when you turn a tool or inquiry into an ideology," he wrote on Facebook, "and then use that as a politically motivated paradigm that colours how you understand and reason about everything. We can give an excuse to non-Muslims and say they have nothing else to anchor themselves onto. But for a Muslim to buy into this nonsense and neglect the Quran and Sunnah and the whole Islamic tradition, there are only two things that can be said: 1. Shame on you 2. May Allah guide you and open your eyes before it's too late.

"It's all a political show," he lamented, "put together by a band of people who don't care for Truth and are led by figures who in some cases proudly declare how they couldn't finish anything they picked up to read. They celebrate ignorance and incoherence. What's even more troubling for me is that Muslims, the people of the Quran and the Sunnah, are falling for this nonsense."

* * *

There were some cracks developing in the liberal coalition Sarsour had built. In November 2018, actress and #MeToo activist Alyssa Milano came out publicly against the Women's March lack of inclusion and alleged anti-Semitism. That opened a chasm.

From Hawaii, Women's March founder Teresa Shook called for the four cochairs to step down. Washington chapter president Mercy Morganfield took to her Facebook page to support the shake-up, despite efforts from Women's March leaders to dismiss her criticism.

The Women's March continued its strange "intersectional" politics and corporate enterprise. The organizing guidelines for the 2019 sister marches noted the presence of police "signal[s] danger to communities," so they wouldn't invite police to participate in events.

Progressives like Morganfield and Shook didn't have a place in this nexus of the Left and Islamists.

CHAPTER 18

Recognizing New Field Marshals

The 2019 election results were in.

Newbie politicians Rashida Tlaib, Ilhan Omar, and Alexandria Ocasio-Cortez had won. Justice Democrats had managed to pull off some key victories in less than two years in operation. Ocasio-Cortez named Saikat Chakrabarti, the dapper Bengali American cofounder of Justice Democrats, as her chief of staff. He had just weathered a storm over a T-shirt he had worn for an interview with NowThis News. It featured the image of Subhas Chandra Bose, a Bengali Indian who lived in the 1930s, through the British-created Bengal famine, which killed more than two million Bengalis. (It also left my father hungry, standing in line for sorghum wheat from the US.) Bose was a fierce Indian nationalist who had gone to Germany in 1941 during World War II to appeal to Adolf Hitler for help to win independence from British colonization of India. He formed the Azad Hind Fauz, or Indian National Army. Critics called Chakrabarti out for wearing a T-shirt honoring a "Nazi collaborator."

For many people in America, they were reading up on these women for the first time, but the Muslim Brothers (and Sisters) knew them well, and their victories were a moment of great celebration for political Islam in America. The CAIR California Political Action Committee, led by Hussam Ayloush, had donated $5,000 to Omar's campaign, and other CAIR chapters had held fundraisers for these two rising Muslim stars in American politics. CAIR was counting on them to push forward a couple of serious issues: their plan to win the land of Israel for Palestinians and to establish the narrative of the West as "Islamophobic." The narratives of these two women's lives, however, belied the notion that Muslims were under attack in America.

* * *

After Omar's election, the US Congress lifted its ban on head covering in the US House. Her campaign office told *MuslimGirl* that she supports the BDS movement despite "reservations on the effectiveness of the movement in accomplishing a lasting solution." A Qatar media outlet published a headline that Saudi Arabia had used an army of trolls to harass Omar and other critics of its regime.

She won key committee assignments: the House Committee on Education and Labor and the House Committee on Foreign Affairs. She joined the Congressional Black Caucus and the Congressional Progressive Caucus.

* * *

These new lawmakers emerged at a time when the Woke Army was gaining new footholds in academia and nonprofits. The money was now starting to roll into the field of "antiracist" studies. In 2018, the Marguerite Casey Foundation, based in Seattle, awarded a $200,000 "gift" to one of the generals in the Woke Army, Ibram Kendi, for a new center at American University (my alma mater) called the "Antiracist Research and Policy Center." The support strategies for the grant included policy, advocacy, and "systems reform."

That year, the Bush Foundation, based in Saint Paul, Minnesota, gave Educators for Excellence, a New York–based nonprofit with six chapters around the country, a $10,000 grant for "sponsorship" of "How to Be an Antiracist Educator: A Conversation with Dr. Ibram

Kendi." The organization promoted a "How to Be an Antiracist" book club with its St. Paul, Minnesota, chapter in April 2020. Kendi had a keynote speech scheduled with the Minnesota chapter in May 2020. The website included a button, "Take the Pledge," agreeing to a pledge to "Commit to live out antiracism for your students."

The next year, the Ford Foundation awarded Kendi a $200,000 grant to create "the National Antibigotry Project" and another $50,000 grant for the "Racial Reporting Initiative" of the Antiracist Research and Policy Center to organize and host a symposium to develop the "Racial Reporting Guidebook."

The next year, the Andrew W. Mellon Foundation gave a nonprofit, Community Music Works, in Providence, Rhode Island, a $150,000 grant to support the "documentation and dissemination" of a "model for antiracist praxis in classical music education."

* * *

The BDS movement was getting beaten up. Its leaders needed new leverage.

Palestinian activists were pressuring Airbnb to stop listing homes in Jewish settlement towns. CAIR weighed in, readying a press release calling on Booking.com to join Airbnb in ending rentals in Jewish settlement towns. Airbnb then backtracked.

In May 2018, the CAIR national council voted to recommend to the CAIR national board that it support BDS. By fall, CAIR leaders like Zahra Billoo, CAIR's executive director for its San Francisco Bay Area chapter, were growing frustrated that CAIR national officers were dragging their feet.

In late November 2018, black activist Marc Lamont Hill gave a speech in the United Nations, marking the International Day of Solidarity with the Palestinian People, drawing calls for his firing as a CNN analyst. He expressed support for the BDS movement and called for a "free Palestine from the river to the sea." For most Israelis, this was not a call for peace but the annihilation of the entire state of Israel.

Billoo responded on Twitter, "From the river to the sea, #Palestine will be free."

CNN quickly fired Hill for his "offensive" remarks.

CAIR executive director Nihad Awad readied an op-ed of support for Hill with Edward Ahmed Mitchell, executive director of the CAIR Georgia chapter. The *Huffington Post* published it. At The Intercept, attorney-turned-journalist Glenn Greenwald complained that Hill's firing represented a "major victory" for the "growing so-called 'online call-out culture' in which people who express controversial political views are not merely critiqued but demonized online and then formally and institutionally punished after a mob consolidates in outrage, often targeting their employers with demands that they be terminated." These firings were a "major defeat" for the "right to advocate for Palestinian rights, to freely critique the Israeli government, and for the ability of journalism and public discourse in the U.S. generally to accommodate dissent."

* * *

While the Sikh American activist and lawyer Arjun Singh Sethi was still on the road selling his book, *American Hate*, Zahra Billoo was at a conference sponsored by American Muslims for Palestine. There, she revealed her true feelings about Israel. "...Let's be real and call it apartheid Israel," she said. "I am not going to legitimize a country that I don't believe has a right to exist."

Communications chief Ibrahim Hooper was annoyed by this outburst and the talking point it gave to CAIR detractors. But Billoo didn't care. She told her colleagues she was speaking from her personal perspective, not in her capacity at CAIR.

* * *

Swearing-in day at the US Capitol was a day of celebration for the Honor Brigade. From around the country, its generals, lieutenants, and foot soldiers descended on Washington, DC, to celebrate the new Muslim congressional representatives who were elected to office.

Linda Sarsour wore a Palestinian *thobe*, or gown, as she mingled in the hallway with other Palestinian Americans. Inside, a Palestinian American comedian wrote, "Palestine," on a yellow sticky note and put it on a map, with an arrow pointing in the direction of Israel.

That night, CAIR hosted a fundraiser for the three new representatives. Nihad Awad took to the podium in his trademark suit and spectacles, blasting against the hate against Muslims that had spiked since Donald Trump's election in 2016.

At her reception, Tlaib took the microphone to rail against Trump, shouting, "We're going to impeach the motherfucker."

Not all in the CAIR system approved of this, as internal debate erupted. One prominent Muslim community activist in Dallas complained that the organization should issue a statement saying it didn't approve of Tlaib's profanity, otherwise it ceded its moral authority to criticize Trump's language. From Southern California, Hussam Ayloush also protested in communications to other officials. CAIR's Zakir Khan called these criticisms a double standard against a woman. CAIR Maryland's Zainab Chaudry, CAIR Seattle's Masih Fouladi, and CAIR New Jersey's Ahmed Al-Shehab opposed CAIR issuing a statement of reproach. And from the San Francisco Bay area, Zahra Billoo was shocked the conversation had even gone on so long.

* * *

While Muslims were getting elected to office, the Honor Brigade was busy getting people they opposed out of government. No position was too small.

In New Jersey, the state chapter executive director, James Sues, dashed out a press release calling for the dismissal of three Republican Hamilton Township municipal employees who had shared Facebook posts he called "racist and Islamophobic." It got picked up by state media outlets, from Insider NJ to the *Trentonian*. In their crosshairs were Robert DiPastina, who worked in the public works department; his wife, Colleen DiPastina, who worked for the Hamilton Police; and Kenneth Enderle, a Hamilton Township engineering aide. The DiPastinas had shared the image of a bearded man wearing a Muslim prayer cap, sitting on a toilet, with the caption, "This is a Muslim. They don't use toilet paper. They use their hand. This is Starbucks. They vow to hire 10,000 Muslims." Enderle had shared a graphic with happy face emojis as the backdrop to a statement, "I haven't seen this many Democrats dressed in white since they created the KKK."

Sues wanted to denounce these three local municipal employees and have them fired.

Across the state line, Ahmed Mohamed, the Yemeni American litigation director at CAIR New York, suggested that his counterparts slow down. Calling for low-level municipal employees to lose their jobs over Facebook posts was more than they had demanded of higher-level elected officials for more egregious offenses. As a trial attorney in the CAIR national office just the year before, Mohamed had learned to pick his battles. But his argument wasn't persuasive. The CAIR New Jersey executive director pushed the button on his press release.

* * *

The requests were flying in for appearances by the Muslim US representatives at CAIR fundraisers. They were celebrities and headliners.

Asma Rehman, national chapter manager at CAIR, corralled the chapters so they would fill out a form to request appearances from Representatives Tlaib, Omar, and André Carson (D-IN) every couple of months. The congressional staffers were booking appearances about six months out. The congressional representatives couldn't accept payments, but community members were encouraged to organize private fundraisers for the lawmakers.

* * *

Meanwhile, lobbyists for the Republic of Turkey from the law firm of Greenberg Traurig, LLP were pounding the pavement, setting up meetings with Representatives Tlaib and Omar, along with Representative Carson, on behalf of Turkey. On Christmas Eve 2018, the

Embassy of Turkey had paid the lobbying firm $425,000 in fees. On March 27, 2019, they doled out another $384,500, for a total of $809,500 over just three months.

* * *

CAIR officials knew they had to keep playing the victim card.

Khaled Beydoun, forty, traveled the country speaking out about "Islamophobia." In 2019, he had released a book, *American Islamophobia: Understanding the Roots and Rise of Fear*, published by the University of California Press. Just months earlier, billionaire George Soros's Open Society Foundations named him among twelve Soros "Equality Fellows." After a two-hour flight from Atlanta, Beydoun, now a University of Arkansas law professor, tweeted that he had been discriminated against on a regional jet operated by Endeavor Air, a wholly owned subsidiary of Delta Air Lines. He took to Twitter to launch his offensive after landing one late Sunday afternoon at Northwest Arkansas Regional Airport in Bentonville, Arkansas. Initially, he had been upgraded from the main cabin to seat 1C as a Platinum-level frequent flier but claimed he was told during boarding that a flight attendant had to sit in 1C, per company policy, because the jump seat wasn't working. He would have to move four rows back to seat 5C, which had just as much legroom as 1C.

Upon landing at gate A9, he alleged that he was waiting for his luggage on the jet bridge when the captain of the flight grabbed him by his jacket and treated him "like a criminal."

"I know that Flying While Brown has always been a concern," he wrote on Twitter. "But now Landing While Brown is also frightening.

"This is Trump's America," he wrote. "It happened in the South, and I'm Arab and Muslim."

In a police report, taken at 4:07 p.m., the pilot, Timothy Hovelsrud, had a very different version of the incident. When Beydoun was moved to seat 5C, he "pulled the 'race card' and complained the seat was empty most of the flight." After all, the flight attendant was working. After deplaning, Beydoun said he wanted to talk to the pilot. Hovelsrud said he told Beydoun he would talk with him further up the jet bridge, motioning for him where to meet. He insisted he did not touch Beydoun.

Beydoun complained that he had had to sit next to a "large man" during the flight and his neck was in pain from leaning into the aisle, away from the man. He had a knee injury and had to sit with his leg stretched out during the flight. He asked the flight attendant if he could be accommodated, but the flight attendant was rude to him too. After landing, the pilot pulled him by the jacket and told him where they would talk.

"Beydoun stated first it was battery, second it was an assault, and third it was condescending because he was 40 years old," the officer wrote in the report.

Beydoun also claimed a grievance that the police officers had interviewed the pilot first. They had to get both sides of the story, they explained.

"True," Beydoun responded.

The officers asked Beydoun if he wanted a warrant for the pilot's arrest.

"No," he responded. He just wanted the situation documented, and he'd seek action against Delta. Later, Delta issued a statement, "We regret that the customer perceived the seat change was anything but procedural. Prior to departure, Delta apologized to the customer for the seat change and provided a goodwill gesture for the inconvenience."

One section of the police report included "Bias Motivation Codes," with options for the police officer to check off Code 24, "Islamic (Muslim)," or Code 31, "Arab," among others.

The police officer chose Code 88: "None."

* * *

The flimsy case of bias didn't matter. In Michigan, CAIR chapter leader Dawud Walid shared Beydoun's cell number with the national network.

Based in Seattle, CAIR leader Masih Fouladi texted Beydoun. In Washington, DC, CAIR communication chief Ibrahim Hooper spoke with him. He assured Beydoun that CAIR would support the American-Arab Anti-Discrimination Committee's complaint.

* * *

Among the reformers, women are some of the fiercest leaders. There are brave young women like Rahaf Mohammed who fled Saudi Arabia in an escape narrated in real time on Twitter; Masih Alinejad, who leads a movement to challenge the compulsory headscarf in Iran; and Yasmine Mohammed, an ex-Muslim, who cocreated a mini-movement with me called "Free from Hijab," turning "World Hijab Day," a construct of a Muslim businesswoman in Brooklyn, into "No Hijab Day." It's not just a piece of cloth we protest. It's an ideology that naive fashion designers and companies, from Nike to Dolce & Gabbana, have normalized with a promotion of the headscarf that more resembles a hijab fetish. Is the hijab a symbol of choice? A symbol of freedom, as its proponents like to argue? No. It's a symbol of a dangerous political ideology.

What the Honor Brigade had done was create a narrative in the world that Muslim women were authentically Muslim if they wore a headscarf. Even CAIR officials described themselves as the "hijab legal defense fund." They won a victory in early 2019 when the international boxing federation changed its rule to allow women boxers to wear headscarves.

* * *

The first two Muslim women elected to the US Congress were leaders in this new generation of Muslim American leaders "unapologetic" for their identities and in their confrontation with America, a declaration that Sarsour asserts often and loudly. In the two months after they were sworn into office in January 2019, Representatives Omar and Tlaib relentlessly criticized their family's adopted country as racist and anti-Muslim; aligned themselves with virulently anti-Israel activists, like Sarsour; and were publicly rebuked for their anti-Semitism. Jewish activists had resurrected a 2012 tweet that Omar had written as a state representative in Minnesota, complaining, "Israel has hypnotized the world, may Allah awaken the people and help them see the evil doings of Israel." *New York Times* columnist Bari Weiss, a strong Jewish American writer who had dared to challenge the anti-Semitism of these Muslim activists, wrote that Omar's statement tied into a millennia-old "conspiracy theory of the Jew as the hypnotic conspirator."

When asked in an interview how she would respond to American Jews who are offended by the tweet, Omar replied, "I don't know how my comments would be offensive to Jewish Americans. My comments precisely are addressing what was happening during the Gaza War and I'm clearly speaking about the way the Israeli regime was conducting itself in that war."

Later, after reading Weiss's commentary, Omar apologized for not "disavowing the anti-Semitic trope I unknowingly used."

But then, days later, she had a series of exchanges about Israel on Twitter with liberal attorney-turned-writer Glenn Greenwald, who had raised funds for CAIR, as a keynote speaker at CAIR fundraisers.

They bantered about support for Israel in the US.

That's when Omar responded, "It's all about the Benjamins baby."

She was referring to Benjamin Franklin on the one hundred dollar bill.

All hell broke loose.

The pressure was getting intense on Representative Omar.

By early afternoon, Hooper drafted a press release. CAIR executive director Nihad Awad recommended deleting any reference to Christian and Muslim Palestinians seeking peace and refer instead vaguely to people of different religious and ethnic backgrounds. That edit made it to the final round. By midafternoon, CBS News reported that Omar "apologizes for tweets widely denounced as anti-Semitic."

What would this controversy mean for the CAIR legislative agenda in the US Congress? Would House Democrats abandon their opposition to anti-BDS legislation?

CAIR research and advocacy director Abbas Barzegar didn't see a problem. CAIR had to just stay on the offensive. The anti-BDS legislation was a threat to free speech. That was the most winning argument they had crafted. Then, also, CAIR had to keep discussing hate crimes, because the idea of "Islamophobia" and anti-Semitism as equally threatening to societies and people was gaining legitimacy. In fact, anti-Semitism was a much more frequent threat. The organization's leaders just needed a stronger offensive strategy. He had some solid ideas. Plan panels with representatives. Run academic panels. Do call-ins with allies. Create workshops.

From the Pacific Northwest, Zakir Khan, the chairman of the board for the Oregon chapter of CAIR, agreed completely. There were an estimated sixty thousand Muslims in Oregon. How about flipping the narrative? And getting a congressional hearing on what law enforcement was failing to do and what far-right hate technology companies were enabling? In the far-left city of Portland, just the week before, he had worked with liberal organizations to get a resolution passed condemning white nationalism and white supremacy. They'd created a strategy to implement with the Oregon Justice Resource Center and the Western States Center, where he was program manager. The year before, Khan had led an effort to get the city of Portland to pull out of the Joint Terrorism Task Force. It had taken a year, but Portland announced that week that it was pulling out.

The Woke Army was learning that if they stuck to their guns, they could win some battles.

* * *

The *New York Post* ran a cover story with the headline "Omar slammed yet again for anti-Semitic tweets."

Early the next morning, things were in a scramble at CAIR headquarters on New Jersey Avenue SE. If mainstream reporters asked about it, what should CAIR's response be?

Don't respond, said CAIR's Michigan chapter chief, Dawud Walid.

Get Jewish Voice for Peace to respond.

The call went out to Jewish Voice for Peace.

* * *

Democratic leaders admonished Omar. House Speaker Nancy Pelosi (D-CA), Majority Leader Steny Hoyer (D-MD), and Majority Whip Jim Clyburn (D-SC) criticized the tweets, calling Omar's anti-Semitic tweets "deeply offensive."

The next day, Omar issued an apology, stating, "I am grateful for Jewish allies and colleagues who are educating me on the painful history of anti-Semitic tropes," adding, "I reaffirm the problematic role of lobbyists in our politics, whether it be AIPAC, the NRA or the fossil fuel industry." She didn't mention Muslim lobbyists.

President Donald Trump said she should resign from Congress.

Omar responded that Trump had long "trafficked in hate" against Jews and Muslims. About that time, the HarperCollins imprint, Dey Street, signed a lucrative contract with her for her memoir.

Omar was attracting fire from all sides until a sophisticated communications network mobilized an aggressive defense for her. It flipped the criticism, with the goal of transforming Omar from an anti-Semite into a victim of racism and "Islamophobia." It weaponized fear and distrust to divide and alienate Muslims from America. The tactics had been honed over a decade by the mini-United Nations for Muslim countries, the Organization of Islamic Cooperation. Muslim world leaders had decided in late 2005 to leverage allegations of "Islamophobia" to push an attack on the West and defense of "true Islam." The Honor Brigade had been fifteen years in the making, and they kicked into action.

The Honor Brigade presented a rich paradox because US practitioners such as Sarsour and Omar were happy enough to align themselves with liberal causes such as feminism and transgender rights—even though such stances would never be tolerated in Muslim countries and in fact contradicted their own religiously conservative interpretations of Islam and their thinly veiled support for Islamist governance. Being gay in many Muslim nations is a capital offense. Indeed, while happy to march for women's rights in the US, they have little to say about the lack of such rights in Muslim countries.

And it's interesting to note their political alliance and the American progressives who—save for the Honor Brigade's claim to victimology—have zero tolerance for religious governance.

* * *

The anti-Semitic tropes promoted by Omar were very familiar to Muslim reformers. For over a decade, we had been called everything from "Zionist media whore" to agents of the Israeli government because we had publicly challenged treating women as second-class citizens, Islamic law in politics and governance, and violent expressions of Islam. Many of the attacks came from anonymous social media accounts hiding their real identities. The Council on American-Islamic Relations was stoking divisiveness, polarization, and hate.

* * *

On a Saturday night in Birmingham, Alabama, in mid-February 2019, 1960s radical activist Angela Davis, then seventy-five, stepped forward from backstage to receive an award that the Birmingham Civil Rights Institute had originally rescinded among uproar over Davis's support of the Boycott, Divestment, Sanctions movement. In the front row that night, Linda Sarsour, a big fan of Davis, filmed Davis as she strode onto the stage to a standing ovation and shouts of "We love you!"

Birmingham Civil Rights Institute president Andrea Taylor, a black woman, had announced in October 2018 that she would be "thrilled" to honor Davis with the institute's Fred L. Shuttlesworth Human Rights Award for "giving voice to those who are powerless to speak." Then, in early January, the institute said Davis did not meet "all of the criteria" for the award. Birmingham mayor Randall Woodfin said protests came from the "local Jewish community and some of its allies."

Sophie Ellman-Golan, the white Jewish staffer at the Women's March from its start, blasted the decision to rescind the award on Twitter as "disgraceful," and blamed "the many Christian Zionists in Alabama." Author Marc Lamont Hill, who just lost his post as a CNN contributor, tweeted that the decision was "shameful."

Behind the lectern, Davis lauded "all of the young women in Congress, women like Ilhan Omar, for telling it like it is."

That night, Sarsour tweeted out her fifty-eight-second clip with the message, "Birmingham welcomes Dr. Angela Davis HOME today. No one gets to dictate who our leaders are and which are worthy of honor. #AngelaDavisDay #iconllllll."

* * *

The Honor Brigade had a tried-and-true solution to turn the tables on this debate: call out the critics of Representative Omar for "Islamophobia."

They scheduled a press conference and photo opportunity outside the steps of the US Supreme Court, trying to get the US House of Representatives to condemn "Islamophobia," while getting Representative Omar out of some hot water. About a half hour before the press conference, Egyptian American activist Ahmed Bedier, the former executive director of the CAIR Florida chapter, and Arsalan Bukhari, CAIR's national strategic communications manager, arrived at the front steps of the Supreme Court on First Street NE, where one cameraman had set up his camera and microphone stand on the sidewalk, positioned so the majestic US Capitol dome would tower behind the activists as they spoke.

Born in Egypt, Bedier had arrived in the United States at the age of eight, when his father, an economist and statistician, moved his family to the US. After his parents returned to Egypt, Bedier stayed in the US, working as an IT network administrator and then operations manager for a dental practice before opening a dental laboratory in St. Petersburg, Florida. After the 9/11 attacks, a reporter for the *St. Petersburg Times* called Bedier's mosque for comments and interviewed him about his views as a young Muslim in America. The next year, Bedier was inspired to action after police arrested a Florida podiatrist for possession of twenty illegal bombs and a three-page "Mission Template" with a plan to "Kill all 'rags'" at an "Islamic Education Center."

When CAIR opened a chapter in Tampa the next year, it named Bedier its first executive director. After a falling-out, Bedier left to start a 501(c)(3) tax-exempt organization, United Voices for America, to increase Muslim participation in politics. On the day of the new lawmakers' swearing in, Bedier shot videos of Omar and Tlaib, their family, friends, and supporters jostling with each other to take selfies with the new lawmakers. "The thobes are here," he said, in one video, referring to the traditional Palestinian robes many women were wearing to their ceremonies.

Moving quietly around the cameramen and smiling warmly, Bukhari had just moved to the CAIR national headquarters in Washington, DC, from Seattle, where he had been the executive director of the CAIR Washington State chapter. He had lobbied editors at the *Seattle Times* to stop using the words "terrorism" and "Islamism," alleging the words unfairly smeared Muslims.

A few minutes before the scheduled start of the press conference, there was a flurry of motion a half of a block north, at the intersection of First Street NE with Maryland Avenue NE. A group of about twenty-five people had walked out of the Methodist Building, led by the star of the show, Sarsour, with a bright green headscarf tightly wrapped around her head, over a long, puffy down jacket. She brought the group to stand in a huddle behind the microphones attached to a folding luggage handcart. The CAIR executive director stood in the front row. The American Muslims for Palestine leader stood to the side.

One by one, the speakers defended Tlaib and Omar from allegations that they were anti-Semitic in a well-crafted script. They accused their detractors of racism and Islamophobia, casting Tlaib, Omar, and Muslims as victims. Allies from two ultra-liberal but anti-Israel Jewish organizations joined the chorus. Rabbi Alissa, deputy director of a nonprofit Jewish Voice for Peace, stepped forward in a long, puffy winter coat and lent her voice of support for Omar. She was cofounder of the Nakba Education Project, to inform people about the *nakba*, the word used for the "humiliation" of Israel's birth. Natalie Bamdad, an organizer at IfNotNow, also rallied for Omar. Though small in membership and denounced as radical and anti-Israel by mainstream Jewish organizations, outfits like Jewish Voice for Peace and IfNotNow give propaganda cover to groups like CAIR, especially when CAIR is accused of anti-Semitism.

"Like many young Jews I grew up hearing stories about persecution of my people," she said, looking up from notes, "and I am now fearful of rising Islamophobia, racism, and anti-Semitism." It was a well-rehearsed plot twist. For almost two decades, since the 9/11 attacks, Muslim leaders had learned to frame themselves as the victims. Now, they had Jewish allies telling the world that Muslim grievances were as important, if not more, than anti-Semitism.

Suddenly, a small group of well-coiffed, well-dressed women arrived and stood at the edge of the reporters, watching impatiently. At one moment, one of the women, Rabia Kazan, a Turkish American journalist and activist, yelled that Tlaib and Omar were a problem. They were anti-Semitic. They represented an ideology of political Islam. The women were members of the Middle Eastern Women's Coalition. Kazan, forty-two, had grown up seeing the growing Islamist influence in Turkey, which was famously led by the secular Mustafa Kemal Atatürk after its creation. She had reported undercover from Iran and published a book, *The Angels of Tehran*, about the legal prostitution industry in Iran, with child marriages, temporary marriages, and secret second wives. In 2010 she had moved to the US and removed her headscarf, which her family had forced her to wear since she was seven. She had seen firsthand the dangers of religion unchecked in society. She had launched a campaign, "This is Not My Allah," against Islamic extremism, including its expression of anti-Semitism. But, on this day, Sarsour and her team looked askance at the women, including Kazan, and ignored them.

* * *

The staged press conference over, Sarsour instructed the group to walk to Pelosi's office in the Longworth House Building to deliver a letter of support for Omar and Tlaib and demand that Speaker Pelosi oppose the "Islamophobia" allegedly targeting the representatives. In the office, Sarsour led the group into the crowded reception room and talked to the young man behind the desk to state their case. He listened politely, jotting a few notes. They moved from Pelosi's waiting room to Omar's office in Room 1517, where they met aides inside the reception area. For me, this was a reporting assignment, like so many I had done since arriving in the nation's capital for the first time in the summer of 1984, when I was a sophomore at West Virginia University. I had covered lobbyists for the biking, textile, and steel industries, among many others.

As they strode down the wide marble stairwell toward Tlaib's office at Room 1628 in the Longworth House Building, they paused so CAIR communications official, Arsalan Bukhari, could film their approach for Facebook Live with the dramatic flourish of the moment. They in fact did cut an impressive, if unsettling, image. Sarsour stood in the middle, flanked by leaders of the American Muslim establishment. Bedier, the former executive director of CAIR Florida, waved his hand and told Bukhari, "Be sure to get us walking through the door."

A former staff reporter for the *Wall Street Journal*, I stood by the door, reporting on the day of lobbying. The public pronouncements by Omar and Tlaib made it clear that they had little affection for the secular country that saved them from the semi-failed states from whence their families came, and they had created their own PR messes by dishing out their own anti-Semitic tropes. Sarsour—a woman who never fails to see "Islamophobia" under every rock—was striding down the hall to come to buck up her friends.

As she stood outside the Tlaib's congressional office in the marbled halls of the US Longworth House Building in March 2019, Sarsour ordered: "Don't let her be one of the first ones in. Do you all hear me?"

"Her" was me.

Around her were the scions of the Muslim establishment in America and their liberal allies, representatives of an array of organizations that take full advantage of the tax exemptions and benefits accorded to nonprofits. In the middle of the scrum outside Representative Tlaib's office, Nihad Awad, fifty-eight, the cofounder and executive director of CAIR, listened to Sarsour's command, turned quietly to his aides, and smiled curtly.

Beside him, Ahmed Bedier, the former executive director of the CAIR Florida chapter, grinned, respectfully pausing to let Sarsour complete her instructions.

Nearby, Osama Abu Irshaid, a stout Palestinian American activist and national director of American Muslims for Palestine—a staunchly anti-Israel group with a history of anti-Semitism—stood by and watched. Next to him, Taher Herzallah, the bespectacled Palestinian American associate director of outreach and community organizing for American Muslims for Palestine, listened as Sarsour acted as a gatekeeper to Tlaib's office. A 2011 graduate of the University of California at Riverside and a former CAIR intern, Herzallah was one of the Irvine 11 prosecuted for disrupting a 2010 speech by Israeli Ambassador Michael Oren at UC Irvine. Prosecutors alleged the protesters asserted a heckler's veto. In a leather jacket and hoodie, Hezbollah had called Oren a "mass murderer," punching into the air before police escorted him out. One student settled his case before a jury in Orange County, California, convicted Herzallah and nine other students to three years of informal probation and fifty-six hours of community service. A local Muslim community leader called the convictions "another reaffirmation that Islamophobia is intensely and extensively alive and thriving in Orange County."

* * *

Sarsour continued in Arabic, her words later translated from a videotape, "Do you all hear me?"

She turned a steely gaze to the huddle of men and women around her and issued an order to one of them: "Come stand here."

"Yes," responded Jinan Shbat, a Palestinian American activist and national events and outreach manager for CAIR. Writing in an online blog with the pen name "Jinan Deena," she had chronicled the trials and tribulations of her life as a single woman for years. Now, she was taking marching orders from Sarsour.

As she moved into position, Sarsour quickly turned on her heels and stepped through the door, followed by the others in her lobbying delegation.

Standing just over five feet tall in pink leather boots and a gray Gap knit cap, I stepped forward to follow the group inside. Before I could take a second step, CAIR's outreach manager, dressed in a bright yellow coat, Palestinian checkered scarf, and tight headscarf, jabbed her elbow into my body, blocking my path. This was a public space, and I was as entitled to be there as they were. I tried to step around her.

A tall man with a cold poker face slipped into the doorway beside Shbat, blocking my path. He was Mongi Dhaouadi, a former executive director of CAIR Connecticut. A Tunisian American, he now worked as senior program manager at the Center for the Study of Islam and Democracy Inc., which promotes political Islam. The CAIR outreach manager accused me of pulling her tightly wrapped headscarf, although I was nowhere near her head, at least eight inches shorter than her, and my hands were full.

Others Muslim activists and their allies stood by silently as these current and former CAIR officials body-blocked me in their self-appointed jobs as bouncers in the halls of Congress. I didn't know much about them that day, but I was about to learn much more.

One, an immaculately dressed young man, was Mohamed Gula, director of the Virginia chapter of Emgage, a newly formed nonprofit that was a reincarnation of an older group, Emerge USA, dedicated to electing Muslims to power. Such a goal wouldn't be intrinsically negative in a secular society, but Emgage was endorsing and promoting only Muslims who ascribed to a political agenda that denied the reality of Islamic extremism, promoted a culture of victimhood among Muslims, and promoted an anti-Semitic, anti-Israel agenda.

"I know what you're doing," I said as the former CAIR Connecticut executive director shoved me into the hall. He could push me out of the room, but he couldn't bully me into silence.

After Sarsour ordered the aides to block me, she stepped inside the front office, where staff greeted her. Outside, after meeting's end, the former CAIR Connecticut official and CAIR's government affairs director, Robert McCaw, laughed, amused, at blocking the door.

The former CAIR Connecticut leader pointed his phone at me. He'd just connected online with someone in Tunisia and turned his camera to me, flashed a wry smile at me, and said, "Say hello to Tunisia." Since its independence from France in 1956, Tunisia was unique among the countries with a majority of Muslims in their population, because the country was governed with a separation of mosque and state. Since a twenty-six-year-old Tunisian street vendor sparked the Arab Spring revolution in 2011, a new political party seeking to govern Tunisia with the tight fist of Islam had sought to come to power. Tunisia had been rocked by terrorist attacks by violent Islamists. The former CAIR Connecticut executive director was promoting the Islamist movement in Tunisia.

Sarsour and a few others stayed together, spilling out onto the sidewalk, animated in conversation. Elsewhere, the Democratic lobbying organization MoveOn.org retweeted a tweet from Tlaib that she stood with Omar. And a cacophony of voices spread their messages of support.

The group walked past a row of townhouses on Capitol Hill until they reached a three-story building with a brick façade and circular driveway lined with pink and white pansies. They turned off the sidewalk onto the driveway to walk up the front step. They were at 453 New Jersey Avenue SE, at the corner of North Capitol Avenue SE. It was a 3,300-square-foot home that had been converted into a suite of offices, blinds drawn over most of the windows.

Across the front façade hung a wide banner with the words, "Muslims Register Here." They entered a door off the circular driveway with four letters on the blue awning: C-A-I-R.

* * *

For years, the Honor Brigade had denied a radicalization problem within Islam. And now its lieutenants wanted to bring back to the West "ISIS brides," women who had gone to Syria to marry ISIS fighters.

CAIR leader Hassan Shibly launched a campaign to return an ISIS bride, Hoda Muthana, invoking Western principles of due process, constitutional protections, and other buzzwords to appeal to the left. Was such a return of a radicalized woman safe? Probably not. This alliance of the Honor Brigade with extremists was a troubling sign of future problems. It revealed a symbiotic connection between the ideology of the extremists and the regressive orthodoxy of the American Muslims who felt sympathy for them. The Honor Brigade ostensibly steered clear of breaking criminal law, but it was worrying that they were culpable in promoting an ideology—or, at a minimum, the people who believed in that ideology.

Shibly's advocacy for the ISIS bride caught his counterparts at CAIR off guard. He'd gone rogue. CAIR officials drafted a statement from CAIR executive director Nihad Awad reprimanding Shibly for not getting approval from CAIR leaders to take the ISIS bride's case. From Southern Californian, Hussam Ayloush protested that issuing a statement would just muddle things. Other staff at chapters from Michigan to Georgia protested that releasing the statement would be akin to airing the organization's dirty laundry. Don't do it, they argued.

At the US federal courthouse in Alexandria, Virginia, CAIR's government affairs director, Robert McCaw, and Shibly joined CAIR lawyers, including Lena Masri, to argue another case: against a registry documenting passengers on a no-fly list. (McCaw stood outside the courtroom, calling me an "Islamophobe.")

Inside, Shibly sat on the plaintiff's side. He told the story of allegedly being harassed as he crossed the US-Canada border with his family once.

* * *

That week, the strategy of flipping the narrative successfully won a congressional hearing, as lawmakers held a hearing in the Cannon House Building on the "rise of white nationalism."

Front and center were the Honor Brigade's members of the Woke Army.

As the hearing began, McCaw, the CAIR government affairs director who had been harassing me on numerous occasions, slipped into the hearing room and spotted a familiar face, Medea Benjamin, the cofounder of radical left-wing CodePink.

"I want to sit next to Medea!" he shouted.

She smiled widely in return.

Next to her, sat her partner-in-protest, Ariel Gold, and beside her sat representatives from Emgage. Speech after speech, the Democratic lawmakers extolled the talking points of "critical race theory," setting the ideological frame for a race war that the activists lapped up.

* * *

The next morning, a beaming Rep. Ilhan Omar strode across the East Lawn of the US Capitol, a blue binder in hand, and slipped quietly into a line beside Democratic Rep. Judy Chu of California. Standing beside Chu, Rep. Rashida Tlaib flashed a smile of welcome and reached across to greet Omar with a fist bump. The cameras were set up so the white marble Capitol dome rose behind the representatives. Delaware Democratic Rep. Chris Coons looked over, smiling.

At the podium, Indiana Democratic Rep. André Carson turned with an open hand to greet Omar.

The red-green alliance stood steadfast behind Carson and the other legislators. Over the past two years, it had effectively solidified.

The phalanx of men and women carried signs that read "#NoBanAct, Muslim Advocates," the organization that had spearheaded much of the attention to the hearing the day before on white nationalism. Its executive director, Farhana Khera, stood beside Coons. When Carson finished, she took her turn in front of the lectern.

CAIR government affairs director Robert McCaw stood silently behind the politicians. The lawmakers, lobbyists, and activists continued the mantra that ReThink Media had scripted months ago, insisting the Trump administration had instituted a "Muslim ban," creating wounds that didn't exist, and perpetuating a false narrative of Muslims as victims.

* * *

The next week, American Muslims descended on Capitol Hill for National Muslim Advocacy Day. It was organized by the leaders of the US Council of Muslim Organizations, led by Oussama Jammal, executive director of the group. One of its main organizations was CAIR.

Inside, its founding members included the key players in the Honor Brigade: CAIR, American Muslims for Palestine, Islamic Council of North America, the Muslim Alliance in North America, and Muslim American Society, as well as Muslim Legal Fund of America, Muslim Ummah of North America, and The Mosque Cares project. It had an office on F Street NW in Washington, DC, blocks from the White House, and another office in Bridgeview, Illinois, near many in the Muslim and Palestinian diaspora. Its mission was to "open effective communication and coordination spectrums" between American Muslims with "one clear, communal voice."

CAIR's McCaw stood in the back, like a field marshal. (When I arrived, he kicked me out, telling Jammal, "This is Asra Nomani. She is the Islamophobia network.")

Outside, a driver nosed a black SUV to the curb. Hussam Ayloush, the executive director of the CAIR Southern California chapter, peeked out the window.

He studied the scene for a moment, and then the driver of the SUV pulled back out onto the road, driving away.

A group of men walked toward the archway. Imraan Siddiqi, the former gold seller and then executive director of the CAIR Arizona chapter, was one of them. (He looked over at me, later tweeting out a photo of me, stating that he momentarily considered interviewing me.)

* * *

During Friday prayers, on the Ides of March, March 15, a gunman attacked Muslims at mosques in Christchurch, New Zealand, livestreaming his brutal murder spree on Facebook.

It was a tragedy, but the propaganda arms for the Honor Brigade saw it as an opportunity. Three days later, their press release included the secretary general of the Muslim World League, Muhammad bin Abdulkarim Alissa's statement to end hate: "To address the scourge extremism and Islamophobia, we need governments and faith organizations around the world to work together to encourage religious tolerance and understanding and prevent all forms of incitement and hatred, including all types of hatred leveled against any religion or ethnicity." He had traveled to New Zealand from the league's headquarters in Mecca, Saudi Arabia.

Meanwhile, the governments of Saudi Arabia and Qatar continued their religious propaganda, inciting hate against Jews, the West, Christians, and any Muslims who weren't orthodox Sunnis.

* * *

In Washington, DC, ReThink Media kicked into overdrive with media placements that it bragged about to clients.

In Seattle, Masih Fouladi, executive director of the CAIR chapter in Seattle, was on his way to a *Captain Marvel* release when his phone started to buzz. He landed a quick op-ed in Crosscut. He told the story of connecting mosque leaders with law enforcement officials to arrange extra security details. He shared a Facebook post, "12 Ways You Can Combat Islamophobia."

Among them, "Name the problem: Islamophobia," take action to repeal the "Muslim ban," and sign a petition to change "violent, Islamophobic city names." The Change.org petition claimed twenty-two cities and towns in Mexico, Spain, Cuba, Guatemala, and Colombia had the name, "Matamoros," which it claimed means "Kill Muslims." The word actually means "killer of Moors."

Shaun Kennedy, twenty-nine, campaign director and cofounder of Jetpac, had placed a piece in Religion News Service. He had founded Jetpac as a nonprofit to train American Muslims to run for political office. Kennedy was born in Australia to white, working-class, low-income parents with Scottish, Irish, and English ancestry. He had even written that he was racist in his teens, ridiculing classmates from the indigenous Māori culture, but chose to fight "white supremacy." He became a lawyer and moved to the US in early 2015 as a political consultant.

Wardah Khalid, founder of Poligon National, placed a piece in *Bustle*, asking politicians to "show solidarity" with Muslims in the wake of the Christchurch shooting. ReThink Media promoted a graphic with symbols of Judaism, Islam, Christianity, the Māori culture (a fern leaf), and the message, "Kia Kaha (Stay Strong)."

* * *

In March 2019, Democratic Minnesota Gov. Tim Walz introduced a conference at the Metropolitan State University in St. Paul, Minnesota, on "Islamophobia." In its introduction, a C-SPAN announcer noted, "The Justice Department has listed CAIR as an unindicted conspirator, saying the group helped fund HAMAS."

Abbas Barzegar, research and advocacy director at CAIR National, then launched into a chronicling of the "Islamophobia industry." He raised alarm bells about "donor advised funds," housed in philanthropic organizations, providing "dark money" to nonprofits.

* * *

One of the organizations born out of the Muslim Brothers who had established institutions in the US from their base at 500 Grove Street was the Islamic Circle of North America, known as ICNA. Active since 1968, the Muslim Brothers officially registered it in 1971.

In the spring of 2019, their officials hosted an annual conference at the Washington, DC, convention center. There, Leila Al-Arian, the daughter of Sami Al-Arian, the deported professor of Islam from the Holy Land Foundation scandal, was speaking in defense of Muslim prisoners. (In the back of a mostly empty conference room, I sat quietly, listening. Suddenly, Al-Arian pointed me out to the audience as an "Islamophobe" in their midst. Off to my right, watching the couple's two young sons, her husband leaped forward in the row in front of me and dashed toward me with wide eyes and a snarling, angry grimace. He stood in front of me, leaning across the row of chairs in front of me, hurling his finger at me and shouting, "Leave! Leave! Leave!" (I didn't.)

A convert to Islam, Al-Arian's husband was Jonathan Brown, the new director of the Prince Alwaleed bin Talal Center for Muslim-Christian Understanding at Georgetown University, overseeing the Bridge Initiative, which published reports on "Islamophobia," including one targeting me personally. Brown was the heir to the empire that John Esposito had built at Georgetown with money from his donors at 500 Grove Street and overseas. With the network of Muslims spitting out "critical race theory," the Bridge Initiative had been churning out reports and articles promoting the thesis of Muslims as a race to be protected against "systemic racism." (Its work included defamatory dossiers on Muslim reformers, including me, largely repeating the smears of LoonWatch.) Bridge Initiative staff saw "Islamophobia" everywhere, publishing a paper, "On the Intersections of DACA and Islamophobia," connecting "Islamophobia" with the immigration policy for "Dreamers," called "Deferred Action for Childhood Arrivals." They also avoided taking ownership of extremist interpretations of Islam, for example, writing a paper, and "Mental Illness: A Key Factor in Terror."

Brown was the fair-skinned golden boy of the community at 500 Grove Street, and he was a fierce defender of the Islamist status quo.

* * *

The next day, on Easter Sunday, Linda Sarsour led a session at the conference on organizing. (She barred me from entry.) Across the hall, Georgetown's Jonathan Brown moderated a session with a charismatic sheikh waxing on and on about fighting "Islamophobia."

Across the world, a terrible tragedy had just shaken Sri Lanka. Muslim extremists slaughtered Christian worshippers at Easter services. At the conference, young volunteers handed conference-goers slick, color flyers inviting them to a "Rally Against Hate, Bigotry, and Islamophobia." It was sponsored by the alphabet soup of organizations that had grown out of the work of the Muslim Brothers at 500 Grove Street: ICNA Council for Social Justice, American

Muslims for Palestine, CAIR, Muslim American Society-PACE, Muslim Ummah of North America, Muslim American Society-DC, ICNA Virginia Islamic Center, and Dar Al-Hijrah Islamic Center (where the 9/11 hijackers and Anwar al-Awlaki had prayed).

At the appointed time, attendees started congregating at the corner of 9th Street and L Street NW for the meeting point. The executive director of the CAIR Maryland chapter eyed me and asked me if I would be harassing protesters. I said certainly not. I asked her if CAIR officials would be harassing me, as they had been doing at events I had been trying to cover.

Sarsour did an interview with a TV news crew before getting the protesters assembled for the hike to the White House. As they moved, she stood camera-ready, front and center among the leaders, behind the main banner. Along the way, Dalia Mogahed, the pollster with convenient statistics for the network, crossed paths with the protesters but continued on her way. At the White House, the speeches were a collection of angry outbursts, one representative from a Turkish American organization even calling for blasphemy laws. For just about one minute, the group acknowledged the tragedy in Sri Lanka. For the rest of the hour, it was their usual litany of grievances against the West and Israel.

* * *

One of the attendees at the "Islamophobia" conference was listed as "Ghulam-Nabi Fai," representing the Kashmiri American Council. The FBI spelled his name a little differently: Syed Ghulam Nabi Fai. He was the former Temple University student whose professor, Ismail al-Faruqi, had been brutally murdered. The FBI had convicted Fai for not admitting he received $3.5 million from the government of Pakistan.

At the "Islamophobia" conference, Fai presented a paper that elicited great interest from the Pakistani press, which included an article on his talk. *Today's Zaman*, an English-language newspaper in Turkey, also wrote about his appearance. The American Muslim Taskforce on Civil Rights and Elections rallied to support him with a press release. An unclassified cable from the US Embassy in Turkey marked, "For Official Use Only" and leaked by WikiLeaks, said conference speakers represented a "wide cross-section of Islamic Scholars throughout the world," and they were "nearly unanimous in declaring that Islamophobia is deeply rooted in the West and used numerous examples of Western intolerance and discrimination—ranging from the Crusades to the Danish Cartoon controversy—to highlight what they characterized as the West,s [*sic*] irrational fear of Islam." Islamophobia was "described as 'more serious' in the wake of the September 11th attacks and the War on Terror." Many speakers "accused U.S. and other Western leaders of manipulating fear of Islam to justify wars in Iraq and Afghanistan as well as domestic legislation that discriminates against Muslims."

The cable was titled: "Going On The Offensive Against Islamophobia."

* * *

ReThink media was back on the road. This time, CAIR's former director of the Department to Monitor and Combat Islamophobia, Corey Saylor, and young communications aide Gracie Farese zipped to Orlando, Florida, with Guthrie Graves-Fitzsimmons, associate director at ReThink Media, to train activists for Muslim, Arab, Sikh, and South Asian rights.

Rasha Mubarak, a Palestinian American Muslim activist and national committee chairwoman of the Florida Young Democrats, and Begüm Becerik, the daughter of Turkish immigrants to the US, had helped organize the training. Mubarak was building a consulting and organizing business, Unbought Power, to promote "Black and Brown liberation." Becerik later joined CAIR's Florida chapter as its outreach and events coordinator.

Farese had success stories to report, getting media hits for the "Islamophobia" narrative. Farese had met Amin Aaser, founder of Noor Kids, at spokesperson training in Minnesota the summer before. Now, Minnesota Public Radio had recently published an interview with him on the effects of "Islamophobia" attacks, policies, and rhetoric on the lives of Muslim children.

* * *

To drive home parallels with Japanese Americans, CAIR organized a tour of the internment camps in which the US had held citizens of Japanese ancestry.

During World War I, there were many instances of German Americans being lynched by mobs. In World War II, countless Japanese families were summarily placed in internment camps by an executive order from Franklin Delano Roosevelt. When viewed in this context, Trump's actions were not the same, but CAIR was exploiting the harsh experience of Japanese Americans to invoke sympathy for American Muslims.

* * *

President Trump tweeted a video of Ilhan Omar with footage of the 9/11 attacks. The *New York Post* published a cover photo of Omar with the World Trade Center towers.

The Yemeni American Merchants Association, working in lockstep with CAIR, announced a boycott of the *New York Post.* Soon enough, the activists pulled together a rally on Capitol Hill, featuring radical activists Angela Davis and Barbara Ransby, one of the cofounders of the Black Lives Matter movement, stepping forward to support Ilhan Omar.

* * *

In May 2019, Angela Davis spoke online to a panel at the University of Massachusetts–Amherst, her dark Afro from her activism in the 1960s now like a halo of white around her face. The panel title was "Not Backing Down: Israel, Free Speech & the Battle for Palestine Rights." She threw a black-and-white checkered Palestinian scarf over her shoulder and greeted her fellow activists. "Hi Linda," she said in her distinct accent, greeting Palestinian American activist Linda

Sarsour. "We stood together in Birmingham and a few days ago we were together in Washington participating in an action in defense of Ilhan Omar. Thank you for your invaluable work."

She listed her grievances. "We are experiencing a new historical conjuncture in social justice organizing. The demand for human rights and justice for Palestine no longer remains on the margins of our struggles here in the United States. This demand is moving to the very center of progressive political agendas."

She brought up the intersection of critical race theory and the new Woke Army.

"One cannot for example say that Black lives matter without challenging the occupation of Palestine and the policies and practices of the state of Israel."

She saluted the BDS movement. She challenged the notion of the "anti-Semitic Left," putting quote marks around the concept.

* * *

For months, Al Jazeera reporter Simon Boazman interviewed key players in the Honor Brigade to produce a project for Al Jazeera Investigations on "Islamophobia Inc." It was dripping of contempt for America, painting a portrait of an America at war with Muslims and trying to link "Islamophobia" with violence against Muslims—while for decades refusing to acknowledge the link between hateful rhetoric among Muslims, including from Qatar, and violence.

The Al Jazeera investigation revealed its disturbing finding in its second installment of its series. Almost 80 percent of funders for the "Islamophobia network" had "vocally or financially supported causes that promote the state of Israel."

In a large conference room, Rebecca Vilkomerson, executive director of Jewish Voice for Peace, sat with hands clasped and said it was "extremely distressing" that Jewish groups were funding "Islamophobia." A strategy to "silence and to bully and to intimidate" was part of a "long-range strategy" to keep American Muslims from being a strong political force and justify pro-Israel policies "at the same time Israel is assaulting Palestinian human rights."

CAIR's executive director, Nihad Awad, stated, "Anti-Muslim entities are motivated by their blind support to the state of Israel and their fear that the growth and development of American Muslims will help Americans and the American administrations adjust their positions to be more fair and just to the Palestinian people."

* * *

By the summer of 2019, the Muslim Brothers found a new pathway to pressing their agenda in California—this time in America's public school classrooms.

In 2016, the state of California had passed a law calling for the creation of "ethnic studies curriculum." By August 2019, the Muslim Brothers had gotten their ideological biases into a new "Ethnic Studies Model Curriculum" for its public schools. The drafting committee included advocates of the anti-Semitic Boycott, Divestment, and Sanctions campaign with a mission to eliminate the state of Israel. Three of the eighteen members on the advisory committee in developing the Ethnic Studies Model Curriculum included academics Gaye Theresa Johnson, Theresa Montaño, and Samia Shoman, all pushing anti-Israel views. Years earlier, Shoman had worked with anti-Israel activist Hatem Bazian and others to get an "Arab and Muslim ethnicities and diaspora studies" minor in the College of Ethnic Studies at their alma mater, San Francisco State University—a birthplace of "ethnic studies" in America. Two years earlier, Johnson, a professor of Chicano and African American studies at the University of California, Los Angeles, had conducted an interview with black activist Angela Davis in a book she co-edited, *Futures of Black Radicalism*, headlining the interview, "Angela Davis on Black Lives Matter, Palestine, and the Future of Radicalism." Montaño was vice president of the California Teachers Association and a professor of Latino studies at California State University, Northridge, and she had signed the US Campaign for the Academic and Cultural Boycott of Israel petition, supporting an academic boycott of Israel.

The "Arab American Studies Course Outline" included teachings with these headings: "Direct Action Front for Palestine and Black

Lives Matter," "Call to Boycott, Divest, and Sanction Israel," and "Comparative Border Studies: Palestine and Mexico." The curriculum also included studying about Minnesota Rep. Ilhan Omar, Michigan Rep. Rashida Tlaib, Women's March cofounder Linda Sarsour, and the late Columbia University professor Edward Said. The sample course models included references to the establishment of Israel in May 1948 as *nakba*, the Arabic word for "the catastrophe," and the term of reference in all anti-Israel propaganda for the founding of Israel. It also included a rap song, "The Real Arab Money," by Iraqi Canadian rapper Narcy, with the lyrics: "In Palestine, kids can't shop at these malls.... My nation on my back, look how proud we are.... America bustin' nuts on Saudi Riyals."

The sample course material included another song by Shadia Mansour, with the lyrics, "Get out Yankees from Latin America, French, English and Dutch, I love you Free Palestine."

The curriculum went on and on about "Islamophobia." It excluded one form of bigotry that outnumbered anti-Muslim incidents. The curriculum did not include anti-Semitism.

The course challenged stereotypes about Arab people, including characterizing Palestinians as "terrorists" who "blow up airlines," "destroy Israel," and "drive the Jews into the sea." A song with the lyrics, "I love you, Free Palestine," was in the curriculum, along with the lyrics, "As the saying goes, 'The situation must be threatened, but in reality, the situation must stop'; For every free political prisoner, an Israeli colony is expanded."

For the second year in a row, the Islamic Society of North America held its annual conference in Houston at the George R. Brown Convention Center over Labor Day weekend, and Uncle Bernie was in the house.

This year, the organization had its biggest success since its birth over four decades earlier. Two Democratic presidential candidates—Bernie Sanders and Julian Castro—spoke on the main stage to some seven thousand Muslims, the first time presidential candidates ever addressed the conference. Even pop culture showed up: icon Trevor Noah was there. He led the Friday night entertainment, interviewed by none other than Mehdi Hasan, the acidic host on Qatar's Al Jazeera TV network.

The usual suspects were in the conference lineup: Linda Sarsour; CAIR's A-team of executive director Nihad Awad, San Francisco Bay Area executive director Zahra Billoo, and Florida executive director Hassan Shibly; and others. UC Berkeley's Hatem Bazian was there on his tried-and-true topic of "Islamophobia." There were many panels on mental health, all standing room only. There was a panel on women and mosques. (It had been fifteen years since I introduced my "Islamic Bill of Rights for Women in Mosques" at a conference of the Islamic Society of North America, eliciting the first death threat against me, and the issue was very much not resolved.)

* * *

Later that fall, on September 7, 2019, at the Hyatt Regency in Arlington, Virginia, American Muslims for Palestine held its annual fundraiser dinner.

There, women in tight headscarves and floor-length robes stood outside the lobby, waiting for others to join them. Volunteers guided guests to the escalator, where the registration table was set up two floors below. There, CAIR official Jinan Shbat registered guests.

Inside, the room was filled with familiar faces. Ahmed Bedier, the former CAIR Florida executive director who had walked the halls of Congress with Sarsour, took the microphone as the night's emcee. Also present was Taher Herzallah, one of the Irvine 11 prosecuted for interrupting the Israeli ambassador's speech. Guests were waiting for the headliner: activist Marc Lamont Hill, whose star power had increased in this crowd after CNN fired him.

Instead, a surprise speaker stepped onto the state behind the podium. She was a young woman in a white headscarf who introduced herself by saying, "My name is Abrar Omeish, and I am running for Fairfax County School Board at-large."

She was a darling, literally, of the Muslim Brothers at 500 Grove Street, the daughter of Esam Omeish, one of the board members at Dar Al-Hijrah Islamic Center—the one who had hired Anwar al-Awlaki and gotten booted from a Virginia political appointment because of his anti-Semitism.

She launched into her agenda to change the curriculum in Fairfax County on issues related to Israel, Islam, and Palestinians.

Omeish, it would turn out, wasn't concerned about failing schools or lifting lagging students up to standards. Her talk was about what she characterized as the lies of American public education, which she considered to be pro-Israel, anti-Palestinian. She spoke of a teacher fired from her position for promoting the Boycott, Divestment, Sanctions (BDS) movement, the controversial economic and political program—and cause célèbre of worldwide leftist organizations—that would pave the way for Palestinian statehood by crippling or destroying Israel economically.

"When we talk about the Palestinian issue, and it affects us deeply and families are affected, and we know how important it is to us," she said. "These are conversations that start in the classrooms.... When they (students) open a textbook, they read Muslims, terrorists."

Palestine as a "word may not even be mentioned in the books," she said, continuing, "These are things that we have to get attention to on the local level right here.... I really want to wake up our community."

Omeish also woke up her audience with the revelation that seats on the Fairfax County School Board were not exactly local-yokel politics. The district controls a budget of $3 billion—over half the county's total spending—and with that "big money" comes the prospects of powerful influence, she explained.

In attendance at the meeting, I was stunned by the arrival of a school board candidate at such an obviously anti-Israel event. I took out my iPhone and started videotaping her campaign speech. Taher Herzallah stood in front of my camera to block my view of Omeish, but the message was clear.

As my reporting would show, a network of Muslims in America had their eyes now set not only on the corridors of power in the nation's capital—with Rep. Ilhan Omar and Rep. Rashida Tlaib in office—but they were now gunning for local school board races so they could walk the halls of America's schools, asserting influence in our classrooms. And not confining themselves to anti-Israel campaigning, they were immersing themselves in a convenient new ideology—"critical race theory."

CHAPTER 19

Unmasking

In September 2019, internet service providers started receiving subpoenas in my lawsuit to identify the people behind the anonymous LoonWatch disinformation campaign.

And the roads were leading back to one common organization: the Council on American-Islamic Relations, or CAIR.

When Amir Saheb got notice from DreamHost that it had received a subpoena seeking his real identity, he retained Ibrahim A. Moiz, a lawyer at NOVA Business Law Group LLP on Chain Bridge Road in Fairfax, Virginia. Saheb had an important job to protect. Two years earlier, he had landed a job at the consulting firm and defense contractor Booz Allen Hamilton. Its human resources team had somehow missed his anonymous writings as "Mujahideen Ryder" and "Ibn Percy," supporting al-Qaeda terrorists and calling for an Islamic state in the United States. Edward Snowden, the young man who had leaked America's secrets to the world and been lionized by lawyer-writer Glenn Greenwald, had also worked at Booz Allen Hamilton.

Moiz was a former civil rights and operations director at the CAIR chapter in Maryland. In 2010, former clients of CAIR's Maryland and Virginia chapter, based in Herndon, Virginia, not far from the hub of Islamist organizations at 500 Grove Street, filed lawsuits against CAIR, alleging CAIR had defrauded clients, failing to provide promised legal services and hiding the fact that a "Resident Attorney" wasn't actually a lawyer.

In 2013, then Virginia Gov. Terry McAuliffe named Moiz to the Board of Funeral Directors and Embalmers. In 2017, McAuliffe named him to the Real Estate Board. According to a 2017 IRS filing, CAIR had paid $125,885 to his law firm, NOVA Business Law Group LLP, for legal services.

That year, Moiz was running for county supervisor in Loudoun County, tapping votes from the community that the Muslim Brothers had set up in the 1980s. Over the years, Moiz had been a regular donor to Democratic candidates, including Virginia Gov. Ralph Northam. With ambitions for Palestine, the Honor Brigade network knew all politics was local.

Two days *after* the deadline for filing a motion to quash the subpoenas, a lawyer appeared and said she was representing clients impacted by subpoenas sent to Twitter and WordPress. She was Lena Masri, CAIR's national litigation attorney.

* * *

On Election Day 2019, at the Elks Lodge off Little River Turnpike in Fairfax, Virginia, there was electricity in the air. The Democratic Party was on the verge of winning back the state House of Representatives for the first time in twenty years.

A few blocks away, at the home of the Omeish family, young women in headscarves were parking on the side of the road and dashing through the darkness to the back of a home. Inside, they stepped into a war room for political Islam in America, and the mood was joyous and festive. That night, Abrar Omeish, twenty-four and single, with no children, had just won a seat on the Fairfax County School Board. In the run-up to the election, she had galvanized the local Muslim community to flood a local school so she'd win the nod for the at-large school board position, unseating a stalwart in the Korean American community. Now, she had won in the general election, running on the slate supported by the Democratic Party.

A delivery man brought pizza for the festivities.

Now, K-12 education, reaching youths from kindergarten through twelfth grade, was one of the next frontiers for the Woke Army, including the Honor Brigade, not just in the US but worldwide.

In September, the journal *Whiteness and Education* published the article "Reading Islamophobia in education policy through a lens of critical race theory: a study of the 'funding freeze' for private Islamic schools in Australia," with "whiteness as property" as a keyword. The paper said it "draws on critical race theory to explore the reproduction and enactment of Islamophobia in education policy."

For the Omeish family, this was sweet revenge.

Twelve years earlier, in 2007, when Abrar Omeish was a preteen, her father had been publicly shamed when then Virginia Gov. Tim Kaine pulled him from the immigration commission because of his views on Israel. Two years later, in 2009, he ran for state assemblyman for the thirty-fifth district of the Virginia House of Delegates. He raised $143,734, with his third-highest contributor being his pals at the International Institute of Islamic Thought, based in Herndon, Virginia, with a donation of $3,500. He also got donations from the businesses connected to the network at 500 Grove Street, including Reston Investments, Mar-Jac Investments Inc., and Sterling Management Group Inc. His daughter canvassed for votes for him. Still, he lost.

Now, his daughter had the opportunity to impact change as an *elected* public official.

He had reason to celebrate.

So did the new crop of Muslim PACs and nonprofits that had emerged in recent years. Emgage Action PAC listed Omeish's win among its "monumental victories." It took credit for helping elect fifty candidates endorsed by the Emgage Action PAC in Virginia, Michigan, and Pennsylvania. The list included mostly local races where they'd infuse local politics with their radical agenda. This included new jobs from the city council of Dearborn Heights, Michigan, to the school board in Prince William County, Virginia.

And at the Elks Lodge in Fairfax, Virginia, local representatives of Emgage Action PAC cheered the Democratic sweep of the Virginia legislature. They had both stood silent and bemused as Linda Sarsour had her assigned bouncers block my way into Rep. Rashida Tlaib's office. Now, they were grinning from ear to ear.

* * *

Standing amid the balloons and loud music at the Elks Lodge in Fairfax County, Virginia, was Aarti Tikoo Singh. As we had driven from my house to the Omeish homestead and then to the Fairfax County Democratic Party victory party, she had been doing a podcast on the controversy raging in her home state of Jammu and Kashmir, on the northeast tip of India, bordering Pakistan and China.

Singh was a progressive feminist and a journalist at the time with the *Times of India*, the country's largest English language newspaper. She had just endured a grueling experience in the US Congress, not much unlike the experiences that Zuhdi Jasser and Ayaan Hirsi Ali had endured, facing attack from Democratic representatives prepped by the Honor Brigade to silence, discredit, and ignore us. She was born into a Hindu family in Kashmir, known as Pandits, the word from which pundit comes. In 1990, as Pakistan directed its militants, battle-hearty from their victory over the Soviet Union in Afghanistan, to try to seize the land of Kashmir from India, her parents packed her into a truck with other girls from their town to find refuge in Srinagar, the capital of the state of Jammu and Kashmir. Her family followed, living for years in poverty as refugees in their own country. Her uncle and his wife lived in canvas tents in a refugee camp on the outskirts of town, and Aarti stayed with them on weekends to give their young son and her cousin solace and friendship.

Singh had testified in a very measured tone at a House Foreign Relations Committee subcommittee hearing on human rights issues in South Asia, describing the tragedy of ordinary Muslims in Jammu and Kashmir, including journalists, shopkeepers, and schoolchildren murdered by Pakistani-sponsored Muslim extremists. She testified to the dangers of the extremism, violence, and murder that the state of

Pakistan exported to the northern state of Jammu and Kashmir for three decades, starting in 1989. Minnesota Rep. Ilhan Omar would have none of it. She read word for word from a script in front of her, insinuating that "Ms. Singh" was a "mouthpiece" for the government of India, covering up their human rights abuses in Jammu and Kashmir while twisting facts, misrepresenting truths, and spinning creative "narratives."

The new Woke activists had their sights set not only on faraway lands such as Israel, but also India, fast moving to becoming the world's largest population of Muslims. Earlier in the year, the Honor Brigade had released a report from its base at UC Berkeley. Called *Islamophobia in India: Stoking Bigotry*, the report was led by Hatem Bazian, the Palestinian American director of UC Berkeley's Islamophobia Studies Center and its Islamophobia Research and Documentation Project. The same organization that refuses to engage in any discussion of "Muslim extremists," "Islamic terrorism," and "Muslim nationalism" went after "Hindu fanatics," the 2018 Bollywood film *Padmaavat* with "expected Orientalist sets," and the "rise of Islamophobia in India."

From Arizona to New Jersey, CAIR officials drafted press releases and did press interviews railing against India. From Phoenix, KJZZ quoted CAIR Arizona's executive director, Imraan Siddiqi, saying, "We're hearing just by second-hand reports that there are [*sic*] live ammunition that are [*sic*] being used on peaceful protesters." The article quoted him saying the "oppression" had led to the "rape and torture of Kashmiri citizens." CAIR's government affairs director, Robert McCaw, who seemed to hold a personal grudge against me, shared an Intercept article with colleagues at CAIR, demonizing India and Singh.

* * *

Ten days later, as headliners from the American Muslim community arrived in Arlington, Virginia, for a banquet commemorating CAIR's twenty-five-year anniversary, Omeish sent out a special invitation to Rep. Ilhan Omar and other dignitaries. Sure enough, the next morning, Ilhan and the rest retraced the route of the teens and crossed the driveway into the war room for political Islam.

Whether in politics, academia, the media, or nonprofit work, it had become good for business to put "Islamophobia" in your pitch. In the Soros philanthropy empire, the Proteus Fund handed out hundreds of thousands of dollars to nonprofits that supported the work of the network.

By late 2019, various foundations had doled out $6,024,132 in grants to fight "Islamophobia" in some form or the other. Over the years, thirty-five grant makers had provided the $6 million in eighty-six grants to sixty-seven recipients. The Soros philanthropy empire continued to be a cash cow for nonprofits on this issue. One of its affiliates, the Proteus Fund, has continued issuing grants. The year before, that included $30,000 to the Justice for Muslims Collective to expand its Resist Islamophobia Coalition. Spirit of Peace United Church of Christ in Sioux Falls, South Dakota, got $30,000 for its South Dakota Voices for Peace coalition to leverage social media in its "grassroots, intersectional organization" efforts, building a model for "combatting anti-immigrant bigotry and Islamophobia in rural America." Teaching for Change, based in Washington, DC, got $10,000 to create curriculum called "Islamophobia: A people's history teaching guide project."

* * *

It took Google fifteen years to take down the "Dr. Maxtor" website run by the physician Javad Hashmi, but in November 2019 when you typed in "DrMaxtor and Zionist media whore" into Google, you got no hits.

The website was gone. Screenshots of pages were still on a website called the Wayback Machine, an unofficial "internet archive" that acts like a photo album of images from websites all over the world. It had been fifteen years since "DrMaxtor" had first started his character assassinations of Muslim reformers trying to challenge orthodoxy. I had filed numerous complaints to Google, reporting the pages as violating Google's policies but to no avail. Now, either Google or "DrMaxtor" had deleted the blog.

This taunting and harassment—cyberbullying—was merciless and painful. When anyone engages in the court of public opinion, we are supposed to develop thick skins. But the mystery of this person who picked away at details of lives like a vulture upon a carcass was very disturbing. His creepy behavior wasn't just uncomfortable but terrorizing. His creation is just one example of what can go so wrong with the internet. And the resolution of the case is a window into how the recklessness and abuse of the internet can be corrected. About fifty people used about ten websites and about thirty social media accounts to run their disinformation campaign and character assassination assault. Using the powers of our courts, cyberforensics, and old-school sleuthing, that insidious disinformation network is about to be dismantled.

When the attacks on me began, my son was two, barely reached my hips, and was driving a battery-operated Jeep Wrangler across our lawn in Morgantown, West Virginia. My son was eighteen years old, head and shoulders taller than me and with a driving learner's permit in his wallet, by the time I unmasked my character assassins. He told me once that to be an upstander, not a bystander in life, it meant challenging bullying and harassment. In my case, that meant challenging the Honor Brigade. What does it mean in your life? In whatever form an Honor Brigade manifests itself in our lives, exploiting the many ways the internet is broken to terrorize, I am here to tell you: we can fight back. The potential is in all of us to go beyond being bystanders and instead choosing to be upstanders to make the world a better place.

Javad Hashmi had been shut down on one platform. He had retreated from another. He was about to come out of the shadows.

CHAPTER 20

Facing a Woke Army

By late 2019, woke Muslims were parroting the language of "critical race theory," fair-skinned Muslims even self-describing as "white passing." They had perfected the art of attaching themselves to any grievance in the "critical race theory" repertoire—including "transphobia"—to push their narrative of "Islamophobia."

For example, speaking at a young adult book conference, new author Nadine Jolie Courtney, a blonde, fair-skinned Muslim born to a Jordanian Syrian dad and a white, blonde Catholic mother, yelled her pitch about her book, *All-American Muslim Girl*, to librarians and booksellers walking by: "It's about a white-passing Muslim girl who, faced with Islamophobia, decides to start actively practicing the Islamic religion she knows little about. It's fiction, but based on my own life." She wrote about the "insidious Islamophobia" she witnessed being a "white-passing" Muslim.

In Chicago, CAIR Chicago executive director Ahmed Rehab and his crew exploited the moment. His Iraqi American friend, Laith Saud, now forty-one, ventured to a protest. It reminded him of the protests at Tahrir Square during the Arab Spring. He was struck by the diversity of the protesters.

At the *Chicago Monitor* that he had founded years earlier, Rehab penned a column, "The Tokenization of Martin Luther King Jr." Saud wrote a piece, "Why is the Confederate Statue Still Found Nationwide?"

* * *

The beachheads for Islamists were now infusing themselves with the rhetoric of "critical race theory." In February 2020, the Bridge Initiative posted a "factsheet" on "white genocide conspiracy theory." In March 2020, the Bridge Initiative hired Nena Beecham, with "critical race theory" among her research interests, as a senior research fellow.

In Canada, York University's Centre for Feminist Research hosted a lecture and workshop, "Anti-Blackness, Islam and Islamophobia," exploring the "intersections between Islamophobia, race, and anti-blackness," as part of its "Spotlight on Islamophobia" series. Among the featured speakers: Yusra Khogali, the cofounder of Black Lives Matter Toronto, who a few years earlier had tweeted a prayer to Allah that she not kill white people.

A new opportunity arrived during a Friday night episode of *RuPaul's Drag Race*, a show featuring "drag queens," or men dressed as women, competing for a top prize. Actor Jeff Goldblum was a guest judge for the week's theme, "Stars & Stripes."

A contestant wore a large Afro wig over a black gown, saying the costume was an "homage to black culture," from the Black Panthers to Black Lives Matter: "I'm showing all my blackness for you."

Another contestant wore a caftan with a midnight blue headscarf, outlined with fifty silver stars. "You can be Middle Eastern, you can be Muslim, and you can still be American," Jackie Cox, an Iranian Canadian, said in a voice-over.

After she walked the runway, Goldblum asked her, "Are you religious, may I ask?"

"I'm not," Cox replied. "To be honest, this outfit really represents the importance that visibility for people of religious minorities need to have in this country."

The actor continued: "Is there something in this religion that is anti-homosexuality and anti-woman? Does that complicate the issue? I'm just raising it and thinking out loud and maybe being stupid."

Woke Muslims jumped to action. Muslim Advocates, one of the advocacy groups growing in prominence, demanded Goldblum apologize, issuing a statement from its public advocacy director, Scott Simpson, invoking the "homophobia, transphobia, and misogyny within all major religions" and alleging the question amounted to "anti-Muslim bigotry." To his credit, Goldblum didn't apologize.

That spring, Ibram Kendi scheduled a panel, "On Islamophobia," in its #AntiracistBookfest, with Palestinian American activist Linda Sarsour as one of the panelists, hawking her new book, *We Are Not Here to Be Bystanders.* Soon after, with Kendi moving to Boston University and the cancellation of events with COVID-19, the new Boston University Center for Antiracist Research organized its second "annual" National Antiracist Book Festival in DC, for April 2021, with Sarsour again on the playbill.

* * *

The radical Muslim lobby was positioning itself for the 2020 election.

In New Jersey, Amani Al-Khatahtbeh, the cofounder of *Muslim Girl*, stepped into her parents' electronics shop in New Jersey to make a big announcement, using a high-profile interview with television journalist and celebrity Katie Couric on *Teen Vogue* online. She had ditched the oversized headscarf that she had made her trademark and wore a funky tight scarf with her bangs peeking through. She announced her run for US Congress in New Jersey's Sixth Congressional District, running against Rep. Frank Pallone, chairman of the US House Energy and Commerce Committee. She'd launched her website, branding herself a "born-and-raised Jersey girl" and "proud child of immigrants," who was a "leading critic of the Trump administration's policies towards communities of color."

The night before she submitted her campaign petition, she got a special call from Rep. Ilhan Omar, cheering on her candidacy. Now twenty-seven, Al-Khatahtbeh kept talking about the "diverse," "immigrant" community of her district, including her (and my father's) alma mater, Rutgers University. Couric didn't ask Al-Khatahtbeh about her controversial anti-Israel position nor her anti-Semitism. Four years earlier, in a memoir, *Muslim Girl: A Coming of Age*, she had refused to even refer to the founders of Israelis as Jews, only calling them "white Europeans." That year, she published an article on the *MuslimGirl* website, "Israel's Organ Harvesting and the UK's BDS Movement," written by "Yelenalel," an unidentified writer. In the *Tablet*, the Jewish magazine, New York writer John-Paul Pagano said the article was a "rehash of professional anti-Semite Alison Weir's riff on the blood-libel—a conspiracy theory in which Israel occupies Palestinian territory in order to murder the locals and loot their body parts." Two years later, she rejected an award from Revlon because Israeli actress Gal Gadot was a Revlon celebrity, and Gadot's "vocal support of the Israel Defense Forces' actions in Palestine goes against MuslimGirl's moral and values."

Pagano lamented, "The implicit assumption here is that honoring a young Muslim woman means embracing stomach-turning extremes of racism, anti-semitism and conspiratorial lunacy. Luckily, in reality, nothing could be further from the truth. The cultural ignorance and condescension displayed by misguided people who honor outspoken bigots as token 'representatives' of large population groups is both a symptom and a cause of bigotry."

None of that was documented in the media blitz she enjoyed. She even landed an article in *Harper's Bazaar* online. She announced she was launching a "Quaran-Tour," on the digital campaign trail.

* * *

In Massachusetts, physician Javad Hashmi, who had spent a good part of the past sixteen years as a character assassin, was about to launch his makeover. He had embedded himself in the Ghamidi Center of Islamic Learning, an organization dedicated to spreading the teachings of a moderate Pakistani scholar, Javed Ahmed Ghamidi.

During the month of Ramadan, starting Friday, April 24, Hashmi sat in front of a camera, using Zoom to take class participants on a "fascinating journey through the evolution of theology, philosophy, and religious thought in classic as well as modern Islam."

The class was free, but the physician who had raised money on IndieGoGo with a fake identity again asked for donations, writing: "Much Needed Donations Strongly Encouraged."

He was finally out of the closet. He didn't have to hide behind fake identities anymore. But he had to keep his double life a secret. Revealing his undercover operation could blow the credibility he had carefully curated.

Two weeks into this project, Hashmi waited patiently for his livestream to begin, his image popping up in the top right corner, his hair carefully manicured and his voice clipped.

"I didn't scare you guys away, so I appreciate you coming back," he started.

At the end, he invited participants to subscribe to his YouTube channel, Javad "Jay" Hashmi.

On May 6, Hashmi had someone special helping him: his retired dentist sister, Sara H. Deen. She would appear on the Facebook page's comment board, herding questions. Of the mystical interpretation of Islam, called Sufism, he said he found it "problematic." He said he'd try to present a "charitable" view of Sufism. He lauded his father as a "great man" beyond the Sufi sheikhs. "I am not a corpse or empty cup," he said. "I'm a Ferrari."

He played a choppy YouTube video of Pakistani rock star Salman Ahmad from the band Junoon. He liked the music, he admitted.

Ironically, he brought up The Kominas, a punk band from the early 2000s supported by the progressive Muslims Hashmi had spent years attacking and degrading anonymously in his character assassination and disinformation campaign.

CHAPTER 21

Exploding into an American Intifada

At the corner of East 38th Street and Chicago Avenue in the Powderhorn Park neighborhood of Minneapolis, a tall, middle-aged black man in a black tank top hanging loosely over his pants stepped inside Cup Foods. His name was George Floyd.

It was just before 8:00 p.m. on Memorial Day, Monday, May 25, and the world was in the grips of a public health pandemic with the spread of the deadly coronavirus. About fifteen minutes earlier, a friend of Floyd's had just handed a cashier a bill that the cashier ran through a money-counting machine, which flagged it as counterfeit. The cashier handed the bill back to the friend.

Now, Floyd handed a twenty dollar bill to another cashier, who accepted it.

Cigarettes in hand, Floyd walked out slowly and slipped into the driver's seat of an SUV parked outside on Chicago Avenue. The teen cashier ran the new bill through a money-counting machine, which flagged it as potentially counterfeit. The cashier followed him outside, demanding that he return the cigarettes. He refused.

Another employee, who had arrived in Minnesota from West Africa the year before, called 911.

According to the official police transcript, the operator asked: "How can I help you?"

The caller responded: "Umm. Someone comes our store and give us fake bills, and we realize it before he left the store. And we ran back outside. They was sitting on their car. We tell them to give us their phone, put their [inaudible] thing back and everything—and he was also drunk and everything—and return to give us our cigarettes back and so he can, so he can go home, but he doesn't want to do that, and he's sitting on his car cause he is awfully drunk, and he's not in control of himself."

The caller gave the details of the blue van in which Floyd sat on East 38th Street.

Operator: "What's he look like, what race?"

The caller answered, mixing up his gender pronouns: "Um, he's a tall guy. He's like tall and bald, about like six...six and a half, and she's not acting right so and she started to go, drive the car."

Operator: "Is it a girl or a boy that did this?"

Caller: "It is a man."

Operator: "Okay. Is he white, black, Native, Hispanic, Asian?"

Caller: "Something like that."

Operator: "Which one? White, black, Native, Hispanic, Asian?"

Caller: "No, he's a black guy."

Operator: "Alright."

The official transcript includes "(sigh)" from the operator.

* * *

At 8:08 p.m., two newly minted Minneapolis Police Department recruits, Thomas Lane and J. Alexander Kueng, arrived in squad car 320. It was only Kueng's third shift as a full officer.

Officer Lane ordered Floyd out of the parked car, pulled Floyd out, and handcuffed him, walking him to the sidewalk and seating him on the ground.

"Are you on anything?" Officer Lane asked Floyd.

Officers Derek Chauvin and Tou Thao arrived soon after in another squad car.

The officers tried several times to put Mr. Floyd in a squad car, but he fell and said he wouldn't go inside. Floyd said several times he couldn't breathe.

The officers tried to get him inside the squad car again.

At 8:19 p.m., for some reason, Chauvin pulled Floyd out of the car, and he fell to the ground handcuffed. Kueng held Floyd's back down while Lane held his legs. Chauvin put his left knee on Floyd's neck.

Lane said, "I'm worried about excited delirium."

"Excited delirium" means extreme agitation and aggression that come from being in an altered state, often as a result of taking illegal drugs, especially stimulants such as cocaine or methamphetamines.

Chauvin said, "That's why we have him on his stomach."

Drawn by shouts of bystanders yelling at the cops, another teen cashier watched in despair, calling the Cup Foods owner in panic that police were killing a man.

"Who are you talking about?" he asked.

She repeated, "Mike! Mike! They're killing him, the guy, they're killing him."

"Make sure you record it and call the cops on the cops."

At 8:24:24, Floyd stopped moving.

At 8:27:24, Chauvin removed his knee from Floyd's neck.

Kueng checked Floyd's pulse. "I couldn't find one," Kueng told the other officers.

Floyd was dead.

* * *

Within hours, headlines of shock and horror crisscrossed the globe. A black man had died under the knee of a white police officer on his neck. The pundits took to the airwaves to declare this a sign of the "systemic racism" that plagued America as an outgrowth of "white supremacy" and "state-sponsored structural racism."

Within days, there was rioting on the streets from Portland, Oregon, to Brooklyn, New York, with looting, arson, and murder. Within weeks, protesters toppled statues, forced the renaming of high schools, and turned America upside down with demands that America's "racism problem" be fixed—immediately.

However, the details of the people involved in this cursed sequence of events defy the narrative of the killing as an act of "white supremacy," as preached by the activists, agitators, academics, and pundits who stoked riots, demonstrations, and more tragedy with their vitriol. The details didn't fit neatly into the black-and-white narrative ideologues were trying to spin. But they moved quickly to get people on script.

What had emerged in America was not a black-and-white struggle for justice, but rather the intersection of many maleficent paradigms that threaten to subvert the entire fabric of America. They make up a cult that is the Woke Army, and they are trying to apply their bankrupt ideology of "critical race theory" to undermine societies.

* * *

Alex Kueng, the officer who first responded to the call and then held Floyd's back down, was born to a white mother and an absentee black father from Nigeria. When he watched protesters block a highway years ago, he had turned to his mother, Joni Kueng, fifty-six, a math teacher, and said, "Don't you think that needs to be done from the inside?"

"That's part of the reason why he wanted to become a police officer—and a black police officer on top of it—is to bridge that gap in the community, change the narrative between the officers and the black community," his mother told a *New York Times* reporter. He grew up with four at-risk black children his mother adopted. On May 22, just three days before Floyd's killing, Kueng became one of about eighty black police officers on the force of almost nine hundred officers. One of his brothers knew Kueng's complex "origins story," as it's called in "critical race theory." But it didn't matter anymore. An activist in the Black Lives Matter movement, he went on Facebook Live with a local leader of the NAACP to demand the arrest of the police involved—including his brother.

* * *

Officer Derek Chauvin's partner, Tou Thao, was born in 1986 in the United States, his family among Hmong refugees from Cambodia fleeing war and persecution. His story, too, shattered the black-and-white narrative of the Woke Army. In Southeast Asia, the Hmong are a nomadic farming ethnic minority from which the CIA recruited members to fight the United States' "Secret War" against communist forces in Cambodia. When communist forces seized the capital of Cambodia, Laos, in 1975, contributing to the end of the Vietnam War, the US cut off aid to the Hmongs, stranding them behind enemy lines. The US allowed many to enter the country as refugees, and traumatized by war and largely destitute, the Hmong were resettled in public housing in two areas of the country: around Fresno, California, and around the Minneapolis-St. Paul area, with a population of about ninety thousand Hmong citizens, just about the same percentage of African American residents, according to US Census data. Hmong Americans rank the lowest among Southeast Asian American groups across a number of income categories, with 60 percent of them living in low-income conditions and more than one of four, or 28.3 percent, living in poverty—more than double the national rate of 11.8 percent and higher than the 20.8 percent poverty rate of African Americans.

But in the politics of "critical race theory," the data didn't matter. Because of the success of some Asians in society today, Asians had become "white adjacent."

But these theories didn't trickle down to police officer Tou Thao. He was trying to improve his odds. After graduating from high school in 2004, Thao attended North Hennepin Community College in nearby Brooklyn Park, Minnesota, but didn't graduate. Trying to build bridges in the local Hmong community, the Minneapolis Police Department hired the young man, fluent in Hmong, as a community services officer in 2009. Laid off during budget cuts, he was recalled in 2011 and hired in 2012 as a full-time officer, wearing badge No. 7162.

* * *

The Cup Foods owner was Mahmoud "Mike" Abumayyaleh, thirty-five, whose Muslim Palestinian American family traced its roots to Hebron in the West Bank. His father, Hamadeh, immigrated to the US from Jerusalem and opened Cup Foods in 1989 in the Longfellow neighborhood filled with businesses owned by blacks and immigrants. He sold hot food, phone cards, and *halal* meat, killed according to Muslim rules of slaughtering animals.

In 2012, the younger Abumayyaleh bought the store with his three sons, Samir, Adam, and Mahmoud. Samir was among a list of fifty Minneapolis landlords with the most housing code violations, topping at ninety-five violations between 2013 and March 2016, across forty-two units, totaling 2.3 violations per unit, according to City of Minneapolis data compiled by the *Minneapolis Star Tribune*.

The Cup Foods awning promoted its wares: "Phones & Accessories," "Mexican Food," and "T-Shirts." Abumayyaleh started working in the store when he was ten. Customers called his father "Pops." He was active in the local Arab American community. His nephew was half black, half Palestinian. The teen cashier was black. The Cup Foods owner soon faced death threats from activists angry that his staff had called 911. He had to flip the narrative. Fast.

He fired the black teen cashier who had called 911. He shared his security footage with NBC and went on air to explain. On Facebook that night, Abumayyaleh lamented, "I and my PR crew, were bamboozled, by NBC." They didn't tell his side of the story.

He needed help. Immediately.

He knew just who could help him: a fellow Palestinian American, Linda Sarsour. Born in Brooklyn to Palestinian parents, she had built a brand since the 9/11 attacks on America as an "unapologetic Muslim" activist, using it as early as 2010 and once even joking she should trademark the phrase. Her father owned a corner store in Brooklyn. She'd spent a decade cultivating relationships within the black community to catapult to the national stage after President Donald Trump's election in 2016, as a cofounder of the Women's March, protesting Trump, and a leader of the "Resistance."

She quickly set about enlisting her army of activists to flip the narrative, taking to Facebook to admonish her thousands of followers to not curse the Palestinian American Muslim store owner but to go after the real culprits: the cops. "There has been a lot of misinformation on the internet about the store owner and the details of the events that unfolded before George Floyd was murdered," she started. The store owner was a "Palestinian American," she said. He didn't sell alcohol or pork, she reassured them. He wasn't at the store when Floyd walked into the store.

A "17-year-old African American teen" made the call to 911 and was "absolutely traumatized" by the tragedy, she wrote.

She now closed with her pleas: "We can argue that police should have never been called, it wasn't worth it and that would be my position. But they were and MURDER/DEATH should never have been the result and that is the issue here."

Turn your anger on the cops, she said.

When rage turned on Sarsour for outing the black teen cashier, she edited her post to delete the teen's race. But her job was accomplished.

The store owner got support from Jaylani Hussein, a local official from the Minnesota chapter of the Council on American-Islamic Relations, who argued that "we need to be focused on the four police officers and having them be jailed with no bail until full charges are brought against them." This time, even CAIR couldn't figure out how to thread this needle. Dawud Walid, executive director of the CAIR Michigan chapter, said that "it is unreasonable to say to the store owners just take one for the team or look the other way when someone is allegedly committing a crime, and that's irrespective of their skin color. On the other hand, if it's something minor or insignificant or perhaps even a misunderstanding, then the store owner should also be aware that calling the police for a small matter could actually lead to the beating or the death of a human being."

Abumayyaleh appeared on TRT World, a Turkish media channel, with Jamar B. Nelson, a black "spokesman for the company."

A friend of Sarsour, Dean Obeidallah, a Palestinian American comedian who has been a frequent headliner at CAIR events, spun the story for the gullible *Daily Beast*, writing a column headlined "How Floyd case could finally unite blacks and Muslims."

The enemy remained the same: the "intersections of oppression," as Obeidallah quoted his old pal, Sarsour, saying.

* * *

Immediately, a network of organizations—from Democratic political operatives to partisan activists at groups ranging from MoveOn to Black Lives Matter—wrote grant proposals, raised money, mass-produced signs, and shot out digital dispatches to supporters to seize the moment.

They had an icon in the Woke Army network, Keith Ellison, the Minnesota attorney general, to champion their message in the courts. A convert to Islam in his twenties, he had built a career on identity politics and racial conflict, befriending activist Linda Sarsour, campaigning for polarizing lawmakers Rashida Tlaib and Ilhan Omar, and championing the cause of Islamist anti-Semitic groups like the Council on American-Islamic Relations, American Muslims for Palestine, and the Boycott, Divestment, Sanctions movement that sought the destruction of Israel.

Facts or morality couldn't get in the way of the mission to reap chaos. In St. Paul, Minnesota, rioters took to the streets, including a busy corridor, University Avenue, where Hmong refugees had started businesses. Kongsue Xiong, forty-six, a Hmong business owner in St. Paul, watched as looters destroyed his building and had flashbacks to his childhood, when he escaped Laos for the jungle and saw people killed as communist forces torched villages. Another businessman, Rob Yang, forty-four, watched as looters walked into his store and stole every shoe off the racks. His life flashed before him as he stood, numb.

* * *

The first Friday after Floyd's killing, another one of the legacy organizations of the Muslim Brothers on Grove Street dove into the moment.

The Islamic Circle of North America, whose members had marched to the White House to protest against Trump, organized an online webinar, "Police Brutality: Structural Racism." Pakistani American Rameez Abid, communication director of ICNA's Council for Social Justice, introduced the evening: "This is a problem that has been rampant for a long time."

Black American Khalid Griggs, associate chaplain for Muslim life at Wake Forest University, spoke, along with Islamic Circle of North America board member Musab Abdali.

* * *

In Brooklyn, the next night, May 30, a fan of Linda Sarsour's got the message.

Driving past the 88th Precinct station house of the New York Police Department in the Fort Greene neighborhood of Brooklyn, young lawyer Urooj Rahman, thirty-one, pulled a black-and-white keffiyeh, the scarf that has become a symbol of Palestinian nationalism, up over her face, just her eyes peeking out, and she tossed a Bud Light bottle filled with gasoline and stuffed with a rag into an NYPD police cruiser. Fortunately, the cruiser was empty. The explosive concoction is known as a "Molotov cocktail," a pejorative term the Finnish military used during World War II to mock Soviet politician Vyacheslav Molotov.

She had come a long way from the young Muslim girl who immigrated to the US from Pakistan with her family. Police gave chase and pulled Colinford "Colin" Mattis, thirty-two, the driver of the van and also an attorney, over on Willoughby Street. In the back seat, police found a gasoline container and another Molotov cocktail in production.

In her mugshot, Rahman wore a T-shirt with the graphic of a fist clenched and the message "The Struggle Continues Regardless."

Indeed, her comrades in the struggle stepped forward to get her and her lawyer friend released on bail. Salmah Rizvi, a former Obama administration official in the US State and Defense Departments, guaranteed her bail. And Palestinian American activist Linda

Sarsour's activist nonprofit, MPower Change, joined a coalition of Muslim, Arab, and South Asian groups organized to free the two Molotov cocktail activists. The coalition described itself as working on "social justice," "civil liberties," and "the fight" against "structural Islamophobia," "anti Muslim," and "anti-Black racism." The coalition also included the Islamic Circle of North America Council for Social Justice, with orthodox anti-gay, anti-Semitic Muslim leaders.

The coalition protested the "politically and racially-motivated" federal charges against the two lawyers, claiming they "instill fear and stifle protest by Black, South Asian, and Muslim protestors."

In a real stretch, they alleged the prosecution against these two protesters of "state violence" is rooted in a "longstanding history of anti-Black racism" and "structural Islamophobia." Federal prosecutors offered a plea deal to the Brooklyn attorneys, but in July 2021, US District Judge Brian Cogan set a date of March 2022 for a trial after plea talks stalled.

But the new nexus was in place.

Radical Muslims, radical leftists, and radical blacks lit the match to foment a race war.

* * *

People in positions of power were going to make sure that the story was written their way. At the *Washington Post*, Karen Attiah was an outspoken black editor born in 1986 to parents with roots in Nigeria and Ghana. She had earned her BA in communications studies from Northwestern University in 2008, moving to Ghana as a Fulbright Scholar, and she had graduated with an MA in human rights and journalism from Columbia University in 2012. After bouncing around a number of assignments, she moved to the *Washington Post* in 2014 and two years later was named the editor of Global Opinions, an influential online section of the newspaper that published international columnists.

Four years earlier, she had skewered white actress Louise Linton's *Telegraph* article, "How My Dream Gap Year in Africa Turned into a Nightmare," as "defining work of the White-Savior-in-Africa genre for the digital age," also criticizing "basically everything" that *New York Times* columnist Nicholas Kristof, a white man, "writes about war-torn countries."

During her tenure, she had groomed writers who pushed the new Woke agenda. She recruited Saudi journalist Jamal Khashoggi to write columns promoting the Muslim Brotherhood agenda of Islam in political governance before his horrific murder in Istanbul by a Saudi hit squad. She'd also recruited writers in India to promote the new Woke "paradigm." One week after Floyd's killing, at 2:31, early into her morning, she tweeted out to her followers: "One thing that will be painfully clear over the coming days: The lack of basic understanding and expertise in media of race relations, critical race theory, grassroots movements and other related forces that have shaped American society."

"*Critical race theory.*"

There were those words again.

She followed up four days later, retweeting her message and saying, "I hate being right."

* * *

The Honor Brigade was not going to waste the moment.

On June 18, 2020, with a banner image of the Dome of the Rock mosque in Jerusalem, American Muslims for Palestine sent its followers an announcement that it had "joined the ongoing and much-needed dialogue" to end the "never-ending plague" of "systemic anti-Black racism," with a new monthly online series, #LetsTalkBLM, featuring "prominent Black leaders" with "intersectional solidarity activists" sharing their "life experiences," "socio-political perspectives," and "practical solutions" for creating an "anti-racist society."

* * *

The next day, on Friday, Juneteenth, the day that marked the end of slavery, Muslims4Abolition held a 1:00 p.m. Friday prayer and rally on E. 88th Street in Manhattan at Gracie Mansion, the residence of New York City Mayor Bill de Blasio, to "abolish bail, abolish jails, abolish the police, abolish prisons." In case there was any confusion on their politics, their advertisement said the event was "open to all, minus cops & Zionists."

On Twitter, @MPower_Change, the organization started by the now ubiquitous Linda Sarsour, promoted the rally with the hashtag #DefundNYPD. "Bring your own mask, prayer mat, and art supplies," they encouraged.

* * *

To mark the one-month anniversary of George Floyd's murder, the government relations manager of the Council on American-Islamic Relations, Robert McCaw, a white Muslim convert representing CAIR as its government affairs director, stood outside the organization's headquarters on Capitol Hill and pulled the white curtain on a new banner spread across the building's front façade.

"BLACK LIVES MATTER," it read, with the image of George Floyd and the names of blacks allegedly killed by police.

"Allahu akbar!" a man shouted from the crowd, amid applause.

From a lectern moved onto the circular driveway in front of the banner, Nihad Awad, the Palestinian American executive director of CAIR, heralded protesters who have "filled the streets," political leaders debating "important political justice proposals," once considered "radical," protesters dismantling statues symbolizing "white supremacy," and corporations, sports leagues, and house of worships condemning "anti-black racism in their midsts." Floyd's murder was part of a "racist system," he declared, punctuating his remarks with white-gloved hand.

He quoted the prophet Muhammad, with no mention of the word "slavery," which is codified in the Qur'an in many verses. He concluded, "May God grant us success in our efforts to promote justice for black Americans and for all," as the Facebook Live camera panned wide.

It was in the "for all" that this radical Muslim wing of the Woke Army opened the door for its wider and true cause: its anti-Semitic aim to destroy the state of Israel.

* * *

Sure enough, four days later, the call went out from Linda Sarsour.

"Courageous" members of Congress, including Reps. Alexandria Ocasio-Cortez, Rashida Tlaib, Pramila Jayapal, and Betty McCollum, and Sen. Bernie Sanders, had just introduced a "historic letter" calling for an end to "U.S. funding to Israel apartheid."

Sarsour's organization, MPower Change, joined US Campaign for Palestinian Rights, Adalah Justice Project, and "more" to "seize this moment" and "call on our government to divest from violence," from "defunding police at home" to "divesting from militarism abroad."

"As the Movement for Black Lives has shown us," she wrote, turning the cause into a pronoun and harnessing the emotional energy attached it, "we know a better world is possible...."

The Woke Army had been decades in the making, and it was now kicking into action.

* * *

Very quickly, as the calls for justice turned to violence, looting, mayhem, and destruction—a retired black police chief in St. Louis was brutally murdered by black looters at a pawnshop—it was evident something more nefarious was at play. A network of radicals—a veritable band of violence-prone left-wing ideologues—was not interested in finding justice for George Floyd. Rather, they were weaponizing his tragedy to stoke racial tensions if not an actual race war. They had in their crosshairs the very ideals of democracy and liberalism.

And the global network of her fellow Muslim activists was ready to push the narrative she wanted: it was time to destroy the system.

In Ontario, Canada, a young Muslim student, Hareer Al-Qaragolie, born in Baghdad to Iraqi parents, penned a column for her student newspaper about realizing that being "white-passing" was a "privilege," making it so that her "pale appearance had made life in Canada easier."

UC Berkeley lecturer Hatem Bazian, a stalwart in the Honor Brigade, sat before his camera in his office, a wall of books on bookcases behind him, to speak on "Islam, Muslims, and Question on Race," launching into a tirade against "racist frames," saying racism should be written onto death certificates as "a cause of death." Now sporting salt-and-pepper hair, he wore a black turtleneck under a blue jacket with leather patches over the elbows, looking very professorial. He used a laundry list of Woke Army buzzwords, blaming "omission," "erasure of history," "blaming the victim," "media misinformation," "reinforcing stereotypes," "whataboutism," "indifference," and criticism of the "family life" of black single mother households. He called for "equity" and "liberation," invoking the Muslim proclamation of faith, "No god but God," as an equalizer against racism.

"Look at the anger," he said, invoking Islam as a vehicle for *adab*, or good manners, with no "rancor" against others, but there shouldn't be "silence" against "structural racists" and others. He committed to act on six action items some black leaders sought from Muslims—including a "letter of solidarity with the black community," a "Day of Outrage" at mosques, workshops and "courageous conversations" on "anti-blackness," calls to the Minneapolis district attorney, and protests for "equity"—plus adding another item: stopping the intersection of Muslims and blacks at the "counter of a liquor store," owned by Muslims.

"You want to quote Malcolm, then walk like Malcolm and act like Malcolm and make transformative change like Malcolm," he closed, ending by saying, "*JazakAllah khair*," Arabic for May Allah reward you.

* * *

Watching all this, Muslim reformer Irshad Manji recalled the response Muslims had of her first book, *The Trouble with Islam*, when she was smeared, attacked, and despised by fellow Muslims. In a blog on Heterodox, a new platform, she wrote, "The 'Muslim fragility' that I witnessed pained me. Most of my co-religionists did not want to hear about the need to change ourselves. Despite backing up my case with passages from the Qur'an, I was met mostly with denial, consternation, condemnation, and, on occasion, violent threats." She added, "It took me years to appreciate that humans, universally, respond badly to being blamed. The primitive part of our brains give [*sic*] rise to the ego, and the ego kicks in as a shield whenever we feel threatened. For tough conversations to succeed, emotional defenses must be lowered all-around. Only then can people tap into the more evolved part of their brains, allowing reason to co-exist with emotion rather than being bulldozed by it."

She concluded, "This is why shaming white people for being fragile is both misleading and toxic."

* * *

Even orthodox Muslims became foot soldiers for the Woke Army.

The Salafi online website, MuslimMatters, added a black banner to its website with #BlackLivesMatter across it and a message, "Click here to donate to NAACP, Reclaim the Block and/or Color of Change." Its editor, Hena Zuberi, had mocked me when I had written my *Washington Post* column about "Uncle Ruslan," the uncle of the Tsarnaev brothers, who had orchestrated the Boston Marathon bombings.

Now, she published a confession on her "internalized racism" and a tutorial on "Structural Racism," "Systemic Racism," and "Whiteness." She pushed training by the "Muslim Anti-Racism Collaborative" and declared, "Racism is a disease of the heart." She sold her readers the laundry list of books of the industry supporting the Woke Army: *The New Jim Crow: Mass Incarceration in the Age of Colorblindness* by Michelle Alexander; *Race Matters* by Cornel West; and *The Racial Healing Handbook: Practical Activities to Help You Challenge Privilege, Confront Systemic Racism, and Engage in Collective Healing* by Anneliese A. Singh, chief diversity officer at Tulane University. On Twitter, @AnnelieseSingh was all about #Academics4BlackLives #antiracism #racialhealing #reparations #liberation. She promoted @Academics-4BlackLives training on "White Terrorism & Black Resistance."

* * *

Linda Sarsour was ready. She had been working closely with Keith Ellison's son, Jeremiah Ellison, a city councilman in Minneapolis. Ellison was leading an effort to defund the police in Minneapolis. Sarsour was continuing her parallel years-long campaign in New York City. On Saturday, June 6, 2020, she marched with thousands of protesters from 110th Street and Central Park West at Frederick Douglass Monument to Washington Square Park, calling on New York City Mayor Bill de Blasio to cut police funding. The next day, he announced a defunding.

Two days after the march, Sarsour appeared on the *The Quarantine Report*, on far-left media outlet Democracy Now! with host Amy Goodman to applaud the decision by the Minneapolis City Council. Perched on a brown sofa, the back covered with a floral tapestry, she wore her trademark tight headscarf, this one green, and now wore eyeglasses. She first thanked her partners in the Woke Army. "The credit is to Communities United for Police Reform, the Justice Committee, the New York Justice League, The Gathering for Justice, Until Freedom, the many groups in New York City who have been doing police reform work for decades, and in the last for years have continued to pressure Mayor Bill de Blasio, who ran on a police reform platform, to actually make transformative change," she declared.

With footage of "DEFUND THE POLICE" being painted in yellow on the streets of New York, she remained militant in her demand to "defund the police," her battle cry for years, since NYPD police officers investigated Muslims at local Brooklyn mosques for their extremism. The campaign against NYPD surveillance had led to settlements with the city and the dismantling of its "demographics unit."

The defunding movement now branded itself as "abolitionists."

* * *

By late June, Kimberlé Crenshaw @SandyLocks tweeted out another take on her mantra, this time writing, "Intersectionality is not additive. It's fundamentally reconstitutive. Pass it on." And pass it on, her trusted friends did.

Among the retweets: Open Society's Alvin Starks.

And she earned a retweet from a former editor at MuslimahMediaWatch.org, which had been doling out content for the Honor Brigade for years.

* * *

In the crowd of Muslims aligned with the new Woke Army, Rutgers University assistant professor Noura Erakat, a Palestinian American activist, listed "critical race theory" among her areas of expertise.

Palestinian activists churned out artwork, cartoons, articles, and protest signs connecting their cause to George Floyd's killing. Drawing for *Mondoweiss*, Palestinian artist Carlos Latuff drew a cartoon of a young black man rising out of a map of the United States, with a white police officer's gun pointed at his head, and he gives a fist bump to a young Palestinian man with a keffiyeh scarf around his neck, a T-shirt emblazoned in the colors of the Palestinian flag, with an angry Israeli security official's rifle at his neck. The Jewish star sat on the police officer's helmet. Students for Justice in Palestine in Chicago quickly shared the cartoon on its Facebook page.

Based in Chicago, American Muslims for Palestine promoted a Friday prayer and protest—calling it a "Jummah + Rally" event—with "Muslims for Abolition" on Friday, June 12, at the corner of 37th Street and Martin Luther King Jr. Drive. The announcement featured a graphic of a protester holding a sign with a quote from the prophet Muhammad, saying, "Fear the prayer of the oppressed, there is no barrier between it and Allah." For another rally the next day, American Muslims for Palestine shared a poster with "Arabs for Black Liberation" across the top, above drawings of women in headscarves with fists pumped in the air, holding signs that read, "Arabs Say Now Is The Time To Stop Police Crimes" and "Protect Black Lives." In small print, the artist, Dana Zituni, got credit, and organization logos sat beside the website URLs for the sponsoring groups: Arab American Action Network and the Chicago Alliance Against Racist and Political Repression, both based in Chicago. The Chicago Alliance was founded in 1973 out of the movement to free "all political prisoners" and radical activist Angela Davis when she was held in jail for conspiracy to murder. In November, it was assembling to rebrand as the "National Alliance," featuring endorsements from the plethora of "intersectional" causes from among Muslims exploiting the political dynamic, including Stand With Kashmir and US Palestinian Community Network. This rally was going to be in the rear parking lot of Jerusalem Banquets on S. Harlem Avenue in Bridgeview, Illinois.

American Muslims for Palestine announced a new monthly online webinar, #LetsTalkBLM, featuring "prominent Black leaders" and "intersectional solidarity activists" sharing their "life experiences" and "socio-political perspectives" and providing "practical solutions to build a just and an anti-racist society."

Their hashtags: #PalestineConnectsUs #BlackLivesMatter.

Hesham Shehab, a staffer at the Counter-Islamist Grid, a project of the Middle East Forum run by historian Daniel Pipes, cowrote with Benjamin Baird, director of the project, an honest refection on this activism amid the history of racism against blacks by Arab Muslims. Born in 1960 into a Muslim family in Lebanon, Shehab says the Muslim Brotherhood in Lebanon, Al-Gama'a al-Islamiyya, recruited him when he was thirteen, and he grew up steeped in their radicalism. He was committed to seeking revenge for the killing of his brother by Christian militia during the Lebanese civil war, when he started learning more about Christianity, eventually converting to the faith. Now a Lutheran minister in Chicago, he had reached out to me earlier in the year to invite Zuhdi Jasser and me to speak in Chicago about the Muslim Reform Movement. He'd written a courageous piece for *American Thinker*, criticizing the *Chicago Tribune* for a puff piece on hijab, quoting one Muslim woman describing it as "flat-out feminist." He had quoted my analysis of the headscarf as a tool of political Islam.

Now, he wrote with Baird: "Islamists are using the Floyd tragedy to advance an intersectionalist worldview which imagines the U.S. and Israel as the common enemy of all oppressed people," they wrote. "In doing so, pro-Palestinian activists whitewash the normalization of anti-black hate within their own communities, while simultaneously paying lip service to the cause of racial justice and equality. Such transparently exploitative motives do lasting damage to the black civil rights movement and racial reconciliation."

* * *

By late June, black leaders started coming to the same conclusion, and Palestinian leaders started warning their rank and file to tone down their parallels between the Palestinian and black causes.

Hatem Bazian took to Facebook again to share a Zoom video on "Racism: Neoliberalism, Militarism and Police Violence," calling on Muslims to reject "whiteness" and harken back to the "alliances" of black activists and Muslims. Filming in a wingback chair, he referenced Malcolm X visiting Gaza. Now, however, he cautioned the "comparison" between the struggle of Palestinians and blacks had a "time and a place," otherwise it became a "silencing act."

"It does begin to appear…that we are trying to jump in front of a discourse…," he said.

* * *

On Sunday evening, Karen Attiah, the Global Opinions editor for the *Washington Post* who had groomed Islamist writer Jamal Khashoggi, before his murder, posted this message on Twitter: "The lies & tears of White women hath wrought:—The 1921 Tulsa Massacre—Murder of Emmet Till—Exclusion of Black women from feminist movements—53% of white women voting for Trump. White women are lucky that we are just calling them 'Karen's'. And not calling for revenge."

* * *

By late July, Emgage Action's Emgage PAC endorsed candidates for the 2020 election from state legislatures to the presidency, giving Biden its seal of approval.

They exploited the new rules in racial politics.

In Arizona, CAIR's top official in the state, Imraan Siddiqi, reached across the nation to launch an attack on Andy Ngo, a young Vietnamese American writer, who had drawn fire with investigative work exposing Antifa activists in his hometown of Portland, Oregon. An Asian American writer and photographer, Ngo walked into the artillery of the Woke Army for daring to defy their new world order.

And the new poster girl of the Woke Army, Rep. Ilhan Omar, relished the attention of her newfound power. In a purple headscarf, Omar stood before a lectern, her eyes downcast, carefully reading her speech from prepared remarks, word for word: "We cannot stop at the criminal justice system. We must begin the work of dismantling the whole system of oppression wherever we find it."

* * *

You didn't have to look far to find the real target of ire for the Islamists. The government of Qatar kept stoking racial division in the United States to feed its hate of Israel.

Dena Takruri, a Palestinian American senior presenter and producer at @AJPlus, the slick propaganda arm of Al Jazeera, shared with her Twitter followers an AJ+ video she'd produced, saying, "U.S. police are being trained by Israel, learning and bringing home the tactics the state uses to control the occupied Palestinian population that has no civil rights." Stefanie Fox, executive director of Jewish Voice for Peace, was her first interview, as images of Israel police flashed across the screen. Wearing a black-and-white keffiyeh, symbolizing the Palestinian intifada, Ajamu Dillahunt, a "student and activist" with Demilitarize! Durham2Palestine, spoke about the "brutalization" of police. She drew "parallels" between police responses from Standing Rock to Gaza. First, she slipped into typical anti-Israel rhetoric, challenging its founding, and then chronicled training from "pro-Israel" groups. She flashed to Ferguson, Missouri, claiming the use of tactics "mirroring" strategies by "Israeli forces against Palestinians." She flashed "from #Gaza to #Ferguson" tweets from Palestinians. "Who could forget" police response to the DC protesters following George Floyd's killing?" she asked. A bit after minute seven in the video, she then targeted NYPD surveillance of Muslims and its "racist" stop-and-frisk policy. She highlighted Durham, North Carolina, as a victory, with the activist saying the "oppressed" people in Israel and the US could fight back. North Hampton, Massachusetts, is another victory, she said. The activist called for a "new era in black and Palestinian solidarity." The executive producer was Shadi Rahimi.

Zahra Noorbakhsh, host of the podcast *Good Muslim, Bad Muslim*, shared the video on her Twitter account, @ZahraComedy, shouting, "FINALLY PEOPLE ARE TALKING ABOUT THIS!!!" She credited CAIR San Francisco Bay Area chapter executive director Zahra Billoo, previously removed from the Women's March board for her anti-Semitism, for explaining the topic to her.

* * *

A couple days later, the "activism" erupted again on the streets, this time in a "Day of Rage" organized by the controversial Palestinian group, Al-Awda, based in Coral Springs, Florida, which demands a "right of return" of Palestinians to Israel, linking their grievances to Black Lives Matter. In Brooklyn, with Palestinian flags flapping all around, one protester yelled, "The United States of America and all of its puppet governments will be no more!"

Nerdeen Kiswani, a former leader in Students for Justice in Palestine and now a founder of a new group, Within Our Lifetime, yelled: "We don't want a fake Palestinian state that they give us while Israel still exists. The land that Israel exists on is still stolen. The 1948 lands are still stolen. Jaffa, Haifa, and Tel Aviv—originally named Tel Rabi'a—was stolen. We don't want to just go back to our homes in Gaza and the West Bank. We want all of it!"

"Death to Israel! Death to America!" yelled another protester.

* * *

By 4:26 p.m., Rashad Robinson, president of Color of Change, tweeted out, "Met with Mark Zuckerberg and @Facebook leadership today. It was a disappointment. They have had our demands for years and yet it is abundantly clear that they are not yet ready to address the vitriolic hate on their platform." He earned 41,200 likes.

Mustafa Dustin Craun @DustinCraun, one of the cofounders of @MPowerChange, retweeted the message. LoonWatch was still alive on Facebook. So was the Facebook page called "Zuhdi Jasser is a Clown."

* * *

Every issue returned to Palestine. When dozens of writers, including J. K. Rowling, wrote an open letter in *Harper's Magazine* protesting "cancel culture," Democratic New York Rep. Alexandria Ocasio-Cortez @AOC wrote to her 7.5 million followers, "Many of the people actually 'cancelled' are those long denied a fair hearing of their ideas to begin w/," listing then "Palestinian human rights advocates," followed by "Abolitionists," "Anticapitalists," and Anti-imperialists." Her tweet was much loved by anti-Semitic, anti-Israel activists.

The next week, the US Campaign for the Academic and Cultural Boycott of Israel held a second session of its summer webinar series on "Palestine and BDS in the age of COVID-19 and Black Lives Matter." The guests this time were Ghada Karmi, an honorary research fellow and instructor at the Institute of Arab and Islamic Studies at the University of Exeter in the UK; Kristian Davis Bailey, cofounder of Black for Palestine; Mohammed Nabulsi, an organizer with the Palestinian Youth Movement; and Terri Ginsberg, assistant professor of film at The American University in Cairo. The subject of the talk was "Black Lives Matter and Israeli Annexation: Anti-Apartheid, Anti-Colonial Perspectives."

Meanwhile, the Birmingham Civil Rights Institute awarded Angela Davis its highest award.

* * *

An eighteen-year-old Muslim teen complained that her headscarf was "forcibly removed" when she was arrested during a Black Lives Matter protest for multiple charges, including battery of an officer and resisting with violence. (Prosecutors later closed the case without action. By September 2021, the young woman was regularly posting TikTok videos without any hair covering.) In Turkey, a journalist claimed, "Pandemic of racism has only reemerged in the U.S."

Established a decade earlier with money from the Muslim groups at 500 Grove Street, the Ali Vural Ak Center for Global Islamic Studies at George Mason University in Fairfax County, Virginia, organized a webinar that exploited George Floyd's killing and COVID-19, calling the webinar "The Pandemic of White Supremacy: Making Black Muslim Lives Matter in a Covid-19 World." It was part of a series, "Covid-19 and Muslim Religiosity." Donna Auston, a Rutgers University professor and a convert writing under the Twitter handle @TinyMuslimah, spoke with Ahmet Tekelioglu, a research fellow at the George Mason Center for Global Islamic Studies and editor in chief of *Maydan*. The graphic was a face mask with the image of a mosque printed on it.

The Muslim lobbying group that had helped elect Muslims, Emgage, was on fire. And unfiltered. Its CEO, Wa'el Alzayat, pounced on the Trump administration possibly rehiring Steve Bannon, writing a tweet to Trump, saying, "You're an asshole. See you in November." He organized a "Million Muslim Voters" online conference with headline news: an endorsement of Democratic presidential candidate Joe Biden.

First, Alzayat showed a new ad that featured the stars of the Muslim brigade, including Rashida Tlaib, Ilhan Omar, and Linda Sarsour, arms crossed defiantly, the US Capitol Police on red alert. Then, Sarsour joined CAIR's Nihad Awad and others to discuss politics. She spoke from her typical talking points. Then, another panel. Finally, Emgage founder Khurrum Wahid took to the camera, flanked on both sides by potted plants, and introduced Biden.

* * *

It didn't take long for the protests to take a direct turn toward anti-Semitism.

Two weeks after Floyd's death, rapper Ice Cube tweeted a mural, "Freedom for Humanity," painted on a wall in the East End of London, illustrating elderly white bankers, several with oversized noses, playing the game of Monopoly on the backs of people of color. The mural creator, MEAR ONE, mocked the "older white Jewish folks" who "had an issue with me portraying their beloved #Rothschild or #Warburg etc. as the demons they are." Former British Labour Party leader Jeremy Corbyn initially supported the mural.

Ice Cube, too, dug in his heels when critics called him anti-Semitic, sharing a photo of the statue of King David on Mount Zion in Jerusalem with the message, "WE ARE THE CHOSEN PEOPLE." Comedian Chelsea Handler, star Madonna, and actors Jameela Jamil and Jessica Chastain approvingly shared videos of Louis Farrakhan, well known for his anti Semitism.

In New York City, Jewish writer John-Paul Pagano was a liberal, but he had courageously called out the darlings of the left who were spewing anti-Semitism. Even then, he watched in shock. He counted them. Rappers. Actors. Comedians. TV personalities. Professional athletes. One after the next. By late July the number was ten. It was "destructive blindness," he wrote in the *Tablet*. "'Anti-racism,' as it is conceived and practiced today—months after a wave of intermittently murderous attacks on Jews in and around New York—has not just a shallow understanding of the peculiarities of Jew-hatred, but no inclination to confront it when expressed by people who have suffered racism themselves," he explained.

He noticed a disturbing conspiracy theory that he called "racist replacement theology." That black people were the "real Jews," while white Jews were fakes who had exploited the Bible to advance themselves.

The sick thinking was seeping into the protests. On the Fourth of July, a black militia, "Not Fucking Around Coalition," walked through the streets of Georgia in an open-carry demonstration. Its founder, "Grand Master Jay," had once posted a fake Hitler quote: "Negros...are the True Hebrews." Retired and current NFL and NBA players joined the fray, repeating anti-Semitic conspiracy theories.

British rapper Wiley defended TV personality Nick Cannon who put forward similar ideas on a podcast. Wiley tweeted, "ISRAEL is a black peoples place." And he warned, "Jewish People I know Who You ARE."

On the left, aligned with Islamists, white writer Max Blumenthal, the son of Clinton operative Sidney Blumenthal, lamented on Twitter how "corporate media & Jewish establishment outrage" over "petty incidents of Black anti-Semitism...invariably omits critical social & class context & winds up reinforcing racist power dynamics."

CHAPTER 22

Waging a War on America's Children

In the Commonwealth of Virginia, the Muslim Brothers had installed one of their own to a coveted seat as the Virginia secretary of education, and nobody had really paid attention.

His name was Atif Qarni, and he was the perfect poster boy for their penetration into public office. Born in Pakistan, he arrived in the United States as a young boy. A mediocre student in Prince William County, Virginia, outside the nation's capital, he took an unorthodox path for young immigrant Muslims. He signed up for the US Marines. But it was a stable living after the 9/11 attacks, as America went to war in Afghanistan and then Iraq. Qarni set off for a deployment in Iraq. He earned an undergraduate degree at a low-rent online college, eventually heading to local George Mason University and a career in public school teaching—again, not a very orthodox path for a Muslim man in America.

A middle school social studies teacher, Qarni ran for state office, first running to be a Virginia state delegate, before losing, and then trying a run for the state senate, again losing. But he had some important investors: the Muslim Brothers at 500 Grove Street doled out money for his political races. His list of political contributions, in fact, read like it could have been the list of companies and individuals cited in the raid at 500 Grove Street. Mar-Jac Investments Inc., carrying the same Mar-Jac name as the halal chicken slaughterhouse purchased by the Muslim Brothers in the 1980s, gave him $6,000 in one campaign, while doling out $81,650 to local and state races, including other Muslim candidates, from Babur Lateef, a Pakistani American, who was Prince William County School Board chair, to Esam Omeish's failed bid for state delegate and the winning school board campaign of his daughter, Abrar Omeish. Also housed at 500 Grove Street, Reston Investments gave money to Qarni as part of the $96,550 it has donated to Democratic candidates, large and small, Muslim and non-Muslim. Another donor from 500 Grove Street, Sterling Management Group Inc., has pumped $92,646 into candidates over the years, including Qarni.

Qarni also snagged a donation from Asim Ghafoor, who listed his affiliation with the Islamic Institute of Islamic Thought at 500 Grove Street, where he was the former political director. Speaking about Muslims in the United States in a radio debate before the 2000 election, Ghafoor once declared, "We are here not just to be nice to people, not to say great things about people, but to bring truth and justice and Islamic ways to this country...you should rule by Islam. Otherwise, you're a *kafir*," the Arabic word for a nonbeliever.

The businesses and businessmen at 500 Grove Street had come a long way since the Muslim Brothers had established them some four decades earlier.

Together, they lined the campaign coffers of state delegates, US representatives, and county board supervisors. Qarni's donors masked their Islamist interests with the innocuous-sounding names they had of investment funds and their old standby: the halal chicken slaughterhouse. When he lost his second state race, Qarni penned an op-ed for the *Washington Post* blaming one issue: "Islamophobia."

Qarni leveraged his loss to win a political appointment to higher office. And it worked.

Shekar Narasimhan, founder of the Asian American Pacific Islander Victory Fund, had doled out $1,000 for one of Qarni's statehouse ambitions and once bragged to a local political leader that he had forwarded Qarni's name to Virginia Gov. Ralph Northam to name as his education secretary. It was quite the rise to power for a middle school teacher. A Hindu from India, Narasimhan told the local leader he didn't care that Qarni had raised money with Islamist interests. He was "Asian," and that was good enough for him.

By the summer of 2020, Qarni had a golden opportunity in front of him. In the weeks after the tragedy of George Floyd's death, the Virginia governor faced a potential race problem. The year before, Northam had admitted he was in a "clearly racist and offensive" photograph in his 1984 medical school yearbook, showing a man in blackface and another man in a white Ku Klux Klan hood and gown. He had refused to say whether he was the man in black face or the KKK hood. Northam had saved his job by ingratiating himself with black leaders around the state and moving from a centrist Democrat to a friend of the far left. He had capitulated to calls to remove the monuments to Confederate generals, and he had placated calls to bring "social justice" to Virginia. Now, with racial sensitivities ignited, he risked the blackface debacle blowing up again. Qarni had the perfect solution: he would exploit the moment to push the issue of "equity" at the state's top schools, called Governor's Schools.

In return, Qarni could realize the vision of the Muslim Brothers to upend curriculum in America's schools, so that America's children could finally learn about "true Islam," the ills of Israel, and the vision of a reborn Palestine. America faced the perfect storm, and the philosophy of Wokeism was the perfect cover for Islamism. They were two ideologies born out of tribalism, and now they could use this ideology of "critical race theory" to embed the ideology of Islamism into the minds of babes.

It was the perfect realization of the dream of the Muslim Brothers who established their hub in Herndon, Virginia, so many years ago.

* * *

They had to move quickly and used the cover of the COVID-19 pandemic disaster, with its social distancing and online virtual meetings, to pass new policies.

My son happened to be a rising senior at one of those schools in Qarni's crosshairs: Thomas Jefferson High School for Science and Technology, named America's No. 1 high school by *US News and World Report* in 2020. For me, as an immigrant Muslim single mother "of color" from India, it was a moment of relief and joy when my son emerged from a rigorous merit-based admissions process, including taking a tough math and science test, to be named to the school's Class of 2021.

As I chased the Honor Brigade and challenged terrorists and those who fund them, my son's school was an emotional reprieve where I drank sugar cane juice at a back-to-school night and worked the front office, greeting the school's mostly Asian immigrant families who called the school home. I connected with them because our stories were so similar, overcoming the odds to pursue the American Dream. In the late 1990s, many families from China, India, and other nations arrived in Northern Virginia to save America from the threat of the "Y2K bug" and boost the country's technology infrastructure. Their children were born in the early 2000s and were now my son's classmates. I called them "Y2K kids." Either through nature or nurture, they were brilliant in science, technology, engineering, and math, known as STEM. But, for the emboldened Woke Army—with a member of the Honor Brigade as its secretary of education—our kids were the wrong side of brown. The activists were obsessed with removing the merit-based admissions process and replacing it with a race-based system that would increase the number of black and Hispanic students, not through merit, accomplishment, or education but by simply lowering the admissions standard to juke the numbers. It was racist, lazy, and offensive.

* * *

On June 7, 2020, I became an accidental activist against the Woke Army in schools.

To the great shock of parents and students at the school, the school's white principal, Ann Bonitatibus, dispatched an email to us with a "call to action," lecturing us to check our "privileges" and calling on us to consider replacing the school's Colonial mascot as a "symbol that perpetuated racism," and gerrymander the admissions process so the school's demographics would match the racial demographics of the county. That meant one thing: a targeted hit on the school's Asian families, which made up 70 percent of the student demographics.

I watched in shock. We weren't people of simple "privileges." We had endured our own struggles, some parents fleeing communism in Eastern Europe, others escaping the Cultural Revolution in China. A mother, Helen Miller, wrote an email to the principal, angry she had thrust her politics on our community, tone-deaf to the fact that families everywhere were struggling through COVID-19.

The next morning, Helen sent a letter to the principal, telling her that her activist agenda was off the mark: "After not sleeping at all last night, I'm hopping mad!!"

Another mother, Suparna Dutta, dispatched a letter with her husband to the principal, noting: "Your message espouses a sham, reductionist view of history and the problems of inequality and injustice which, in our view, belittles the intelligence and values of many of your students and their parents."

The day of the principal's letter, a local Democratic political operative named Lowell Feld published a false headline on the blog *Blue Virginia*, which he'd started, dedicated to "Virginia politics from a progressive and Democratic perspective." He didn't respond to requests for comment. The headline claimed "ZERO African Americans" had been granted admission to the school. *Washington Post* reporter Hannah Natanson tweeted out the false information, soliciting outrage. The headline is still up.

Helen's husband, Glenn Miller, told me: "You have to understand only three words to understand what's happening right now," he said. "Critical. Race. Theory." He had been a student at Harvard Law School in the 1980s as Derrick Bell and Kimberlé Crenshaw started building the cult of "critical race theory."

I started investigating "critical race theory." The pieces started falling into place. I could finally understand everything I had confronted over almost two decades with the increasingly influential Woke Army.

* * *

Over the years, Islamists had exploited "critical race theory" to racialize any criticism of Islam or Muslims as "Islamophobia" and press their grievances.

Now, it was their opportunity to pounce to further their own agenda.

In my parents' home in Morgantown, West Virginia, as my son did school remotely, I sat before the video camera on June 19 and testified to the Fairfax County school board, all twelve members endorsed by the Democratic Party, warning the school board that we were facing an assault on our school.

A week later, I testified again. We faced an industry that I called Woke Inc. It used "critical race theory" as a vehicle to enter into K-12 schools. I warned the school board members that this was a movement that was trying to destroy the very fabric of our community.

Dutta also spoke to the school board for the first time ever, expressing her opposition to the new activism in schools. She was so nervous she couldn't figure out how to turn on her video, but yet she persisted.

Little did we know the school board was in on the hijacking of our school, along with the school principal and a radical group of school alumni that had banded together to create a group called "TJ Alumni Action Group."

They had an important daughter of the Muslim Brothers on their side: Abrar Omeish, who had just a year earlier stood before the fundraiser of American Muslims for Palestine, promising to change curriculum so that it would be friendly to the cause of Palestine. She had won the race to Fairfax County School Board, to the chagrin of many.

* * *

The entire network of the left, its donors, and its nonprofits were cashing in on this movement.

The Southern Poverty Law Center, or SPLC, which had defamed Muslim reformer Maajid Nawaz as an "anti-Muslim extremist" and paid him a $3.3 million settlement, was churning out curriculum, coined "Teaching Tolerance," pushing "critical race theory" in K-12 schools. And now Muslim organizations were getting in on the racket. Out of Northern California, Islamic Networks Group started pumping a new curriculum to schools steeped in "critical race theory."

And in Virginia, Education Secretary Atif Qarni led a public campaign to overhaul the state's social studies curriculum. Behind the scenes, as summer continued, he presided over a secretive task force to overhaul admissions to TJ. By summer's end, parents had learned what was quietly happening behind the scenes. But Qarni had important allies on his side: state delegates funded by the companies headquartered at 500 Grove Street, not to mention the Prince William County School Board chair, Babur Lateef, the recipient himself of donations from the businesses at 500 Grove Street. Lateef also had an important position on the board of the TJ Partnership Fund, a nonprofit that raised money for the school. He personally lobbied his board members to run interference for Qarni and win support for the new "equity" changes to the school.

As corresponding secretary of our school's Parent Teacher Student Association, I advocated for action. One day, Qarni's executive assistant contacted the PTSA president to invite two representatives from the PTSA at a "listening session." Word got to Qarni through Lateef's network that I would be one of the speakers. Qarni's executive assistant set up a phone call with the PTSA president. Qarni had important news to share, he told him, when they talked. I was a member of a hate group designated by the Southern Poverty Law Center.

Surprised by the news, the president asked: What hate group?

The answer was simple: the Muslim Reform Movement.

The hand of a lieutenant in the Honor Brigade had reached into a high school in Northern Virginia to spread its toxic disinformation trying to hijack progress—not to mention, decency and civility. In California, the Honor Brigade was working with the left to continue its campaign to infuse anti-Semitic, poisonous "ethnic studies" curriculum into America's schools. The intention was clear:

to flip the hierarchy of human value, so that Muslim supremacists could leapfrog to the top of the pecking order. The Honor Brigade had used LoonWatch to advance its agenda and now thought they didn't need it anymore, because they had penetrated mainstream media outlets like the *New York Times*, the *Washington Post*, and CNN. They were back in the White House with new appointments to the new Biden administration.

They had realized all this success because of a dream by some Muslim Brothers who stood before barren land at 500 Grove Street. What they knew—and what America must remember—is that this country is worth defending.

And the Muslim reformers who have survived character assassinations for almost two decades will continue fighting to defend this country that we love.

Will you?

CHAPTER 23

Courage is Contagious

In September 2020, a group of about two hundred students, parents, alumni, and concerned local residents flooded the sidewalk in front of Thomas Jefferson High School for Science and Technology. This was no back-to-school event. It was a rally to save the soul of the school itself. And the future of America.

The rally included parents from China, India, South Korea, and the far corners of the world. They stepped forward, one by one, to describe their families' journeys—from marching in Tiananmen Square decades ago to arriving in the United States with only dollars in their pockets.

"I came here for freedom," said Yuyan Zhou, a Chinese American mother who had spent eight years as a TJ parent. "Moral courage is the only solution for this madness. Stand up for your rights. Stand up for your values. Fight for the future of our students!"

And what was the "madness" Zhou described?

It was the growing power of the Woke Army. Since early June, the small but vocal group of TJ alumni had successfully worked with activist school board members, state education officials, politicians, and even TJ's principal to undermine the school's selective admissions process. Their language consistently channeled fashionable academic doctrines from "critical race theory" that presuppose that all of society's institutions are embedded with implicit forms of white supremacy.

Parents like Zhou were now experiencing traumatic flashbacks to their childhoods when government leaders shamed them during the brutal Cultural Revolution of the 1960s and 1970s, as Mao Tse-tung, the leader of the Chinese Communist Party, waged a bloody purge of the nation's intellectuals, weaponizing an army of youth into a paramilitary movement called the Red Guards. Children would turn in their parents, teachers, and other adults for holding ideas that questioned Mao.

For all the demonization of Republicans for opposing "critical race theory," it's Democratic political operatives who were pushing "critical race theory," from school boards to social studies classrooms. Through the fall and winter, our parents held protests at the school and testified to the school board, state legislature, and office of the Virginia Education secretary, Atif Qarni, only to be dismissed, smeared, muted, and treated like dirt.

Fellow mother Suparna Dutta had also become an accidental activist, rallying parents to our protests. One morning, as a group of our Coalition for TJ parents, including Dutta, readied to speak to Virginia Gov. Ralph Northam, we got bad news. Northam was cancelling the meeting. For many of our parents, they overcame cultural barriers, challenging authority, and their activism came from a place of moral courage. As Asian parents, we faced disparaging references to us as "Asian tiger moms," so one day I thought: let us embrace our sacred duty as "mama bears" and "papa bears," and our new moniker was born.

At home in Virginia in spring 2021, as Democratic and Republican lawmakers canvassed to win the nomination for governor and lieutenant governor, our parents organized debates. In a universe very far from the battle to challenge Islamist extremists, the Democrats were no-shows.

None of the Democratic candidates appeared. We asked McAuliffe's campaign for a meeting. His staffer told one of our members that the campaign had a suggested contribution of $25,000 for a one-hour virtual visit. Our group balked.

Meanwhile, a Republican candidate for governor, Glenn Youngkin, met with our parents, expressing his support for a merit-based admission to TJ. When Youngkin won the Republican Committees' nomination, Dutta raised her hand to volunteer to lead an Educators for Youngkin Coalition. She worked tirelessly, organizing webinars and door-knocking for Youngkin, going from being an anonymous mother to introducing him to a crowd of about five hundred cheering supporters in his last campaign stop in Fairfax County.

This was a world very far apart from challenging Islamic extremism, but an important pattern was emerging. Parents had to stand up unapologetically against smears of being called "racist" to defend their values. Everywhere, mama bears and papa bears were facing a national network of activists and educrats in the Woke Army hijacking schools with their agendas, segregating students by race into "affinity circles," and demanding children take "privilege" tests.

And the Muslim Brothers were going to make sure that they exploited this new hierarchy of human value.

* * *

On the occasion of Eid, marking the end of the holy month of Ramadan on the Islamic calendar, Fairfax County school board member Abrar Omeish posted a selfie with two brothers and expressed the agenda of the Muslim Brothers of decades ago: the anti-Semitic destruction of the state of Islam.

"Hurts my heart to celebrate while Israel kills Palestinians & desecrates the Holy Land right now. Apartheid & colonization were wrong yesterday and will be today, here and there," she wrote, in a May 2021 tweet.

Amidst anger over her tweet, she didn't back down. Like her mentors Rashida Tlaib and Ilhan Omar, Omeish doubled down, and local members of the Fairfax Democrats and the Islamist network in Northern Virginia rallied for her "free speech" rights at a protest outside a school board meeting at Luther Jackson Middle School in Fairfax, Virginia.

When I arrived, I saw familiar faces in the outer circle, surrounding the protesters: elder representatives from among the Muslim Brothers who had built their base in Northern Virginia, starting at 500 Grove Street. A young CAIR organizer bellowed from behind a megaphone against the "Zionists," and behind her stood Nihad Awad, the cofounder of the Council on American-Islamic Relations.

The Muslim Brothers no longer depended on their anonymous disinformation LoonWatch page to push their propaganda. They got on the evening news that night.

Even when the Muslim activists were hit by scandal, few journalists paid attention. In late June 2021, nine anonymous staffers of Muslim Advocates blew the whistle on alleged abuse, harassment, and intimidation by the organization's infamous codirector, Farhana Khera. They noted: "None of Farhana's accolades would have been possible without us—our intense work, our strategy, and our intelligence. Muslim Advocates is the powerhouse it is today not because of Farhana, but despite her. And rather than lifting up our efforts, Farhana and Naheed fostered an environment of mistreatment."

* * *

Just before the twentieth anniversary of the 9/11 attacks, Virginia Education secretary Atif Qarni—propped up by the Muslim Brothers at 500 Grove Street—endorsed a training webinar by educator Amaarah DeCuir and posted on the official YouTube channel of the Virginia Department of Education.

In the nearly two-hour lecture, DeCuir told teachers to avoid calling the 9/11 hijackers "terrorists," simply calling them "extremists," but with no discussion of religion.

"It's going to be important as we begin to plan our 9/11 lessons in a way that does not seek to reproduce anti-Muslim racism," she said. "We're not going to reproduce a false assumption of Muslim responsibility for 9/11. We're just going to begin right there and name that there is no responsibility and therefore we're not going to use this space to try and untangle this."

The Virginia Department of Education was now engaged in state-sponsored propaganda work for the Honor Brigade.

"We're also not going to reproduce what's understood as American exceptionalism—this understanding that America is a land at the top of a beautiful mountain and that all other countries, nations, and people are less than America," she said.

After an outcry by us, as parents, the Virginia Department of Education took down the video. But that didn't deter the Woke Army and its Honor Brigade.

From the dais on September 11, 2021, Fairfax County school board member Abrar Omeish refused to vote for a 9/11 resolution honoring the victims of 9/11 and the first responders.

"The token phrasing around 9/11 is 'Never Forget,'" she said. "As a nation we remember a jarring event, no doubt, but we chose to forget, as this resolution does, the fear, the ostracization, and the collective blame felt by Arab Americans, American Muslims, Sikhs, and Hindus and all brown or other individuals that have been mistaken for Muslims since that day over the past two decades."

Omeish was doing her job in the Honor Brigade, playing the victim and the wound collector. Across the country, CAIR Chicago's executive director was playing his part—now out in the open, out of the shadows of the LoonWatch disinformation network he had created. He published an op-ed in *USA Today*, laying out the same talking points of grievances that Omeish had outlined. "All in all, an emergent Islamophobia cottage industry that extended from outlandish blogs and think tanks to the halls of power defined a generation of Muslims as well as my entire career."

* * *

Something very powerful was opposing the Woke Army: a legion of parents.

In late September 2021, in an unprecedented move, the National Association of School Boards sent President Joe Biden a letter seeking the federal government's law enforcement help in investigating parents who engaged in "domestic terrorism" and "hate crimes." They demanded invoking the Patriot Act—written after the 9/11 attacks to investigate terrorists—against protesters at school board meetings.

The Woke Army had used "critical race theory" to turn the world upside down.

That night, I recorded a video message from my kitchen, wearing a shirt I had made myself: "I'm a mom not a domestic terrorist."

Twenty years investigating terrorism allowed me to know the difference.

But, four days later, the Biden administration shockingly responded with the US attorney general, Merrick Garland, responding with a letter saying he would use the powers of the FBI to investigate protesters at school board meetings.

The Honor Brigade and the Woke Army remained mum on this new surveillance of parents. They were in on the strategy.

But our nation finally found the outrage that pushed us over the edge. We rejected the criminalization of parenting, and when Democratic candidate for governor, Terry McAuliffe, said parents don't have a right to determine what schools should teach, in a debate with the Republican candidate, parents were galvanized against the Woke Army.

* * *

On election night 2021, Suparna Dutta stood in the Westfields Marriott ballroom in Centreville, Virginia, at the election watch party for Republican gubernatorial candidate Glenn Youngkin. She embraced friends, old and new, as I did a TV interview about our parents' campaign, wearing a shirt to which I'd added the words: "Mama Bear Movement."

Later, Dutta stood in front of the stage, shoulder to shoulder with so many parents whom school board, school, and state education officials have ignored, belittled, and dismissed since June 2020. The results scrolled across the TV monitors. Youngkin was the winner, and the crowd roared approvingly, including Dutta.

She and this new movement of "hopping mad" mama and papa bears had defeated the Woke Army that had been silencing us for so long. With the DJ pumping out rock band Huey Lewis and the News's 1980s hit song, "The Power of Love," Dutta was grinning ear to ear.

As Youngkin shook hands with his fans after his acceptance speech, he saw my shirt, interlocked his fingers together as if in prayer, and, with his hands clasped, declared, "Way to go, mama bears! You guys were awesome."

Indeed, nearby, Dutta was a manifestation of awesome: humble, courageous, resilient, and determined. "I'm so happy," she said, grinning.

In the coming days, Democratic strategist James Carville admitted in an interview with PBS that it was "stupid Wokeism" that led to the loss.

* * *

Across the country, in Boston, a physician named Javad Hashmi had been living a lie since mid-October 2004 when he first adopted the fake name, "Dr. Maxtor" to pen screeds against the West, Israel, America, Christians, and progressive Muslims.

Later settling on the identity of "Danios," he had helped Ahmed Rehab and Muhammad Tauseef Akbar, from the Chicago office of the Council on American-Islamic Relations, build a website named LoonWatch, the largest disinformation network by American Muslims on the web.

The little problem for his ego: hardly anyone knew it.

That was about to change, but, first, Hashmi had to lay a trap for the No. 1 target of his animus: the author Robert Spencer.

* * *

Hashmi returned to a previous challenge that had disturbed his pal, CAIR Chicago's executive director, Ahmed Rehab. Back in October 2010, Rehab had sent his Muslim friends a Google Group email with the subject line: "Robert Spencer Challenges me to a Debate."

Rehab had penned a blog making fun of Spencer's challenge, writing: "And now for some irony. Spencer, you are claiming you are ready to debate anyone but that alas no one wants to debate you because no one can. But, is this actually true? Does the name Danios of Loonwatch ring a bell [*sic*] Spencer? You may be burying your head in the sand hoping no one will notice, but a simple Google search on 'Robert Spencer debate' reveals your hypocrisy."

He linked to a LoonWatch column by "Danios," with the headline "Robert Spencer is a chicken."

In it, "Danios" had written, "How come you are ignoring an invitation from another blogger who has challenged you numerous times and whose articles shredding your arguments to pieces are all over the web without a peep of a rebuttal from you? Are you conceding defeat? Are you 'running away?'"

Later, in an email to Rehab and their friends, Iranian American author Reza Aslan dismissed Spencer's challenge: "Robert Spencer is a clown and the only legitimate response to clowns is laughter. Debating him would be like debating a child. It is a useless enterprise."

* * *

But Javad Hashmi hadn't let go of this idea. By the fall of 2021, he was fully engaged with a Twitter handle. He deployed his credentials to trick Spencer into believing he was a well-intentioned intellectual with a difference of a point of view.

Spencer agreed.

The afternoon of Saturday, December 4, 2021, at 1:00 eastern time, Hashmi faced off against his sworn enemy. After pretending to embrace "reform," he returned to the old divisive, judgmental, anti-American, anti-Christian, anti-Semitic, and anti-Israel views of his alter ego, "Danios." Christianity was extremist. If Christians wanted to terrorize Muslims, all they had to do was sign up for the US military. Jews enjoyed the benefits of "whiteness."

And now, at 4:08 p.m., with some five thousand followers, Hashmi stepped out of the closet with this declaration on Twitter: "A decade* [*sic*] ago I dedicated myself to this task, writing as Danios of LoonWatch, & today the task has been completed. God is truly great. I am very pleased with how that went." He had no explanation for his asterisk.

In another tweet, he taunted Spencer, writing: "I almost said at the end of the debate, 'Danios sends his regards.'"

Understandably, Spencer was taken aback. "Danios! You took advantage of my good will and friendliness, and deceived me by not informing me that you were this vile smear merchant from the murky past."

Later, at 4:29 p.m., he wrote: "You've outed yourself as a liar, thief, & fraud."

Incredulously, Hashmi reveled in his deceit.

To Spencer, he said, "Robert, you're absolutely right that I played possum so you wouldn't pull out of the debate. It took a lot of restraint on my part."

His old friends from his days writing behind a mask emerged to congratulate him.

Disgraced Iranian American author Reza Aslan wrote: "In which @DrJavadTHashmi reminds us once again what an ignorant tool Robert Spencer is." Years earlier, Aslan had taped a YouTube video to help Hashmi raise money on IndieGoGo.

Hashmi responded: "Thank you for the retweet Prof. Aslan."

White writer and Islamist apologist C. J. Werleman called him "brilliant."

Even author Mustafa Akyol defended Hashmi and encouraged folks: "Do watch his debate...."

Hashmi was not finished. "I'll come for the Majid [*sic*] Nawaz's too. First, the Sam Harris types, as well as the ex-Muslim crowd. I'm coming."

That evening, just before 9:00, Spencer recalled that I had said I knew the real identity of "Danios"; I hadn't revealed it because I hadn't yet corroborated it.

Hashmi responded again, in deception: "I don't know Asra. I think we had a couple emails back & forth many years ago."

We had never communicated with his real identity. Just his fake identity.

The next day, December 5, 2021, at 1:52 a.m., Shahed Amanullah, the former technology advisor in the Obama administration and the architect of many Muslim websites, including the Brass Crescent Awards given to LoonWatch and "Danios," emerged. He shared Hashmi's proud admission with this one-liner: "I've been sitting on this well-kept secret for most of the last decade."

@LoonWatchers had been tweeting again, but on this issue, they remained silent publicly.

* * *

As a young man, in the fall of 2004, Javad Hashmi had exploited the weaknesses of the internet to become an internet mercenary with his friends in the Council on American-Islamic Relations and other organizations, first, for the Honor Brigade and then for the Woke Army, aligning with the far left to attack America, the West, Israel, and progressive Muslims. For all of the talk about accountability among social media companies, these character assassins of disinformation were still operating freely. LoonWatch's 17,100 tweets were still online. Javad Hashmi waved his Harvard credentials like a Good Housekeeping seal of approval.

But, just like with the power of parents, their deception, divisiveness, and ideological indoctrination will not be allowed to prevail in America.

The eternal price of freedom is vigilance.

CHAPTER 24

Woman. Life. Freedom.

When a young woman named Mahsa Amini ventured with her family from their home in the town of Saqcz in the Iranian province of Kurdistan for Tehran, it was for a simple holiday to the big city. Tehran is divided into twenty-two districts that cover about 280 square miles, about the area of Chicago. About sixteen million people live in Tehran (about the population of Tokyo) in a nation of about eighty-four million people, the 17th most populated country in the world, just ahead of Turkey and Germany.

On the night of Tuesday, September 13, 2021, when Mahsa and her brother walked out of the Shahid Haghani Metro Station near the National Museum of the Islamic Republic and Holy Defense in Tehran, Iran, vice squad officers of the Gasht-e Ershad, or "Guidance Patrol," suddenly blocked Mahsa's path and reprimanded her for being "dressed inappropriately" in tight pants and incorrect headscarf, according to Brigadier-General Hossein Rahimi, the head of Tehran's police, even though she was wearing a black gown and scarf.

In that moment, the so-called Morality Police in Iran were acting as proxies for the Woke Army, which had waged disinformation campaigns for decades to protect regressive interpretations of Islam, including the false notion that women must cover their hair.

Mahsa's brother, Kiaresh Amini, explained to the police they were from out-of-town and begged the officers to let them go. But the officers grabbed Mahsa and shoved her in the van, her family says, while one agent restrained her brother by twisting his arm behind his back.

The officers told him: we are taking her to a "re-education class" at the Vozara Street Detention Center, four miles away. They drove Mahsa, certainly frightened and traumatized, the fifteen minutes to the headquarters of the morality police, on Vozara Street, past an expressway named for the Iranian intelligence chief Qasem Soleimani, killed by the U.S. for murders in the Middle East.

There, according to CCTV footage released by Iranian authorities, claiming to document Mahsa's last steps, the young woman walked through the detention facility into a room packed with rows of chairs and women. Inside, a woman of authority, shrouded in a veil and gown, tugged at Mahsa's headscarf before the young woman collapsed to the floor.

Outside, her brother heard screams from inside, he later recounted to Iranian journalists.

As family members, including Mahsa's brother, frantically banged on the door, security officers pummeled them with batons and tear gas. An ambulance sped out of the building. Mahsa's brother desperately showed photos of his sister to young women scrambling out of the building. One told him Mahsa was in her arms.

Shocked, Mahsa's brother bolted and ran the few blocks to the neighborhood's government-run Kasra Hospital.

Inside, Mahsa was intubated so she could breathe with an intravenous drip and bandages on her face.

That night, the family recalled, doctors told them they couldn't save her.

Within hours, this beautiful symbol of light and youth had been extinguished.

For many, her death was a shock, but for those of us fighting the tyranny of an extremist interpretation of Islam, we know that her death sentence was written in 1979 when thugs, cleric, and tyrants took power in Iran. What's more, something that many folks don't want to admit as they rush to join the movement of brave women, men, girls, and boys marching in the streets with a simple chant, "Woman. Life. Freedom," is that a deadly alliance of illiberal progressives in the West has run cover for Muslims who promote and accept Islamic theocracy and shut down voices of Muslims and ex-Muslims protesting the tyranny of regimes like Iran, Saudi Arabia, and Qatar.

Mahsa's death didn't have to happen.

But a Woke Army has denied freedoms to people the world over, making excuses for Muslims who accept Islam in governance. Their lies have denied people freedoms the world over since 1979. These enablers come in many forms, and many of them wear a Western secular face. In that world, where nothing—including the truth—may be said or written that might possibly be judged as "Islamophobic," the challenge to Islamic extremism has been muted.

This Orwellian distortion has been as semantically disingenuous as it has been dangerous, and it provides cover to repressors disguised as emancipators. *Atlantic* magazine published a feature by disgraced writer Reza Aslan, who had led the movement in the United States to allege "Islamophobia" was behind every attempt to discuss Islamic extremism honestly. I had debated him in 2008 when he blurted out, "You're confused," when I raised issue about women's second-class status in too many Muslim communities. The *Los Angeles Times* opened its pages to an apologist, "hijab fashion blogger" Hoda Katebi, who blamed "Western imperialism" rather than the tyranny of clerics for the oppression of women in Iran. I had debated her in 2016 in Chicago on the issue of hijab when she downplayed the injustices women face in Iran as having any relationship to the regime's dangerous brand of Islam, but there again blamed "Western imperialism." The audience laughed at her, and Aslan's team lost the debate, but here they were, still peddling their disinformation.

Aslan and Katebi may be just tiresome blowhards, but when the arbiters of Western progressiveness help to codify repression as normality, they empower and encourage tyranny.

Incredulously, as women and girls defied the morality police in Iran, the Boston City Council passed a resolution to declare Mahsa Amini's birthday "Boston Hijab Day."

In the days since Mahsa's killing, the people of Iran have exploded in righteous anger. A grieving sister cut locks of her hair at the graveside of her brother, killed in anti-regime protests. A white-haired woman waved her headscarf in the air during protests. The hope for throngs of protesting Iranians is that the death of Mahsa Amini harkens the overdue death of the Islamic Republic of Iran. After years of trying, I finally succeeded in booking the brave activist Masih Alinejad on comedian Bill Maher's HBO show and there she railed against the gender apartheid that is the regime in Iran.

And Masih uttered a rallying cry for the movement: "We are all Mahsa Amini."

Mahsa's death is personal to me. It hits me hard, as a Muslim woman born in India and raised in the United States, with the freedom to dress as I please, and as a Muslim reformer who has faced the disinformation campaign of the Woke Army for two decades now. The ringing alarms of Mahsa's life support system echo in my ears and in my heart. Can any person of conscience fail to be moved by the heartbreaking video that captured her final moments at Kasra Hospital in downtown Tehran? This isn't how a woman's life is supposed to end.

I was thirteen years old, growing up in Morgantown, West Virginia, in the foothills of the Appalachian Mountains, when Khomeini rose to power in 1979. It was a victory for the theocrats of the minority Shia sect of Islam. A few weeks later, on International Women's Day, March 8th, 1979, women marched from Tehran University through the city, and an estimated 100,000 other women.

"Freedom is not Eastern or Western," they chanted. "It is universal!"

Now, finally, the shameful killing of Mahsa Amini reveals the moral incongruence of the Woke Army and lays bare the moral depravity of their disinformation and unholy alliances. Finally, those who gave them cover cannot do so. Former First Lady Michelle Obama issued a statement supporting the women and girls of Iran, and so did Oprah. CNN and MSNBC finally covered with sympathy our struggle against the tyranny of Islamism. And former President Barack Obama admitted in a podcast that he made a "mistake" in listening to those who told him to refrain in his support for protestors in Iran in 2009.

For two decades, I have personally experienced the gaslighting of the Woke Army's disinformation campaign. And it continues—with leaders from the Organization of Islamic Cooperation meeting in Ankara, Turkey—to wage their next war against "Islamophobia."

But with the tragedy of a young woman named Mahsa Amin, there is a clarity from which we can never allow the Woke Army to return the West to confusion.

Defeating the Woke Army is long overdue, for the sake of freedom the world over.

GRATITUDE

When I embarked upon this book, I thought it would be a simple Nancy Drew mystery. It ended up a journey—through identity, fear, and darkness to emerge with truth and light.

I have so many people to thank who gave me strength, moral clarity, and faith. My mother, Sajida Nomani, never allowed me to reel in the shame that I faced from the earliest days in our family's struggle for an Islam of grace. My father, Zafar Nomani, was hurt by the attacks upon his daughter but was never deterred in his support for women's rights and tolerance. My niece, Safiyyah, and nephew, Samir, walked with me into the "men's section" of the mosque in Morgantown, West Virginia, as children and buoyed my spirits always. My brother, Mustafa, arrived on these shores with me, wearing matching striped clothes on a TWA jet we flew with only each other as companions, to be reunited with our parents in America. The journey has not been easy, but he remains a beacon of light.

It is with my family's support that I went to Ayaan Hirsi Ali with the vision for this book, and she graciously introduced me to her agent, Susanna Lea, who shepherded this book to the only book publishing editor who could fully understand it. In Adam Bellow, I found this editor. As I disappeared into so many rabbit holes, he championed this book's fruition. I thank him for seeing me through this journey to completion, for without editors of incredible will there would be no published authors. I thank the team at Post Hill Press for seeing this book to publication.

My first editor at the *Wall Street Journal*, Ken Wells, remains my most trusted writing coach today, and I thank him for his intellectual courage and clarity. Thank you to attorney Charles Glasser for emerging as a shield who made this book stronger. And thank you to intrepid researcher Madeleine Steppel for spending a summer with me, following the cybertrail on these villains hiding behind masks.

To my dear friends—Pam Norick and Vasia Deliyianni—I thank you for always believing in telling this story and sustaining me with your encouragement. To the accidental activists—Suparna Dutta, Harry Jackson, Glenn Miller, Helen Miller, Yuyan Zhou, and so many others—I thank you. Gratitude also to Luke Rosiak, James Lindsay, Peter Boghossian, and so many others for helping me connect the dots on the Woke Army. If you know who I am, I know who you are: part of the collective consciousness changing the world for good. I do not stand alone. None of us do. We stand together.

In early 2013, when I began this book, my son, Shibli, was a boy of just ten years old. He absorbed a reality no child should have to witness of his mother in tears, broken some moments by the barbs and arrows slung her way. "They are terrorists of the mind," he told me one day, as he wiped away my tears in a Dairy Queen parking lot. He drove with me in a blue Mustang from Southern California to Northern California, dodging rocks falling along Route 1, as we did reconnaissance on the masked suspects in the Honor Brigade. In the writing of the book, Shibli went from boyhood to manhood, writing his own story. It has been my honor to be a part of it. I thank my dear son for always being by my side, a support and an inspiration. And I thank all of you for being a part of our journey.

ABOUT THE AUTHOR

Asra Q. Nomani is a former *Wall Street Journal* reporter and cofounder of the Pearl Project, which investigated the murder of journalist Daniel Pearl. She is a cofounder of the Muslim Reform Movement, a human rights group, and cofounder of Coalition for TJ, a civil rights group. She is senior fellow in the practice of journalism at the Independent Women's Network, investigating indoctrination in schools.

Printed in Great Britain
by Amazon

47978722R00228